THEATERS OF PARDONING

CORPUS

The Humanities in Politics and Law

JURIS

Series editor: Elizabeth S. Anker, Cornell University

CORPUS JURIS: THE HUMANITIES IN POLITICS AND LAW PUBLISHES BOOKS AT THE INTERSECTIONS BETWEEN LAW, POLITICS, AND THE HUMANITIES—INCLUDING HISTORY, LITERARY CRITICISM, ANTHROPOLOGY, PHILOSOPHY, RELIGIOUS STUDIES, AND POLITICAL THEORY. BOOKS IN THIS SERIES TACKLE NEW OR UNDER-ANALYZED ISSUES IN POLITICS AND LAW AND DEVELOP INNOVATIVE METHODS TO UNDERTAKE THOSE INQUIRIES. THE GOAL OF THE SERIES IS TO MULTIPLY THE INTERDISCIPLINARY JUNCTURES AND CONVERSATIONS THAT SHAPE THE STUDY OF LAW.

THEATERS OF PARDONING

Bernadette Meyler

CORNELL UNIVERSITY PRESS ITHACA AND LONDON

First published 2019 by Cornell University Press

Library of Congress Cataloging-in-Publication Data

Names: Meyler, Bernadette, author.
Title: Theaters of pardoning / Bernadette Meyler.
Description: Ithaca [New York] : Cornell University Press, 2019. |
    Series: Corpus juris : the humanities in politics and law |
    Includes bibliographical references and index.
Identifiers: LCCN 2019007604 (print) | LCCN 2019011012
    (ebook) | ISBN 9781501739392 (e-book pdf) | ISBN
    9781501739408 (e-book epub/mobi) | ISBN 9781501739330 |
    ISBN 9781501739330 (hardcover) | ISBN 9781501739347
    (pbk.)
Subjects: LCSH: Theater—Political aspects—England—
    History—17th century. | Clemency in literature. | Pardon—
    England—History—17th century. | Pardon. | English drama
    (Tragicomedy)—17th century—History and criticism. |
    Politics and literature—England—History—17th century. |
    Law and literature—England—History—17th century. |
    Political plays, English—History and criticism. | Politics in
    literature.
Classification: LCC PR678.L38 (ebook) | LCC PR678.L38 M49
    2019 (print) | DDC 822/.409—dc23
LC record available at https://lccn.loc.gov/2019007604

In memory of my mother, Joan Meyler,
whose exceptional love, generosity, and forgiveness
touched so many and so deeply

CONTENTS

ACKNOWLEDGMENTS

In writing this book, I have made wonderful friends and incurred many debts, only the deepest of which I can acknowledge here. I began pondering the themes of pardoning and sovereignty as well as their connection to early modern drama while a graduate student in English at the University of California, Irvine. Julia Reinhard Lupton, J. Hillis Miller, and Jacques Derrida furnished extraordinarily generous and incisive mentorship, and I benefited greatly from conversations with Wolfgang Iser, Victoria Kahn, and Richard Kroll along the way. Late-night confabulations with graduate school friends and colleagues Jason Smith, Steven Miller, and Jeff Atteberry have left their mark throughout this work.

When my interests turned increasingly toward law, I found George Fisher, Tom Green, Bob Weisberg, Janet Halley, and Martin Stone invaluable interlocutors, and I am extremely grateful for their efforts to bring me up to speed in matters of legal history and law and literature. During my time at Cornell University, Annelise Riles, Rayna Kalas, and Philip Lorenz provided suggestions that were key to the arguments of particular chapters. I was also fortunate to benefit from the sustained advice of Peter Brooks, Daniel Heller-Roazen, Hendrik Hartog, and Oliver Arnold during the year I spent as a fellow in the Law and Public Affairs Program at Princeton and am indebted to the program for the time and intellectual camaraderie it afforded me. As I completed the book at Stanford, I enjoyed the encouragement of David Sklansky, Rick Banks, Barbara Fried, and Rich Ford. A number of scholars whom I encountered at conferences or through other academic exchanges opened up new paths of thought and gave me valuable research suggestions; these include, among many others, Lorna Hutson, Bradin Cormack, Julie Stone Peters, and Kathy Eden.

I could not have completed this book without the support of close friends and interlocutors, some of whom witnessed the birth of the project and others whom I met along the way. Amalia Kessler, Ben Heller, Elizabeth Anker, Kenji Yoshino, Amanda Claybaugh, Martin Puchner, Jim Whitman, Dan Edelstein, Robert Katzmann, Henry Turner, Alex Krulic, Susanna Blumenthal, and Avlana Eisenberg have all lent me their ears and imagination on topics both clearly germane and those seemingly more remote.

I have also profited from the insightful and meticulous labors of my research assistants Daeyeong Kim, Stephen Wu, and Will Evans. Sonia Moss of the Stanford Law Library has engaged in heroic efforts to help me secure relevant documents. I greatly appreciate Mac Graham's assistance in researching the books from Sir Edward Coke's library at Holkham Hall and am indebted to the Earl of Leicester for granting me permission to examine the materials there. My wonderful administrative associate Eun Sze has helped with everything conceivable. I am grateful, too, to former Stanford Law School dean Liz Magill for giving me the resources to complete this project. For the past decade Elizabeth Anker has been a cherished friend, and it is a joy to be able to publish this book in the series she edits. I am additionally obliged to Amanda Heller for her painstaking copyediting and to David Luljak for making indexing a pleasure.

Throughout the writing process, my family has sustained me. Matt Smith has encouraged me to complete this book and furnished the love and support that made it possible to do so. My daughters, Calliope and Minerva Smith, allow me to contemplate and hope for a world where forgiveness will have a more prominent place and friendship will be paramount.

My parents, John and Joan Meyler, were there at every turn to converse about my ideas, copyedit my drafts, drive me somewhere on short notice, take care of my children, and generally shower me with love and kindness. My mother's mother, Helen Fischer, also enthusiastically supported all of my endeavors, including this one. When my mother died in 2015, my father heroically stepped in to take care of my grandmother until she too passed away in 2018. My mother's life ended much too soon, with projects uncompleted that she wished to see consummated, including this one. As she was dying, I told her that I planned to dedicate this book to her, and it gives me some comfort to do so now.

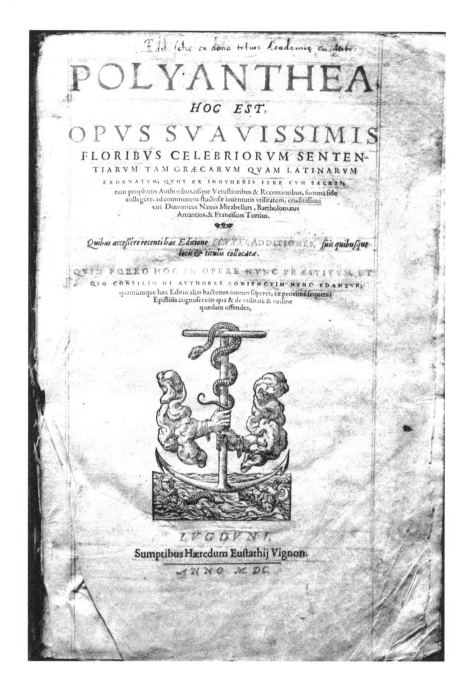

POLYANTHEA,

HOC EST,

OPVS SVAVISSIMIS

FLORIBVS CELEBRIORVM SENTEN-
TIARVM TAM GRÆCARVM QVAM LATINARVM

EXORNATVM, QVOS EX INNVMERIS FERE CVM SACRIS,
tum prophanis Authoribus, iisque Vetuftioribus & Recentioribus, fumma fide
collegere, ad communem ftudiofæ iuuentutis vtilitatem, eruditiffimi
viri Dominicus Nanus Mirabellius, Bartholomæus
Amantius, & Francifcus Tortius.

*Quibus acceſſere recenti hac Editione CCXXX ADDITIONES, ſuis quibuſque
locis & titulis collocata.*

QVID PORRO HOC IN OPERE NVNC PRÆSTITVM, ET
QVO CONSILIO HI AVTHORES CONIVNCTIM NVNC EDANTVR,
quantúmque hæc Editio alias hactenus omnes fuperet, ex proxime fequenti
Epiftola cognofces:in qua & de vtilitatè & ordine
quædam offendes,

LVGDVNI,

Sumptibus Hæredum Euftathij Vignon.

ANNO M. DC.

FIGURE FM.1 / *Polyanthea* (copy of Sir Edward Coke), photo by Mac Graham, located at Holkham Hall

THEATERS OF PARDONING

INTRODUCTION /
Theaters of Pardoning

As president of the United States, Donald Trump has insisted on his power to pardon and has remitted punishment in a number of controversial cases. In the summer of 2017, he pardoned former Maricopa County, Arizona, sheriff Joe Arpaio, who had been convicted of contempt of court. Arpaio, a state official, had violated people's constitutional rights by encouraging traffic patrols to target individuals they suspected were not in compliance with federal immigration laws. A judge had ordered him to cease this program, but he refused, and continued to resist judicial authority for a number of years.[1] Fast-forward almost a year to President Trump's 2018 pardon of two ranchers who had been convicted of arson on federal lands in the West. Dwight Hammond Jr. and his son Steven had become catalysts for the takeover of an Oregon wildlife refuge by those opposing federal power over the area.[2] In the interim, Trump tweeted, "I have the absolute right to pardon myself."[3] Throughout this period, Trump eschewed involvement of the Department of Justice's Office of the Pardon Attorney in the process, instead preferring to pardon friends or people he had seen on television.[4]

Trump's manner of wielding the pardon power encapsulates several themes of this book. Most notably, Trump has asserted his "absolute power" through pardoning and avoided any bureaucratic elements introduced into the process

---

1. Tom Jackman, "How Ex-Sheriff Joe Arpaio Wound Up Facing Jail Time before Trump Pardoned Him," *Washington Post,* August 25, 2017, https://www.washingtonpost.com/news/true-crime/wp/2017/08/25/how-ex-sheriff-joe-arpaio-wound-up-facing-jail-time-before-trump-pardoned-him/?utm_term=.af8d59a0b82d.

2. Elizabeth Landers, "Trump Pardons Ranchers Whose Case Sparked Bundy Takeover of Oregon Refuge," CNN.com, July 10, 2018, https://www.cnn.com/2018/07/10/politics/hammonds-trump-pardon/index.html.

3. Caroline Kenny, "Trump: 'I Have the Absolute Right to Pardon Myself,'" CNN.com, June 4, 2018, https://www.cnn.com/2018/06/04/politics/donald-trump-pardon-tweet/index.html.

4. Tucker Higgins, "Trump Brings the Power of the Pardon to His Battle with the Justice Department," CNBC.com, June 1, 2018, https://www.cnn.com/2018/06/04/politics/donald-trump-pardon-tweet/index.html.

in recent years. Pardoning here manifests his exceptional status in relation to ordinary law in a manner that recalls the sovereignty of early modern kings. By insisting on an ability to pardon himself, Trump also violates a long-standing common law prohibition against judging in one's own case. While sovereigns in this book sometimes pardon treason contemplated or committed against themselves despite this precept, they never pardon themselves. Furthermore, by overturning a criminal contempt conviction and pardoning those asserting federalism claims against the national government, Trump has waded into conflicts over the separation of executive and judicial powers and constitutional interpretation. Finally, Trump has cannily recognized the theatrical power of pardoning. He has built pardons upon personal dramas and stories and has kept the public on tenterhooks—will he or won't he?—with his suggestion of the possibility of pardoning himself.

To get at the root of these issues and controversies as well as their persistence in contemporary democracy, one must, I argue in this book, turn back to an earlier setting, that of seventeenth-century England, where modern views about the pardon power and its relation to liberal constitutionalism were established and where alternative possibilities burgeoned before being dismissed. The project aligns in this respect with the approach of political theorists like Richard Tuck or literary critics like Victoria Kahn, who have found seventeenth-century England fertile ground for understanding our own political settlement as well as the paths not pursued.[5]

Recovering seventeenth-century thought about pardoning and its dramatic manifestation in what I am calling "theaters of pardoning" can aid us in understanding both the sources of residual reluctance regarding exercises of the pardon power and the value of something like pardoning, as opposed to the seemingly related practices of compassion or empathy, for which Martha Nussbaum and Robin West have advocated.[6] On the one hand, the close connection between

---

5. Barbara Shapiro has also helpfully brought to light the importance of a range of sources, including drama and poetry, to understanding seventeenth-century English political culture. Barbara Shapiro, *Political Communication and Political Culture in England* (Stanford: Stanford University Press, 2012).

6. Martha Nussbaum has often argued for an ethic of compassion, including in *Political Emotions: Why Love Matters for Justice* (Cambridge: Harvard University Press, 2015); *Upheavals of Thought: The Intelligence of Emotions* (Cambridge: Cambridge University Press, 2001); *Poetic Justice: The Literary Imagination and Public Life* (Boston: Beacon Press, 1995); and *The Therapy of Desire* (Princeton: Princeton University Press, 1994). Robin West defends a return to empathy in judging against the rise of a new paradigm of judicial reasoning in "The Anti-Empathic Turn," *NOMOS LIII*, ed. James Fleming (2011): 243–88.

pardoning and sovereignty—already posited in the late sixteenth century by Jean Bodin—solidified through the contests over power between king and Parliament in seventeenth-century England, ultimately eclipsing other figurations of pardoning. On the other, these theaters of pardoning emphasize the particularly political significance of pardoning, which is elided by the interpersonal dimensions of compassion and empathy; formally, the performance of pardoning calls for an audience to consider the legitimacy of the laws and exceptions that are staged rather than soliciting concern for or identification with characters.

In order to address the roots of pardoning's treatment in politics today and uncover what new formulations of pardoning might contribute, this book examines the role of theaters of pardoning—a form of tragicomedy—in the drama and politics of seventeenth-century England. Historically, it argues, shifts in the representation of pardoning tracked the transition from a more monarchical and judgment-focused to an increasingly parliamentary and legislative vision of sovereignty. On stage, a transformation surreptitiously took place from individual pardons of revenge to more sweeping pardons of revolution. The change can be traced from Shakespeare's *Measure for Measure*, where a series of final pardons interrupts what might otherwise have been a cycle of revenge, to later works like John Ford's *The Laws of Candy* and Philip Massinger's *The Bondman*, in which the exercise of some form of mercy prevents the overturn of the state itself. In the political arena, the pardon correspondingly came to be envisioned in increasingly law-like terms, culminating in the idea of a general amnesty, or "Act of Oblivion," that obsessed King Charles I from the beginning of his reign and was finally implemented by the Restoration Parliament under his son King Charles II.[7] This apparent assimilation of pardoning with lawgiving did not eliminate its connection to sovereignty but instead displaced sovereignty from the king onto Parliament.[8]

---

7. The book focuses on particularly visible instances of pardoning or the failure to pardon rather than comprehensively examining pardoning practices, as in Krista Kesselring's sixteenth-century study *Mercy and Authority in the Tudor State* (Cambridge: Cambridge University Press, 2003), or examining the entire compass of interactions between king and Parliament over pardons, as in Cynthia Herrup's analysis of the reigns of James I and Charles I, "Negotiating Grace," in *Politics, Religion and Popularity in Early Stuart Britain: Essays in Honor of Conrad Russell*, ed. Thomas Cogswell, Richard Cust, and Peter Lake (Cambridge: Cambridge University Press, 2002), 124–42. These more concrete instantiations of pardoning are, of course, relevant to this book, but the primary object of analysis remains the symbolic representation of the relation between pardoning and sovereignty in seventeenth-century England and the circulation of that representation between the political and dramatic spheres.

8. This argument bears a connection with Eric Santner's thesis in *The Royal Remains*. Drawing on Ernst Kantorowicz's classic discussion of the king's two bodies—mortal and symbolic—and its role

The association between pardoning and sovereignty simultaneously put pressure on the emerging conception of the common law as an autonomous and self-authorizing source of law.[9] Building on recent work emphasizing the extent to which the ancient Greek influence on early modern English law and political theory has been underestimated, this book examines the role of sources like Plato's *Laws* as well as anthologies such as *Polyanthea Nova*, which collected classical materials under a variety of topic headings, in establishing both ideas about the independence of law and the goal of law as the benefit of the polity as a whole.[10] A similar blind spot regarding the influence of ancient Greek

---

in the medieval theory of kingship in *The King's Two Bodies: A Study in Medieval Political Theology* (Princeton: Princeton University Press, 1997), Santner contends that the age of revolutions led not to the disappearance of the king's two bodies but rather to "the 'metamorphosis' of the King's Two Bodies into the People's Two Bodies." Eric Santner, *The Royal Remains: The People's Two Bodies and the Endgames of Sovereignty* (Chicago: University of Chicago Press, 2011), 8. I similarly argue that sovereignty did not simply disappear or become transmuted into "disciplinary power" or "biopower," as Michael Foucault would have it on one reading of his work—though not the one Santner accepts—but instead remained despite a change in the figure to whom it was attached.

Rather than focusing on "the people" as the new locus of sovereignty, I turn in this book to the governmental form that claims for the people took in mid-seventeenth-century England, that of Parliament. In his classic *Inventing the People*, Edmund Morgan argued for the replacement of the fiction of the divine right of kings with the sovereignty of the people. Edmund Morgan, *Inventing the People: The Rise of Popular Sovereignty in England and America* (New York: Norton, 1988), 54. In doing so, however, he explained the crucial role of Parliament as the embodiment of that sovereignty. Indeed, as he wrote, "in endowing the people with supreme authority, then, Parliament intended only to endow itself" (65). The particularity of that form of sovereignty has had significant implications for the development of the modern British polity as well as the parts of the former British Empire that retain an emphasis on legislative sovereignty.

9. The timing of this development is disputed, but scholars largely agree that it can be recognized in the early seventeenth century. As Conrad Russell writes: "Professor Pocock noted that 'between 1550 and 1600 there occurred a great hardening and consolidation of common law thought.' His dating may be a trifle early, but that such a hardening can be seen in the mind of Coke is surely undeniable." Conrad Russell, "Topsy and the King: The English Common Law, King James VI and I, and the Union of the Crowns," in *Law and Authority in Early Modern England: Essays Presented to Thomas Garden Barnes*, ed. Buchanan Sharp and Mark Charles Fissel (Wilmington: University of Delaware Press, 2007), 68.

10. In *The Greek Tradition in Republican Thought*, Eric Nelson has established the importance of Greek thought—and its divergence from Roman republicanism—in Sir Thomas More's *Utopia* as well as James Harrington's *Oceana*. As he elaborates the differences between Greek and Roman conceptions of justice, the "view of justice as 'balance among elements' leads Plato to endorse policies that would straightforwardly violate the Roman principle of justice," adding that "Platonic justice is holistic, and is inextricably linked to an overall conception of nature and order." Eric Nelson, *The Greek Tradition in Republican Thought* (Cambridge: Cambridge University Press, 2004), 13. Christopher Brooks likewise emphasizes that "although much of the historiography on the relationship between legal and political thought over the past century or so has stressed the relative insularity of English common-law thinking, this misses the point that the Elizabethans in particular embraced classical and continental learning with some enthusiasm and used

materials—as opposed to their Roman reception—has characterized scholarship on early modern drama, which has perhaps been overly affected by Ben Jonson's reference to Shakespeare's "small Latin and less Greek." As I contend in this book, the legal deployment of Greek sources allows us to uncover the hidden debt to these materials in seventeenth-century drama as well as law. In both contexts, the ancient Greek sources are mustered in support of an alternative account of law and mercy as operating to the benefit of the state, conceived as including its full range of subjects or citizens, rather than serving the primary purpose of glorifying the sovereign.

By analyzing the interconnections between the audiences of drama and the actors of politics in seventeenth-century England, the book also intervenes in debates about the relationship between law and literature.[11] It posits that, through raising the threat of tragedy but insisting on a comic ending by the imposition of pardoning, theaters of pardoning as a genre enabled spectators to safely rethink the foundations of the state. Furthermore, the historical context of early Stuart

---

it to develop a more thoughtful appreciation of the nature and history of their own institutions." Christopher Brooks, *Law, Politics and Society in Early Modern England* (Cambridge: Cambridge University Press, 2008), 82. Addressing the influences on Thomas Hobbes, Ioannis Evrigenis also demonstrates that Greek sources were more important than Roman to the philosopher's work. Ioannis Evrigenis, *Images of Anarchy: The Rhetoric and Science in Hobbes's State of Nature* (Cambridge: Cambridge University Press, 2016), 10–12.

11. Within the past two decades, a wealth of scholarship has connected Shakespeare and other early modern drama to the law with increasing historical and theoretical rigor. The works that have most influenced my own approach in this book include Oliver Arnold, *The Third Citizen: Shakespeare's Theater and the Early Modern House of Commons* (Baltimore: Johns Hopkins University Press, 2007); Bradin Cormack, *A Power to Do Justice: Jurisdiction, English Literature, and the Rise of the Common Law* (Chicago: University of Chicago Press, 2007); Lorna Hutson, *The Invention of Suspicion: Law and Mimesis in Shakespeare and Renaissance Drama* (Oxford: Oxford University Press, 2008); Julia Reinhard Lupton, *Citizen-Saints: Shakespeare and Political Theology* (Chicago: University of Chicago Press, 2005); Holger Schott Syme, *Theatre and Testimony in Shakespeare's England: A Culture of Mediation* (Cambridge: Cambridge University Press, 2011); and Luke Wilson, *Theaters of Intention: Drama and the Law in Early Modern England* (Stanford: Stanford University Press, 2000). Although not as centrally concerned with drama, Victoria Kahn's *Wayward Contracts: The Crisis of Political Obligation in England, 1640–1674* (Princeton: Princeton University Press, 2004) treats the literary and cultural contexts of the emergence of an obsession with contract in seventeenth-century England and demonstrates the political salience of contract in legitimating governmental orders.

These endeavors are, of course, only among the more recent installments in a venerable tradition of scholarship that has attended to Shakespeare and the law, in some cases to the point of identifying the works of Shakespeare as those of another—legal—author, like Sir Francis Bacon. Sir Dunbar Plunket Barton's 1929 *Links between Shakespeare and the Law* (London: Faber & Gwyer, 1929) refrains from adopting such an extreme stance, and may prove the most informative of such treatises, discussing both Shakespeare's allusions to the law and lawyers—including Sir Edward Coke—and the performance of his and other Elizabethan and Jacobean dramas at the Inns of Court.

rule furnished a unique opportunity for drama to serve a constitution-building function.

This introduction situates the succeeding chapters within the context of developments in early modern law and literature, which have emphasized the historical interrelations among the institutions and actors of law, drama, and politics.[12] At the same time, it takes up the challenge to older historicist literary approaches posed by recent returns to consideration of form and examines how the specificities of genre might affect the kind of political intervention these plays produced.[13]

Scenes of Reception

The audiences of early modern England were multiple and multiply engaged between the juridico-political and dramatic spheres. While acted upon and interacting with episodes of pardoning, they conveyed the connections drawn between sovereignty and pardoning in the playhouse to the public square and back again. Particularly close links subsisted between the participants in and spectators of drama and law; the same individuals even assumed these various capacities at disparate times. Shakespeare's *Twelfth Night* and *Comedy of Errors*, among other plays, were performed at the Inns of Court, and the budding lawyers of the Inns themselves staged masques and entertainments.[14] Even the moots,

---

12. For a broader discussion of this historical turn, see Bernadette Meyler, "Law, Literature, and History: The Love Triangle," *UC Irvine Law Review* 5, no. 2 (June 2015): 365–92.

13. Caroline Levine insists on the value of conjoining the study of form with politics, writing: "It is the work of form to make order. And this means that forms are the stuff of politics." Caroline Levine, *Forms: Whole, Rhythm, Hierarchy, Network* (Princeton: Princeton University Press, 2015), 3. For one analysis of the varieties of "new formalisms," see Marjorie Levinson, "What Is New Formalism?," *PMLA* 122, no. 2 (March 2007): 558–69.

Valerie Forman has emphasized the significance of form with regard to tragicomedy in particular in *Tragicomic Redemptions: Global Economics and the Early Modern English Stage* (Philadelphia: University of Pennsylvania Press, 2008). Forman presents one of her goals as that of "redeeming genre itself—which of late has been relegated to the poor cousin of historical context—as important to the study of literary and cultural history." She does this by insisting on tragicomedy as a test case for "the historicity of form in both senses: that form develops within specific historical contexts and that form makes historical interventions" (18). My analysis here of theaters of pardoning presents a similarly dual role for the historicity of form.

14. Adwin Wigfall Green discusses the interconnections between the spheres in detail in *The Inns of Court and Early English Drama* (1931; New Haven: Yale University Press, 1965), while Robert Pearce treats the Inns of Court masques and holiday revels in *A History of the Inns of Court and Chancery* (London: Richard Bentley, 1848), 81–128. Jessica Winston's *Lawyers at Play: Literature, Law, and Poli-*

aimed at instructing these burgeoning practitioners in their trade, boasted a theatrical dimension.[15] The regular theaters, including the nearby Blackfriars and the Globe, also attracted members of the legal profession as well as a range of other spectators.[16] Several of the playwrights, like John Marston or John Ford, had themselves studied—or at least lived—at the Inns, and some of their works bear the marks of this apprenticeship.[17] The norm of openness of judicial proceedings—reaffirmed by Sir Edward Coke—may also have allowed playwrights to sit in on cases being decided.[18]

The legal practitioners of early modern England were thus furnished with ample opportunity to view and debate the content of contemporary plays, and the approaches of different playwrights may themselves have been influenced by the proximity of contexts for legal experiences. The range of those who could have derived legal and political conclusions from drama was not, however, restricted to those who studied law for professional purposes. Just as Shakespeare's works depict a wide variety of participants in the legal arena, from

tics at the Early Modern Inns of Court, 1558–1581 (Oxford: Oxford University Press, 2016) examines how the Inns emerged as a literary center during the sixteenth century.

15. John Baker, "The Third University of England," in The Common Law Tradition: Lawyers, Books, and the Law (London: Hambledon Press, 2000), 3–28. Building on the Inns of Courts' tradition of moots and the less official practice of debating cases over dinner, Karen Cunningham has argued for the theatrical relevance of moots, contending, in particular, that Shakespeare's Measure for Measure should be interpreted as a kind of moot. Karen Cunningham, "Opening Doubts upon the Law: Measure for Measure," in A Companion to Shakespeare's Works, vol. 4, ed. Richard Dutton and Jean E. Howard (Oxford: Blackwell, 2003), 316–32.

16. Andrew Gurr, The Shakespearean Stage, 1574–1642, 3rd ed. (Cambridge: Cambridge University Press, 1992), 11–12, 16–17, 216–18.

17. Philip Finkelpearl furnishes an account of Marston's particular connection with the Inns of Court and its relation to his writing in John Marston of the Middle Temple: An Elizabethan Dramatist in His Social Setting (Cambridge: Harvard University Press, 1969). Finkelpearl also lists a number of writers who lived at the Inns during the sixteenth and seventeenth centuries, including "More, Ascham, Turbervile, Googe, Gascoigne, Sackville and Norton, North, Lodge, Fraunce, Raleigh, Harington, Campion, Donne, Bacon, Davies, Marston, Ford, Beaumont, Shirley, Davenant, William Browne, Wither, Denham, Qarles, Carew, Suckling, and Congreve" (19). The poet and playwright John Ford was admitted to the Middle Temple in 1602 and lived there for a considerable period. Gilles Monsarrat, "John Ford: The Early Years (1586–1620)," in The Collected Works of John Ford, vol. 1, ed. Gilles Monsarrat, Brian Vickers, and R. J. C. Watt (Oxford: Oxford University Press, 2012), 12–38.

18. According to one account of Westminster Hall, "the business of the courts attracted a huge variety of visitors who included sightseers such as Lady Margaret Hoby in 1600, and law students." J. F. Merritt, The Social World of Early Modern Westminster: Abbey, Court and Community, 1525–1640 (Manchester: Manchester University Press, 2005), 162. As John Baker has noted, however, the courts at Westminster were rather makeshift and operated in the interstices of the other activities of the venue. J. H. Baker, "Westminster Hall, 1097–1997," in The Common Law Tradition: Lawyers, Books, and the Law (London: Hambledon Press, 2000), 247–62. As a result, access may have been more theoretically available than practically sought.

criminals, to constables, to jurors, to justices of the peace, to the Lord Chief Justice, to the king, the spectators of his plays included those involved with the law in a lay capacity as well as the sovereign.

Many spectators may indeed have experienced the law as individual jurors rather than as trained participants. Members of all classes could attend the early modern theater, and "amphitheatres, baiting-houses, prize-fights and whore-houses were always within reach for the great majority of the working population as well as the wealthy."[19] At the same time, however, a number of plays also boasted royal audiences at court, including Shakespeare's *Hamlet*, *Measure for Measure*, and *Merchant of Venice*, the last of which King James ordered to be played again in 1605.[20] Both James and his son King Charles I permitted their wives to participate in masques and other amateur theatricals, to the opprobrium of some subjects, including William Prynne, who excoriated such activity in his infamous 1633 anti-theatrical screed *Histriomastix*. Both James and Charles also manifested an active involvement in the world of drama, and the latter even annotated copies of others' dramatic writings.[21] More broadly, a natural alliance proposed itself between the sovereign and the stage in the theatrical displays of a monarchy justified on the basis of the divine right of kings.[22] Another form of deliberation that drama spawned was thus that of royal lawmakers themselves, who could evaluate the impact of legal determinations like theirs within the world of the play.

Although the various kinds of spectators often frequented diverse venues, and the types of entertainments that they witnessed sometimes differed in either the subjects represented or the lavishness of the presentation, the plays of early modern England were, in many instances, designed to be accessible to several types of audience members. Nor were those who could attend live performances the only ones to engage with dramatic works. Particularly with the closure of the theaters in 1642, the publication of new plays became a crucial vehicle for the interchanges between drama and politics.[23] Furthermore, a number of tragi-

---

19. Gurr, *The Shakespearean Stage*, 12.

20. Alvin Kernan, *Shakespeare, the King's Playwright: Theater in the Stuart Court, 1603–1613* (New Haven: Yale University Press, 1995), 30–31, 53; John Astington, *English Court Theatre, 1558–1642* (Cambridge: Cambridge University Press, 1999), 182–83.

21. Gurr, *The Shakespearean Stage*, 20.

22. Kernan, *Shakespeare, the King's Playwright*, 1–23.

23. Both Dale Randall's *Winter Fruit: English Drama, 1642–1660* (Lexington: University Press of Kentucky, 1995) and Susan Wiseman's *Drama and Politics in the English Civil War* (Cambridge: Cambridge University Press, 1998) treat the remarkable amount of drama produced during this period.

comedies that had remained in manuscript were printed for the first time in the 1650s, some speculate in conjunction with a royalist resurgence.

The convertibility characteristic of some drama of the period manifests itself quite vividly in the alternate openings of Ben Jonson's 1614 play *Bartholomew Fair*. On the one hand, Jonson composed a poetic "Prologue to the King's Majesty," emphasizing the variegated quality of the play's characters by proclaiming:

> Your Majesty is welcome to a fair;
> Such place, such men, such language and such ware,
> You must expect: with these, the zealous noise
> Of your land's faction, scandalised at toys, . . .
> These for your sport, without particular wrong,
> Or just complaint of any private man,
> Who of himself or shall think well or can,
> The maker doth present: and hopes tonight
> To give you for a fairing, true delight.[24]

King James, for whom the play was performed, is here offered a bird's-eye view of controversies characteristic of those experienced in his state—although the play supposedly refrains from representing any actual "private man" or slandering such an individual by pointing out his misdeeds. At the end, the king is asked to render judgment from above; as the Epilogue observes, "This is your power to judge, great sir, and not/ The envy of a few" (Epilogue 9–10).

On the other hand, the prose Induction, for the production at the Hope in Southwark, insists on the "grounded judgements" of the spectators, punning on the relationship between the status of those standing beneath the stage, in the arena, and the idea of a well-anchored verdict; in this manner, the play is supposed to be comprehensible to the ordinary spectator, "for the author hath writ it just to his meridian, and the scale of the grounded judgements here, his playfellows in wit" (Induction 66–68). Not simply one ordinary spectator is envisioned here, however; in contrast to the singular vantage point of the king, the Induction emphasizes the multiple perspectives of the popular audience, composed of those who have paid "six penn'orth, . . . twelve penn'orth, . . . eighteen pence, two shillings," or even "half a crown," and of the "curious and envious"

---

24. Ben Jonson, prologue to *Bartholomew Fair*, in *The Selected Plays of Ben Jonson*, vol. 2, ed. Martin Butler (Cambridge: Cambridge University Press, 1989), lines 1–4, 8–12; hereafter cited parenthetically by line.

and "favouring and judicious" as well as the "grounded judgements and under-standings" (Induction 87–89, 103–4).

The author requires an initial covenant and "articles of agreement" with the audience members, but this contract covers only the conditions for spectator-ship, not attendees' ultimate verdicts on the play (Induction 75–185). Those judgments remain part of the exercise of the spectators' "free-will," an exercise that the language of the Induction seems to analogize not only with the activity of judges but also with that of jurors.[25] The character of the "Scrivener" insists that "every man here exercise his own judgement, and not censure by contagion," and "not . . . be brought about by any that sits on the bench with him, though they indict, and arraign plays daily" (Induction 113–14, 121–23). By maintain-ing that every man should judge according to his own conscience, a word the Induction itself uses elsewhere, and that he should not indict without search-ing it, the Scrivener appeals to the standard of judgment applied by the early English jury, as well as alluding to judges sitting on the bench.[26] According to this Induction, the collective judgment of the common audience consists in a sum of individual decisions, which combine into a verdict through popular "suffrage" (Induction 180).[27]

Sometimes the plays explicitly appealed to the mercy or clemency of those who might sit in judgment. In William Habington's *The Queene of Arragon*, performed at court in 1640, the "staging of a queen who is deeply mistrusted and despised by her people chimed with the perilous position of England's own queen consort, Henrietta Maria," as Rebecca Bailey has argued.[28] Although gen-erally sympathetic to the plight of the royal family, the play could have stirred

---

25. At the end of *The Alchemist*, the character Face similarly invokes the rhetoric of jury trial, telling the spectators, "I put myself/ On you, that are my country." Ben Jonson, *The Alchemist*, in *The Selected Plays*, vol. 2,5.5.162–63. Jonas Barish has also noted that "Jonson seemed to think of the good audience as a kind of jury, assembled to render a verdict on a work of art." Jonas Barish, *The Antitheatrical Prejudice* (Berkeley: University of California Press, 1985), 134.

26. For a discussion of the rhetoric of conscience in English debates about the role of the jury, see Thomas A. Green, *Verdict According to Conscience: Perspectives on the English Criminal Trial Jury, 1200–1800* (Chicago: University of Chicago Press, 1985). James Q. Whitman also considers how the religious understanding of conscience affected early modern judges' and juries' approach to their task in *The Origins of Reasonable Doubt: Theological Roots of the Criminal Trial* (New Haven: Yale University Press, 2016).

27. The term, of course, possessed a different nuance than it does in an era of democracy; Rob-ert Cawdrey's 1604 word list glossed it as "consent, or voice, or helpe." Robert Cawdrey, *The First English Dictionary, 1604: Robert Cawdrey's* A Table Alphabeticall, ed. John Simpson (Oxford: Bodleian Library, 2007), 143.

28. Rebecca Bailey, "Staging 'a Queene opprest': William Habington's Exploration of the Politics of Queenship on the Caroline Stage," *Theatre Journal* 65, no. 2 (May 2013): 198; William Habington,

unwelcome considerations and comes armed with material appealing to the king's mercy. In the Prologue, Habington writes:

> But you have mercy sir; and from your eye,
> Bright madam, never yet did lightning fly;
> But vital beams of favour, such as give
> A growth to all who can deserve to live.
> Why should the authour tremble then, or we
> Distresse our hopes, and such tormentors be,
> Of our own thoughts? since in those happy times
> We live, when mercy's greater than the crimes.[29]

And in the Epilogue:

> We have nothing left us but our blushes now
> For your much penance; and though we allow
> Our fears no comfort, since you must appear
> Judges corrupt, if not to us severe:
> Yet in your majesty we hope to find
> A mercy, and in that our pardon sign'd.
> And how can we despair you will forgive
> Them who would please, when oft offenders live?
> And if we have err'd, may not the courteous say,
> 'Twas not their trade, and but the Author's play?[30]

Despite the author's sense that mercy and pardoning are undeserved, he insists that the reception of his play as well as its content must fit within a tragicomic genre. Referring to the precedents according to which "oft offenders live" as well as "those happie times/ We live, when mercy's greater than the crimes," Habington confirms the possibility of a merciful acceptance of the play.

These examples raise questions about what variety of judgment or mercy was called for on the part of these plays' audiences and its proximity—or lack thereof—to legal judgment. In *The Invention of Suspicion*, Lorna Hutson makes the case for a close link between the legal and dramatic exercise of judgment in

---

The Queene of Arragon, A Tragi-Comedie, in *A Select Collection of Old English Plays*, 4th ed., ed. W. Carew Hazlitt, vol. 13 (London: Reeves & Turner, 1875), 322–409.

29. Habington, *Queene of Arragon*, 326.
30. Habington, *Queene of Arragon*, 409.

the period. Examining the connection between the epistemological positions of the spectator and of the juror in sixteenth- and seventeenth-century England, she contends that an "appeal to the audience as lay judges . . . throw[s] the emphasis simultaneously on to the audience's intellectual capacity to puzzle out what the plot presents as 'evidence' and on its ethical arbitration of what that evidence implies." Hence, for Hutson, "sixteenth-century English revenge tragedy, while not presenting us with competing narratives of the facts as such, nevertheless makes a similar open-ended appeal to our capacity as equitable moral arbiters of the case."[31] Under this account, audience members were asked to approach the dramatic spectacle as though they were jurors deciding a case by reasoning from the evidence before them.

Puzzling over the surprising lack of representation of common law procedure in early modern drama, and particularly the absence of jurors from the early modern stage, Holger Schott Syme has resisted the conclusion that the audience furnishes a substitute deliberative body, the proxy jury reasoning through the evidence presented. As Syme writes: "It is true, of course, that spectators are often apostrophized in terms evoking notions of judgment in early modern prologues and epilogues. But they are not called on to assess the veracity of the narrative; they are asked to deliver a (kind) verdict on the worth of the play. . . . Even when [audiences] judge characters, they do not judge from the same plane as other characters in the play might; instead they pronounce from without."[32] Hutson has formulated a characteristically elegant response, emphasizing the audience member's "process of judging and conjecturing motives for the staged action as the complex story unfolds."[33]

Taking seriously Syme's concern, however, that audiences judge on a different plane from the characters, and returning to Jonson's own move from judgment to suffrage, one might see in that conversion a transition from the specifically legal to the political, a passage from the precise compass of a verdict on evidence to the affirmation or disapproval of a system represented as a whole. While the language of judgment remains, the sphere in which it is exercised is no longer that of the law courts but instead that of the polity broadly conceived. While Victoria Kahn sees a political dimension to the contract between author and

---

31. Hutson, *Invention of Suspicion*, 69–70.

32. Holger Schott Syme, "(Mis)Representing Justice on the Early Modern Stage," *Studies in Philology* 109, no. 1 (Winter 2012): 79–80.

33. Lorna Hutson, "Proof and Probability: Law, Imagination, and the Form of Things Unknown," in *New Directions in Law and Literature*, ed. Elizabeth Anker and Bernadette Meyler (Oxford: Oxford University Press, 2017), 149.

reader or spectator as arising later, with English Civil War writers' "explicit [analogy between] the reader's consent to the literary contract [and] an individual's consent to the political contract,"[34] this book contends that the theaters of pardoning of the early seventeenth century already involve their spectators in a form of political rather than simply legal judgment.

The several types of audiences would have approached the plays treated in this book in a manner informed by their particular legal and political vantage points. *Measure for Measure* and *The Bondman* were both performed before kings—but were also staged for "groundlings" and republicans of the mid-century Interregnum. The specific perspective of the viewer presumably influenced his interpretation of each play's political significance. If the king could see in a pardon the means for further securing his own sovereignty, the ordinary subject might view the prospect of revolution that some plays raised as an opportunity for rethinking the state.

A New Genre

A brief perusal of the literature on dramatic genres of the seventeenth century might make it seem that every conceivable variety has been identified and catalogued, from city comedies to disguised ruler plays.[35] And yet the vast number of tragicomedies between 1604 and 1660 that end with pardoning has so far been overlooked.[36] More than forty-five examples exist in which some kind of remission of punishment assumes a central role at the end of the play, whether taking the more common form of an exercise of mercy and pardoning, extending to the abrogation of an unjust law itself, as occurs in *The Partiall Law*; involving a "general pardon," as in John Fletcher's *The Pilgrim*; or assuming the guise of a "general Indemnity," as happens in the closet drama *The Female Rebellion*.[37]

---

34. Kahn, *Wayward Contracts*, 18.

35. See, for example, Brian Gibbons, *Jacobean City Comedy* (London: Routledge, 2017); Kevin Quarmby, *The Disguised Ruler in Shakespeare and His Contemporaries* (Oxford: Routledge, 2016).

36. Although the title of Janet Spencer's article "Staging Pardon Scenes: Variations of Tragicomedy" seems promising in this regard, she focuses her argument exclusively on the examples of Shakespeare's *Richard II* and *Measure for Measure*. She does, however, identify the potential for the tragicomic representation of pardons to undermine royal sovereignty. Janet Spencer, "Staging Pardon Scenes: Variations of Tragicomedy," *Renaissance Drama* 21 (1990): 58.

37. *The Partiall Law: A Tragi-Comedy by an Unknown Author*, ed. Bertram Dobell (London: Published by the editor, 1908); John Fletcher, *The Pilgrim*, in *Dramatic Works in the Beaumont and Fletcher Canon*, vol. 6, ed. Fredson Bowers (Cambridge: Cambridge University Press, 2008), 205; *The*

This figure does not even count the numerous plays in which punishment is avoided explicitly in service of a comic outcome, like several tragicomedies in the Beaumont and Fletcher canon, such as *The Fair Maid of the Inn*, which insists, "This day that hath given birth to blessings beyond hope, admits no criminal sentence."[38] It also generally omits works in which some pardons take place but other deaths are permitted.[39]

Despite the contingency of many plays' receptions on the particular audience members' characteristics, the generic structure of theaters of pardoning served the somewhat consistent function of destabilizing audience judgments, from wherever those judgments emanated. These theaters of pardoning stand in relation to tragedy; although they approach close to a tragic outcome, a set of final pardons, delivered by a *deus ex machina* figure, renders them tragicomedies instead. This *deus ex machina* may seem alternately a character intervening in the narrative or a function of the plot itself. The intrusion of the event of pardoning from outside the established universe of the play unsettles the tragic structure of knowledge and instead invites the audience to reimagine the world represented.

Some of the plays might also be considered romances, or pastoral romances—including the 1602 translation of *Il Pastor Fido* and Richard Fanshawe's 1647 version, *The Faithfull Shepherd*, as well as Cosmo Manuche's *The Banish'd Shepherdess*.[40] As Victoria Kahn has demonstrated, Fanshawe, among others, deployed the form of pastoral romance as a mechanism for justifying subjects'

Female Rebellion: A Tragicomedy (Glasgow: W. Anderson Eadie, 1872), 77. See Appendix A for an annotated catalogue of all the plays in question and a description of how they were selected.

38. John Fletcher et al., *The Fair Maid of the Inn*, in *Dramatic Works in the Beaumont and Fletcher Canon*, vol. 10, ed. Fredson Bowers (Cambridge: Cambridge University Press, 2008), 658.

39. Thomas Killigrew's *Claracilla* (performed between 1635 and 1636 and published in 1641) furnishes an interesting example of this kind of play. A usurper and a traitor are both killed during the course of the action—the latter by his own hand—but there are a number of pardons, and the king's daughter Claracilla, whom Seleucus, the second villain, had attempted to undermine, grants the latter forgiveness before he dies. In this play, the king too asks for pardon from Claracilla, whom he had attempted to entrap. Thomas Killigrew, *Claracilla: A Tragae-Comedy* (London: Thomas Cotes, 1641). Appendix A, listing theaters of pardoning, does not, however, exclude some plays with deaths early on that do not seem relevant to the endings. Likewise, it includes a number of works that remit the death penalty but prescribe alternatives such as exile or confinement in a monastery, or contain conditional pardons.

40. John Dymock (?), *Il Pastor Fido, or the Faithfull Shepherd* (translating Giovanni Battista Guarini's *Il Pastor Fido*) (London: Thomas Creede, 1602); Richard Fanshawe, *The Faithfull Shepherd* (translating Guarini) (London: R. Raworth, 1647); Cosmo Manuche, *The Banish'd Shepherdess*, in Patrick Kennedy Canavan, "A Study of English Drama" (Ph.D. diss., University of Southern California, 1950).

obligation to their king through the passions rather than coercion.[41] Focusing on the act and contexts of pardoning, however, illuminates additional political as well as generic features of these plays, including how they tackle responsibility for past rebellion or transgressions and the guise that they envision royal power assuming.

Considered from a purely juridico-political vantage point, pardoning already involves a theatrical scene. This is apparent from the entire history of pardoning's description within political philosophy, ranging from the texts of Jean Bodin through those of Immanuel Kant. In each instance, pardoning assumes a "spectacular" quality, phenomenally displaying the majesty of the sovereign. According to Michel Foucault's description of its function, pardoning—even more than punishment—actualizes what he terms the "super-power" of the sovereign, his affirmation of a personal excess over the criminal.[42] The exception constituted by the pardon, far from undermining the power of the classical sovereign that is staged in the scene of execution, underlines his supremacy over the individual malefactor; it permits him the acclamation of the people as though he had returned to them a life already forfeited. Jacques Derrida similarly speaks of "the theatrical space in which the grand forgiveness, the grand scene of repentance . . . is played, sincerely or not."[43]

At the same time that philosophy describes the appearance and staging of pardoning, however, it reserves the sovereign in the wings. Even for Foucault, who most emphatically insists upon the visibility of power in the classical age, the pardon arrives not with the person of the sovereign but by letter—conveyed from outside the scope of the play by a messenger; as he writes: "The sovereign power that enjoined [the executioner] to kill, and which through him did kill, was not present in him; it was not identified with his own ruthlessness. And it never appeared with more spectacular effect than when it interrupted the executioner's gesture with a letter of pardon."[44] The political theater of pardoning thereby traces an elaborate relation between the presence and the absence of the sovereign.[45]

---

41. Victoria Kahn, "The Passions and the Interests in Early Modern Europe: The Case of Guarini's *Il Pastor Fido*," in *Reading the Early Modern Passions: Essays in the Cultural History of Emotion*, ed. Gail Kern Paster, Katherine Rowe, and Mary Floyd-Wilson (Philadelphia: University of Pennsylvania Press, 2004), 236–37.

42. Michel Foucault, *Discipline and Punish*, 2nd ed. (New York: Vintage, 1995), 51.

43. Jacques Derrida, *On Forgiveness*, in *On Cosmopolitanism and Forgiveness*, trans. Mark Dooley and Michael Hughes (London: Routledge, 2001), 29.

44. Foucault, *Discipline and Punish*, 53.

45. Several of the plays in Appendix A, such as Thomas Heywood's *The Captives* (1624) or the anonymous *Dick of Devonshire* (1626), stage the actual arrival of a pardon by letter. Thomas Hey-

Certain plays likewise stage theaters of pardoning as politico-juridical moments dramatically depicted. Each play discussed in this book contains at least one scene of judgment followed by pardoning. At first glance, these moments simply appear to represent the legal verdict and subsequent pardon thematically. Yet the structure of the sovereign's pardon itself already entails a certain theatricality; given between the fact of his presence and the imperative for his withdrawal, the pardon unhinges the sovereign from a law that finds itself defined as positive insofar as it is posited apart from him. In each instance, the pardon delineates a relation between the law and the sovereign that the drama allegorizes. From the beginning, then, the staging of the pardon belongs not exclusively to the sovereign but to the play itself—implicating its theatrical form. Although it would be easy to view these pardons only as legal acts that can be located and analyzed within each play, they more crucially serve to connect the procedures of law with those of literature and link the audiences of both.

Neither tragedy nor comedy nor a simple combination of the two, theaters of pardoning constitute a kind of tragicomedy—one that undercuts the tragic unity valued at least since Aristotle's *Poetics*. It is helpful to situate theaters of pardoning within a post-Aristotelian context for two reasons. Historically, the Renaissance reception of Aristotle by such theorists of tragicomedy as Giovanni Battista Guarini and Giraldi Cinthio paved the way for English tragicomedy, the earliest writers of which were, as Tanya Pollard has argued, "scholars steeped in the classics."[46] John Fletcher's 1608 *The Faithful Shepherdess*, classified here as a theater of pardoning, "signaled [its] debts to Guarini not only in [the] play but in [its] account of tragicomedy in the play's preface."[47] Formally, Aristotle's account of tragedy furnishes a paradigm against which to understand the operations of tragicomedy—including its peculiar form of reversal and the kinds of judgment that it encourages in its spectators. The plays discussed, however, do not enact a particular, pre-formulated version of tragicomedy but instead progressively define the theater of pardoning.

---

wood, *The Captives* (London: Malone Society, 1953); *Dick of Devonshire* (Oxford: Malone Society, 1955).

46. Tanya Pollard, "Tragicomedy," in *The Oxford History of Classical Reception in English Literature*, ed. Patrick Cheney and Philip Hardie, vol. 2, 1558–1660 (Oxford: Oxford University Press, 2012), 425. As Sarah Dewar-Watson has shown, sixteenth-century theorists of tragicomedy attempted to bolster its prestige by positing a set of classical antecedents. Sarah Dewar-Watson, "Aristotle and Tragicomedy," in *Early Modern Tragicomedy*, ed. Subha Mukherji and Raphael Lyne (Cambridge: Cambridge University Press, 2007), 15–27.

47. Pollard, "Tragicomedy," 426.

In revising Aristotle's recommendations aimed at ensuring the unity of the tragic form, Renaissance writers like Giovanni Battista Guarini and Giraldi Cinthio simultaneously imported a Christian perspective and reinforced some of the divisions that Aristotle's *Poetics* had suggested. Although only descriptive in its original formulation, the *Poetics* has functioned as a privileged object of subsequent opposition, especially in its post-seventeenth-century incarnation as a series of dramaturgical rules. Among the theses that have been attacked, three in particular have provided focal points for the work of subsequent theorists of the theater. These can be identified as Aristotle's description of the requisite reversal (*peripeteia*) and recognition (*anagnôrisis*), his comments about what kinds of characters (*ta êthê*) tragedy should depict, and the mandate of unity in space, time, and action that has been attributed to him.[48] Examples of drama deviating from each of these principles can be found in the seventeenth century as well as subsequently, but Renaissance accounts of tragicomedy and theaters of pardoning themselves respond principally to strictures about action, reversal and recognition, and character. Whereas the articulation of tragicomic genre in Guarini's *Compendio della poesia tragicomica* separated such internal or "instrumental" concerns from tragicomedy's "architectonic" end—the catharsis peculiar to it—theaters of pardoning demonstrate the fundamental coherence between the instrumental and the architectonic. By undermining the security of the epistemological judgment that tragic spectators attain, these plays do not induce affective responses that would remain juxtaposed with the audience's exercise of reason, but instead produce feelings out of the impasse that rational judgment reaches.

The works of two more recent thinkers on tragedy assist in connecting the characters' recognition with that of the audience and elaborating their epistemological valences. Tragedy itself has often been interpreted epistemologically, viewed as entailing judgment both on the part of the characters and on that of the audience. Kathy Eden, writing in the Aristotelian tradition, emphasizes the relevance of judgment to the nature of tragic recognition, or *anagnôrisis*. Operating without Aristotle's explicit aid, Stanley Cavell has instead discerned

---

48. The extent to which Aristotle's text endorsed such unities has often been debated, and their systematic articulation has generally been attributed to seventeenth-century French writers like Pierre Corneille. The character Eugenius in John Dryden's "Essay of Dramatic Poesy," arguing for modern over ancient drama, claims that the unity of place was invented by "the French poets" (and that the unity of time was historically neglected). John Dryden, "Essay of Dramatic Poesy," in *Sources of Dramatic Theory I: Plato to Congreve*, ed. Michael J. Sidnell (Cambridge: Cambridge University Press, 2008), 274.

in tragedy—specifically Shakespearean tragedy—stagings of and responses to modern skepticism. From them it is possible to derive an account of the resemblance between the experience of figures within the play and that of the audience, as well as a diagnosis of the nature of the knowledge attained—or the disappointment of the desire for knowledge suffered—through recognitions.

In both the final section of *The Claim of Reason* and *Disowning Knowledge in Six Plays of Shakespeare*, Cavell argues for "an epistemological reading of Shakespearean tragedy," and maintains more generally that "tragedy is the story and study of a failure of acknowledgment, of what goes before it and after it— i.e. . . . the form of tragedy is the public form of the life of skepticism with respect to other minds."[49] As Cavell reminds us, acknowledgment (of other minds) cannot simply be reduced to knowledge (of external objects); employing the language of recognition, he stresses that "acknowledgment 'goes beyond' knowledge, not in the order, or as a feat, of cognition, but in the call upon me to express the knowledge at its core, to recognize what I know, to do something in the light of it, apart from which this knowledge remains without expression, hence without possession."[50] The urgency of the problem of skepticism as it is staged by tragedy does not subsist, for Cavell, absolutely, but instead resides within a specifically modern historical situation. Already indicating the historical inflection of his study in *The Claim of Reason*, he asserts, in introducing *Disowning Knowledge*, his "intuition . . . that the advent of skepticism as manifested in Descartes' *Meditations* is already in full existence in Shakespeare, from the time of the great tragedies in the first years of the seventeenth century, in the generation preceding that of Descartes."[51] Cavell thus implicitly intervenes in a conversation about the historical transmogrification of genre—or more specifically, in this case, of tragedy—and claims that the early seventeenth century furnishes a unique epistemological setting.

Cavell ends the same introduction with a reading of *Antony and Cleopatra* which views the play as figuring world catastrophe—the catastrophe of skepticism— while simultaneously emphasizing the text's affinity with Shakespeare's romances. Although Cavell does not explicitly demonstrate how *Antony and Cleopatra* constitutes a romance rather than a tragedy, the significance of the label emerges from his discussion of what occurs *after* the world has been

---

49. Stanley Cavell, *Disowning Knowledge in Six Plays of Shakespeare* (Cambridge: Cambridge University Press, 1987), 1; Stanley Cavell, *The Claim of Reason: Wittgenstein, Skepticism, Morality, and Tragedy* (New York: Oxford University Press, 1982), 478.

50. Cavell, *The Claim of Reason*, 428.

51. Cavell, *Disowning Knowledge*, 3.

withdrawn from Antony, or what he describes as "the shrinking of the world, from him, from itself." Corresponding to the place of a conventional tragic recognition, which it disappoints, "the recession of the world," Cavell explains, "is this play's interpretation of what I have called the truth of skepticism, that the human habitation of the world is not assured in what philosophy calls knowledge." Interpreting the conclusion of the play as a wedding, Cavell discovers, however, a renewed and distinct role for theatricality that Cleopatra herself reveals following the withdrawal of the world; as he writes, "I say that Cleopatra's desire in her conclusion is to present the world, make a present of it, to Antony; to return or represent it by presenting, finding out new ways of representing, her satisfaction by him; and I find that this requires the theatricalization of the world, hence her enacting of it." The theatricalization that Cleopatra performs for Antony is also that which the play generates for its spectators; thus, "Antony's subjection to mood is ours, this theater's." As Cavell asserts more generally, "It is the work of this theater to present itself as an instance of the ceremonies and institutions toward which our relation is in doubt, exists in doubt, is unknowable from outside."[52]

If Cavell furnishes a sense of the centrality of epistemology and the connection between epistemological relations within the play itself and between the play and the audience, Kathy Eden provides the most concrete juridical explanation of the epistemology of recognition, "isolating the Aristotelian correspondence between legal and poetic procedures in a single element of tragic structure—the *anagnôrisis* or tragic discovery." She demonstrates the similarity between how Aristotle ranks different types of proof in the *Rhetoric* and in the *Poetics*, emphasizing that, in both texts, "Aristotle . . . gives priority to rational argument over physical proof" and that probability "is responsible for the best recognitions." The characters' judgments, which depend exclusively on such ratiocination, differ slightly in nature from those of the spectators. According to Aristotle's description, tragedy should affect the audience psychologically by exciting pity and fear. Taking into account this axiom, Eden asserts that the viewers' judgments are aided by the concomitant activity of their emotions; as she writes, "Aristotle's stand on these matters represents a general attempt to include the emotions in the activity of making ethical judgments, whether in the law court or the theater."[53]

---

52. Cavell, *Disowning Knowledge*, 20–21, 25, 37, 29.
53. Kathy Eden, *Poetic and Legal Fiction in the Aristotelian Tradition* (Princeton: Princeton University Press, 1986), 9, 18, 19, 100–101.

While these judgments may correspond to tragedy in the theater, they correlate with equity in the legal sphere. Looking to the intention of the legislator—and especially that of the actor—the equitable judgment mitigates punishment through pity for the person.[54] Moving to Renaissance versions of Aristotle, Eden demonstrates that the classical understanding of equity is converted into a specifically Christian distinction between the Old Testament and the New—between the letter of the law and its overcoming by the spirit.

Cavell's and Eden's accounts of tragedy both reveal the juridico-epistemological dimension of recognition and the extent to which it affects the spectators as well as the characters in the play. Although theaters of pardoning modify tragic structure, subverting Aristotelian principles, they too create a juridico-epistemological effect. In such plays, pardoning intervenes in sequence after judgment but undermines its security. Arriving almost too late, in a time out of joint, it engenders a second reversal—and with it a version of recognition. Often granted by a figure who appears from above—or as a stranger—this pardoning may seem to be the gift of a god.[55]

Plautus's *Amphitryon*, the first play to use the term *tragicomoedia* and a text that is taken by some as the prototype of the genre, expressly derives its comic outcome from Jupiter.[56] These two determinations of pardoning—its divine aspect and its ability to generate a new recognition and reversal—partake at once of character and of plot. Nor can the two be divided. Precisely the discontinuity between the nature of the god and that of the other characters permits the former to reconfigure the theatrical terrain.

Elaborating his assertion that "tragedy is the representation [*mimêsis*] of an action [*praxeôs*] that is serious [*spoudaias*] and complete [*teleias*] and has a certain magnitude," Aristotle enumerates the genre's several component parts.[57] Foremost among these he ranks plot (*muthos*)—or "the arrangement of the events [*pragmaton*]"—since it is the "representation [*mimêsis*] of the action [*praxeôs*]."

---

54. An alternative version of equity, one associated with the law itself rather than the judge who interprets more mercifully than literally, appears in another strain of writings on equity, one taken up, in part, by Thomas Hobbes, as discussed in chapter 6.

55. There is no contradiction between representing the intruder as a stranger and as a god since there is a venerable tradition (Jewish and Greek) of the stranger as God.

56. The *Amphitryon* seems to have been of at least some interest in early seventeenth-century England; a manuscript called *The Birth of Hercules* translated the *Amphitryon* into English between 1600 and 1606, adapting it in the process.

57. Aristotle, *The Poetics*, trans. Stephen Halliwell (Cambridge: Harvard University Press, 1991), 22. I have drawn from the Halliwell translation as well as the Butcher translation in Aristotle, *Poetics*, trans. S. H. Butcher (New York: Hill and Wang, 1961), but modified both in places.

Second in place is classed "character" (*êthos*), which determines the quality of the actors (*prattontes*). As the color (or *pharmakos*), as it were, of tragedy, the character merely fills in the preexisting sketch (*graphê*). In discussing each of these elements, however, Aristotle reaches a point where they overlap. He specifies that character must, in tragedy, be both ethically good (*chrêstos*, also serious, *spoudaios*) and better (*beltion*) than the norm—like the larger-than-life pictures of Polygnotus. Although the demand for a certain status is combined here with the ethical component of character, and Aristotle even writes of the hero that "he must be one who is highly renowned and prosperous," he acknowledges the possibility that a slave might be "good" in the sense that he suggests—and thus, presumably, capable of being included in a tragedy.[58] This potential was overlooked by subsequent critics, who rapidly assimilated Aristotle's comments on character to prescriptions about what kinds of individuals tragedy could represent.

In his chapter discussing character, Aristotle emphasizes that it must, like plot, fulfill the criteria of probability and necessity. The analogy he raises between plot and character rapidly transforms into what seems to be an excursus on plot within this otherwise character-focused section. As Aristotle writes:

> It is clear therefore that the untying [*luseis*] of plots should emanate from the plot of itself and not by means of a machine [*mechanê*] as in the *Medea* and in the *Iliad* with respect to the embarkation. For the *mechanê* should only be used for things that lie outside the play, either what happened before and is therefore not such a thing as man knows [*eidein*], or what happens later and must be foretold [*proagoreusein*] and announced; for all things we give to the gods to see [similar to "know"]. But there must be nothing illogical [*alogon*] in the incidents, or if not, it must lie outside the tragedy, as in Sophocles' *Oedipus*.[59]

The *mechanê* here refers both to the machine itself and, synecdochically, to the deity arriving within it, later and in Latin dubbed the *deus ex machina*. Aristotle's prohibition against the *mechanê* commences as a statement about plot but concludes as a point about character—and the god associated with the machine.

In both cases, knowledge is at stake. Suggesting that tragedy can appositely circumscribe human knowledge while giving back to the gods precisely what is due to them, Aristotle provides an epistemological picture according to which human beings can arrive at appropriate and fairly unproblematic judgments.

---

58. Aristotle, *The Poetics*, trans. Halliwell, 23–24, 54–55.
59. Aristotle, *The Poetics*, trans. Halliwell, 56–57.

The plot must adhere to that logic familiar to the spectators and remain confined within their perspective. The gods, since they observe from a farther remove (where knowledge is given *up* [*apo*] to them)—synchronically seeing the context and realization of the events depicted—should not interfere lest they disturb the unity of this theater, the unity of the spectator's temporally conditioned synthesis. In the scope of their knowledge and vision, these gods are too much "better"—than us, or than the other characters—to do more than fill in outlying incidents. The disruption of the organic logic of the plot and its unity, initially attributed to the *mechané*, is thus eventually personified in the figure of the god who knows too much.

The shift within this passage from the *mechané* itself to the person of the god, from the intrusion of the literal machine to the knowledge of its occupant, elides another reading, one focused on plot rather than character, and on the performative rather than the constative dimensions of the play. In both of the examples that Aristotle mentions, Homer's *Iliad* and Euripides's *Medea*, machines literally appear, unaccompanied, even if assisted, by gods. Although in referring to the embarkation Aristotle presumably designates the appearance of Athena, who urges the Greeks to remain at Troy, the reversal itself in the *Iliad* occurs through the contrivance of the horse, left behind as the Greeks supposedly depart. Likewise, in the *Medea*, Medea herself arrives at the end in a *mechané* not occupied by but instead given to her by a god. This escape mechanism, like a pardon, enables her to elude punishment but not to avoid judgment—or at least, not that of the audience. When Medea returns from offstage carried aloft in the machine, it is to announce her imperviousness to the operations of the penal law—the logic of cause and effect associated with crime and its punishment. The *mechané* in these instances functions as a force against which the operations of probability and necessity are ineffectual, a force that ignores the power of logic and cognition. Not tied to the personified character of the deity, it subsists on the level of the plot itself, intruding within and disrupting a sequence that it would be possible to anticipate. Emerging from a discussion of character and ultimately reinscribed within that compass, Aristotle's treatment of the *mechané* thus also involves a performative break associated with the plot itself.

This intertwining of plot and character through the figure of the *mechané/deus ex machina* emerges with particular clarity in a passage from the prologue of Plautus's *Amphitryon* delivered by Mercury, the messenger god of money. At the same time, however, the *Amphitryon* moves a step further toward reifying its characters rather than viewing them as personified agents of the plot. Serving Jupiter and impersonating the king Amphitryon's slave Sosia in the play, Mercury explains the tragicomic genre in terms of a disparity in character between gods and slaves, but also implies a change from tragedy to comedy that depends on both knowledge and performance. As Mercury announces:

> Now first I'll tell you what I've come to ask,
> Then what's the subject [*argumentum*] of this tragedy.
> Why do you frown? Because a tragedy
> I . . .? Being a god, I will change it [*commutauero*].
> The same thing, if you like, I will make from tragedy
> Comedy and let be in the very same verses.
> Would you not like that? But I am stupid,
> As if I did not know what you wanted, being a god.
> I . . .
> I will make it mixed [*commixta*] tragedy [*tragico*] and comedy
>   [*comoedia*].
> For to make constantly a comedy
> A play where kings and gods come . . .
> What therefore? Since a slave [*seruus*] has some part here,
> I will make it be, as I said before, a tragicomedy [*tragicomoedia*].[60]

Mercury emphasizes both the aspects of divinity that Aristotle had noted, the gods' comprehensive knowledge (cognizing even the desires of the audience) and their performative power (transforming the genre of the play). As he explicitly states, however, this change leaves every line intact. What then constitutes the difference? The alteration is effected by Mercury's own statement—and that of Jupiter at the conclusion. These speech acts serve to recontextualize the play, undermining the security of a tragic outcome on the level of language as well as on that of plot.

During the course of the drama, several characters (including Jupiter himself in the guise of Amphitryon) invoke the name of the king of the gods, but the characters are not alerted to the futility of these promises and oaths until the conclusion of the play, when Jupiter reveals himself. Likewise, Jupiter converts the plot from tragic to tragicomic by elaborating his perspective on the events of the play, explaining that the infidelity of Amphitryon's wife, Alcmena, cannot be considered culpable since it was divinely coerced. As he instructs Amphitryon: "Live as you used to live with Alcmena,/ In love and mutual trust. She did no

---

60. Plautus, *Amphitryon*, trans. Constance Carrier, in *Plautus: The Comedies*, vol. 1., ed. David R. Slavitt and Palmer Bovie (Baltimore: Johns Hopkins University Press, 1995), ll. 50–63; hereafter cited parenthetically by line.

wrong—/It was my strength" (literally, she had to submit to me) (1141–43). Just as the fact of Jupiter's involvement in the plot alters the nature of the oaths sworn upon his name, his absolute power changes the quality of Alcmena's admittedly inadvertent actions. The assertion of divinity—both initially by Mercury and subsequently by Jupiter—is thus also a proclamation of tragicomedy rather than tragedy. In theaters of pardoning, the pardon serves a similar function, but rather than exculpating the condemned, it usually only remits their punishment.

At the same time that Mercury announces his and Jupiter's capacity to change the genre of the play, he describes why it must remain tragicomedy rather than becoming comedy. If at first he espouses a performative production of genre, he then shifts to a constative definition. While the omniscience and capacity of the gods allowed them to negate the tragic quality of the plot, their presence also renders pure comedy impossible. As Mercury explains, the very fact that the *Amphitryon* involves kings and gods as well as slaves prevents the play from being categorized as comedy. Guarini confirms this suggestion, asserting, "These specific differences are proper to tragedy: persons of high rank, serious actions, terror, and pity; and these to comedy: private persons and affairs, laughter, and witty remarks."[61] For both Plautus and Guarini, however, tragicomedy combines high and low characters in more than one sense. In the *Amphitryon*, Mercury is a god yet plays the part of the slave Sosia; a further representational abyss is opened by Mercury's suggestion that the actor himself may only be a servant (1020). By merging the god with the slave in a single individual, the play likewise raises the suggestion that even gods or kings may carry out private as well as public activities. As Guarini writes on this subject, citing the example of the *Amphitryon*: "Do princes always sit in majesty? Do they never deal in private matters? Certainly they do: why then cannot a high-ranking person appear on the stage when he is not engaged in matters of great importance?"[62] This vision of tragicomedy as actualizing both of the king's two bodies, the political and the personal, is confirmed by the circumstances under which Jupiter disguises himself as Amphitryon—the pursuit of his desire for Alcmena.[63]

When the pardon—coming on the scene as a *mechanê*, a *deus ex machina*, or both—occasions a second reversal, accompanied or not by one or more

---

61. Giambattista Guarini, "Compendio della Poesia Tragicomica," in *Sources of Dramatic Theory I: Plato to Congreve*, ed. Michael J. Sidnell. (Cambridge: Cambridge University Press, 1991), 150.

62. Guarini, "Compendio," 151.

63. Ernst Kantorowicz furnished the classic discussion of the king's two bodies and its role in the medieval theory of kingship in *The King's Two Bodies* (1997). Since then, his analytic framework has furnished a model and jumping-off point for many other studies.

recognitions, it further defies Aristotle's instructions. As Aristotle writes with reference to the reversal and recognition involved in the complex plot, which he values above the simple one, "These things should happen through the very arrangement [*suntaxis*] of the plot [*muthos*], so that out of what has happened before comes either by necessity [*anagkê*] or according to probability (*to eikos*) what happens later; for there is a great difference between what happens because of something and what happens after it."[64] Not only does the *mechanê* of the pardon generate a second reversal, a possibility that Aristotle never mentions, but also it interferes with the organic logic of the plot, intervening between cause and effect. Either personified or simply the place of a break within the plot, the pardon belongs not just to the god or sovereign but to the plot itself as its openness to the unexpected.

For the characters, pardoning does not necessarily transform the original judgment. But for the audience it does. As part of the plot, pardoning sets up the possibility of the new. The tragicomedies, as well as the political and philosophical responses to proto-revolutionary and revolutionary events discussed in this book, demonstrate how the very act of pardoning constitutes the precondition for the establishment of a new political ground and allows for the reconfiguration of the existing terrain.

There are several close cousins of theaters of pardoning, but they differ in certain crucial respects. First, theaters of pardoning depart from the equitable understanding of tragedy that Kathy Eden elaborates. Second, they can be distinguished from the vision of compassion that Martha Nussbaum has advocated as both the appropriate response to tragedy and the basis for creating scalable connections among individuals throughout the world. Finally, they fail to fulfill the dream of a pure forgiveness without hope of reciprocation advocated by Jacques Derrida and others.

The equitable judgment involved in Eden's account of tragedy might initially appear to verge on theaters of pardoning. In theaters of pardoning, however, the play's judgment of the character is not altered by the pardon, but the consequences of judgment are instead suspended. Likewise, to the extent that equity involves relaxing what would otherwise be a negative judgment about the effects of a perpetrator's actions in light of his or her less than culpable intent, theaters of pardoning often stage the opposite scenario. In many, the intent of revenge or revolution remains despite the actor's failure to pull off a murder, assassination, or rebellion. It can be this intent that winds up being the object of mercy. The

---

64. Aristotle, *Poetics*, trans. Halliwell, 64–65.

contrasts between equity and theaters of pardoning are developed in more detail in chapters 1 and 6 in the discussions of Shakespeare's *Measure for Measure* and Thomas Hobbes's *Dialogue between a Philosopher and a Student of the Common Lawes.*

Nor do theaters of pardoning involve compassion in Martha Nussbaum's sense. Nussbaum has articulated an influential account of tragedy—and the novel—as generating compassion, a feeling that might encourage a moral relation scalable not only within communities but even to remote parts of the world. In developing her account of compassion, Nussbaum draws on Stoic thought, particularly Seneca's vision of clemency, while rejecting the Stoic "extirpation of the passions."[65] Under Nussbaum's model, compassion "has three cognitive elements: the judgment of *size* (a serious bad event has befallen someone); the judgment of *nondesert* (this person did not bring the suffering on himself or herself); and the *eudaimonistic judgment* (this person, or creature, is a significant element in my scheme of goals and projects, an end whose good is to be promoted)."[66] As with equity, the "judgment of *nondesert*" may not be—and frequently is not—present in theaters of pardoning. Even more important, however, the pardoning involved in these plays does not generally entail the eudaimonistic judgment Nussbaum describes. Some plays instead draw on a different thread of the Stoic tradition that emphasized clemency for the benefit of the polity as a whole rather than compassion for a particular individual. Political consciousness hence trumps fellow feeling. The disparities between clemency and compassion feature prominently in chapter 4, treating Philip Massinger's *The Bondman*, a play that self-consciously situates itself within a Stoic frame.

By the same token, to the extent that pardoning is aimed at the future or intended to achieve a pragmatic end, it may fail to fulfill the most stringent requirements of forgiveness from a philosophical perspective. As Jacques Derrida argued, a "forgiveness worthy of its name . . . must forgive the unforgivable, and without condition."[67] In that respect, "one could never . . . found a politics or law on forgiveness." The political pardon instead represents an act of sovereignty; indeed, "what makes the 'I forgive you' sometimes unbearable or odious, even obscene, is the affirmation of sovereignty. . . . Each time forgiveness is effectively exercised, it seems to suppose some sovereign power." Only a forgiveness that

65. For the development of this line of reasoning, see Martha C. Nussbaum, "Equity and Mercy," *Philosophy and Public Affairs* 22, no. 2 (Spring 1993): 83–125; *The Therapy of Desire*, 316–438; and *Upheavals of Thought*, 354–400.

66. Nussbaum, *Upheavals of Thought*, 321.

67. Derrida, *On Forgiveness*, 39.

exceeded the frame of the political—even if subsequently reinscribed in it—would actualize the pure version of the concept. There may, indeed, be a space for such forgiveness in the aftermath of revolutionary violence—a forgiveness that is, as Derrida insists, "*unconditional but without sovereignty*"—but it will almost always, as demonstrated in the chapters that follow, be co-opted by a pragmatic plan for the future, and a new grounding of the state.[68]

While, in many of the instances discussed, the pardon similarly effects a renewal of the state, the dramatic structure of the tragedies out of which tragicomedy emerges altered over the course of the seventeenth century. At the commencement of the reign of James I, the central paradigm remained that of revenge, but this revenge itself became progressively generalized into the threat of revolutionary violence, culminating in the English Civil War and the execution of James's son King Charles I. Corresponding to this evolution from the personal level of revenge to the political construction of revolution is the transition from a more monarchical, judgment-focused conception of sovereignty to a more parliamentary, and legislative, vision. The danger of revolution, as opposed to revenge, thus becomes not the peril it poses to the body of the king but rather its act of striking at the very source of legality and lawgiving.

The Chapters

Chapter 1, "Dramatic Judgments: *Measure for Measure*, Revenge, and the Institution of the Law," sets the stage by analyzing Shakespeare's play as paradigmatic of what I call "theaters of pardoning." It locates the play dramatically within the tradition of revenge tragedy, beginning with Aeschylus's *Oresteia*, and the negation of that revenge through pardoning. It situates the play politically within the attempt to conceptualize the institution of law, an institution that, the chapter argues, the play presents as more judicially than legislatively determined. Although pardoning is foregrounded late in the action, the bulk of the tragicomedy implicitly examines the role of sovereignty in judgment, staging a conflict between a more bureaucratic, institutional conception of judgment and a vision of judgment as emanating from a sovereign decision on the law as well as its application.

As I contend, both *Measure for Measure*'s reflections on sovereignty, pardoning, and judgment and its staging of the relationship between early modern

---

68. Derrida, *On Forgiveness*, 38, 58–59.

tragicomedy and ancient tragedy appear in greater relief against the backdrop of the early modern jurist Sir Edward Coke's *Reports*, which were in the process of appearing at the time when the play was first performed. Particularly salient are two features of Coke's work that helped to render it what Michel Foucault argued was the first "historico-political discourse." As early as 1602, Coke had attempted to dismiss the claim that English common law had been altered by or even generated out of the Norman Conquest by appealing to a more archaic, ancient Greek source of law; in a 1607 conference with King James, he then asserted limitations on the monarch's power to judge in person. Coke's elaborate genealogy of the common law was articulated before *Measure for Measure* was first performed, and his views opposing the king's power to judge in person emerged several years after the play. Shakespeare's play was, however, engaged in a dialogue with both of Coke's propositions, I argue, responding to the former and auguring the latter.

Included among the audiences of *Measure for Measure* was King James I himself. Chapter 2, "Emplotting Politics: James I and the 'Powder Treason,'" considers the significance of this circumstance for interpreting James's response to the Gunpowder Plot of 1605—sometimes deemed the first act of terrorism in the West. Only months after the play was performed before him, James invoked the rhetoric of measure for measure in addressing the Gunpowder Plot. James's reaction to the event assumed a dramatic form, and he attempted both to inscribe the unprecedented crime within the conventional structure of revenge tragedy and to interpret it according to a model of tragicomedy indebted to John of Patmos's apocalyptic Revelation, which, as a teenager, he had translated from the Greek.

Despite echoing the language of *Measure for Measure*, King James refrained from pardoning the conspirators and thereby following the paradigm presented by the play. While taking the advice of Jean Bodin's *Six Books of the Republic*, perhaps as well as *Measure for Measure*, and avoiding judging in person, he nevertheless neglected the power that both sources indicated might be conferred on the sovereign by pardoning. Instead, he insisted on another version of tragicomedy—one in which the elect would be saved and all others condemned. In applying this generic structure, the king suggested that Parliament be entrusted with judging the conspirators, thus imaginatively displacing his sovereignty onto it. Whereas James could have reinforced his own sovereignty in this instance by pardoning, he instead contributed to the power of Parliament at this early moment of his monarchy.

Chapters 3 and 4 turn to two plays staged toward the end of James I's reign, each of which involves the reformulation of a polity threatened with dissolution through some modification of pardoning; both present alternatives to the sovereign pardon contemplated in *Measure for Measure*, alternatives that suggest new bases for constructing the state. Chapter 3, "Non-Sovereign Forgiveness: Mercy among Equals in *The Laws of Candy*," examines *The Laws of Candy*, now generally acknowledged to be primarily the work of John Ford. Set on the island of Crete (Candy), the play draws in part on Plato's *Laws*, which itself takes place in Crete and features a dialogue among Cretan, Spartan, and Athenian lawgivers. Within the play, a law granting honor to one who has been acclaimed military victor by his fellow soldiers comes into conflict with a law punishing ingratitude with death. This latter law provides for its own suspension by a grant of forgiveness between individuals. *The Laws* undergirds the quasi-constitutional significance of law as a force beyond sovereignty in the play as well as the tragicomedy's concerns with ambition, excesses of wealth, and the difference between war among and within states. *The Laws of Candy* concludes with a sequence of grants of non-sovereign forgiveness—enabled by law—that represents a new foundation of the state.

Philip Massinger's *The Bondman* furnishes the subject of chapter 4, "From Sovereignty to the State: The Tragicomic Clemency of Massinger's *The Bondman*." Here too the polity—Syracuse in this instance—is nearly overturned but through different means, a slave rebellion that occurs when most are away, fighting abroad; a representation of the widespread abuses within the city sets the scene for this event early in the play. The dedication of *The Bondman* to Philip Herbert, the Earl of Montgomery, introduces the language of clemency, a Stoic concept most fully elaborated in Seneca's *De Clementia*, which Thomas Lodge had newly translated in 1614. Drawing on Seneca's vision, *The Bondman* centers both generically and politically on clemency. Clemency infuses the play's mode of tragicomedy and presents a vision of politics that prioritizes the general welfare of the state over any particular form of rule. The play hence displaces focus from the sources of sovereignty onto the stability of the state, allowing the work to appeal to audiences across the seventeenth-century political spectrum.

In one sense, *The Laws of Candy* and *The Bondman* imagine the transformation of pardoning in relation to a potentially revolutionary threat. Only a year after the first performance of *The Bondman*, King James's Lord Keeper referred, when addressing Parliament, to the imperative of forgetting the conflict of Greek with Greek; this speech would augur James's son Charles's subsequent obsession with acts of oblivion—a form of general amnesty erasing the record of the underlying events rather than simply remitting punishment. At the same time, the plays do not simply show a stage in the evolution of the pardon power. Although fitting within the seventeenth-century trajectory of the generalization of pardoning and its transfer from king to Parliament, they simultaneously suggest a set of alternative visions, those of non-sovereign forgiveness and Stoic clemency.

Chapter 5, "Between Royal Pardons and Acts of Oblivion: The Transitional Justice of Cosmo Manuche and James Compton, Earl of Northampton," turns to royalist drama of the 1650s following the closure of the theaters, focusing on playwright Cosmo Manuche and his patron, the Earl of Northampton. Manuche's *The Just General* attempts to return to a model of pardoning more akin to that found in *Measure for Measure*, enhancing the power of the sovereign through a display of mercy. It is noteworthy, however, that the title of the play focuses not on the king but on his subordinate, the general. This displacement of attention to those entrusted with carrying out a program of loyalty or its opposite characterizes Manuche's *The Banish'd Shepherdess*—which remains in manuscript—as well. In that play, much of the action is taken up with tormenting the minions of a fled usurper who are gradually realizing that their heyday is at its end and attempting to figure out how they can reconcile themselves with the ruler whom they had previously shunned. Both of these works are centrally concerned with transitional justice, a topic dwelt on by a manuscript in Compton's hand (see Appendix B) found bound with *The Banish'd Shepherdess* at Castle Ashby. This brief and incomplete expository piece devotes itself to advocating "an act of indemnitie, or of oblivion stille it what you please," explaining the advantages such an act would present not simply for Cavaliers but for the state itself. Taken together, both works attempt to restore pardoning to the hands of the king and evince an emerging concern with a form of transitional justice that considers how to reintegrate not rebel leaders but their followers within the state.

The Bondman was not only performed on the eve of the Restoration to stir republican sentiment against the return of King Charles II but was also revived extensively on the Restoration stage. Chapter 6, "Pardoning Revolution: The 1660 Act of Oblivion and Hobbes's Recentering of Sovereignty," turns to the moment of the Restoration and from drama to political theory. Many of the writings of the philosopher Thomas Hobbes were inflected by his royalist leanings. Despite his royalist tendencies and support for the restoration of Charles II to the English throne, however, Hobbes's writings fundamentally altered the existing conception of sovereignty after the English Revolution in a way that would prove deleterious to the continued power of the monarch. If King James I had emphasized his capacity to judge over his ability to make and promulgate laws, Hobbes instead grounded sovereignty in lawgiving and envisioned the king's equitable power of judgment as derivative of this more fundamental mark of majesty. In doing so, Hobbes turned the conception of sovereignty toward the generality of lawgiving rather than the singularity of judgment, a displacement that paved the path for the transfer of sovereignty from king to Parliament.

The 1600 Act of Oblivion passed by Parliament after the restoration of King Charles II, at his behest—an act Hobbes himself analyzed in his *Dialogue between a Philosopher and a Student of the Common Lawes*—provides a particularly striking example of how this transfer unfolded on a conceptual level. In this instance, something like the pardon, which represented the act of sovereignty most closely linked with the singularity of the monarch, was itself generalized and transferred to Parliament instead of being exercised exclusively by the king. Charles I's obsession with oblivion had culminated in a final letter to his son, the future King Charles II, written as the first Charles awaited execution; this letter urged Charles II to pass an Act of Oblivion as soon as he was restored to the English throne. The latter took this admonition to heart and began negotiating for such a step before even setting foot on English soil from his exile in France. The crucial aspect distinguishing oblivion—and its cousin amnesty—from regular pardons, in addition to its generality, was the fact that it required the legal forgetting of the revolutionary events.

In reformulating sovereignty and contextualizing the Act of Oblivion within that reformulation, Hobbes posited a particular role for philosophy itself in providing a ground for the political sphere. Perhaps because of the political and legal disruption that the English Revolution represented, Hobbes sought a new foundation, one that emanated from philosophy. Whereas a jurist like Sir Edward Coke had been able to theorize the obligations of the common law and its relation to the sovereign from within the compass of law itself, Hobbes insisted on stepping outside and, like Socrates, addressing the law as a foreigner to it. For the first time in the English tradition, then, rather than being constituted through dramatic and political interventions, the law is examined by a secular discipline beyond its bounds, philosophy announcing and delimiting for law—and even for sovereignty—its proper place.

Although the philosophical account of sovereignty that Hobbes provided has enjoyed a substantial post-history in continental Europe, it nevertheless bears the traces of its English origins. The oppositions between equity and common law, king and Parliament, and judging and lawgiving—all connected with a particular set of English legal and political institutions—pervade Hobbes's *Dialogue*. While his efforts to undermine and transmute these binaries enable Hobbes's theory to attain the abstraction of philosophy, the residues of their influence remain within his conception of sovereignty. On one reading, the *Dialogue* could be seen as representing Hobbes's efforts to enact his own oblivion on Sir Edward Coke and the body of early seventeenth-century English legal theory for which his name stands. While Hobbes may have thereby succeeded in directing the attention of subsequent philosophy toward his own vision of sovereignty and away from its precursors, the oblivion was necessarily rendered incomplete by the *Dialogue*'s own indebtedness to its seventeenth-century English context. Names and details may have succumbed to amnesia, but certain patterns and paradigms remain.

In order to excavate the grounds of Hobbes's conception of sovereignty— a conception that has influenced the entire subsequent history of political theory—it is therefore necessary to examine the seventeenth-century ferment out of which this understanding emerged. It is the aim of this book not only to furnish such a genealogy but also, in doing so, to help unsettle the dominance of sovereignty in the post-Hobbesian tradition, as the Postlude suggests. Only with the displacement of the connection between pardoning and sovereignty could another form of forgiveness potentially emerge out of hiding into the political sphere.

1

DRAMATIC JUDGMENTS /
Measure for Measure, Revenge, and the Institution of the Law

At the commencement of *Measure for Measure*, the ruler of Vienna, Duke Vincentio, absents himself from the city for an indefinite duration without providing reasons for his departure. Two individuals, named Escalus and Angelo, seem potentially appropriate as substitutes, but, again for reasons unknown at the outset, Vincentio chooses Angelo over Escalus. Once in power, Angelo immediately revives an old law against lechery that had fallen into desuetude and condemns the character Claudio to death for violating it by impregnating Juliet;[1] he also issues a "proclamation" mandating that "all houses [meaning houses of prostitution] in the suburbs of Vienna . . . be plucked down" (1.2.88–89). It soon transpires that Angelo's reign is one of tyranny when he himself attempts to seduce Claudio's sister, the virtuous novice Isabella, in exchange for remitting her brother's life (2.4), a remission he ultimately fails to furnish.[2] Despite verging on tragedy at various points, the play achieves a comic conclusion when the Duke returns, abandoning the disguise of a friar that he had donned, and pardons almost all of the offenders (5.1). Justice itself seems to require at least one

---

1. As Claudio says of Angelo's role in his punishment,

This new governor
Awakes me all the enrolled penalties
Which have, like unscour'd armour, hung by th' wall
So long, that nineteen zodiacs have gone round,
And none of them been worn; and for a name
Now puts the drowsy and neglected act
Freshly on me: 'tis surely for a name.

William Shakespeare, *Measure for Measure*, ed. J. W. Lever, 2nd ser. (London: Arden Shakespeare, 1994), 1.2.154–60; hereafter cited parenthetically.

2. It is not incidental that the request for mercy here, as in other Shakespeare plays, comes from a woman. As Cynthia Herrup has explained in "The King's Two Genders," pardoning came in masculine and feminine versions in the seventeenth century, and the challenge that kings often proved unsuccessful at facing was that of transforming feminine mercy into a masculine form. Cynthia Herrup, "The King's Two Genders," *Journal of British Studies* 45, no. 3 (July 2006): 493–510.

of these pardons, that of Claudio, who was condemned under a law of which he lacked proper notice. Pardoning Claudio—the first object of the law's revival—at the end of the play appears to be the only way that the law can remain in force without those newly implementing it appearing unjust.

At first blush, then, *Measure for Measure* addresses several problems with lawgiving. It not only invokes the kind of legislation by proclamation that the jurist and politician Sir Edward Coke[3] would later condemn in relation to King James I—and would claim was already illegitimate in the reign of Henry VIII—but also suggests the potential wrongfulness of prosecuting an individual under a long-dead law. The play has indeed been interpreted along these lines, viewed as involving the injustice to an individual that a law itself may generate or as prefiguring the imminent controversies between king and Parliament over the location of legislative authority.[4]

The principal events of the play, however, involve not lawgiving but scenes of judgment and pardoning, ones that draw upon a particular juridical conception of early modern kingship. The work of several Elizabethan theorists of the state revealed, as Debora Shuger has contended, a juridic rather than a constitutional understanding, in which "to govern is to dispense justice; that is the king's primary role and it is also why the throne he sits on and the sword he bears are God's."[5] King James himself adopted this stance, observing that "Kings are properly judges" and advising his son, the future King Charles I, on the centrality of judgment to the capacity of a king.[6] Nevertheless, as Coke's writings demonstrate, the identification of judgment with the sovereign did not remain

---

3. Coke served in such diverse positions as attorney general, chief judge of the Court of Common Pleas and King's Bench, and member of Parliament during the reigns of Queen Elizabeth, King James I, and King Charles I. For more biographical details about him, see Allen D. Boyer, *Sir Edward Coke and the Elizabethan Age* (Stanford: Stanford University Press, 2003); and Catherine Drinker Bowen, *The Lion and the Throne: The Life and Times of Sir Edward Coke, 1552–1634* (Boston: Little Brown & Co., 1990).

4. As Craig Bernthal has noted, emphasizing how the play depicts the connection between the law and those condemned under it: "The crimes in *Measure for Measure* are, in a sense, manufactured by the imposition of a long dead statute, a practice which Bacon warns against. The imposition of the statute creates a problem so that the state can flex its muscles by asserting control." Craig Bernthal, "Staging Justice: James I and the Trial Scenes of *Measure for Measure*," *Studies in English Literature, 1500–1900* 32, no. 2 (1992): 256–57. Focusing on the institutional location of the legislative power, Louise Halper has argued that *Measure for Measure* should be interpreted in light of the conflict between king and Parliament in early modern England. Louise Halper, "*Measure for Measure*: Law, Prerogative, Subversion," *Cardozo Studies in Law and Literature* 13, no. 2 (Fall 2001): 221–64.

5. Debora K. Shuger, *Political Theologies in Shakespeare's England: The Sacred and the State in* Measure for Measure (New York: Palgrave, 2001), 72–73.

6. Shuger, *Political Theologies,* 73–74.

uncontested during the course of James's reign; indeed, some of the most significant disputes to occur under his rule involved the relation between royal and judicial authority and between the prerogative and common law courts. It is perhaps not surprising, then, that even in a play performed shortly after James's ascension to the throne, questions concerning theories of judgment and the proper location of judicial power should be paramount.

The juridico-political treatment of pardoning as well as its dramatic place in *Measure for Measure* render the play the paradigmatic example of a theater of pardoning. Within it, the sovereign pardon resembles a judgment yet manages to escape many of the problems that contemporary legal and political theorists identified with the sovereign's act of judging in person. Reaffirming the Duke's majesty and suppressing the threat of revolution, the pardon remains the act of a singular sovereign, prudently managing his power. The pardon here permits the sovereign's withdrawal, although that withdrawal occurs in person.

As individualized determinations on the law and its exceptions, the Duke's final pardons leave the audience uncertain as to whether the law will continue in force after the end of the play, perhaps under the jurisdiction of Escalus and his minions, or whether lawlessness will reign, subject to the Duke's whim.[7] *Measure for Measure*'s form of tragicomedy thereby thrusts judgment back upon its audience more definitively than ancient analogues like the *Oresteia*, which ends on a note affirming the establishment of legal institutions.

At the same time, two additional dimensions of pardoning are suggested by Shakespeare's play. On the one hand, the potential violence of the sovereign pardon appears in the pardons of the characters Isabella and Lucio, calling the mercy of pardoning into question. On the other, the possibility emerges of an act of pardoning not based on prior knowledge. By identifying the drawbacks of the sovereign pardon, the play allows the audience to ask whether an alternative kind of pardoning could occur, one that might neither affirm the power of the king nor rely on the certainty of judgment. Not until later in the seventeenth century, however, would answers to these questions begin to be sketched.

The stakes of the play are rendered perspicuous only in the final scene, which is the first to explicitly mention sovereignty and conjoin it with pardoning. Focusing on that scene, in the first section of this chapter I analyze the intimate relation between pardoning and sovereignty in *Measure for Measure*. While sovereignty and its connection with pardoning are foregrounded late in the play, the bulk of the play implicitly examines the role of sovereignty in judgment. In

---

7. The later play *The Partiall Law* furnishes a contrast on this point.

particular, as I argue in the second section, it stages a conflict between a more bureaucratic, institutional conception of judgment and a vision of judgment as emanating from a sovereign decision on both the law and its application.

This clash remained not simply hypothetical in early modern England; several years after *Measure for Measure* was performed, Coke would elaborate on the reasons why the king lacked the power to judge in person. Prioritizing the institution of the common law and the role of judges steeped in accumulated wisdom, Coke sought to circumscribe King James's sovereignty. In doing so, he historicized that very sovereignty, as I contend in the third section, dismantling the inherited authority of the English monarchy by looking back before the origins of its power in the Norman Conquest. To the extent that the Norman Conquest brought both French and Roman principles onto English soil, Coke examined the palimpsest of English custom not only for an immemorial ancient constitution but also for Greek roots that preceded any Roman sources. Explicitly associating an institutional version of the common laws with Greek antecedents, Coke suggests an early modern notion of Greece that furnishes an alternative to the divine right conception of monarchy and sovereignty.

At the same time, Coke's invocation of ancient Greek drama indicates that the dominance of Roman plays in the Elizabethan and Jacobean periods did not succeed in entirely suppressing the Greek theatrical tradition. Indeed, certain structural analogies link Aeschylus's *Oresteia* with *Measure for Measure*, including the extent to which both works contend with the relation between law and a cycle of revenge. The final section of this chapter elaborates on these resemblances while also suggesting the possibility that the *Oresteia* may have had a more direct influence on the composition of *Measure for Measure*. Regardless of the degree of actual indebtedness, a detailed comparison of the two plays indicates the specifically modern quality of theaters of pardoning as a genre and the intimate connection of that genre with the concept of sovereignty.

Measure for Measure as a Theater of Pardoning

In *Measure for Measure*, pardoning itself conforms to a juridical model and is intimately associated with sovereignty. Although the play has often been read as a meditation on sovereignty, the first and last occasion for the appearance of the word—or any associated terms—corresponds with the commencement of pardoning in act 5, scene 1, the final episode of the tragicomedy. There Isabella, arguably the least blameworthy figure in the story, introduces the series of pardons by requesting one herself. Following the revelation of the Friar as the Duke,

Isabella begs, "O, give me pardon,/ That I, your vassal, have employ'd and pain'd/ Your unknown sovereignty" (5.1.385–95). The line breaks in the middle, at the end of her succinct request, to allow the Duke to respond in almost the same breath, "You are pardon'd, Isabel" (5.1.385). "Your unknown sovereignty" and "You are pardon'd, Isabel" share the space of a single line, sovereignty ineluctably paired with pardoning here. The Duke's sovereignty furnishes both the reason why Isabella must be pardoned and the precondition for the politico-juridical success of the pardons she and others receive.

The pardons the Duke delivers at the conclusion of the play partake of a structure similar to that of the judgments preceding them. Like judgments, each pardon is issued individually and considers the circumstances of the particular case. The procedure for pardoning Angelo renders apparent the more general paradigm. The first model of justice—and mercy—that the Duke proposes is one of uniformity. As he contends in a passage justifying the title of the play:

> The very mercy of the law cries out
> Most audible, even from his proper tongue:
> 'An Angelo for Claudio; death for death.
> Haste still pays haste, and leisure answers leisure;
> Like doth quit like, and Measure still for Measure.' (5.1.405–9)

Far from being opposed to law, mercy here constitutes an organ of it. The antecedent of "his" remains ambiguous, mercy either ventriloquized through the "proper tongue" of the law or itself personified. This mercy attends to the victims of Angelo's crimes, including Claudio, who is presumed dead, and Isabella, as his surviving sister. The words spoken by this mercy of the law resemble those of Aeschylus's Furies, pursuing Orestes as the murderer of his mother; called forth by blood guilt, the Furies in the *Eumenides*, the final play of the *Oresteia*, theatrically embody the principle that is figuratively voiced in *Measure for Measure*.

This vision of mercy is, however, presented only to be supplanted. Once Mariana and Angelo return from their hastily performed marriage, Mariana persuades Isabella to supplicate the Duke for Angelo's life. In her appeal, Isabella invokes a logic that resembles that of equity but functions in a sense as its opposite.[8] She first raises the "as if" of the equitable fiction, asking the Duke, "Look,

---

8. Several critics have contended that equity lies at the heart of *Measure for Measure*. Debora Shuger includes an extended discussion of the theory of equity and the courts of equity in *Political Theologies in Shakespeare's England*, 72–101, and a number of others have pointed out specific connections. As Andrew Majeske has persuasively argued, though, the pardons at the end of *Measure for Measure* remain more disruptive than equitable and controvert the possibility of reading the play as

if it please you, on this man condemn'd/ As if my brother liv'd" (5.1.442–43). Rather than continuing by asserting that Angelo's intention failed to meet the requisite level of culpability—as she would in a conventional turn to equity—Isabella in fact points out the opposite. If Claudio still lived, Angelo's bad intent would remain simply an intent rather than a criminal act. Hence,

> For Angelo,
> His act did not o'ertake his bad intent,
> And must be buried but as an intent
> That perish'd by the way. Thoughts are no subjects;
> Intents, but merely thoughts. (5.1.448–52)[9]

Whereas the equitable judgment would insist on mitigating or increasing punishment in light of the perpetrator's intent, Isabella suggests that the Duke should focus instead on completed acts. This passage appears to furnish the basis for the Duke's "apt remission" (5.1.496), subsequently directed toward Angelo once it is revealed that Claudio does, in fact, live.

Remission in this instance depends on a scene of judgment featuring reasoning about the individual malefactor. Whereas mercy at first seemed to constitute an aspect of the law itself and heeded the interests of the victims of crime, the form of pardoning that eventually occurs relies on the personal act of the sovereign. The pardon, like a judgment, is triangulated. In the typical context of judgment, the judge assesses the merits of one individual's claim against another or of the state's allegations against a defendant. As a prelude to Angelo's pardon, the sovereign hears a plea for mercy delivered by an aggrieved party and decides to forgo punishment.

The judgment-like quality of the pardon does not furnish the sole instantiation of judgment in the scene. It remains significant that the pardon occurs only after condemnation. Unlike the equitable judgment, which considers mitigating factors in the first instance and reduces the penalty accordingly, the Duke's pardon of Angelo is preceded by a determination of guilt. Generically, this feature of the Duke's pardons distinguishes *Measure for Measure* from a work like the *Eumenides*, in which the jury's equal votes for and against Orestes lead to his acquittal. Instead, Angelo is condemned but given impunity.

---

simply endorsing equity over justice. Andrew Majeske, "Equity's Absence: The Extremity of Claudio's Prosecution and Barnardine's Pardon in Shakespeare's *Measure for Measure*," *Law and Literature* 21, no. 2 (2009): 169–84.

9. This passage also refers to Angelo's attempted seduction of Isabella herself, which miscarried when he bedded Mariana instead.

Not all of the pardons in the final scene of *Measure for Measure* share this structure. Both the first and the last, in fact, eschew triangulation in favor of a relation between two, and in each the Duke becomes a judge in his own case. At the commencement of the sequence, Isabella asks the Duke's pardon for imposing on his sovereignty; at the end, the Duke "forgive[s]" (5.1.517) the character Lucio, who had slandered him when in disguise, even though he had initially proclaimed of Lucio that "here's one in place I cannot pardon" (5.1.497). In both cases, the Duke contends with an individual who supposedly abused the Duke's position, whether through "employ[ing]" him in her service, as Isabella did, or by casting unsubstantiated verbal accusations. Each is pardoned, yet not without a condition, as both are obliged to marry. Whereas Isabella's reward—or punishment—consists in wedding the Duke, Lucio's involves "marrying a punk" (5.1.520). Although different in degree, these resolutions are perhaps not entirely different in kind; Lucio vehemently protests against his fate, but Isabella's silence about her own marriage has often been construed as itself a manifestation of resistance.[10]

In each instance, the transgression that requires pardoning arises from the fact of the Duke's sovereignty. Lucio's slander would not constitute the grave offense of a *scandalum magnatum*—a form of treason in early modern England, discussed later in this chapter—were the Duke solely a private individual. Likewise, Isabella would not bear any culpability for her use of the Friar were he not also the Duke. The results of the Duke's judgments in these cases concerning his own "place" or sovereignty are those that seem most sinister in the play. Lucio views the condition on his pardon as equivalent to "pressing to death,/ Whipping, and hanging" (5.1.520–21), and we are never allowed to hear Isabella's views on her own marriage. The residual violence of these pardons complicates the comic ending of the play precisely by emphasizing the sovereign aspects of the sovereign pardon. Deploying his sovereignty to pardon offenses against that very sovereignty, the Duke attaches conditions that insist upon his continued power over his subjects' persons. Marriage itself, the most intimate of relations, is not freely chosen, despite the Duke's request of Isabella that she "be . . . as free to us"

---

10. This is, for example, the interpretation of Barbara Baines in "Assaying the Power of Chastity in *Measure for Measure,*" *Studies in English Literature, 1500–1900* 30, no. 2 (1990): 283–301. Isabella's silence has often furnished the opening for inventive stagings of the final scene, such as that in the Theatre de Complicité's 2004 London production of the play, which ended with a series of curtains unfurling to display a bed upon the Duke's statement "What's yet behind, that's meet you all should know" (5.1.542). David Nicol, "Review of *Measure for Measure,*" *Early Modern Literary Studies* 10, no. 2 (September 2004): 13.1–8.

(5.1.386). At the end of the play, the Duke refuses to maintain the abstract legal relation of judge to parties and instead insists on becoming involved in the lives of his subjects as a participant, a circumstance most clearly demonstrated by his pending marriage to Isabella.

Considering these purported offenses equitably also suggests a very different result from an equitable assessment of Angelo's guilt. With respect to Isabella, intent is clearly absent, with no indication earlier in the play that she sees through the Friar's garb to the Duke's sovereignty; hence, even if her act of employing him in her service would be a fault if she were aware of his sovereignty, her lack of awareness should, under an equitable interpretation, render her entirely blameless. As argued at more length later in this chapter, Lucio's mental state remains more impenetrable: the audience member is left uncertain as to whether Lucio was merely jesting with the Duke, whom he recognized in disguise as the Friar, or whether he was, in fact, culpable of voicing malicious imputations about the Duke and delivering them in earnest to someone he believed was a third party. Equity would dictate an acquittal in Isabella's case, whereas it might be stymied in that of Lucio.

The pardons the Duke provides at the end of the play are juridical in form, but not all partake of the ideal judicial structure; instead, some involve the Duke judging in his own case. Use of the term "forgive" rather than "pardon" (5.1.517) with respect to Lucio, and the substitution thereby of a word bearing ethical significance for that pertaining to the juridico-political, may mark this very difference. The nature of these final pardons—with the exception of Isabella's—further distinguishes them from equitable determinations. Unlike an equitable adjustment of punishment based on lack of culpability, the pardons apply to agents who acted with malicious intent (Angelo) and with indiscernible intent (Lucio). In addition, whereas the equitable judgment simultaneously accounts for the crime and its mitigation, these pardons largely follow after judgment (Angelo), or at least after an impasse in judgment (Lucio).

While considering the legal dynamics of the particular pardons the Duke grants indicates how *Measure for Measure* situates pardoning in relation to judgment, the pardons also function as a structural feature of the play. Analyzing them from that perspective serves both to give shape to several relations between pardoning and sovereignty and to demonstrate the disparity between the genre of theaters of pardoning and close earlier analogues, including the *Oresteia*, which, like *Measure for Measure*, is in dialogue with a logic of revenge that its ending appears to subvert.

At first blush, *Measure for Measure* seems to contravene Foucault's claim that pardoning entails the withdrawal of the sovereign. The pardons take place not from afar but on Duke Vincentio's dramatic and visible return to Vienna when his disguise is ripped off in full view of the audience. Yet issuing the pardons arguably permits the Duke to withdraw *in person*, allowing for the peaceful rees-tablishment of his sovereignty. Under this reading, the pardons, far from mani-festing the spirit of "remission" (5.1.496) that Vincentio purportedly finds within himself, instead represent a canny and ultimately successful device for legitimiz-ing his rule. Admonishing Barnardine, the unrepentant, drunken murderer whom he also releases from custody, the Duke advises, "Pray thee take this mercy to provide/ For better times to come" (5.1.482–83). The future-oriented logic of this statement applies more broadly to the play's other pardons, which aid not just their recipients' projects but Vincentio's own. Through pardoning, Vincentio assumes control over those who might otherwise foment strife—including Lucio and Isabella herself. The condition on these individuals' pardons—that of marriage—also folds them more securely into the social fabric and suggests the possibility of their relegation to the private sphere, out of the public eye. Vincentio hence eases back into sovereignty by eschewing a more obvious dis-play of force and instead pardoning.

The pardons also hold implications for the play's genre. As in the *Oresteia*, the conclusion of *Measure for Measure* seems to reject the logic of revenge implied both by its title and by some of the events that take place within it. Also as in Aeschylus's trilogy, violence appears to have been tamped down by the end, and the conclusion could be considered less tragic than comic. There remain, however, substantial differences between the modes of achieving such resolu-tion within the two dramatic contexts. Whereas a new order, represented by the establishment of the court of the Areopagus, arises in the *Oresteia*, it is not clear whether the end of *Measure for Measure* augurs a retreat back into the old regime or the commencement of a different one. While it is possible to interpret the Duke as simply furnishing pardons to soften the impact of the newly rigorous enforcement of the law, one could also read the pardons as suggesting a return to the chaotic lenity that had characterized the initial years of the Duke's reign. The conclusion of *Measure for Measure* furnishes no guidance in choosing between these alternatives. This discrepancy between the endings of *Measure for Measure* and the *Oresteia* carries implications for the audiences' perceptions of the plays; if in the *Oresteia* the resolution furnishes the comfort of a permanent institution, the end of *Measure for Measure* casts judgment back upon the audience and asks the spectators to decide on the future.

Likewise, in Aeschylus's trilogy, revenge appears to be clearly replaced by law, whereas in Shakespeare's play, some of the pardons retain a striking resemblance to acts of revenge. As with revenge, the Duke's pardons of both Isabella and Lucio occur without the mediation of a legal or quasi-legal judgment: Isabella is, as already observed, hardly deserving of punishment, and, under equity, would be found innocent, while Lucio's intent to slander rather than tease remains uncertain. Hence the Duke's pardons in both of these cases are relational in nature, furnished by the Duke as the one injured without a third party's assessment of guilt. Although culminating in the opposite outcome, these pardons thus remain analogous in structure to revenge. This does not, however, exhaust the similarity. The scene of Lucio's pardon, the very last in the play, stages the humiliation potentially entailed by receipt of a pardon. Through insisting on Lucio's marriage to a "punk," the Duke drastically diminishes his status within the commonwealth and casts him not into jail but into disgrace. The pardon thus visibly subjugates Lucio to Vincentio's sovereignty.

It may be sovereignty itself, and its arrival as a concept within the early modern period, that differentiates the plots of the *Oresteia* and *Measure for Measure*. The *deus ex machina* of Athena, who can assist in establishing the institution of the Areopagus then withdraw into the background, is no longer available in seventeenth-century England. She is instead replaced by the sovereign, here the Duke, who retains ultimate responsibility both for institutions and for their enforcement. Unlike the ancient institutions left in place by the gods for mortals to maintain, justice in Vienna remains subservient to Vincentio's whim, liable to be established and then swept aside within the compass of the same play, if not the same day.

In contrast with the power of Athena, whose wish can rule mortals by force regardless of its merits, the Duke's sovereignty remains at least partly dependent on the acclamation of the people; without their support, or that of the auxiliary nobility, Vincentio might be swept aside as summarily as some of the rulers in Shakespeare's history plays. Precisely because the Duke is not a god, he can fall; the rebellion or revolution of mere mortals could conclude his reign. The luster of the Duke's reputation furnishes his chief weapon against this threat and, hence, must be carefully managed. Pardoning provides the principal mechanism for doing so in *Measure for Measure*.

These aspects of sovereignty hold implications for the two possible aftermaths of the play. On the one hand, the Duke's act of pardoning the first instances of the law's renewed application could absolve the law of its relation to the sovereign's intention, the motive force behind it, and generate a gap between sovereign and law. To the extent that the final pardons leave the laws in place while furnishing individual exceptions to their implementation, they mark a growing chasm between the sovereign and the legal institutions of Vienna. Under this scenario, the pardon, while securing the Duke in the good graces of his subjects and restoring his reputation, would simultaneously serve to limit his continued power within the legal system, which might carry on judging without his further intervention. In this case, the Duke would bear a greater resemblance to Athena than is initially apparent.

On the other hand, the final pardons might indicate the ascendancy of sovereignty over law, these pardons presaging a chain of similar acts to follow, which would cumulatively negate whatever legality remained present in Vienna. The Duke as sovereign would thereby conflate rule with exception and affirm his power over law by condemning law itself rather than his subjects to death.

Sovereign and Institutional Judgments

At stake in these disparate futures facing the city in the aftermath of *Measure for Measure* are several discrete visions of judgment, ones that map roughly onto the sovereign and the institutional. While Escalus can be read as embodying the institutional perspective, both Angelo and the Duke represent disparate elements of the sovereign approach. Only through analysis of these underlying models can the role of pardoning in relation to judgment be fully understood.

For reasons pertaining to both the history of its production and its overarching dramatic structure, critics have often viewed *Measure for Measure* as treating claims of sovereignty by divine right and staging a thinly veiled version of the newly ascended King James I in the character of Duke Vincentio.[11] The other characters' implicit theories of justice have remained somewhat neglected, however, including,

---

11. Debora Shuger furnishes a detailed account of the early modern political and religious theory, on the one hand, and contemporaneous legal and political institutions, on the other, which intersect *in Measure for Measure*'s representation of sovereignty. Shuger, *Political Theologies*, passim.

      Those who specifically identify the Duke with James often rely on the idea that *Measure for Measure* articulates principles that the king had propounded in *Basilikon Doron*—a text originally completed in 1598 but republished and promoted in London in 1603, after James had been proclaimed Elizabeth's successor. King James VI and I, *Basilicon Doron*, in *Political Writings*, ed. J. P. Sommerville (Cambridge: Cambridge University Press, 1994), xxx. The connections between *Basilikon Doron* and *Measure for Measure* were most fully elaborated in Louis Albrecht, *Neue Untersuchungen zu Shakespeares* Mass für Mass (Berlin: Weidmannsche Buchhandlung, 1914). J. W. Lever's introduction to the Arden edition provides a useful encapsulation of motifs that Shakespeare's play appears to have adopted and adapted from James's treatise; these include "the duty of rulers to display virtue in action" and the importance of "the principle of temperance, or of the Aristotelean mean." Shakespeare, *Measure for Measure*, ed. Lever, xlviii–xlix. Lever also notes the resemblance between James's signature activities and those of the Duke—like James's public acts of mercy.

in particular, those of Angelo and Escalus.[12] During the course of *Measure for Measure*, a series of judgment scenes are staged, which range from censuring venial sin to condemning slander, the latter potentially an offense against the sovereign capacity of the Duke. As successive trials unfold in the play, several characters assume the role of judge, and each enacts and exposes his particular conception of legality. None of these models seems quite sufficient, however, and the text points out the inadequacy of each at the same time that it supplements their shortcomings with a set of pardons. Although these final pardons reestablish harmony, the audiences of the play are left not with a positive sense of the justice that can be achieved but rather with an account of the inadequacy of the alternatives.

From the very commencement of *Measure for Measure*, the character Escalus—identified as an "ancient lord"—is associated with legal institutions. Indeed, the virtues of something like the "artificial reason" of the common law emerge in Escalus's methods, and he is described in a manner that could recall Sir Edward Coke himself. As the Duke addresses Escalus:

> Of government the properties to unfold
> Would seem in me t'affect speech and discourse,
> Since I am put to know that your own science
> Exceeds, in that the lists of all advice
> My strength can give you. Then no more remains
> But that, to your sufficiency, as your worth is able,
> And let them work. The nature of our people,
> Our city's institutions, and the terms
> For common justice, y'are as pregnant in
> As art and practice hath enriched any
> That we remember. (1.1.3–12)

A number of words in this passage resonate with the language of the common law. Only here, in all of Shakespeare, appears the word "institution," which would be featured the next year in John Cowell's Latin treatise reconciling Justinian's *Institutes* with English common law and which would also later be used in the

---

12. There are a few notable exceptions to this tendency. Ian Ward has observed that—in addition to the Duke—both Angelo and Escalus become justices during the course of the play; as he remarks, "There are three magistrates in *Measure for Measure*, and each presents a distinct approach." Ian Ward, *Shakespeare and the Legal Imagination* (London: Butterworths, 1999), 85. Likewise, Kenji Yoshino interprets *Measure for Measure* as a play about judging, and he examines the three methods of judgment entailed, concluding that Shakespeare endorses Escalus's approach over the others. Kenji Yoshino, *A Thousand Times More Fair: What Shakespeare's Plays Teach Us about Justice* (New York: HarperCollins, 2001), 59–88.

title of Coke's own *Institutes of the Laws of England*.[13] In the folio, the phrase "cities institutions" is itself italicized—usually a typeface reserved for Latin or quotations, suggesting the status of the phrase as part of a specialized language. The invocation of "common justice" on the subsequent line likewise recalls the "common law," and the posited relationship between "art" and "practice" resembles Coke's insistence on the relevance of long experience to excellence in judging. Although Escalus is not himself chosen as the Duke's deputy, he does possess a "place," and, speaking with Angelo, explains "A power I have, but of what strength and nature/ I am not yet instructed" (1.1.79–80). Without stretching too far, we might see this power as an adjudicatory one. By failing to involve Escalus in the prosecution of Claudio and then ignoring Escalus's advice about the case, Angelo could then be seen as tyrannously usurping a judicial power that would better assume a bureaucratic form.[14]

Escalus's mode of judgment is not, however, represented in an entirely positive light throughout the play. Escalus endorses a judicial model predicated on identification with both the status and the interior state of the accused. This

---

13. As Cowell explains the forms of common law and their relation to so-called civil institutions:

> The civill law of *England*, (usually called Common Law) is, [Greek letters] polu'sêmon, and hath a threefold Acceptation. For first, it is taken generally for that Law which the *English* use, distinguished from that of the *Romans*, and other Nations. Secondly, It is taken for these two Courts of *Judicature*, commonly called the Upper Bench, and the Common Pleas. For when we say, the cognisance of any cause belongs to the Common Law, we did not intend to any Court Baron, County Court, Pypowder Court or any such Court, but to one of these two Judicatories, who do most strictly judge all causes according to the rule of the Common Law. Although there be many cases in which, both in the Chancery and Exchequer, Process are issued upon Originall Writs, and judgment given according to common Law. And thirdly, it is taken for that Law which we tearm Statute Law.

John Cowell, *The Institutes of the Lawes of England* (London: Thomas Roycroft, 1651), 3–4.

14. The play likewise represents Escalus as concerned about the integrity of the systems of judicial administration. When he encounters the clearly incompetent constable Elbow, Escalus makes plans to replace him:

> Esc. Come hither to me, Master Elbow: come hither, Master constable. How long have you been in this place of constable?
> Elbow. Seven year and a half, sir.
> Esc. I thought, by the readiness in the office, you had continued in it some time.—You say seven years together?
> Elbow. And a half, sir.
> Esc. Alas, it hath been great pains to you: they do you wrong to put you so oft upon't. Are there not men in your ward sufficient to serve it?
> Elbow. Faith, sir, few of any wit in such matters. As they are chosen, they are glad to choose me for them; I do it for some piece of money, and go through with all.
> Esc. Look you bring me in the names of some six or seven, the most sufficient of your parish.
> (2.1.254–70)

tendency evinces itself with particular clarity in act 2, scene 1, where he sets the scene of judgment. At the commencement of this episode, before the trial of Pompey, a bawd, opens, Escalus provides two reasons why Angelo should treat Claudio mercifully. First specifying that "this gentleman,/ Whom I would save,/ had a most noble father" (2.1.6–7), Escalus continues by insisting,

> Let but your honour know . . .
> Had time coher'd with place, or place with wishing,
> Or that the resolute acting of your blood
> Could have attain'd th'effect of your own purpose,
> Whether you had not sometime in your life
> Err'd in this point, which now you censure him. (2.1.8–15)

Considering the worth of the judge as well as the accused, Escalus here passes almost seamlessly from a comparison based on Claudio's "place" to one grounded in his "purpose," or intention. Here the discrepancy between "purpose" and "effect" manifests itself through a spatiotemporal discontinuity, or an impeded extension in time.[15]

Angelo, by contrast, rejects both these modes of analogy, first responding to Escalus's own speech by asserting, "The jury passing on the prisoner's life/ May in the sworn twelve have a thief, or two,/ Guiltier than him they try" (2.2.19–21). In other words—if we emphasize the term "may"—Angelo explains that any attempt to compare the judge's interior purpose with that of the accused will not provide sufficient, or even relevant, material for a judgment, and that this lack impedes identificatory judgment enough that it should not occur.[16] He then claims subsequently, in dialogue with Isabella, "Were he my kinsman, brother, or my son,/ It should be thus with him" (2.2.81–82).

---

15. The temporal aspect of "purpose" here recalls Augustine's use of the term "intentio" in Book 11 of his *Confessions*. As he writes in a passage discussing the act of utterance, "So much of it as is completed has already sounded, and what remains will sound, and thus will become completed, until the present intention [*intentio*] conveys the future into the past." Augustine, *Confessions II* (Cambridge: Harvard University Press, 1988), 274; the translation is my own.

16. Escalus's assertion that the judge should consider his own shortcomings in rendering judgment recalls equitable decision making. Under at least one understanding of equity, the judge considers his relationship of obligation toward the plaintiff in rendering a decision, and arrives at a verdict in the absence of adequate standards of measurement. Likewise here, the judge is asked to compare himself with the accused, and evaluate their internal similarities, quantities that one cannot precisely calculate. As Kathy Eden writes, "The equitable man pities and pardons the *hamartêma* [error] of a man like himself, just as the spectator at a tragedy is bound to do." Kathy Eden, *Poetic and Legal Fictions in the Aristotelian Tradition* (Princeton: Princeton University Press, 1986), 59.

The disparity between Angelo's and Escalus's judicial procedures then lit-eralizes itself in the former's incapacity to achieve any closure when faced with the "misplacing" constable Elbow and far from transparent situation that fol-lows. After asking several questions, including an inquiry that attempts to correct Elbow's accusation against "two notorious benefactors" into one against "male-factors," Angelo abandons the interpretive effort to Escalus, and finally departs the premises, claiming, "This will last out a night in Russia/ When nights are lon-gest there. I'll take my leave,/ And leave you to the hearing of the cause;/ Hoping you'll find good cause to whip them all" (2.1.133–36). This statement simultane-ously establishes Angelo's inability to elicit facts and judge when the crime is not immediately evident, and his concomitant desire to ensure punishment. Escalus, attending carefully to each individual's testimony, unlike Angelo, still reaches an impasse, however, since neither the plaintiff nor the defendants present tenable objects of identification, and he cannot elicit satisfactory answers from Elbow. Although Escalus recognizes that someone is culpable, he proves unwilling to pass judgment since supplied with insufficient information and tends instead toward lenity.[17] Thus he pardons the defendants for the future, and he allows their motives time to reform. Apparently only continued repetition of the crime after they have been clearly informed as to the nature of the law can, in his view, finally confirm the malevolence of their intentions.

Several of Escalus's comments from this scene illuminate the fraternity cemented by equality which he espouses, the actualization of which ultimately results in a flawed type of judgment. Like the Duke, who in act 1, while still in agreement with Angelo's perspective, observes "Liberty plucks Justice by the nose,/ The baby beats the nurse, and quite athwart/ Goes all decorum" (1.3.29–31), Escalus juxtaposes Justice with an opposite that, through its negation, demon-strates what the term "Justice" itself means for him. Inquiring, "Which is the wiser here, Justice or Iniquity?" (2.1.169–70), Escalus suggests the commen-surability of justice and equity, a correlation that he realizes Angelo does not acknowledge; in act 3, scene 2, he contrasts his own stance with that of Angelo, of whom he still speaks using the language of kinship, asserting that "my brother-justice I have/ found so severe that he hath forced me to tell him/ he is indeed Justice" (3.2.246–48). Escalus here describes the separation between the

---

17. As Escalus instructs Elbow, "Truly, officer, because he hath some offences in him that thou wouldst discover if thou couldst, let him continue in his courses till thou know'st what they are" (2.1.182–85). Toward the end of the scene, Escalus releases Pompey with a warning, simply telling him not to offend again: "In requital of your prophecy, hark you: I advise you, let me not find you before me again upon any complaint whatsoever; no, not for dwelling where you do" (2.1.241–44).

individual justice who functions within the law, inside a system where his role can also be fulfilled by "brother-justices," and the one who, like Angelo, enters the scene in a personal capacity; while the former retains a working partnership with personification—going so far as to dine with a character designated only as "Justice" (2.1.275–76)—the latter attempts to incorporate Justice within himself, disguising his mortal frame as a perfect concept.

For the moment, however, it is Escalus's very affiliation with Angelo as a "brother-justice" that will occasion problems. When the Duke, still disguised as a friar, in act 5 denounces the state of Vienna, Escalus's allegiance to his fellow rulers, both Duke Vincentio himself and Angelo, causes him to ignore the methodical pursuit of justice and instead cry out: "Slander to th'state! Away with him to prison!" (5.1.320–21). Since the testimony provided in this scene is almost as contradictory as that which Escalus had attempted to sort through in the earlier trial he conducted, yet those maligned by the concealed Duke's statements are individuals with whom Escalus retains an identificatory bond, he condemns everyone who brought a complaint without trying to discern whether he or she has committed perjury or spoken the truth. The "pity" or mercy by which Escalus claimed to have "wrought" is exposed here as a gesture based on the logic of identification, and not one that will lead inevitably toward a just outcome.

Angelo, however, views the world and constructs verdicts according to the paradigm of Christian, and particularly Puritan, religious tenets,[18] a perspective revealed especially in act 2, scene 2, immediately following the trial over which Escalus presides. Surrounded by semantic fields associated with Puritanism, like the terms "precise" or "seemer," Angelo himself enacts a predestinarian vision through the attitude toward speech acts that he assumes. His very name, while conjuring angelic associations, would also denote "I announce" in Greek and names the very problem that he creates: the difficulty of proclaiming the law at the same time as instituting it and condemning on the basis of it. In this case, as in that of the objects of Angelo's judgments, an illusion of transparency coats the relevant speech acts, which seem to name and do immediately and on their surface. As Angelo remarks, "What's open made to justice,/ That justice seizes . . . 'Tis very pregnant,/ The jewel that we find, we stoop and take't,/ Because we see it; but what we do not see,/ We tread upon, and never think of it" (2.2.21–26). The fact that he conflates announcing the law with enforcing it, as though the latter followed immediately from the former, is additionally demonstrated by his

---

18. In the Arden edition of *Measure for Measure*, Lever notes some of the language associating Angelo with Puritanism; see the notes to 1.3.50–54.

response to Isabella in act 2, scene 2: "It is the law, not I, condemn your brother" (2.2.80). Far from indicating that Angelo maintains an unobtrusive role in the process of judgment, this statement signals that he has committed the tyrannous act of assuming for himself at the same time the functions of making a law and executing judgment upon it, rather than attempting to mediate between the generality of law and a particular factual situation through evaluating each context individually.

Likewise, while he would appear to eschew considerations of intentionality, deeming them contained within the crime, Angelo himself displays an excess of volition. Again in act 2, scene 2, when Isabella asks that he divorce punishment of Claudio from that of Claudio's crime, he replies, "Condemn the fault, and not the actor of it?/ Why every fault's condemn'd ere it be done/ Mine were the very cipher of a function/ To fine the faults, whose fine stands in record,/ And let go by the actor" (2.2.37–41), insisting on his own agency as sovereign embodiment and executor of the law. Subsequently Isabella aptly describes Angelo's "purpose surfeiting" (5.1.105), revealing the intentional overflow that characterizes his speech acts.

Angelo's statement that the "fine stands in record," while susceptible to a secular interpretation based on the preexistence of a paradigm of punishment prescribed by a particular law, also alludes to a divine temporality, by which every sin, since already encompassed within God's knowledge, could be seen as condemned in advance, but would at the same time require a type of human recognition accomplished only by censuring the criminal. Given this vision of time, delay serves no possible function, so Angelo insists on the immediacy of Claudio's punishment, almost collapsing the moment of (necessarily verbal) judgment into that of (physical) execution. No pardon appears possible according to this scenario, and, as Angelo tells Isabella, referring to Claudio, "He's sentenc'd, 'tis too late" (2.2.55). Nor does Angelo see himself as an exception to this rule when in act 5 he finds the Duke privy to his nefarious actions; as he then implores:

> O my dread lord,
> I should be guiltier than my guiltiness
> To think I can be undiscernible,
> When I perceive your Grace, like power divine,
> Hath looked upon my passes. Then, good prince,
> No longer session hold upon my shame,
> But let my trial be mine own confession.
> Immediate sentence, then, and sequent death
> Is all the grace I beg. (5.1.364–72)

Any vision of pardon is here supplanted by the frame of an inexorable logic of automatic punishment, one that must be negated by the temporal fold allowing Claudio to return to life, or return on stage alive.

Angelo hence espouses an immediacy in the relation between law and its execution that bypasses the procedural aspects of judgment, an immediacy that the play represents as tyrannical. Furthermore, the surfeit of will connected with both Angelo's imposition of punishment on Claudio and his attempted seduction of Isabella stands as a negative contrast to Escalus's more bureaucratic mode of judicial inquiry. The methodical quality of the common law and common-law institutions emerge as powerful counterparts to the workings of tyranny; yet they remain insufficient as embodied in Escalus because of the status-based emphasis of his approach. Examining the contrast between Angelo's and Escalus's judicial orientations suggests a nascent common law justification for prohibiting the king from judging in person; at the same time, however, the common law itself does not emerge from the play's representation unscathed.

After examining the excesses of Escalus's identifications and Angelo's orientation toward exteriority, we might be tempted to see Duke Vincentio, who seeks the hidden behind what is manifest, as constituting a holy *deus ex machina* and providing the only viable model of judgment. Such a conclusion would, however, too hastily ignore the fact that the Duke himself had engineered the entire situation, in a sense inciting all the nefarious deeds that have occurred during the course of the play.[19] As his own rhetoric demonstrates, the Duke has in certain respects criminalized himself through reviving the dead law and thereby injuring his subjects. This culpability can be erased only through the sovereign's act of pardoning, which reinstates his own majesty, serving the sovereign himself rather than the individual remitted from punishment.

---

19. Although many have viewed the Duke as a figure for the divine, some writers on the play have questioned his anointed status. For example, Huston Diehl notes that "when, in the final act, [Shakespeare] makes his own activity as dramatist visible through a Duke who constructs fictional narratives, traffics in substitutions, manipulates desire, cleverly scripts comic endings, and seeks to reform his audiences, he depicts his central character as an imperfect, even a bungling playwright." Huston Diehl, "'Infinite Space': Representation and Reformation in *Measure for Measure*," *Shakespeare Quarterly* 49, no. 4 (1998): 410. Likewise, Arthur Little claims that "the play invites its audience to mock and pull back from the Duke's construction of himself as its one and only serious subject. The play challenges its offstage audience not to heed the absolutism demanded by a measure for a measure but to fancy at least that some kind of critical difference exists between a punishment and a marriage. The play's real mockery seems to be directed at the Duke." Arthur Little Jr., "Absolute Bodies, Absolute Laws: Staging Punishment in *Measure for Measure*," in *Shakespearean Power and Punishment*, ed. Gillian Murray Kendall (London: Associated University Presses, 1998), 125.

Throughout the middle of *Measure for Measure*, the Duke assumes the religious role of friar, and he confesses various individuals—albeit in the sacred rather than juridical sense—attempting to learn their most intimate secrets and intentions. This effort proves successful in almost all cases except that of Lucio, whose motives always remain to some extent concealed. In act 5, the Duke accuses and convicts him of "slander," reinforcing his judgment with the words "yet here's one in place I cannot pardon" (5.1.497), a phrase that refers the crime of slander to the Duke's status as sovereign—his place—and almost implies the idea that majesty cannot pardon sedition against the state. Several lines later, employing the more personal term "forgive," he addresses Lucio with the words "Thy slanders I forgive, and therewithal/ Remit thy other forfeits" (5.1.517–18), an alteration in diction that might imply a personal forgiveness rather than political pardon of defamation.

In act 1, however, the Duke had already expressed worries about slander to Friar Thomas as he explained why he had substituted Angelo in his own place, claiming, "I have on Angelo impos'd the office [of again enforcing the law];/ Who may in th'ambush of my name strike home,/ And yet my nature never in the fight/ To do in slander" (1.3.40–43). This statement associates slander with a mortal, and even revolutionary, violence that it shares only with the law's verbal reestablishment and imposition. Angelo's sentencing of Claudio can be identified as his act of "striking home" (as though in a duel), while Vincentio has artfully parried the counterthrust that would "do him in." Because the Duke has ceded only his position as sovereign (his "name") rather than his own person (his "nature") to Angelo, he imagines in advance, however, that he will avoid the fatal wound; only Angelo's nature, not his own, will be subject to slander. The results of Angelo's reanimation of the law confirm the Duke's fears about what might have happened had he himself taken on the task of imposing legal order; indeed, Angelo speaks to Isabella of his judgment as "the sentence/ That you have slander'd so" (2.4.109–10).

The sovereign's fear of generating slander through imposing the law recalls sixteenth-century French political theorist Jean Bodin's rationale for recommending that the king avoid judging in person. As Bodin claimed in *The Six Books of the Republic*, doing so might disfigure the king's reputation, as will be discussed in chapter 2. The representation of the Duke thus also suggests the advisability of divorcing the sovereign from the exercise of judgment, but for a reason different from that embodied in Escalus: to save the honor of the King rather than to establish the autonomy of the common law system.

Within the play, several passages explore the relationship between the law and a force that animates it, endowing the law itself with varying degrees of life. As the Duke asserts, employing metaphors mixed between plant and animal:

> We have strict statutes and most biting laws,
> The needful bits and curbs to headstrong jades
> Which for this fourteen years we have let slip;
> Even like an o'er-grown lion in a cave
> That goes not out to prey. Now, as fond fathers,
> Having bound up the threatening twigs of birch
> Only to stick it in their children's sight
> For terror, not to use, in time the rod
> Becomes more mock'd than fear'd: so our decrees,
> Dead to infliction, to themselves are dead. (1.3.19–28)

While the law initially appears "biting," implying an executive power of its own, its carnivorous and leonine force has been mitigated through the intrusion of vegetation, represented by the overgrowth encompassing the lion. Even plant life is finally denied the law when the twigs, separated from their natural existence by being bound into a rod, are deprived of any effect at all through the allegorical father's refusal to use them. The implication at this point is that the laws must in some way regain life, but they can do so only by parasiting off an individual's—for example, Angelo's—intentionality. Speaking of Angelo himself, Lucio resumes the image of the lion, asserting, "He [Angelo], to give fear to use and liberty,/ Which have for long run by the hideous law/ As mice by lions, hath pick'd out an act" (1.4.62–64). Finally expressing his own stance, Angelo then urges at the very commencement of act 2, "We must not make a scarecrow of the law,/ Setting it up to fear the birds of prey/ And let it keep one shape till custom make it/ Their perch, and not their terror" (2.1.1–4). Here the image of the inanimate rod becomes converted into another bundle of sticks, the scarecrow, which Angelo insists on making move as though human. These passages emphasize the difficulty entailed in setting the law in motion as though intentional or animate despite its "death" to even itself. Although Angelo's proclamation and judgment of Claudio appear to solve this problem, they do so only through the involvement of his own intentionality.[20]

---

20. When the Duke speaks as "the mercy of the law," requiring "Measure still for Measure," a logic that his subsequent pardonings call into question, he resorts to personifying the law and displacing his own agency onto it. What his statement demonstrates, then, is that when the law talks, its only language is the *lex talionis*.

Returning to the Duke's attempt to foist the problem of reviving the laws onto Angelo, one can see that Vincentio has indeed provided some justification for slander, a motive of which Lucio could avail himself. As M. Lindsay Kaplan observes, several of Lucio's comments indicate that he might be cognizant of Duke Vincentio's identity, even when he maligns the disguised Duke to his face.[21] The presence of this possibility casts the Duke's omniscience into question, yet it is this very omniscience that allows commentators to consider the Duke divine in both capability and mercy. The manner in which Lucio slanders the Duke to his face, and yet in his symbolic absence, emphasizes this point. During the play, Lucio only defames the Duke when speaking with the Duke himself in his disguise as a friar. In one respect, then, Lucio might not be construed as slandering the Duke at all, because he is not spreading rumors about the Duke's nature to a third party but rather addressing the Duke himself. At the same time, by slandering the sovereign in his absence, or perpetrating a *scandalum magnatum*,[22] Lucio verges on committing a revolutionary offense.

The Duke's observation that Lucio is "one in place I cannot pardon" also takes on an additional significance. To the extent that Lucio's slander pertains to the Duke's office—or his "name"—the Duke may opt not to pardon his attack against the state. If, however, the slander refers merely to the private person of the Duke—his "nature"—Vincentio might not only forgive but also be prevented from himself judging. In discussing the problems caused by the sovereign's act of judging in person, Bodin emphasizes that they are particularly pronounced when the sovereign judges in his own case.[23] Instead, the king—or in this instance, the Duke—is left to forgive.[24]

Perhaps appropriately for a play whose title connects it with the biblical injunction "Judge not, that you be not judged. For with the judgment you

---

21. M. Lindsay Kaplan, *The Culture of Slander in Early Modern England* (Cambridge: Cambridge University Press, 1997), 92–108.

22. *Black's Law Dictionary* defines *scandalum magnatum* as "actionable slander of powerful people; specif., defamatory comments regarding persons of high rank, such as peers, judges, or state officials." Henry Campbell Black and Bryan A. Garner, eds., *Black's Law Dictionary*, 7th ed. (St. Paul: West, 1999), s.v. "*scandalum magnatum*." Describing the origin of the crime, Kaplan writes, "During the reign of Edward I, provision was made in 1275 to punish rumors defaming the reputation of a state official in the statute of *scandalum magnatum*—slander of a magnate." Kaplan, *Culture of Slander*, 21.

23. This point is elaborated in chapter 2.

24. It may be worth noting here that the Duke awaits Isabella's approval in the final scene before granting pardon to Angelo; this sequencing accords with Coke's concern that the king avoid pardoning when doing so might give away a right possessed by another of his subjects. In addition, it recalls the deference to female requests for mercy that Cynthia Herrup has noted in "The King's Two Genders."

pronounce you will be judged, and the measure you give will be the measure you get" (Matthew 7:1–2), *Measure for Measure* stages several theories of judgment. Inquiring as to the relation between the institution of the law and its implementation, the play examines both the sovereign and the common law versions of judgment. While suggesting reasons why those trained in the "cities institutions" might exercise greater judicial discernment than the sovereign and why the ruler himself might, for reputational reasons, avoid taking on the judicial capacity, the play also directs the spectators' attentions to the flaws in each of these positions. Despite the advantages of expertise that they possess, those appointed judges may run the risk of excessive lenity toward individuals of their own status and, in turn, rush to judgment against those perceived as undermining the state. Likewise, while the sovereign may preserve himself from slander by refraining from judging in person, his act of imposing this office on another may itself represent an injustice.

In one respect, pardoning furnishes the only resolution that can preserve the sovereign's majesty. Simultaneously, however, the pardon absolves the law of its relation to the sovereign's intention, the motive force behind it, and generates a gap between sovereign and law. To the extent that the final pardons leave the laws in place while furnishing individual exceptions to their implementation, they mark a growing chasm between the sovereign and legal institutions. Furthermore, to the extent that the sovereign's pardon resembles a judgment, even pardoning may render him culpable of judging in his own case, as discussed in the opening section of this chapter. Although pardoning appears to solve the problems that arise from the sovereign's judgment, it may simultaneously separate the sovereign from the law and itself become subject to the same critique as the sovereign's act of judging.

Coke, the Greeks, and the Common Law

If Bodin suggested reasons why statecraft itself might dictate that the sovereign refrain from judging in person, Sir Edward Coke attempted to establish that the king could not judge in person according to the laws and customs of England. Although Coke's argument to this effect postdated *Measure for Measure* by several years, he had already commenced the effort to generate a history of the common law that would circumvent the sovereign by the time of the first performance of the play in 1604. This history was aimed at historicizing sovereignty by affirming its Roman-Norman roots and circumventing it through appeal to earlier origins, including even those of ancient Greece. Examining in more detail the history behind Coke's common law justification for cabining the king's power not only helps to illuminate the rationales for the institutionalized vision of judgment gestured to in *Measure for Measure* but also indicates one place for Greece within the early modern imaginary.

In *Society Must Be Defended*, a seminar delivered at the Collège de France in 1975–76, Foucault identified Coke as one of the central figures in constructing the first modern "historico-political discourse" in seventeenth-century England, a discourse that attempted to recover the genesis of sovereignty, or the multiple accounts thereof.[25] At stake in the creation of a new historico-political discourse was the assertion of a particular kind of national—or, as Foucault puts it, race—struggle and the resuscitation of an earlier right in opposition to the power claimed by the king.[26] The genre that this historico-political discourse adopted broke sharply from extant Roman models of history; explaining why the new

---

25. Michel Foucault, *Society Must Be Defended*, trans. David Macey (New York: Picador, 2003), 50–56. *Measure for Measure*, among other Shakespeare plays, has been glossed by a number of critics in a Foucauldian manner, which emphasizes the discourse of violence and the Duke's surveillance of the other characters throughout the play. The extant work, however, often falls prey to Lorna Hutson's critique of employing Foucault to understand early modern English drama. As Hutson has persuasively argued, Foucault's accounts of criminal procedure are influenced by the French inquisitorial tradition rather than the English model, and hence obscure aspects of the English judicial system. According to Hutson: "The Foucauldian genealogy depends on a history of prosecution techniques and a system of proof in early modern criminal law that is specifically French. Where Foucault portrays an *ancien régime* epistemology of judgment based on a 'system of "legal proofs"' . . . known only to specialists' and speaks of 'the singularity of this judicial truth,' the sixteenth-century English epistemology of judgment could rather be said to be based on the participation of lay persons (justices, victims, neighbours, jurors) in deciding what was to count as knowledge." Lorna Hutson, *The Invention of Suspicion: Law and Mimesis in Shakespeare and Renaissance Drama* (Oxford: Oxford University Press, 2008), 6.

Unlike *Discipline and Punish*, however, Foucault's seminars, including *Society Must Be Defended*, demonstrate an attunement to the specifically English context of judicial thought and valuably place this thought within a theory of the relationship between historical and political discourses. In this respect, *Society Must Be Defended* resembles J. G. A. Pocock's classic *The Ancient Constitution and the Feudal Law: A Study of English Historical Thought in the Seventeenth Century* (Cambridge: Cambridge University Press, 1987), although emerging out of a very different tradition and set of concerns.

Pocock's own reliance on Coke as a primary exponent of early seventeenth-century common law thought has been hotly contested, most notably by Glenn Burgess, who has claimed that "the attitude to the history of English law expressed by Sir Edward Coke was both untypical and confused." Glenn Burgess, *The Politics of the Ancient Constitution: An Introduction to English Political Thought, 1603–1642* (University Park: Penn State University Press, 1992), 58. Subsequent commentaries, such as Alan Cromartie, *The Constitutionalist Revolution: An Essay on the History of England, 1450–1642* (Cambridge: Cambridge University Press, 2006), have, however, confirmed the importance of Coke's role and influence within seventeenth-century English debates about law and politics. This book demonstrates Coke's influence without claiming that his position represented the vantage point of all common lawyers.

26. Foucault, *Society*, 69, 105–7.

approach constituted an anti-Roman "counter-history," Foucault elaborates that under it, "the history of some is not the history of others. It will be discovered, or at least asserted, that the history of the Saxons after their defeat at the Battle of Hastings is not the same as the history of the Normans who were the victors in that same battle. It will be learned that one man's victory is another man's defeat." Rather than partaking of "the Roman history of sovereignty," this genre resembles a "biblical history of servitude and exiles," in which the "goal is not to establish the great, long jurisprudence of a power that has always retained its rights, or to demonstrate that power is where it is, and that it has always been where it is now," but "to demand rights that have not been recognized, or in other words, to declare war by declaring rights."[27] Instead of insisting on the continuous inheritance of power, this historico-political discourse unearthed a subterranean right in order to bring it back to life.

As Foucault observes in the French context, displacing the Roman form of history entailed the construction of new genealogies of the state. Hence, from the Middle Ages through the Renaissance, "a story . . . circulate[d] . . . [that] tells how the French are descended from the Franks, and says that the Franks themselves were Trojans who, having left Troy under the leadership of Priam's son King Francus when the city was set on fire, initially found refuge on the banks of the Danube, then in Germany on the banks of the Rhine, and finally found, or rather founded, their homeland in France. . . . [T]his legend completely elides both Rome and Gaul." Only during the later seventeenth century, however, was the "theme of national dualism," which had somewhat earlier characterized the English historico-political discourse, introduced in France as well. Entailed by the elision of Rome was the possibility of repositioning France on the stage of world history. Rendering France and Rome "two branches that grow from the same trunk" endowed the king of France with the same kind of sovereignty as the Roman emperor and suggested that "because France is Rome's sister or cousin, France has the same rights as Rome itself."[28]

In specifying the right asserted by the new historico-political discourse in England, Foucault turns to Coke and contends that it consisted in "a set of Saxon laws." As he maintains:

> The major influence here was a jurist called Coke, who claimed to have discovered [*The Mirrors of Justice*] . . . [and] made it function as a treatise on Saxon right. Saxon right was described as being both the

---

27. Foucault, *Society*, 71, 73, 77.
28. Foucault, *Society*, 115, 117.

primal and the historically authentic—hence the importance of the manuscript—right of the Saxon people, who elected their leaders, had their own judges [the manuscript has "were their own judges"], and recognized the power of the king only in time of war; he was recognized as a wartime leader, and not as a king who exercised an absolute and unchecked sovereignty over the social body. Saxon right was, then, a historical figure, and attempts were made—through research into the ancient history of right—to establish it in a historically accurate form. But at the same time, this Saxon right appeared to be, and was described as, the very expression of human reason in a state of nature.[29]

Although grounded in a historical narrative, the right uncovered turns out to be a natural right. In content, it entails a democratic method of self-governance, including the availability of trial by jury—or, in the manuscript's phrasing, the ability of the people to be their own judges.

In the English context as well, Foucault alludes to the circumvention of Rome by comparing the Saxons both with more ancient antecedents and with biblical history. As he observes, the jurist John Selden "pointed out that it was a wonderful right and very close to human reason because in civil terms it was more or less similar to that of Athens, and in military terms, more or less similar to that of Sparta." Nor did Selden limit his analogy to ancient Greece. He also insisted on the resemblance between the Saxons and the Jews, who were "divers from all other people" and endowed with a "government above all other likest unto that of Christ's Kingdom, whose yoke is easie, and burthen light."[30] Hence a theological-political aspect, as well as a connection with classical Greece, inheres in this representation of the Saxon right.

Had he delved further into Coke, Foucault could, however, have analyzed a much more developed and explicit account of the ancient Greek origins of English right. In his efforts to bolster the credentials of the common law, Coke, in his *Reports*, insisted on its ancient Greek rather than Norman origins. Instead of imposing an alien law, the Norman Conquest—according to Coke—as well as the earlier Roman invasion, instead found in place laws derived from the Greek tradition. As Coke suggests in his preface to the second part of his *Reports*, which appeared in 1602, "If the ancient Lawes of this noble Island had not excelled all others, it could not be but some of the severall Conquerors, and Governors thereof; That is to say, the Romanes, Saxons, Danes, or Normans, and specially

---

29. Foucault, *Society*, 105–6.
30. Foucault, *Society*, 106.

the Romanes, who, (as they justly may) doe boast of their Civill Lawes, would (as every of them might) have altered or changed the same."[31] The aims of Coke's account of the history of English common law were quite similar to those of the French narratives about a Trojan past. In both contexts, the invocation of a more ancient heritage served to displace the significance of Rome. Coke concludes his preface to the third part of the *Reports*, also published in 1602, "Hereby . . . it is sufficiently proved that the lawes of England are of much greater antiquity than they are reported to be, & than any of the Constitutions or Lawes imperiall of Roman Emperors."[32] For Coke, however, the antiquity of the common law further functioned to minimize the impact of the Norman Conquest, which both recalled the earlier intrusion of the Romans and provided an additional vehicle through which the legacy of Roman law might have affected English jurisprudence.

Coke returned to the argument on several occasions, at first only indicating a Greek analogy in the second part of the *Reports*, then recounting a more elaborate genealogy in the third part, and finally, in 1607, defending his initial position and rejecting the influence of the Norman Conquest with the sixth part of the *Reports*. The second part commences suggestively, pairing a vision of the excellence of Greek law attributed to the ancient Greek playwright Euripides with Coke's own praise of English law. According to Coke, "there are (sayth *Euripides*) three Virtues worthy [of] our meditation; To honour God, our Parents who begat us, and the Common Lawes of Greece [*nomous koinous Hellados*]: The like doe I say to thee (Gentle Reader) next to thy dutie and pietie to God, and his anointed thy gracious Soveraigne, and thy honour to thy Parents, yeeld due reverence and obedience to the Common Lawes of England."[33]

Although it can be located in Stobaeus's *Anthologium*, this passage from a lost Euripides play initially presents something of a puzzle in terms of Coke's source, as Stobaeus was not widely referenced during the period. Other books collecting commentary on particular topics from ancient sources were, however, available; these included *Polyanthea* (1600) and *Polyanthea Nova* (1604), compendia that could both be found in Coke's library.[34] Coke evidently pored over *Polyanthea* as

---

31. Sir Edward Coke, *Reports*, in *The Selected Writings and Speeches of Sir Edward Coke*, vol. 1, ed. Steve Sheppard (Indianapolis: Liberty Fund, 2003), 40.

32. Coke, *Reports*, 66.

33. Coke, *Reports*, 39. This fragment of Euripides, 853(N), 211, can be found in Ioannis Stobaei, *Anthologii*, ed. Otto Hense, vol. 3 (Berlin: Weidmannos, 1894), 33.

34. *A Catalogue of the Library of Sir Edward Coke*, ed. W. O. Hassall (New Haven: Yale University Press, 1950), 5. The possibility that *Polyanthea* furnished a source for some of Coke's classical references is raised in Norma Adams's review of the *Catalogue* in *Speculum: A Journal of Medieval Studies*

he began to compile an index to the book—although he unfortunately only managed to make it through words beginning with A.[35] The citation from Euripides occurs in *Polyanthea* in the midst of a multi-page set of quotations about law (*lex*), which drew from a number of other Latin and Greek sources, including many plays as well as philosophical and historical materials.[36]

The only other reference to this passage from Euripides treating "the common laws of Greece" in English writings of the period can be found in Sir Henry Finch's influential *Nomotexnia*—published in law French in 1613 and then in a somewhat more abridged English version in 1627—a work "in which maxims or principles linked according to rules of method formed a comprehensive overview or institution of the whole law." As Wilfred Prest has convincingly demonstrated, a number of extant manuscripts of *Nomotexnia* show the alterations and additions over the course of the 1590s and early 1600s.[37] Strikingly, it is only with the 1604 version, which incorporates references to Coke's *Reports*, that *Nomotexnia* first includes the phrase from Euripides.

Toward the beginning of a chapter treating positive law ("Des Leys Positif"), Finch opines:

> Positive are the laws that each commonwealth makes for itself. And from this comes the grounds and maxims of all common laws, because what we call the common law is not a new or barbarous word. . . . Thus *Euripides* mentions *nomos koinos Hellados*, the common laws of Greece. Thus also *Plato* defines that which he is speaking of as *logismos*, the reasoning faculty, *hos genomênos* (he says), *dogma poleôs koinon nomos epônomastai*, the golden and sacred rule of reason which is called common law [marginal note: Plato lib. 1 de Legibus]. The place there is quite notable, because it shows the fountain and original of common law, it shows the antiquity of the term, in effect all one with that which later, and by a newer name is called *Ius civile* (*quod quisque populus ipse sibi jus constituit*, as *Justinian* defines it) it teaches us that common law

---

28, no. 1 (January 1953): 164–66. Among other Greek materials referenced in the *Catalogue* is a lost "MS of Platoes difinitions in 4o. Lat:/ Edw: Coke (Autogr.)" (*Catalogue,* 61), suggesting Coke's interest in Plato, among other ancient Greek writers.

35. Photo on file with the author. A number of pages in the 1600 edition are marked.

36. Domenicus Mirabellius, *Polyanthea* (Lyon: Vignon, 1600), 474.

37. Wilfred Prest, "The Dialectical Origins of Finch's *Law,*" *Cambridge Law Journal* 36, no. 2 (1977): 328. Prest identifies three principal stages of revision, including an early version of *Nomotexnia* (Rawlinson c. 43), two manuscripts both stemming from the 1590s (Cambridge University Library manuscript Ll. 3.6–7 and Longleat MS. Whitelocke papers, vol. 30), and several representing a third stage, the earliest copy of which was dated August 23, 1604 (Bodl. MS. Eng. Misc. e. 476, f. v.).

is nothing other than reason, but what reason? Not that which each man frames for himself, but reason refined, *Quae cum adoleverit atque perfecta est, nominator rità sapientia*, as *Cicero* says, and as *Plato*, in the place before mentioned, says, when he designates *dogma* opinion or decree; How? *Dogma poleôs koinon*, generally received by the consent of all.[38]

Finch notably adds the reference to Plato's *Laws*, which serves to connect common law with reason—in particular, a form of reason given legitimacy by widespread acceptation.

Coke's own comparison between English and Greek common law remains on the level of analogy in the second part of his reports; only in the third part does Coke explicitly furnish an account of the ancient Greek genesis of English law. In that context, Coke engages in what appears to be a legalistic proof of his contention. Taking up the reports of the chroniclers, whom he generally critiques, Coke urges that if the reader believes anything they say, he agrees that "*Brutus* the first king of this land, as soone as hee had settled himselfe in his kingdome, for the safe and peaceable government of his people wrote a book in the Greeke tongue, calling it the lawes of the Britans, and hee collected the same out of the Laws of the Trojans." Coke then continues the linguistic argument on his own: "That the Lawes of the auncient Britans, their contracts and other instruments: and the Records and judiciall proceedings of their Judges were written and sentenced in the Greeke tongue, it is plaine and evident by proofs luculent & uncontrollable." In the course of his "proof," Coke cites Aeschylus, among other writers, as the source for particular English terms.[39]

As in Foucault's French history, Coke invokes the potentially Trojan content of the laws. Indeed, much of his argument for the Greek antecedents of English law relies not on the transmission of particular legal principles from one context into the other but rather on the linguistic echoes of an ancient tongue. A certain irony arises from this focus on the language of law in establishing its national origins. Coke himself, despite his insistence on the English quality of common law and the Norman Conquest's lack of significant impact, was writing the *Reports* in law French. If anyone should have recognized the possibility of a disparity between the linguistic form of law and the origins of the material expounded in this language, Coke was that person. Yet perhaps undermining French as the

---

38. Henry Finch, *Nomotexnia; cestascavoir, un description del Common Leys dangleterre solonque les rules del Art* (London, 1613), 19 (chap 6, "Des Leys Positif").

39. Coke, *Reports*, 64–66.

language of English law was precisely the aim. If the deployment of Greek terminology in England both preceded the Norman Conquest and continued to
infiltrate the common law, these circumstances could serve to neutralize the
powerful evidence that the French form of English law provided of the significant impact that the Conquest might actually have had. Once he has implicitly
countered the presumption that its French presentation indicates a central aspect
of English common law, Coke thus shifts his avenue of attack; responding, in the
sixth part of the *Reports*, to critics who had doubted his contention in the second
part and who positioned the Norman Conquest as crucial to the development of
English law, Coke adduces examples not of Greek precedents but rather of pre-
Conquest English principles.[40]

Although he refrains from connecting specific aspects of Greek and English
law, Coke does elaborate extensively on the nature of the right enshrined in the
ancient common law. As Foucault suggests, this right helped establish a particular type of resistance against the power of the king. In part, it cabined the
capacity of the king to make law without the consent of Parliament. Even more
centrally, however, it restricted the scope of the king's judicial power. In Coke's
conception of the common law, the institutions of the legal system themselves
subsisted beyond the reach of the king's sovereignty, furnishing an ancient constitution that a present ruler could not alter and that undergirded the subjects'
rights.[41] Rather than being opposed principally to more democratic legislative
decision making, the king's power was contrasted with the right embodied in the
common law and its institutions.[42]

---

40. Coke, *Reports*, 150–52.

41. The conception and stakes of this "ancient constitution," as well as early modern English and
French jurists' role in the development of historiography, were most famously explored by J. G. A.
Pocock in *The Ancient Constitution and the Feudal Law*.

42. Later in the seventeenth century, John Sadler developed the link between English common
law and Greek sources in an even more thoroughgoing fashion, shifting emphasis to a Platonic tradition and simultaneously relying on ancient drama, including the story of Aeschylus's *Oresteia*. As
Sadler opines, "How much our Ancestors owed to the *Grecians*, I do not find expressed by any; most
of our *Plays*, much of our *Works*, and somewhat of our *Laws* seemeth to be *Grecian*." John Sadler,
*Rights of the Kingdom: or, Customs of our Ancestors. Touching the Duty, Power, Election, or Succession
of our Kings and Parliaments* (London: Richard Bishop, 1649), 43. Sadler traces the English practice
of trial by a jury of twelve back to ancient Greece through allusion to the plot of the *Oresteia* as referenced by Pausanias's *Description of Greece*, claiming, "And for the *Grecian* Trials by Twelve, I need cite
no more than the known Histories of *Orestes*, and of *Mars*, tried for *Murther* by a *Jury* of Twelve, (and
quitted only by the equality of Votes,) in that Famous Place which from him was called *Areopagus* or
Mars Hill" (45). Pranav Jain has elaborated on the Platonic elements of Sadler's work in "John Sadler
(1615–1674): Religion, Common Law, and Reason in Early Modern England," *Columbia University
Journal of Politics and Society* 26, no. 2 (Spring 2016), www.helvidius.org.

Two 1607 encounters involving King James I and Coke epitomize how the common law—for Coke—circumscribed the monarch's judicial power.[43] In the case of the *Prohibitions del Roy*, Coke's account of which Robert Cover referred to in "*Nomos* and Narrative" as "one classic formulation of the privileged hermeneutic position" of judges, Coke maintained that the king lacked the power to judge in his own person.[44] According to Coke, when James I asserted this ability, "it was answered by me, in the presence, and with the clear consent of all the Judges of England, and Barons of the Exchequer, that the King in his own person cannot adjudge any case, either criminall, as Treason, Felony, &c. or betwixt party and party, concerning his Inheritance, Chattels, or Goods, &c. but this ought to be determined and adjudged in some Court of Justice, according to the Law and Custom of England." While the king represented his own reason as sufficient to ground his judgment, Coke insisted, like Finch, on a distinction between types of reason, contending that "causes which concern the life, or inheritance, or goods, or fortunes of [the king's] Subjects . . . are not to be decided by naturall reason but by the artificiall reason and judgment of Law, which Law is an act which requires long study and experience, before that a man can attain to the cognizance of it."[45] Only the judges of the common law, who had mastered the methods of legal reasoning, possessed the privilege of judging English subjects. Despite the king's ability to appoint his magistrates, he could not substitute himself in their place.

Even the power to pardon, which might appear to pertain directly to the king's prerogative, was not, according to Coke, absolute. In a note on pardons, also from 1607, Coke observed that "the Law so regards the Weal-publick, that although that the King shall have the suit solely in his name for the redress of it, yet by his pardon he cannot discharge the Offender, for this that it is not only in prejudice of the King, but in damage of the Subjects." In other words, to the extent that other subjects—rather than solely the king—are injured by an action or failure to act, the king cannot excuse the one sued from the obligation he is supposed to fulfill. Nevertheless, in another, undated note on the king's dispensing power, Coke confirmed that "the Royall power to pardon Treasons, Murthers, Rapes, &c. is a Prerogative incident solely and inseparably to the person of the King," which Parliament itself could not restrain.[46]

---

43. Although both of the incidents discussed appear to have occurred in 1607, Coke's notes on the proceedings were only published posthumously in the twelfth part of his *Reports* (1656).

44. Robert Cover, "The Supreme Court, 1982 Term—Forward: *Nomos* and Narrative," *Harvard Law Review* 97, no. 42 (1983).

45. Coke, *Reports*, 479, 481.

46. Coke, *Reports*, 439, 424.

Pertaining not just to the king but to judgment in general, another fundamental principle of the common law was reaffirmed by Coke in *Bonham's Case* in 1610. Quite apart from the controversies about whether *Bonham's Case* provides a precedent for judicial review, it clearly articulates the notion that it is improper for anyone to adjudicate his own case. As Coke writes, "The Censors, cannot be Judges, Ministers, and parties; Judges, to give sentence or judgment; Ministers to make summons; and Parties, to have the moiety of the forfeiture, *quia aliquis non debet esse Judex in propria causa, imo iniquum est aliquem sui rei esse judicem*."[47] Although the rule that Coke cites appears universal in scope, its application to the king would generate particular difficulties. Even if one did not subscribe to the notion that any criminal offense also constituted a violation against the monarch conceived as sovereign, certain acts, like those of revolution or treason, would clearly pertain to the king himself. Were the king to judge these crimes himself, he would thus fall afoul of the prescription not to judge in one's own case.

The same year, Coke, in a conference of the Privy Council, propounded further restrictions on James I's capacity in the legal realm, determining that he could not prohibit new building in London by proclamation. Rather than simply opposing the king's power to that of the king in Parliament, Coke suggested the role of the common law in this controversy. As Coke retrospectively recounts his statement, "the King cannot change any part of the Common Law, nor create any Offence by his Proclamation, which was not an Offence before, without Parliament." Among the precedents for this claim that he draws upon are earlier judges' negative response when "the Whore-houses, called the stews, were suppressed by Proclamation, and sound of Trumpet, &c." under Henry VIII.[48]

A closer examination of Coke's writings thus demonstrates that, more than Foucault suggested, Coke himself participated in the creation of an ancient genealogy for the common law that would precede and circumvent Rome. Furthermore, it reveals the extent to which an assertion of Saxon right against King James I entailed a defense of the domain occupied by the institutions of the common law and a cabining of the king's authority in the judicial arena. Both of these motifs appear in Shakespeare's *Measure for Measure*, first performed between, on the earlier side, Coke's account of the Greek genesis of the common law and, on the later, Coke's resistance to King James's assertion of his prerogative to judge, pardon, and proclaim. Placing *Measure for Measure* within this context suggests that the problems of this problem play may be, in part, ones shared

---

47. Coke, *Reports*, 275.
48. Coke, *Reports*, 487, 489. As the source for this information, Coke cites Holinshed's *Chronicles*.

with the historico-political discourse of early modern English jurists. In particular, the sovereign's act of judging in person was condemned not only in Bodin's statecraft-based approach, aimed at preserving the power of the king, but also in the dominant common law account of the respective authority of legal institutions and the king. Likewise, while the pardon remained the sole province of the sovereign, escaping the critique leveled against the king's judgment in person, it already constituted a point of contention.

The Greeks and the Theater of Pardoning

Measure for Measure may not only presage Coke's resistance to King James's efforts to judge in person but also draw upon the genealogy Coke had earlier constructed linking ancient Greece with early modern England. Just as Coke traced the heritage of the English common law not to Rome but to Greece, Shakespeare can be seen as resuscitating and modifying not simply Seneca's revenge tragedies—staple intertexts of the period[49]—but even Aeschylus's *Oresteia*. As in the *Oresteia*, the interplay between revenge and law is of paramount importance. Indeed, in constructing a "theater of pardoning," *Measure for Measure* stands in direct relation to the classical Greek as well as the Elizabethan tradition of revenge drama. Revenge here, however, becomes generalized into something like revolution through slander, which, although operating on the symbolic plane rather than in the sphere of physical violence, might significantly undermine the sovereign and the state. By pardoning at the end of the play, the Duke thereby averts the possibility of the demise of the polity.

Before we turn to the significance of the structural parallels between the plays, it may be helpful to suggest possible mechanisms for the *Oresteia*'s actual influence on *Measure for Measure*, mechanisms indicating that the homonymy between the names of the "ancient Lord" "Escalus" of Shakespeare's play and the playwright "Aeschylus" might not be purely coincidental. Although it cannot be conclusively demonstrated that Shakespeare was cognizant of Aeschylus's work or a Renaissance adaptation, many commentators have adduced parallels between it and both *Hamlet* and *Macbeth*.[50] In the most developed of such

---

49. For an excellent account of the relation between Senecan drama and Shakespeare, see Gordon Braden, *Renaissance Tragedy and the Senecan Tradition: Anger's Privilege* (New Haven: Yale University Press, 1985), 153–223.

50. Adrian Poole has emphasized how fear affects the attempt to establish a new beginning in both the *Oresteia* and *Macbeth* in *Tragedy: Shakespeare and the Greek Example* (Oxford: Blackwell,

comparisons, Louise Schleiner has traced residues of the *Oresteia* in *Hamlet* and suggested that Shakespeare was at least familiar with a Latin or contemporary version of the trilogy. In particular, she considers as sources both Jean de Saint-Ravy's two-part Latin redaction—which composed part of Ben Jonson's library—and Dekker and Chettle's lost tragedies *Agamemnon* and *Orestes' Furies*, performed in 1599 and probably based on the Saint-Ravy translation.[51] Not merely describing these influences, Schleiner indicates Aeschylean echoes not available from other sources in both the churchyard scene, paralleling the graveyard one of *The Libation Bearers*, and the relationship between Hamlet and Horatio, distinctly resembling that of Orestes and Pylades.[52] John Hale has added to these the opening images of the two plays, *Hamlet*'s watchmen on the ramparts and the *Agamemnon*'s single sentry on the palace roof.[53]

Connecting Ben Jonson's ownership of the Saint-Ravy version with Shakespeare, Schleiner also contends that, even if the bard had not himself attended a performance of Dekker and Chettle's plays or read Saint-Ravy's *Oresteia*, he would have had ample opportunity to learn the contents of these works from his colleagues.[54] More significant, I would suggest, for establishing a relationship between the character Escalus in *Measure for Measure* and Aeschylus the playwright is the fact that Jonson was a devotee of Aristophanes, not just citing the Greek author's works[55] but even structuring *Epicoene* loosely around

---

1987), 15–53. Likewise, John Kerrigan, building on Louise Schleiner's research on possible means by which Shakespeare may have gained familiarity with Aeschylus's trilogy, has convincingly contrasted the dynamics of remembrance in *The Libation Bearers* and Elizabethan revenge tragedy—including *Hamlet*. John Kerrigan, *Revenge Tragedy: Aeschylus to Armageddon* (Oxford: Clarendon Press, 1996), 170–92. Earlier scholarship also insists on the resemblances, although it divides into works that cite the playwrights' "imaginative kinship" (J. T. Sheppard, *Aeschylus and Sophocles: Their Work and Influence* [London: George G. Harrap & Co., 1927], 136) and those that compare specific Aeschylean and Shakespearean passages. J. F. Boyes notes such correspondences not only with *Macbeth* and *Hamlet*, but also with Kyd's *Spanish Tragedy* and Tourneur's *Revenger's Tragedy*, in *Illustrations of the Tragedies of Aeschylus from the Greek, Latin, and English Poets* (Oxford: J. Vincent, 1842), 5–25.

    51. Louise Schleiner, "Latinized Greek Drama in Shakespeare's Writing of *Hamlet*," *Shakespeare Quarterly* 41, no. 1 (1990): 29–48.

    52. Schleiner, "Latinized Greek Drama," 37–45.

    53. John Hale, "Watchmen on the Ramparts: *Hamlet*'s Opening Image," *Hamlet Studies* 17 (1995): 98–101. On a more general level, Inga-Stina Ewbank has drawn connections between various Shakespeare plays, their reception by his contemporaries and successors, and a tradition of responding to Aeschylus's *Agamemnon*. Inga-Stina Ewbank, "'Striking too short at Greeks': The Transmission of *Agamemnon* to the English Renaissance Stage," in *Agamemnon in Performance, 458 BC to AD 2004*, ed. Fiona Macintosh, Pantelis Michelakis, Edith Hall, and Oliver Taplin (Oxford: Oxford University Press, 2005): 37–52.

    54. Schleiner, "Latinized Greek Drama," 32–34.

    55. For example, in the Induction to *Every Man Out of his Humour*, in which Shakespeare himself acted, Cordatus replies to the question of what the play is like, "Faith sir, I must refrain to judge;

Aristophanes' *Plutus*.[56] As a result, Jonson's *Poetaster*, his contribution to the infamous "war of the theaters," and a text that parodies several contemporary playwrights, followed the principles of Aristophanes's *Frogs*.[57] Performed during the 1601–2 season, Jonson's "Comical Satire" inherited from Aristophanes the attempt to dramatize a conflict among figures representing contemporary—or almost contemporary—playwrights, and a trial rendering judgment on them.[58] Jonson did, however, modify this basic formulation in a manner anticipating *Measure for Measure*, providing his writers with less transparent names, more clearly emphasizing the political aspects of the contest, and framing his trial as one of false accusation—a type of slander—rather than simply respective poetic merits; at stake, then, in Jonson's account, as in Shakespeare's, is punishment rather than reward. While the *Frogs* boldly presents Dionysus, the god of theater,

---

only this I can say of it, 'tis strange, and of a particular kind by itself, somewhat like *vetus comoedia*; a work that hath bounteously pleased me; how it will answer the general expectation, I know not." Subsequently the same character mentions Aristophanes by name as one of the practitioners of such *comoedia*, in whom "this kind of poem appeared absolute, and fully perfected." Jonson's knowledge of and affinity for Aristophanes is widely recognized, and has been used to substantiate the latter's availability to the Renaissance; as Anne Barton writes, "Ben Jonson owned several copies of the works of Aristophanes, and could refer to the *vetus comoedia* of the ancient world in terms that assumed at least a measure of familiarity on the part of his readers." Anne Barton, *The Names of Comedy* (Toronto: University of Toronto Press, 1990), 36–37. Jonson's plays are hereafter cited parenthetically from *Ben Jonson*, ed. C. H. Herford and Percy Simpson, 11 vols. (Oxford: Clarendon Press, 1954–1963).

56. Louis Lord, *Aristophanes: His Plays and His Influence* (London: George G. Harrap & Co., 1925), 158.

57. Lord observed: "In the *Poetaster* (1601) [Jonson] adopts Aristophanes' method of literary-political satire. The *Poetaster* follows the *Frogs* in general outline." Lord, *Aristophanes*, 157. C. G. Thayer likewise remarked: "In view of its subject, *Poetaster* seems to be related to *The Frogs* of Aristophanes. . . . There does appear to be some connection, the general terms of which are quite consistent with Jonson's comments in *Every Man Out* about his artistic independence combined with his partial reliance on the tradition of *Vetus Comoedia*." C. G. Thayer, *Ben Jonson: Studies in the Plays* (Norman: University of Oklahoma Press, 1963), 49. Leonhard Rechner also elaborated further upon the two plays' resemblances in *Aristophanes in England: Eine literarhistorische Untersuchung* (Frankfurt am Main: M. G. Martens, 1914), 10–14. More recently, Matthew Steggle situates the connections between *Poetaster* and the *Frogs* within a longer tradition of the reception of Aristophanes in the sixteenth century. Matthew Steggle, "Aristophanes in Early Modern England," in *Aristophanes in Performance, 421 BC–AD 2007: Peace, Birds, and Frogs*, ed. Edith Hall and Amanda Wrigley (London: Modern Humanities Research Association, 2007), 52–65.

58. This emphasis is especially clear from the *Poetaster*'s name at its original performance, which furnished its subsequent subtitle, *The Arraignment*. As Lorna Hutson pointed out to me, in his posthumously published *Discoveries* (1641), Jonson attributed a quotation to Stobaeus that is found verbatim instead in Jacobus Pontanus's *Poeticarum institutionum* (Ingolstadt: David Sartori, 1600). Pontanus himself includes a chapter in his section on tragedy comparing Aeschylus, Sophocles, and Euripides, placing them within a critical contest as Aristophanes had in the *Frogs* (116–19).

deciding between Aeschylus and Euripides, *Poetaster* disguises the targets of its satire behind the names of Latin lyric and epic poets.

By introducing the dynamics of patronage into the plot, Jonson also both places Virgil—Caesar's choice—above reproach and brings to the surface the links between poetry and politics that remained implicit in Aristophanes. In the *Frogs*,[59] the terms of the debate between Aeschylus and Euripides had been those of aristocracy opposed to democracy, grandeur against sophistry, and tradition versus innovation. This dichotomy is emphasized even through the disparate results of popular and "divine" judgment; Aeschylus wins according to Dionysus's decision, whereas previously the "housebreakers" (l. 808) of the underworld had seconded Euripides when he staged a coup against Aeschylus and supplanted him in "the chair for tragedy" (l. 768). The contrast between the methods of the two playwrights as well as between their receptions is already politically coded in Aristophanes, since, as Dionysus himself asserts, a tragedian is needed not simply to enhance the quality of the dramatic festivals but instead primarily "that the city [*polis*] [may be] saved" (l. 1419).

Jonson adopts the political aspects of this precedent but also expands upon them by introducing several of the poets' patrons and, most notably, the figure of the sovereign: Caesar. Horace, whose honor remains intact and enhanced despite the poetasters' calumny, expresses—like Aeschylus—no desire for the esteem of the multitude; instead he proclaims, speaking to Demetrius, but of the poetasters generally:

> Envy me still, so long as Virgil loves me,
> Gallus, Tibullus, and the best-best Caesar;
> My dear Maecenas. While these, with many more,
> Whose names I wisely slip, shall think me worthy
> Their honoured and adored society,
> And read and love, prove and applaud my poems,
> I would not wish but such as you should spite them. (5.3.448–54)

Jonson initially modifies Aristophanes's version of a final judgment though, allowing for a collective process (5.3.404–15) until Crispinus and Demetrius confess their guilt in accusing Horace of a "seditious libel" (5.3.43) against Caesar knowing the charges were false—thus, that they had slandered Horace by accusing him of such slander. After this point, it is Virgil who metes out

---

59. Aristophanes, "Frogs," in *Aristophanes II* (Cambridge: Harvard University Press, 1989), 293–437; hereafter cited parenthetically by line. The translations are my own.

punishments—mitigated at Horace's own plea. Speaking to Demetrius, he asserts: "Th' extremity of law/ Awards you to be branded in the front/ For this your calumny. But since it pleaseth/ Horace (the party wronged) t'intreat of Caesar/ A mitigation of that juster doom,/ With Caesar's tongue thus we pronounce your sentence" (5.3.558–63).

Virgil's authority as "Caesar's tongue"—both the sugared tongue of poetry and the sterner one of judgment—arises from the sovereignty of poetry itself. Responding to Caesar's praise of poetry at the commencement of act 5, Maecenas had proclaimed,

> Your majesty's high grace to poesy
> Shall stand 'gainst all the dull detractions
> Of leaden souls, who, for the vain assumings
> Of some, quite worthless of her sovereign wreaths,
> Contain her worthiest prophets in contempt. (5.1.33–37)

Tibullus had then praised Virgil's works themselves as of "sovereign worth" (5.1.116). The tongue of sovereignty, Virgil still cedes place to Caesar, whose role it is to conclude the play as the last individual to speak (5.3.600–611).[60] Although poetry remains the language of sovereignty, Jonson ensures that purely political figures also appear in his play. The structure of *Poetaster* thus stands between that of the *Frogs* and *Measure for Measure*, which, in a sense, provides a mirror image of the Aristophanic play. Whereas Aristophanes develops the political implications of playwrights' occupation, Shakespeare shows the dramaturgical role of political figures. Furthermore, the tragedians of the *Frogs* find themselves staged in a scene of judgment, while *Measure for Measure*'s characters produce their politics through the very act of judging.[61]

Irrespective of the extent of actual influence, several structural parallels connect *Measure for Measure* with the *Oresteia*, including, most broadly, their shared connection with revenge tragedy. Although the *Oresteia* ends in an acquittal, just as *Measure for Measure* concludes with a series of pardons, it begins with a scene

---

60. The play does not immediately end after Caesar's statement; instead, a final song follows.

61. Inscribing *Measure for Measure* in a line of descent from the *Frogs* through Jonson's *Poetaster* could also explain what I am suggesting is the relative transparency of the names given to Escalus and Angelo, a readability generally more characteristic of Aristophanes than Shakespeare. As Anne Barton writes: "In Aristophanic comedy, a man or woman's name can be the most important thing about them, especially if its meaning is readily decipherable. Aristophanes often drags his contemporaries into a play simply because of their names, which he treats in a strictly cratylic fashion." Barton, *The Names of Comedy*, 21.

of retribution, one that is then repeated in the second play, *The Libation Bearers*.[62] Initially Clytemnestra murders Agamemnon, because he had sacrificed Iphigenia long before the events of the trilogy began, then Orestes wreaks vengeance on his mother by killing her in turn, an act that calls forth those avenging spirits, the Furies or Erinyes, who pursue him until the conclusion of the *Eumenides*, the final play.

If revenge is evident on the surface of the *Oresteia*, it operates on a more subterranean plane in *Measure for Measure*. Although one interpretation of the play's title invokes the "eye for an eye" of revenge tragedy, the tragicomic genre of *Measure for Measure* has deflected analysis from this aspect of its inheritance. Rather than viewing the play as—like *Hamlet*—incorporating and critiquing elements of the revenge tradition, critics have instead, when considering *Measure for Measure*'s political dimensions, focused on the display and imposition of power.[63] Probably the second of Shakespeare's works performed before King James, however, *Measure for Measure* set itself against *Hamlet*, its predecessor, as a modification of revenge, both actualizing the revolutionary potential implicit in the other genre and juxtaposing the model of vengeance with the institution of the law.[64]

During *Measure for Measure*, the Duke employs a substitutive logic akin to that of revenge drama, encouraging the replacement of Claudio with a sequence of other bodies before formally pardoning each reprobate. *Measure for Measure* further raises the threat of revolution through both its structure—Duke Vincentio's replacement, albeit voluntary, by Angelo, and his subsequent restoration[65]—and

---

62. It would indeed be difficult not to consider at least the first two texts in the trilogy the first Western revenge plays. See, for example, the discussions in Anne Pippin Burnett, *Revenge in Attic and Later Tragedy* (Berkeley: University of California Press, 1998), 99–118; and Kerrigan, *Revenge Tragedy*, 3–29.

63. See, classically, Jonathan Dollimore, "Surveillance and Transgression in *Measure for Measure*," in *Political Shakespeare: New Essays in Cultural Materialism*, ed. Jonathan Dollimore and Alan Sinfield (Ithaca: Cornell University Press, 1985), 72–87; or, more recently, several of the essays collected in Gillian Murray Kendall, ed., *Shakespearean Power and Punishment* (London: Associated University Presses, 1998).

64. Alvin Kernan has argued persuasively that *Hamlet* would have been performed before James I at Hampton Court during the Christmas season of 1603. *Measure for Measure* was itself dramatized at Whitehall during the same season the subsequent year—played for the king on December 26, 1604. Alvin Kernan, *Shakespeare, the King's Playwright: Theater in the Stuart Court, 1603–1613* (New Haven: Yale University Press, 1995), 53.

65. Although not emphasizing the revolutionary nature of the motif, Leonard Tennenhouse points out the resemblance between *Measure for Measure* and other nearly contemporaneous plays in which monarchy was usurped rather than willingly and temporarily ceded. Leonard Tennenhouse, *Power on Display* (New York: Methuen, 1986), 156–57. The Duke even encourages Angelo

its use of Lucio's slander, as discussed earlier in this chapter.[66] Within the *Oresteia*, however, revenge is called forth by bloodshed that occurs outside the framework of law, whereas in *Measure for Measure*, Lucio's motives for revenge would stem from the injustice perpetrated by the imposition of the revived law upon Claudio. If, according to the conventional interpretation, the *Oresteia* involves revenge's replacement by law,[67] the structure of the law's activation itself calls forth revenge in *Measure for Measure*.

The trial scenes that both the *Oresteia* and *Measure for Measure* contain also represent an inaugural moment within each context, and both dramas stage the "institution" of the law. While Athena, in instructing the jury members before they judge Orestes, proclaims, "Here is my ruling now, you men of Athens:/ you who judge this first trial of bloodshed./ This shall be for all time to come for the people of Aegeus the judges' council chamber,"[68] the commencement of *Measure for Measure* makes the problem of reintroducing, and in a sense inaugurating, a long-dormant law the crucial issue.[69] Orestes and Claudio, each of whom's sister is crucially involved in his trauma, then become the exemplary objects of a law and at the same time the exception to its enforcement.

---

to think of himself as a revolutionary replacement—until his surprise reappearance, as though by a counter-coup. Still disguised as the Friar, Vincentio, in act 4, informs the Provost of his incipient return but adds, "This is a thing that Angelo knows not; for he this/ very day receives letters of strange tenour, per-/chance of the Duke's death, perchance entering/ into some monastery" (4.2.198–201).

66. The term "revolution" was not yet employed in the modern sense and, even later in the century, still retained the connotation of a return to an established order. As Hannah Arendt writes in *On Revolution*, "The word was first used not when what we call a revolution broke out in England and Cromwell rose to the first revolutionary dictatorship, but on the contrary, in 1660, after the overthrow of the Rump Parliament and at the occasion of the restoration of the monarchy." Hannah Arendt, *On Revolution* (1963; London: Penguin, 1990), 43. Despite the fact of restoration, however, the nature of the government had been ineluctably altered. I am using the word "revolution" in discussing *Measure for Measure* both to highlight this sense of the difference within a return and to emphasize what in the play exceeded revenge but remained still unnamed.

67. Paul Gewirtz, "Aeschylus' Law," *Harvard Law Review* 101, no. 5 (March 1988): 1046.

68. Aeschylus, *The Eumenides*, in *The Oresteia*, trans. David Grene and Wendy Doniger O'Flaherty (Chicago: University of Chicago Press, 1989), ll. 680–83; hereafter cited parenthetically by line.

69. As Simon Goldhill states the prevailing critical view of the *Oresteia*, the trilogy does not simply remain constrained within a revenge model but instead "dramatizes a movement from the sense of *dikê* as retribution to the sense of *dikê* as legal justice." Simon Goldhill, *Reading Greek Tragedy* (Cambridge: Cambridge University Press, 1986), 37. Escalus the character is already associated with Vienna's "institutions" at the beginning of the play, a term that, used only here by Shakespeare, recalls Aeschylus's allegorical "institution" of the Areopagus court of Athens at the conclusion of the *Oresteia*; as the Duke addresses Escalus, "The nature of our people,/ Our city's institutions, and the terms/ For common justice, y'are as pregnant in/ As art and practice hath enriched any/ That we remember" (1.1.9–13).

The historical particularities of the legal institutions concerned are, in addition, important to both works. As Simon Goldhill has elaborated, the representation of the founding of the court of the Areopagus, an aristocratic institution that had been fundamentally altered by the reforms of Ephialtes only four years before the first performance of the *Oresteia*, connects the trilogy tangibly to its contemporary political context, regardless of how one interprets that link.[70] Likewise, as we have seen, *Measure for Measure* takes up debates about common law judging that were current at the time.

In each text, the accused's escape from punishment also crucially happens only through an apparently unnatural intervention into the order of tragedy, one that occurs twice at the last minute. After the jury of the *Eumenides* has considered Orestes's case, it cannot reach a verdict and instead remains tied; as a result, Athena must intrude on the scene. She acquits Orestes for two reasons: because the oracle of Apollo had instructed Orestes to commit the crime, thus absolving him of full intentionality, and because Athena identifies with his situation on account of her own origins and nature (ll. 733–807). Both these rationales entail understanding or empathizing with the mental state of the accused, and thus choosing leniency over revenge. In *Measure for Measure,* the Duke fulfills a function analogous to that of Athena, although he pardons those already condemned rather than acquitting. The Duke's much interpreted *deus ex machina* reappearance in act 5 places him in the same position as the almost immaterial feather to which the Provost refers in an interchange with Abhorson; when Abhorson inquires, "A bawd, sir? Fie upon him, he will discredit our mystery," the Provost replies, "Go to, sire, you weigh equally: a feather will turn the scale" (4.2.26–29). Athena, as incorporeal goddess, had likewise in the *Eumenides* indiscernibly tilted the balance of votes in favor of Orestes.

The temporal disparity between the timing of the institution of the law within the *Oresteia* and *Measure for Measure* nevertheless alters the stakes of that institution itself. The near tragedy of *Measure for Measure*—averted only through the substitution of another head for Claudio's combined with the Duke's final pardons—arises from the law that has been proclaimed at the beginning of the play, not from a preexisting cycle of revenge. The arrival of tragicomedy corresponds not neatly with the law's intervention—as it does in the *Oresteia*—but instead with the Duke's extralegal pardon. Not only his name but also his identificatory jurisprudence and tendency toward leniency suggest Escalus, rather

---

70. Simon Goldhill, *Aeschylus: The Oresteia*, 2nd ed. (Cambridge: Cambridge University Press, 2004), 11.

than the Duke, as the closest analogue in *Measure for Measure* to both the character Athena in the *Oresteia* and the outcome of Aeschylus's trilogy itself. The Duke instead pardons Lucio with no indication of either sympathy with his character or a sense of the equitable justification of Lucio's slanders. Indeed, Lucio's intentions, as discussed earlier, seem triply unfathomable. Neither Duke nor spectator can resolve whether Lucio slanders the disguised sovereign to his face with knowledge of his identity or not, and therefore whether he is in fact slandering him at all; nor can we determine whether he intends merely to impugn the Duke's private person rather than engaging in *scandalum magnatum* and slandering the Duke as sovereign; nor, finally, can we ascertain whether Lucio's words are in fact false. The dynamics of *Measure for Measure*'s theater of pardoning thereby deviate from those of Orestes's acquittal in the *Oresteia*.

The differences may result not only from the inevitable gap between works written millennia apart but also from the specific political situation of early modern England, the juxtaposition between a conception of sovereignty that, under James I, would assume a form increasingly indebted to a notion of divine right, and the rise of arguments for a common law that would persist independent of sovereign influence. Through raising the problem of the relation between the person of the sovereign—in the form of the Duke—and the reinstituted laws, *Measure for Measure* suggests that it is precisely in the space between the sovereign and the laws that the possibility of revolution emerges, a possibility ultimately stemmed by the sovereign pardon. The final pardons of *Measure for Measure* not only turn tragedy into tragicomedy but also perform the Duke's majesty for the characters and spectators. These pardons serve to extricate the Duke from the difficulties occasioned by his act of reimposing the law.

At the same time, the Duke's pardons provide only a contingent solution rather than resolving the epistemological quandaries that the play raises for its audiences. The pardon of Lucio leaves the spectator uncertain about what was actually pardoned and still immersed in speculation as to whether or not revolutionary activity had been on the horizon. Playgoers are, in addition, furnished with sufficient fodder to deliberate the merits of the king's act of judging in person without being led to a particular conclusion through authorial instructions. The tragicomic conclusion of *Measure for Measure* hence serves to restore the state but not the certainty of the spectators. Instead, it provides an incitement for political reflection that might take place outside of the theater, in Parliament, the Inns of Court, the royal palace, or the pub.

By potentially invoking both Coke and Aeschylus in the character of Escalus, *Measure for Measure* establishes a dramatic genealogy stemming from ancient Greece while also suggesting the necessary modification of the "Common Lawes of Greece" within the context of early modern English monarchy. While the laws may remain common, the authority for their establishment has shifted as theories of royal sovereignty have come onto the scene. In reaching back to Aeschylus, the play also indicates that political discourse and theory may not be confined to the realms in which one might expect to find it, and that drama has always been capable of contributing to political thought. Although the spectators of the *Oresteia* were deliberating the reforms of the Areopagus rather than the independence of common law judges, the ancient trilogy and *Measure for Measure* both called upon their audience to reflect imaginatively on contemporary legal institutions. In the following chapter we will see how one such audience member— King James I himself—might have derived insight from *Measure for Measure* in pursuing his political ends.

2

EMPLOTTING POLITICS /
James I and the "Powder Treason"

In the early hours of November 5, 1605, a man who called himself John Johnson was discovered lurking about the Palace of Westminster, the seat of the English Parliament, scheduled to meet there the next day.[1] Rapidly apprehended and subsequently tortured, this individual later identified himself as Guido Fawkes, and is known to posterity as Guy Fawkes. Through the information extracted from him, the state confirmed the existence of a Catholic plot to demolish Parliament, its members, and King James I at the opening of the new parliamentary session. This conspiracy soon came to be designated the "Powder Treason," since it relied for its accomplishment on thirty-six barrels of gunpowder placed in the vault underneath the Parliament building. Many of the corresponding "Powder Men"—the plotters—fled London upon learning they had been discovered, and a few fell victim to the explosion of their own ammunition. The rest were brought to trial—also in Westminster Hall—on January 7, 1606.

Sir Edward Coke, then attorney general for King James, addressed the Lords Commissioners and urged them to judge those who had intended such a revolutionary treason; in a second trial linked with the Gunpowder Plot, he likewise subsequently adjured them to condemn Henry Garnet, a Jesuit who had remained secretly in England, despite James's prohibition against Catholic priests.[2] The case against Garnet rested solely on the fact that the priest had received knowledge

---

1. This account of the Gunpowder Plot and subsequent trials relies on Antonia Fraser, *Faith and Treason: The Story of the Gunpowder Plot* (New York: Doubleday Anchor Books, 1997).

2. For the purposes of discussing the Gunpowder Plot and the subsequent trial, over which Coke presided, I treat James and Coke as sharing a similar—although clearly not identical—vantage point. Although James may already have realized the problems for his prerogative inherent in an insistence on the common law, he remained firmly allied with Coke during the first few years of his reign. Mark Fortier, "Equity and Ideas: Coke, Ellesmere, and James I," *Renaissance Quarterly* 51, no. 4 (1998): 1270–72. Indeed, in *Calvin's Case*, Coke even employed the logic of common law in order to affirm the unity of England and Scotland under James, stating that the king's Scottish subjects could inherit land in England since both English and Scottish men were born under allegiance to the same sovereign.

of the conspiracy through the confession of one of the participants—and that he possessed a book alternatively titled *A Treatise of Equivocation* and *A Treatise against Lying and Fraudulent Dissimulation*. Not surprisingly, both trials ended in conviction—and capital punishment. Memory of the plot and its aftermath has persisted for centuries, and Guy Fawkes Day—or "Bonfire Night"—is still commemorated to this day.

James I's more immediate response to the plot, however, and the alteration in sovereignty that it implied, furnishes the subject of this chapter. First examining the king's assertion of his own sovereignty prior to the plot—and his emphasis on judging rather than lawgiving—I then turn to James's attempt to inscribe the Powder Men within a recognizable genre, that of revenge tragedy. In doing so, the king suggested that Parliament be entrusted with judging the conspirators, thus imaginatively displacing his sovereignty onto it. The way in which James scripted the aftermath of the plot was not uncharacteristic of his interpretive approach, and followed from his apocalyptic vision of history as a tragicomedy that would result in comedy for the elect and tragedy for the rest. Although another—Shakespearean—model of tragicomedy was also available, James remained constrained by his own generic paradigm and declined to adopt it. In responding to the threat of revolution by punishing rather than pardoning, James refused to rethink the state and instead commenced a shift in the place of sovereignty, a shift that ultimately undermined his own broad claims for monarchical authority.

Staging Sovereignty

By the time the Gunpowder Plot took place, James had demonstrated a commitment to conducting himself according to principles of divine right sovereignty, articulating his theories in both *Basilikon Doron* (1599 and 1603) and *The Trew Law of Free Monarchies* (1603). James was significantly influenced by Jean Bodin's *Six Livres de la République*, which decorated his library as early as 1577.[3]

---

3. Jenny Wormald, "*'Basilikon Doron'* and *'The Trew Law of Free Monarchies,'*" in *The Mental World of the Jacobean Court*, ed. Linda Levy Peck (Cambridge: Cambridge University Press, 1991), 43. James possessed the French version of Bodin's work, rather than Richard Knolles's 1606 translation into English, which attempted to combine the expanded Latin edition with the French. In citing Bodin, however, I use the modern reprint of Knolles, the only complete edition in English, and supplement the translation where necessary with the French and with the excerpts on sovereignty that Julian Franklin translated. See Jean Bodin, *On Sovereignty: Four Chapters from* The Six Books of the Commonwealth, ed. and trans. Julian H. Franklin (Cambridge: Cambridge University Press, 1992).

While James's debt to Bodin has long been acknowledged, recent scholarship on the legal and political theory of the early seventeenth century has demonstrated that Bodin's influence was more widespread than previously imagined. Hence Daniel Lee traces a trajectory from Bodin—whom he reinterprets as furnishing a theory of popular sovereignty—to parliamentarians like Henry Parker, writing in the lead-up to the English Civil War.[4] Although Lee looks to English civilians as conduits for Bodin's ideas, he largely neglects the arguments of common law judges like Coke in response to notions of prerogative derived from Bodin. This omission is important because it allows him to downplay the force of a judicial constitutionalism derived from the common law as opposed to the popular constitutionalism he locates in the parliamentarians' thought. In this sense, Ian Williams's article "Developing a Prerogative Theory for the Authority of Chancery: The French Connection" helpfully supplements Lee's work by illuminating the extent to which the stakes of jurisdictional debates among the courts were predicated on interpretations of and opposition to Bodin.[5] Even Williams does not flesh out the full extent of Bodin's influence, however, and he does not consider Coke as a reader of Bodin. Two French versions of Bodin, from 1576 and 1580, appear in the published *Catalogue* of Coke's library, and the book list from Holkham Hall, where what remains of his library has been reassembled, includes an Italian version as well as the expanded Latin one.[6] Most important, the first French edition contains extensive annotations in Coke's hand, particularly in passages pertaining to royal power.[7]

Turning to James's conception of his own power and reception of Bodin, he urged a concept of the king as God's lieutenant on earth,[8] and monarchy itself as the form of government that, since "resembling the Diuinitie, approcheth

---

4. Daniel Lee, *Popular Sovereignty in Early Modern Constitutional Thought* (Oxford: Oxford University Press, 2016), 273–315.

5. Ian Williams, "Developing a Prerogative Theory for the Authority of the Chancery: The French Connection," in *Law and Authority in British Legal History, 1200–1900*, ed. Mark Godfrey (Cambridge: Cambridge University Press, 2016), 33–59.

6. W. O. Hassall, *A Catalogue of the Library of Sir Edward Coke* (New Haven: Yale University Press, 1950); 73; Sir Edward Coke's Ownership List, Holkham Hall library, Norfolk (undated), 6.

7. I do not believe anyone else has remarked on these annotations, which I have inspected at Holkham.

8. This concept is articulated in both *The Trew Law* and *Basilikon Doron*, but also recurs throughout the rest of James's writings. In *The Trew Law*, he speaks of the king as "Gods Lieutenant in earth," and in the sonnet that precedes and epitomizes *Basilikon Doron*, he refers to the sovereign as God's "lieutenant here [on earth]." James VI and I, *The Trew Law of Free Monarchies*, in *Political Writings*, ed. Johann P. Sommerville (Cambridge: Cambridge University Press, 1994), 72; James VI and I, *Basilicon Doron*, in *Political Writings*, 1.

nearest to perfection."[9] Bodin had explained that "nothing upon earth is greater or higher, next unto God, than the maiestie of kings and soveraigne princes, for that they are in a sort created his lieutenants for the welfare of other men"; he also added, "He which speaketh evill of his prince unto whome he oweth all dutie, doth iniurie unto the maiestie of God himselfe, whose lively image he is upon earth."[10] Sovereignty itself Bodin defined for the first time, asserting, "Soueraigntie is the most high, absolute, and perpetuall power ouer all the citisens and subiects of a Commonweale: which the Latines cal *Maiestatem*."[11] This power of majesty James parsed into the three parts that have subsequently become known through separation of powers doctrine: the lawmaking, the judicial, and the executive functions. Despite declaring that "kings were the authors and makers of the Lawes, and not the Lawes of . . . kings,"[12] James—in contrast to Bodin—emphasized the second and third of these categories over the first.[13] Identifying his own singularity as sovereign with the application of the law in individual cases, he envisioned himself as representing both the force of law and the source of judgment.

There were several reasons for James to downplay lawmaking's function in constituting sovereignty despite Bodin's claim that "it is only sovereign princes who can make law for all subjects without exception, both collectively and individually [*en particulier*]."[14] Although James did—unsuccessfully—attempt to endow his proclamations with the force of law, he acknowledged that a certain general applicability inherent in lawmaking rendered it the appropriate province of Parliament.[15] Whereas Parliament was entitled to frame laws, however, James

---

9. James, *Trew Law*, 63.

10. Jean Bodin, *The Six Bookes of a Commonweale*, trans. Richard Knolles (London: G. Bishop, 1606), reprinted in *The Six Bookes of a Commonweale*, ed. Kenneth Douglas McRae (Cambridge: Harvard University Press, 1962), 153.

11. Bodin, *Six Bookes*, 84. As Daniel Lee points out, Bodin draws heavily on Roman models in his account of sovereignty. Lee, *Popular Sovereignty*, 158–86. Nevertheless, Bodin establishes the term for modernity.

12. James, *Trew Law*, 73.

13. The disparity in the two thinkers' priorities manifests itself in the order of their discussions. When treating "the true marks of sovereignty" in book 1, chapter 10, Bodin establishes that the first of these is the power to make law, and opines that all others derive from it: "This same power of making and repealing law includes all the other rights and prerogatives of sovereignty, so that strictly speaking we can say that there is only this one prerogative of sovereignty, inasmuch as all the other rights are comprehended in it." Bodin, *On Sovereignty*, 58. By contrast, James's fundamental premise remains that "[a king's] office is, *To minister Iustice and Iudgement to the people*." James, *Trew Law*, 64.

14. Bodin, *On Sovereignty*, 52.

15. Humphry Woolrych summarizes this episode—and the conflict between Coke and the king that ensued—in his *Life* of Coke. As Woolrych writes: "[Coke] had been called upon by the King's

usually deemed it capable neither of executing them nor of implementing judgments. In *Basilikon Doron*, he warned his son Henry against allowing any such particularity in Parliament. Conceding that the institution could function as a seat of judgment, James maintained that it properly employed this capacity only when judgment had been redefined as lawgiving:

> Onely remember, that as Parliaments haue bene ordained for making of Lawes, so ye abuse not their institution, in holding them for any mens particulars: For as a Parliament is the honourablest and highest iudgement in the land (as being the Kings head Court) if it be well used, which is by making of good Lawes in it; so it is the in-iustest Iudgement-seat that may be, being abused to mens particulars: irreuocable decreits against particular parties, being giuen therein under colour of generall Lawes, and oft-times th'Estates not knowing themselues whom thereby they hurt.[16]

The numerosity of Parliament as a collective body here finds its analogy in the generality of laws that apply to all, with its sphere of knowledge characterized as that of policy rather than person. When attempting to venture into the area of application—that of judgment and execution—Parliament exceeds the parameters of its competence and thereby commits injustice. Its inability to mediate

---

ministers to sanction certain proclamations of the monarch, and to allow them the same force with Acts of Parliament. It was the wish of James to restrain the building of new houses in and about London, and to prohibit the making starch from wheat; and he proposed by the mere virtue of his proclamations, to suppress these practices, and, of course, to inflict penalties for any acts of disobedience to them." Humphry Woolrych, *The Life of the Right Honourable Sir Edward Coke, Knt* (London: J. & W. T. Clarke, 1826), 84. Both the form and material of James's attempted lawmaking recall Angelo's proclamation in *Measure for Measure*, according to which "all houses in the suburbs of Vienna must be plucked down" (1.2.89); the real-life instance can be analyzed along the same lines as the fictional one (see chapter 1).

Responding to James's legislative efforts, Coke and his fellow judges insisted "that the law of England was divided into three parts,—common law, statute law and custom; that the King's proclamation was not any one of those; and that, with regard to the creation of offences, it could not be done in the manner proposed, since there were only two kinds of mischiefs; the one, *malum in se*, against the common law; the other, *malum prohibitum*, against an act of the legislature." Woolrych, *Life*, 85. The judges' reply indicates that the historical generality of the common law as well as the numerical generality of Parliament stand in opposition to the king's particularity, and to his capacity to create laws.

The relationship between the generality of the common law—obtained through a persistent practice of judgment—and the particularity of the king's equitable judgment or pardoning will be taken up again in chapter 6, in the context of Hobbes's *Dialogue between a Philosopher and a Student of the Common Lawes*. Although postdating the Civil War, this text reprises the controversy between equity and the common law as championed by Coke.

16. James, *Basilicon Doron*, 21.

between the generality of lawmaking and the particularity of judgment manifests itself as the failure to know at once the specific and universal consequences of a certain law.

For the king, by contrast, James claims a cognizance of particulars, which remain a secret from others; thus, in *The Trew Law*, he urges that "lest otherwise *Summum ius* bee *summa iniuria* . . . generall lawes, made publikely in Parliament, may upon knowen respects to the King by his authoritie bee mitigated."[17] Although the sovereign must know the reasons for such equitable remedies, his decision is not susceptible to the same public review that characterizes the open discussion of Parliament. If we compare the two passages, it becomes evident that not only does the creation of a general law out of a particular circumstance render Parliament the "in-iustest Iudgement-seat," but also its very capacity to generate a "rigorous" statute—applying without regard to person—means that Parliament will inadvertently transform *summum ius* into the greatest injury. This deficiency—inherent in the generality of lawgiving—can be remedied only by the king's exercise of his equitable powers, or by his act of pardoning, a mark of sovereignty James also discusses in *Basilikon Doron*. A certain asymmetry then emerges between the lawgiving of Parliament and the mitigating judgment of the king; whereas the former provides legal maxims, the latter allows for exceptions from the law. The force of law that James envisions as represented by his scepter derives, in a certain sense, from the sovereign's capacity to furnish a reprieve from the laws. Without the ratification of the king, Parliament's propositions would remain ineffectual; as James writes, "It lies in the power of no Parliament, to make any kinde of Lawe or Statute, without [the king's] Scepter be to it, for giuing it the force of a Law."[18]

The necessity of upholding his reputation also dictated that James should not insist on his capacity to make laws.[19] Since the act of promulgating new laws entails breaking with an extant system, the sovereign, in generating them,

---

17. James, *Trew Law*, 75.

18. James, *Trew Law*, 74–75.

19. Following a well-established tradition, Carl Schmitt distinguishes the basis of monarchy from that of parliamentarism precisely through opposing the honor of the king to "openness and discussion." Carl Schmitt, *The Crisis of Parliamentary Democracy*, trans. Ellen Kennedy (Cambridge: MIT Press, 1996), 8, 48. This constitutive element he presents as so fundamental that "the epoch of monarchy is at an end when a sense of the principle of kingship, of honor, has been lost, if bourgeois kings appear who seek to prove their usefulness and utility instead of their devotion and honor" (8). Proclaiming the end of the parliamentary era, however, Schmitt introduces the replacement of openness and discussion with "public opinion" (6–7). Although this phrase focuses on the perspective of the people rather than the focal point provided by the sovereign, what Schmitt calls public opinion may constitute a transmuted version of honor.

actualizes what within him remains above the law; only as an exception to the law can he apply his formative powers. His exceptional determination, however, always risks becoming exemplary—of furnishing an example that would be perilous to the state if followed by its subjects. Bodin considers this problem in discussing the king's voluntary promise to maintain those laws already in existence and to abide by them himself. According to Bodin, this oath, on the one hand, establishes a principle of strict adherence to the laws but, on the other, opens the possibility that the king himself could commit what Bodin conceives as the greatest crime of his office—perjury. As Bodin observes, "It was no maruell if *Traian*, one of the best princes that euer liued in the world, swore (as is aforesaid) to keep the laws, although he in the name of a soueraigne prince were exempted; to the end by his own example to moue his subiects to the more carefull obseruing of them." He then warns that the king would deny his own sovereignty by adhering to such an oath but also perpetrate the most grievous offense by violating it: "The prince that sweareth to keepe the lawes of his countrey, must either not haue the soueraigntie; or els become a periured man, if he shall abrogat but one law, contrarie unto his oath: whereas it is not only profitable that a soueraigne prince should sometimes abrogat some such lawes, but also necessarie for him to alter or correct them, as the infinit varietie of places, times, and persons shall require."[20] Bodin depicts such deceit as particularly abhorrent because the sovereign "is the formal guarantor to all his subjects of good faith among themselves, and because there is no crime more detestable in a prince than perjury."[21]

James, attempting to resolve the dilemma Bodin had presented, assured his subjects that he would provide an example of lawfulness at the same time as maintaining his sovereign privilege to exceed the law; as he asserts in the *Trew Law*, "A good King, although hee be aboue the Law, will subiect and frame his actions thereto, for examples sake to his subiects, and of his owne free-will, but not as subiect or bound thereto."[22] Furthermore, in a subsequent speech to Parliament, he declared that he intended to rule in accordance with settled laws, and, following Bodin in excoriating those who fail to abide by their coronation oath, remarked that "all Kings that are not tyrants, or periured, will be glad to bound themselues within the limits of their Lawes; and they that perswade them the contrary, are vipers, and pests, both against them and the Commonwealth."[23]

---

20. Bodin, *Six Bookes*, 100.
21. Bodin, *On Sovereignty*, 35.
22. James, *Trew Law*, 75.
23. James VI and I, Speech to Parliament of 21 March 1609, in *Political Writings*, 184. James's discussion in the *Trew Law* of the Scottish coronation oath, which he claims is similar to that of

Both individually abiding by extant law and upholding these laws generally, James essayed to retain the honor required of a sovereign.

For Bodin, the risk that the sovereign will set a bad example also impinges on the king's capacity to render judgment personally, since such an act stages him— and his deficiencies—in public. After articulating a series of arguments traditionally adduced to urge that the sovereign should himself serve as judge, Bodin interposes, "Unto mee it seemeth not onely not necessarie, but not profitable unto the subiects, the prince himselfe to bee unto them the minister of iustice." Following the example of God, of whom he remains the earthly representative, the king should, rather than parading his virtues, withdraw from view. As Bodin states initially, any stain on the majesty of the king will disfigure his reputation irremediably, and assist in propagating injustice among the people:

> The least vice in a prince being like unto a canker in a faire face: and so to doe, what were it els, than in the sight of the people to set up an example of vice, to lead me, to draw them, yea & euen to enforce them to be naught? For there is nothing more naturall, than for the subiects to conforme themselues unto the manners, unto the doings and sayings of their prince; there being neither gesture, action, nor countenance in him, be it good or bad, which is not marked, or counterfaited by them which see him, hauing their eyes, their sences, and all their spirits, wholly bent to the imitation of him.

Responding, then, to those who would emphasize the exemplary character of the sovereign's virtues, Bodin opines that deviation provides an infinitely more potent source of transformation than uprightness itself, remarking, "So much power the prince hath at his pleasure to chaunge and turne the harts of his subiects, but alwayes rather unto vices and vanities, than unto vertues." Thus, despite designating the right of final judicial appeal the fourth "mark" of sovereignty, Bodin envisions the very appearance of the king in applying justice as defiling the picture of perfect justice that he must represent. As the gold standard of justice, the sovereign should withdraw from manifestation and the risk of being counterfeited.[24]

---

every other "Christian" country, suggests the model he has in mind. The clauses include a promise— ensuring continuity—"to maintain all the lowable and good Lawes made by their predecessours: to see them put in execution, and the breakers and violaters thereof, to be punished, according to the tenour of the same." James, *Trew Law*, 65. An escape hatch is, however, offered by the condition that these laws be "lowable and good."

24. Bodin, *Six Bookes*, 502–5.

Not only this flaw in the facade of the king's justice but also a further structural paradox inherent in the relationship between that judgment appropriate to the sovereign and the correct application of the law renders withdrawal from the scene of justice appropriate for the king. According to Bodin, "nothing is so proper unto a prince, as clemencie; nothing unto a king, as mercie; nothing unto maiestie, as lenitie." Nevertheless, generalizing these principles will lead—like the failure to execute the laws—to a paramount violation of justice. As Bodin concludes, "Nothing is more contrarie unto true iustice, than pitie; neither any thing more repugnant unto the office and dutie of an upright judge, than mercie."[25]

In elaborating the king's right to pardon, one of the marks of his sovereignty linked with the right of final appeal, Bodin explains that mercy engenders injustice when the king thereby "sacrifice[s] the civil interest of a subject."[26] The injured individual, not the king, is the only one endowed with the authority to forgive an offense against him. Furthermore, God's interest—identified with natural law—is even more indispensable than that of the subject. Since Bodin believes that "the law of God and nature" prescribes death as the penalty for intentional murder, it becomes impermissible for the king to pardon, or even to remit capital punishment in such cases. As Bodin writes, analogizing the king's relation to his magistrates with God's connection to the king, "If . . . the magistrat deserue capitall punishment, which dispenseth with the law of his king, how shall it be lawfull for a soueraigne prince, to dispence with his subiect from the law of God."[27]

Despite the various analogies Bodin draws between God and the king, a crucial dissimilarity furnishes a partial solution to the paradox: the fact that God cannot judge in person (on earth) while the king can, even if it is inadvisable for him to do so. In instances of treason against the king, unlike intentional murder, no subject has been injured. As Bodin maintains, "Of all the graces and pardons that a prince can giue, there is none more commendable, than when he pardoneth the iniurie done against his owne person." At the same time, he also admonishes every king to refrain from personally administering justice, especially when he has been injured and, therefore, would be a judge in his own case.[28]

---

25. Bodin, *Six Bookes*, 509.

26. Bodin, *On Sovereignty*, 76.

27. Bodin, *Six Bookes*, 31, 174. Andrea Frisch similarly remarks upon Bodin's trepidation about the king's pardon of premeditated murder, finding support in Bodin for her argument that royal pardoning was beginning to lose its legitimacy as a response to the sixteenth-century wars of religion. Andrea Frisch, *Forgetting Differences: Tragedy, Historiography, and the French Wars of Religion* (Edinburgh: Edinburgh University Press, 2015).

28. Bodin, *Six Bookes*, 175, 514.

These two sets of instructions—one requiring the sovereign to recuse himself entirely and the other insisting that he should judge but pardon—appear to contain an irreconcilable contradiction. And yet a path forward emerges from a flaw in the parallel established between God and the king. If the resemblance Bodin described remained in force, the sovereign would be able to withdraw himself from judgment, leaving those who committed treason to be executed. Precisely because it remains possible, if inadvisable, for him to judge in person, he must instead pardon. Caught in the space of incomplete withdrawal, the sovereign has at his disposal only one weapon: mercy.

A Dramatic Exception

In his 1605 address to Parliament in the aftermath of the discovery of the Gunpowder Plot, only the second he had ever delivered to the assembled members, James I skillfully suggested how the very fact the kingdom had been "saved" from a treasonous act could be interpreted in support of his own sovereignty. At the same time, he imagined a scenario that supplied a first step toward conceptualizing Parliament itself as a sovereign entity. Implicitly pointing to the element exceeding reason inherent in a sovereignty based on the principles of divine right, James claimed that the Gunpowder Plot's failure should be seen as God's act of pardoning both him and the entire state of England; this pardon means that James can subsequently embody the ideal theological-political ruler—and thus the only one truly free of divine intervention—initiating God's apocalyptic reign on earth.[29] At the same time, however, James indicated that Parliament would be reconvened once the plotters were apprehended and asked to render judgment against them, since the treason of the Gunpowder Plot had aimed against the very lawmaking capacity embodied in Parliament. Although this unprecedented trial never occurred, envisioning it alone set in motion the conceptual train that would lead to the sovereignty of Parliament. Both of James's lines of argument

---

29. As Alison McQueen observes, following "England's defeat of the Spanish Armada in 1588, . . . the country was increasingly cast as an elect nation with a special role in the end times," and "the failure of the Gunpowder Plot in 1605 was taken as a further sign that England was under divine protection." Alison McQueen, *Political Realism in Apocalyptic Times* (Cambridge: Cambridge University Press, 2018), 114. While James's biography prior to ascending the throne and his early reign rendered him "the focus of . . . apocalyptic hopes," he backed away from an apocalyptic logic later in his reign. McQueen, *Political Realism*, 114–15. For additional discussions of the apocalyptic imaginary of this period, see Paul K. Christianson, *Reformers and Babylon: English Apocalyptic Visions from the Reformation to the Eve of the Civil War* (Toronto: University of Toronto Press, 1978).

rely on generic models derived from drama, the first representing a tragicomedy resolved by a *deus ex machina* conclusion, and the second even more strongly reflecting the influence of revenge tragedy. The distinction between them likewise corresponds to the difference between interpreting what occurred as a "natural accident"—and thus a sign of God's will—and as a purely human intention; precisely because the crime was not actually consummated, both readings are allowed to remain.

Toward the commencement of his speech, James reminds Parliament several times of his contention that the monarchy descended upon him by divine right. The most striking of these allusions takes the form of a comparison, James entreating Parliament, "I must crave a little pardon of you, That since Kings are in the word of god it selfe called Gods, as being his Lieutenants and Vice-gerents on earth, and so adorned and furnished with some sparkle of the Divinitie; to compare some of the workes of god the great king, towards the whole and generall world, to some of his workes towards mee, and this little world of my Dominions." During the course of this analogy, a certain slippage occurs; whereas one would expect the alignment of God as supreme king with particular political kings to result in a claim comparing James's treatment of his subjects with God's actions toward him, James instead decides to consider himself a privileged object of God's deeds. This is particularly significant since translating the anticipated analogy into execution would require James to pardon rather than punish. In fact, James's entire subsequent elaboration of biblical parallels insists that he has been "pardoned" by the *misericordia* of God and allowed to be "purged" rather than destroyed by the Apocalypse. Stating, "It pleased god to deliver mee, as it were from the very brinke of death, from the point of the dagger, and so to purge me by my thankefull acknowledgement of so great a benefite," he insists on the *deus ex machina* success of God's intervention, which results in a "purgation" akin to that achieved in tragic drama that yet refrains from carrying out a fully tragic conclusion. How, then, does James, endowed with the theatrical "sparkle of the Divinitie," emerge from this speech with majesty renewed?[30]

In his speech, two sets of paired events are discussed, both conjunctions leading to the conclusion that James's sovereignty should now be considered free from all external constraints. In opening, James asserts that his first speech was designed to thank Parliament, whereas this one expresses his gratitude "to a farre greater person, which is to god." His salvation by God through the failure of the Gunpowder Plot allows him to postulate further independence from Parliament;

---

30. James VI and I, Speech to Parliament of 9 November 1605, in *Political Writings*, 147–48.

if it had any role in his initial succession, he seems to say, God himself had taken over that responsibility by thwarting the completion of the recent treason. God too, however, has "forgiven" James, and given up his investment in the king's monarchical power through pardoning him during the Apocalypse—or, rather, rendering a positive judgment on his soul. Since the postapocalyptic world no longer fears the judgment of God, James can now operate in a solely political post-history.[31]

When considered according to the logic of punishment rather than forgiveness, the Gunpowder Plot must be thought of as an intentional event rather than a potential "accident" or God-ordained occurrence. This scandal of its intentionality James expresses as a result of its failure to conform to generic norms or to adhere to available dramatic models. As we will see, it is the very "generality" of the terrorist action that defeats extant generic classifications. Censuring the plotters' composition of their "tragedy," James marvels: "How wonderfull it is when you shall thinke upon the small, or rather no ground, whereupon the practisers were entised to invent this Tragedie. For if these Conspirators had onely bene bankrupt persons, or discontented upon occasion of any disgraces done unto them; this might have seemed to have bene but a worke of revenge. But for my owne part, as I scarcely ever knew any of them, so cannot they alledge so much as a pretended cause of griefe." This deficiency of the conspirators' tragedy assumes two related forms, the first linked to the means by which the crime would have been committed, and the second bound up with the generality of its object. Claiming that personal murder "by other men, and reasonable creatures" represents the least despicable, since "who knoweth what pitie God may stirre up in the hearts of the Actors at the very instant?," James opines that the "crueltie" of technologies like gunpowder is immense. Rather than composing a revenge play that might abruptly be transformed into a tragicomedy through a suffusion of pity within the characters—thus not requiring the explicit intervention of God's *misericordia* which James had invoked at the beginning of his speech—the plotters designed a method by which their intention could neither be affected by their changing passions nor reversed. Likewise, rather than being spurred by a

---

31. James, Speech of 9 November 1605, 147. Postulating a Protestant reign on earth between the fall of the Antichrist—identified with the papacy—and the Last Judgment, millenarianism gained conceptual popularity during James's reign. Bernard Capp, "The Political Dimension of Apocalyptic Thought," in *The Apocalypse in English Renaissance Thought and Literature: Patterns, Antecedents and Repercussions*, ed. C. A. Patrides and Joseph Wittreich (Manchester: Manchester University Press, 1984), 101. James's own writings, however, place significantly more emphasis on the role of kings following the Last Judgment than on such an earthly monarchy.

characterological motivation, or a particular grievance against James I, the plotters designed to destroy, in his words, "the whole body of the State in generall. . . . And as the wretch himselfe which is in the Tower, doeth confesse, it was
purposely devised by them, and concluded to be done in this house; That where
the cruell Lawes (as they say) were made against their Religion, both place and
persons should all be destroyed and blowne up at once." Although many revenge
dramas featured attempts to kill a king, these occurred secretly and separately,
not expanding to include more individuals within their scope. Since directed
against the Parliament in its legislative function, and not solely against James
I himself as king, the treason assumed previously unfigured dimensions.[32]

It is this aspect that Sir Edward Coke subsequently emphasized in his opening
remarks at the plotters' actual trial, enumerating the three most horrible aspects
of the scheme—the fact that "this offense is *primae impressionis*" and without
name; its status "*sine exemplo,* beyond all examples, whether in fact or fiction,
even of the tragic poets, who did beat their wits to represent the most fearful
and horrible murders"; and finally its existence "*sine modo,* without all measure
or stint of iniquity." While the third characteristic stems from the "generality" of
the crime, the first two complement each other. The greatest treason previously
envisioned consisted in a *crimen laesae majestatis,* touching the majesty of the
king; this type occurs in revenge tragedy but does not entail dissolving an entire
state as the Gunpowder Plotters attempted, or, as Coke phrases it, "the deletion
of our whole name and nation." Coke's emphasis on the crime's lack of a prior
pattern not only expresses his stance on the relationship between fiction and
politics but also insists on the importance of the conspirators' intentions, the
anomaly of which supposedly caused them to be unimaginable at their historical
moment. The very extravagance of these intentions rendered them like fictions,
so that Coke could almost accurately say "that when these things shall be related
to posterity, they will be reputed matters feigned—not done."[33]

Not only was the Powder Men's act of intending treason treasonous, but
the nature of intention itself, according to Coke, resembles that of treason as
well. Both are conjoined in their indiscernibility, "for treason is like a tree whose
root is full of poison, and lieth secret and hid within the earth, resembling the
imagination of the heart of man, which is so secret as God only knoweth it." The
imagined—or intended—treason both outstrips reality in its genre and defines

---

32. James, Speech of 9 November 1605, 149–50.

33. David Jardine, ed., *Criminal Trials,* vol. 2, *The Gunpowder Plot* (London: Charles Knight,
1835), 65, 122–23.

the concept of treason itself. Coke can thus assert that Father Garnet, the Jesuit tried subsequently for his supposed assistance in the plot, was "a doctor of five DD's, namely, of dissimulation, of deposing of princes, of disposing of kingdoms, of daunting and deterring of subjects, and of destruction." In Coke's mantra, dissimulation and destruction, which frame the series as outgrowths of intention and treason, respectively, retain their relation beyond simple alliteration.[34]

After juxtaposing the two interpretations of the Gunpowder Plot that he presents, James devises a plan for reintegrating the conspirators back into the legal system through incorporating them into a recognizable tragedy. Asserting that he will dismiss Parliament for the season, James insists that he will recall the members when it comes time to prosecute the criminals, and that they themselves will be in charge of executing what he dubs an "extraordinary Iudgement."[35] The structure of this prospective trial would have been even stranger than it might initially seem, since it would have provided Parliament with the right to try those who had (literally) "undermined" its legislative authority, and presumably convict them, thus endowing it with a judicial as well as a lawmaking capacity.[36] It is through appealing to the *lex talionis,* and one version of the biblical "measure

---

34. Jardine, *Criminal Trials,* 67, 262.

35. James, Speech of 9 November 1605, 153.

36. Bodin's elaborate attempt to circumvent the conclusion that the English Parliament can punish demonstrates the incommensurability of envisioning Parliament as judge and upholding the king's sovereignty; in explaining why, despite the privileges accorded Parliament, the sovereignty of English kings remains intact, Bodin writes:

Here someone may object that the Estates of England have the power to punish. . . . I answer that this was done by the ordinary judges of England [seated] in the upper house of Parliament at the request of the lower house. . . . This clearly shows that the Estates as a body have neither power nor jurisdiction, but that the power lies in the judges of the upper house. It would be as if the Parlement of Paris, assisted by the princes and the peers, were present as a separate body in the Estates to judge great cases.

Bodin, *On Sovereignty,* 22. The trial following the Gunpowder Plot did in fact employ some such lords as judges, although not the entire Parliament, and as Coke additionally explained, "The King, out of his wisdom and great moderation, was pleased to appoint this trial in time of Assembly in Parliament, for that it concerned especially those of the Parliament." Jardine, *Criminal Trials,* 66.

In subsequently revisiting and revising his own words, James himself modified them to refer not to a trial but instead to Parliament's act of promulgating an Oath of Allegiance, which required subjects to swear their fidelity to him. Addressing his fellow kings, James enjoined them to consider "if this Treason now, clad with these circumstances, did not minister a iust occasion to that Parliament house, whome they thought to haue destroyed, courageously and zealously at their next sitting downe, to use all meanes of triall, whether any more of that minde were yet left in the Countrey." James VI and I, *Premonition,* in *Workes* (London: Robert Barker, 1616), 291.

Alan Cromartie delves in some detail into the conflicts over parliamentary judicature from Queen Elizabeth through the end of King James's reign in *The Constitutionalist Revolution: An Essay on the History of England, 1450–1642* (Cambridge: Cambridge University Press, 2006), 189–233.

for measure," that James justifies the theory of such an unusual case, which did not, in fact, occur; as he maintains, "So can there not I thinke (following euen their owne Rule) be a fitter Iudgement for them, then that they should be measured with the same measure wherewith they thought to measure us: And that the same place and persons, whom they thought to destroy, should be the just auengers of so unnaturall a Parricide."[37] Attempting to efface the "generality" of the Gunpowder Plot's attack on legislative power, James places weight instead on the particular "place and persons," returning the crime to the regime of revenge tragedy.

In *Homo Sacer*, Giorgio Agamben suggests that the *lex talionis* generates referentiality within the law. After establishing a certain topology of sovereignty according to which the sovereign—here conceived as a single placeholder rather than a psychological individual or lawmaking body—represents the limit point of the law, at the same time within and outside its compass, Agamben focuses on the "relation between law and fact."[38] Here Agamben posits a first phase of the law—perhaps taking place only in the same order of fictionality as the social contract—that relies on the *lex talionis*. He writes:

> The juridical order does not originally present itself simply as sanctioning [meaning, here, prohibiting] a transgressive fact but instead constitutes itself through the repetition of the same act without any sanction, that is, as an exceptional case. This is not a punishment of this first act, but rather represents its inclusion in the juridical order, violence as a primordial juridical fact (*permittit enum lex parem vindicatum*, "for the law allows equitable vengeance" [Pompeius Festus, *De verborum significatione*, 496.15]. In this sense, the exception is the originary form of law.[39]

Rather than being identified with the initial imposition of the law, this "first act" of transgression in one sense occurs "before the law," but in a "before the law" that the law already claims as its own, and that becomes constitutive of it as law.[40] In the structure that Agamben outlines, according to which the law per-

37. James, Speech of 9 November 1605, 154.

38. Giorgio Agamben, *Homo Sacer: Sovereign Power and Bare Life*, trans. Daniel Heller-Roazen (Stanford: Stanford University Press, 1998), 26.

39. Agamben, *Homo Sacer*, 26. One example of this phenomenon occurs in Aeschylus's *Oresteia*, when Orestes is acquitted for murdering his mother, Clytemnestra, after giving the defense that he had killed her only in retribution for her murder of his father, Agamemnon. Although Orestes is tried in what the play designates the first murder trial, his act is, despite its extralegal origins, permitted by the law.

40. One could observe in Kafka's fable "Before the Law" a spatiotemporal conflation of the "before" that also characterizes Agamben's text.

mits those who have been injured—or their relatives, if the act has had fatal consequences—to respond in kind to the perpetrator, a type of mimetic mirroring
emerges; it is through the conceded re-presentation of the original act that the
law secures its referentiality, or, in Agamben's terms, can "create the sphere of its
own reference in real life and *make that reference regular.*" Pardoning and equity
partake of analogous configurations, structures Agamben acknowledges—albeit
in other terms—when distinguishing between the rigid application of the Roman
ius civile and the judge's freedom to determine a more equitable resolution in
certain instances. In these cases, the inscription of the judge's privilege within the
parameters of the law allows for the possibility of pardon.[41]

But how, exactly, can Agamben's account of the *lex talionis* assist us in comprehending the exceptional drama dreamed up by James I? Here Parliament
itself, in "re-presenting" the crime through its retribution, affirms the referentiality of the laws that it has framed and will in future continue to produce—or,
in other words, insists again on its own legitimacy. The revenge that James proposed, however, was not actually commensurate with the offense, but instead
endeavored to return the terrorists within the compass of legally recognized—
one might almost say "legitimate"—crime. Through forcibly introducing the
perpetrators into a representational—and, above all, dramatic—situation, James
appropriated the signification of their contemplated act, creating his own version
of the referent that patched over the presentational event. Putting into practice
one response to revolutionary activity, James insisted on the integration of the
Gunpowder Plot into an epistemological order commensurate with the human
and political, and thus generated a fictional scene in which Parliament would
become endowed with the capacity to judge the treasonous perpetrators. This
particular solution, however, leaves him and the inheritors of his throne vulner-
able to Parliament's judgment, its effort to bring not only religious "accidents"
like the Gunpowder Plot but also the monarch's divine right under its control.

Why, then, did James not himself realize these consequences? The answer lies
in the immediate context of James's rhetorical performance; by producing such
a fictional scenario, he allowed Parliament to retain a sense of importance while
at the same time being summarily dismissed. Of the two dramas presented, the
first consisting in the *deus ex machina* intervention of God's pardon and the second in a revenge tragedy, James perhaps opted privately for the first, and acted
accordingly, yet set his public persona behind the second. What this means is that
salvation is dependent on God, and concerns the monarch, while punishment

---

41. Agamben, *Homo Sacer*, 23–26.

rests upon Parliament, which assumes responsibility for the political carriage of the country. Permitting himself to imagine Parliament as both lawmaking and judging body, James created a new fiction of sovereignty while at the same time responding to the exceptionality of the Gunpowder Plot as *sine exemplo,* in fact or in fiction.

Apocalyptic History (Tragicomedy I)

Although the echoes of John of Patmos's Revelation that resonate throughout James's speech may seem fortuitous, the broader context of his intellectual labors as well as the prevailing religious climate belie the idea that any reverberations could be simply coincidental. Before the age of twenty, James had composed a lengthy *Paraphrase upon the Reuelation*; this volume was destined to remain unpublished until the 1616 edition of James's *Workes,* but a briefer exegetical sermon he wrote in 1588—titled *A Fruitfull Meditation*—situated both James and his kingdom in the midst of apocalyptic history. Subsequently, when James reissued *Triplici Nodo,* an apology for the Oath of Allegiance he had promulgated in response to the Gunpowder Plot, the accompanying *Premonition* to Christian kings again invoked Revelation. Others even viewed the king as specializing in the study of John's text; as the editor of James's 1616 *Workes* opined, "Above all other things, God hath given [the king] an understanding Heart in the Interpretation of that Booke, beyond the measure of other men."[42] Nor did James's memory of phrases from Revelation fail him. Indeed, he abandoned the second Hampton Court Conference in 1606 after interpreting Andrew Melville's comment that King's Advocate Thomas Hamilton was "the accuser of the brethren" as an attempt to designate Hamilton the Antichrist of Revelation.[43] The Gunpowder Plot thus furnished one among several opportunities for James to interpret history itself in accordance with the text of John of Patmos's prophecy, a prophecy that several contemporary Protestant commentators viewed as tragicomic. This apocalyptic version of tragicomedy remains distinct, however, from that of plays like *Measure for Measure*; rather than employing a final reversal—a

---

42. James, Bishop of Winton, "Preface to the Reader," in *Workes.*

43. David Willson, *James VI and I* (London: J. Cape, 1963), 317. The phrase "accuser of the brethren" is employed in reference to Satan, after he has been cast from heaven; as John relates, "And I heard a loud voice saying in heaven, Now is come salvation, and strength, and the kingdom of our God, and the power of his Christ: for the accuser of our brethren is cast down, which accused them before our God day and night" (Revelation 12:10).

pardon—it allows revenge and redemption to sit side by side. The Last Judgment then becomes a tragedy for the condemned, and a comedy for the elect.

Specifically dramatic interpretations of Revelation largely postdated James's work, but the sixteenth-century plays of John Bale and John Foxe emplotted the events it described in tragicomic form.[44] Subsequent, more explicitly interpretive delineations of the text's genre illuminate the range of its possible generic determinations. These often vary depending on the focal point of the commentator; from the perspective of the Antichrist, Revelation describes a tragedy, whereas from the vantage point of God, or of the elect, it represents a tragicomedy. The mode of the drama may similarly seem to diverge according to the points at which it is said to commence and to conclude. The three basic variations in genre that result include tragedy, tragedy framed by the ecstasy of eternal salvation, and tragicomedy.

David Pareus, a principal proponent of the "aesthetic" approach, whose *Commentary upon the Divine Revelation of the Apostle and Evangelist John* influenced Milton,[45] read each of John's visions as a tragedy. This analysis yielded seven mini-dramas, including the tragedy of the Antichrist. Despite adopting a structure similar to that which Julius Caesar Scaliger described in his *Poetices Libri Septem*, Pareus substitutes four acts for Scaliger's five; these approximate the four parts of comedy and tragedy that Scaliger had articulated before referring, almost as an addendum, to the prologue, "which certain critics attribute only to Latin playwrights."[46] In specifying a four-act form for these tragedies, Pareus allows them to represent the entire course of the Christian history that Revelation depicts, which he likewise divides into four "*distances*" or "*periods*."[47] What he designates "universal visions" encompass all four of these periods, whereas the "particular" ones focus on the final two—the oppression of the

---

44. Frank Ardolino elaborates on the apocalyptic tragicomedy of Bale's *A Comedy concerning Three Laws of Nature, Moses, and Christ*, and Foxe's *Christus Triumphans*, a *comoedia apocalyptica* in *Apocalypse and Armada in Kyd's* Spanish Tragedy (Kirksville, MO: Sixteenth Century Essays & Studies, 1995), 52–55.

45. Michael Murrin, "Revelation and Two Seventeenth-Century Commentators," in *The Apocalypse in English Renaissance Thought and Literature*, ed. Patrides and Wittreich, 125–47. Milton explicitly refers to Pareus in both *The Reason of Church Government* and the prologue to *Samson Agonistes*.

46. Julius Caesar Scaliger, *Poetices libri septem*, trans. C. J. McDonough, in *Sources of Dramatic Theory I: Plato to Congreve*, ed. Michael J. Sidnell (Cambridge: Cambridge University Press, 1991), 102. Although Pareus does not mention Scaliger in his *Commentary*, the *Poetices libri septem* provides a useful point of comparison both because it had a wide-ranging influence on Renaissance thought and because Pareus on occasion echoes Scaliger.

47. David Pareus, *Commentary upon the Divine Revelation of the Apostle and Evangelist John*, trans. Elias Arnold (Amsterdam: C.P., 1644), 25, 27.

church until the "*measuring of the Temple*," identified with the Reformation, then the reform of the church and decline of the papacy—which constitute the "Tragedie of Antichrist."[48]

It is, notably, these last-mentioned acts that conform most closely to Scaliger's articulation of dramatic structure. As Scaliger writes of the *catastasis* and *catastrophe*, the third and fourth main elements of comedy, "The *catastasis* contains the activity and the crux of the plot, where the situation is drawn and embroiled in the storm of fortune. This component has not been noticed by many but it is essential. *Catastrophe* is the transformation of the intrigue which has been stirred up into a calmness not anticipated." Supplementing this definition in applying the terms to tragedy, he asserts that "*catastrophe* added death or exile."[49] Pareus similarly details, in reference to his acts, that "*the third* shadoweth out an amplification of calamities, or new and more glorious Combats of the Church under Antichrist," then "*the fourth* parallel to the third, sheweth the *Catastrophe* of all evils, *viz.*, the declining of Antichrists Kingdom, and the casting of all adversaries into the lake of fire: and on the contrary the Churches Victory, and Eternal Glory."[50] Condemnation to the lake of fire can clearly be read as a variety of exile, but the victory of the true church that Pareus notes might seem to contravene a truly tragic structure. Scaliger himself, however, explains that "it was common for both [tragedy and comedy] to have on occasion an outcome mingled with sadness and happiness."[51] Furthermore, as Pareus observes, Revelation generally concerns the tribulations of the church, a properly tragic subject matter: "We must remember, that the forme of this Prophesie is truely Tragicall. For it representeth Tragicall motions and tumults of the adversaries against the Church of Christ, and at length the Tragicall end also of the wicked themselves."[52] Although the true church may experience a happy ending, the travails John details throughout the book as a whole, as well as the Antichrist's ultimate demise, lead Pareus to conclude that the text is fundamentally tragic.

Adopting other dramatic conventions of the Renaissance, Pareus emphasizes principles of decorum and explains that musical choruses divide the acts. Indeed, Pareus's structure may not actually deviate substantially from Scaliger's five-act standard, since Pareus too classifies certain material as "preparatory to

---

48. Pareus, *Commentary*, 25. Pareus is not entirely consistent, however, and is obliged to make an exception and allow four acts for the destruction of the Whore of Babylon.

49. Scaliger, *Poetices*, 102–3.

50. Pareus, *Commentary*, 27.

51. Scaliger, *Poetices*, 103.

52. Pareus, *Commentary*, 26.

the visions"—like a prologue—and explains that other interpreters have been deluded in their attempt to discern prophetic meaning from these passages; as he writes, "They that search for other mysteries in these things, seeme to labour in vaine." Two of Pareus's observations, however, demonstrate a divergence between the genre of Revelation and that of traditional tragedy. Several times he reminds the reader that John's visions constitute a *"Propheticall Drama*," and a "Heavenly *Dramma*, or Interlude," rather than a human one. Likewise, John is identified as the privileged spectator of the play, much like Dante in the *Divine Comedy*; for "the Lord Iesus revealed the same unto Iohn by his Angell, after the manner of a *Dramaticall Representation* . . . exhibiting to Iohns sight or hearing those things in the Heavenly Theater, which God would have him to understand, and us by continuall prayers, meditations, and observations to search out, touching the future state of the Church." The mode of imitation thus differs from that of traditional tragedy, and the subject of imitation is accessible only to the initiated. An Aristotelian form of mimesis, however, applies oddly well in such a system, since, as Aristotle maintained, "it is not the poet's business to relate actual events, but such things as might or could happen in accordance with probability or necessity." According to Pareus, the prophetic tragedy of Revelation, similarly, does not attempt to outline the precise events of the future but instead offers a general schema of history, sketched out in the "Typicall Speeches and Actions" of the characters. Revelation's tragic genre thus assumes a world-historical character, but Pareus refrains from mapping it onto an empirical history.[53]

The problem that the dual ending of Revelation poses for traditional tragedy was also resolved by altering the frame of the drama. Thus, Thomas Brightman, in dedicating his *Revelation of the Apocalyps* to the reformed church, which he identifies as the future bride of Christ, divides the tumultuous body of John's text from its conclusion. As he writes, situating himself and the church in the final days of history, "For now is begun the last acte of a most long & most dolfull Tragedie, which shall overflow with scourges, deaths, ruines: But this Scene being removed, shall come in the place of it the pleasant prospect of a perpetuall peace, accompanied with abondance of all good things."[54] Whereas the turmoils of the textual drama enforce its identity as tragedy, the "perpetuall peace" that follows acquires its quality not simply from its own nature but also in contradistinction

---

53. Pareus, *Commentary*, 20, 26.

54. Thomas Brightman, *A Revelation of the Apocalyps* (Amsterdam: Iudocus Hondius & Hendrick Laurenss, 1611), A3. Audible in Brightman's phrase "perpetuall peace" are both foreshadowings of Kant's text *Perpetual Peace* and echoes of James's insistence on identifying himself as an emissary of peace.

to the tribulations entailed by temporal existence. Although not yet tragicomic, this tragedy finds its limits in the "perpetuall peace" of post-history.

Those who actually designated Revelation a tragicomedy tended either to place emphasis on its plot devices and romance topoi or to reverse Pareus by reading the text from the vantage point of the true church rather than that of the Antichrist. In *The Great Interest of States and Kingdoms* (1646), a sermon delivered to Parliament, Thomas Goodwin followed the former approach, designating Revelation "a *Tragy-Comedy*, which begins with a kingdome given to be won by conquest, and ends with a Coronation of a King, and the marriage of his Bride."[55] Richard Bernard, who published *A Key of Knowledge for the Opening of the Secret Mysteries of St. Iohns Mysticall Revelation* in 1617, a year after the appearance of James's *Workes*, instead suggested that the text's logic would unfold naturally once one discovered the hero. As he writes, "The principall thing to be marked in this tragicall Comedie, (if I may so call it) is the Church of Iesus Christ, that is, consisting of true and faithful Christian beleevers, their doings and sufferings, their battels, and victorie at the length over all their enemies." Although Bernard remains uncertain whether John's work should be deemed a "Comicall tragedie" or a "tragicall Comedie," he does—unlike Goodwin—include the entire text within his generic scheme, speaking of "the great and last Acts whereof the *Plaudite* shall be given to Christ."[56]

Bernard's interpretation is especially interesting in the context of James's endeavors, both because it appeared in such close proximity to the publication of the king's *Paraphrase* and because Bernard often refers to King James's work on Revelation in laudatory terms. Emphasizing the historical topicality that James himself attributes to Revelation, Bernard also cites the Spanish Armada and the Gunpowder Plot as potential tragedies for his hero that were instead diverted and transformed into tragedies for the Antichrist. As Bernard summarizes the moral of this history, "In the mainest arguments they bring to overthrow us, they doe unawares strengthen us; and what they thinke doe serve to make for themselves, in those they be confounded and overthrowne." While reading James's writings on Revelation as demonstrating how the prophecy applies to current events, Bernard simultaneously diagnoses the Gunpowder Plot as one of the foremost such incidents.[57]

---

55. Thomas Goodwin, *The Great Interest of States and Kingdoms* (London: R. Dawlman, 1646).

56. Richard Bernard, *A Key of Knowledge for the Opening of the Secret Mysteries of St. Johns Mysticall Revelation* (London: Felix Kynaston, 1617), 109, 130, 4.

57. Bernard, *A Key of Knowledge*, 16, 17, 128, 291, 23. That these commentaries on and interpretations of Revelation were of interest to contemporaries is indicated by the fact that Coke, in his library,

In James's own account of Revelation, tragicomedy is already implicit as he details Revelation's applicability within the historico-political sphere. Eschewing the notion that "*this Booke is so obscure and allegorique, that it is in a maner unprofitable to be taught or interpreted*," he explains that understanding the text accurately remains crucial, since "*it is the last* Reuelation *of Gods will and Prophesie, that euer was, or shall bee in the World*."[58] Following the same basic outline as most Protestant readings, James diagnoses the Antichrist as the Roman Catholic Church, likewise identifying this institution with one version of the Whore of Babylon. The *Fruitfull Meditation*—although brief—then maps onto human history part of the sequence sketched in Revelation. In chapter 20, John had explained that Satan would be bound for a thousand-year period, during which some would be resurrected and live with God; this period was to be succeeded by the loosing of Satan, who should "go out to deceive the nations" and "gather them together to battle." Defeated, Satan would then be "cast into the lake of fire," and the Last Judgment follow—at which time "death and hell" would also go the way of Satan. The glorious appearance of "a new heaven and a new earth," the marriage of the Lamb, and the new Jerusalem, are announced subsequently in chapter 21. James situated a section of this sequence—from the release of Satan to his destruction—within his own period, articulating a three-level historical hermeneutic. The connection he identifies in this work can be extrapolated to cover James's interpretation of the rest of chapter 20 in his *Paraphrase*; since he claimed that chapter 20 constituted "*the summe and recapitulation of all the former visions*," any historical nexus involving chapter 20 should pertain to the remainder of Revelation as well.[59]

The *Fruitfull Meditation* itself, produced on the eve of the Spanish Armada,[60] establishes the historical signification of chapter 20 through examining its analogical resemblance to other moments in Revelation; James identifies particular terms' references through a nexus of phrases sufficiently similar that he deems they conceal the same signification. As he states, "We are taught to use onely Scripture for interpretation of Scripture, if we would be sure, and neuer swarue from the analogie of faith in expounding, seeing it repeateth so oft the owne phrases, and thereby expoundeth them." James does not, however, simply discern a specific institutional or temporal reference behind each verse of chapter 20 but

---

possessed *Brightman in Apocalipsin* (*Catalogue*, 6) and *Bernard on the Revelation* (*Catalogue*, 8), as well as *Gallus on Apocalipse*.

58. James VI and I, *Paraphrase on Revelation*, in *Workes*, 4–5.

59. James, *Paraphrase*, 63.

60. Willson, *James VI and I*, 80–82.

instead elaborates a more complex interpretive method. This approach proceeds in three stages; first "touching the wordes in them for order sake," James then "followeth the interpretation of the sentence according to the order used in the first part," and finally explains "what we may learne of this place."[61]

James's description of the "order" of the sentences on which he focuses reveals them as the bare bones of a tragic plot—the tragedy of Satan; as he outlines, "First Satan his loosing: next his doing, after he is loosed: and last his unhappie successe." This outline he calls a "paraphrase"—the same level of interpretation that characterizes his longer work.[62] It is this outline that bears the greatest resemblance to the trajectory and fate of the Powder Men.

In his subsequent "interpretation of the sentence," James situates this sequence within human history, refusing a numerological analysis of chapter 20's chronology and instead preferring a reading based on the filled substance of time. Hence he identifies the millennium of Satan's binding not with a literal span of years but with the time in which the teaching of the Gospel remained undiluted. As he states, "This time did endure from Christ a space after Augustine his dayes, when the bloodie Sword of persecution ceasing, the whole Church began to be defiled with diuers heresies, which coming unto a mature and ripe heape, did produce or bring foorth the Antichrist." Claiming that the loosing of Satan names "the arisings of the heresies, and the Antichrist breeding of their smoake," he identifies actions of the Antichrist recounted elsewhere in Revelation and concludes with a lengthy sequence of rhetorical questions designed to indicate that only the pope can be so variously described. The present in which he speaks James thus definitively identifies as the era of Satan's wandering, and, furthermore, the time immediately preceding the great battle—the imminent Armada. His very historical situation James then indicates as the reason for disclosing the meaning of Revelation, a book that conceals as it reveals: "And what is prepared and come forward against this Ile? Doe we not daily heare, and by all appearance and likelihood shall shortly see? Now may we iudge if this be not the time, whereof this place that I haue made choice doeth meane, and so the due time for the reuealing of this Prophecie."[63]

When, in the third part of his sermon, James draws certain lessons from the meaning he has discerned, he includes among these the prediction—based on those verses yet to be fulfilled—that the Catholics would soon be vanquished and

61. James VI and I, *Fruitfull Meditation,* in *Workes,* 80, 74, 76, 78.
62. James, *Fruitfull Meditation,* 74–76.
63. James, *Fruitfull Meditation,* 76–78.

the Last Judgment ensue. Elaborating on this latter point, he writes that "after the great persecution and the destruction of the pursuers, shall the day of Iudgement follow . . . but in how short space it shall follow, that is onely knowne unto God; Onely this farre are we certaine, that in the last estate, without any moe generall mutations, the world shall remaine till the consummation and end of the same." This culminating sequence—the defeat of the Antichrist as papacy, and the Last Judgment—is not, however, to be awaited passively. Instead, James adjures his subjects to pursue these ends themselves, insisting that "God hath promised not only in the world to come, but also in this world to giue us victory over [our Catholic enemies]"; he encourages them that "the stronger they waxe, and the nearer they come to their light, the faster approcheth their wracke, and the day of our deliuery." While consoling his countrymen over the strength of the opponent, he simultaneously urges them to "use lawfull resistance" and press ahead in the destruction of the Antichrist.[64]

Nor does James premise his persuasions simply on his identity as a member of the true Christian commonwealth; instead he presents himself as specially ordained, as king, to interpret and bring to fruition the prophecies of Revelation.[65] In accordance with his frequently reiterated conviction that kings are God's "Lieutenants and Vice-regents" on earth, James insists that John's prophecy designates temporal monarchs as the agents destined to unmask the papacy—and uncover the Whore of Babylon. He articulated this position most explicitly in his 1609 *Premonition to All Most Mightie Monarches, Kings, Free Princes, and States of Christendome.* Directed, in particular, to Rodolphe II, to whose name he appends the epithet "by Gods Clemencie Elect Emperour of the Romanes,"[66] as well as to the other Christian kings, this *Premonition* responds to Cardinal Bellarmine—whom James deems beneath his own majesty—by resort to such a triangulation. Fashioning a community of kings akin to the College of Cardinals which he excoriates, James urges them to resist the pope's attempt to usurp their temporal sovereignty and instead to fulfill the prophecies of John.

Substituting for the generality of Parliament that of the European kings, James in a sense extended the speech he delivered after the discovery of the Gunpowder Plot, urging a united front now not against the plotters, who had undermined the authority of lawmaking through gunpowder, but against the

---

64. James, *Fruitfull Meditation*, 80.
65. Bernard Capp explains the contemporaneous significance of the role of the "godly prince" who would rule in a "millennial golden age" in "The Political Dimension of Apocalyptic Thought," in Patrides and Wittreich, *The Apocalypse in English Renaissance Thought and Literature*, 95.
66. James, *Premonition*, 288.

papacy, which would destroy kings' sovereignty by words. As he admonishes his brother kings, disavowing any special interest, and addressing them in legal terms, "The consideration hereof hath now mooued me to expone a Case unto you, which doeth not so neerely touch mee in my particular, as it doeth open a breach against our Authoritie, (I speake in the plurall of all Kings) and priuiledge in general."[67] Despite the political source of his appeal, however, James invokes Revelation to illuminate the course that kings should adopt.

Throughout his *Premonition*, accurate interpretation is linked with the kings' capacity to execute the laws, including those of the Bible; once his brethren have correctly discerned the meaning of scripture, they will take action, James opines. Thus, providing a rather unconventional interpretation of Revelation's "two witnesses"—whom the Reformation saw as its leaders, and whom the Roman Catholics deemed reincarnations of Enoch and Elias—James views them as the Old and New Testaments; these then become the source of kings' conversion from allegiance to the Roman Catholic Church to what James considers the true Christian faith. Performing a reading of chapter 17, James asserts that

> wee [Kings] shall in the time appointed by God, hauing thus fought with the Lambe, but *being ouercome by him*, that is, conuerted by his Word; wee shall then (I say) *hate the Whore, and make her desolate, and make her naked*, by discouering her hypocrisie and false pretence of zeale; and shall *eate her flesh, and burne her with fire*. . . . And then doeth hee subioyne the reason of this strange change in us: for (saith hee) God *hath put it in their hearts to fulfill his will, and with one consent to giue their Kingdomes to the Beast, till the words of* God *be fulfilled*, according to that sentence of *Solomon*, That *the hearts of Kings are in the handes of* God, *to be turned at his pleasure*.[68]

Employing the language of tragedy—like "discovery" (*anagnoresis*) and "turned" (reversal: *peripeteia*)—James designates the moment of kings' conversion as the crux of the apocalyptic drama. Only after this reversal and recognition have occurred can the fruition of the Antichrist's *catastrophe* follow—the *catastrophe* of which his fellow sovereigns will be the agents.

In this instance, the discovery and reversal occur at once in the least artful manner and according to the most sophisticated of Aristotelian methods. On the one hand, kings are "turned" by God himself, appearing as a *deus ex machina* on

---

67. James, *Premonition*, 289.
68. James, *Premonition*, 316, 325–26.

the scene; such a development contradicts Aristotle's instruction that, as we saw in the introduction, "the unraveling [*lusis*] of the plot should be the result of the plot itself and not produced mechanically [*mêchanês*] as in the *Medea*. . . . The god in the machine should be used only to explain what lies outside the play."[69] On the other hand, kings are "conuerted" by the Word of God, or the interpretation of scripture; this mode of recognition partakes of the two forms Aristotle most fervently exalts, those according to events (*ex autôn tôn pragmatôn*) and those according to inference (*sullogismou*).[70] In order to achieve such a recognition, the royal readers would be obliged first to follow out the sequence of occurrences in John's prophecy or the "order of the words"—the subject of James's *Paraphrase*. They would then, by inference, deduce the historical referents of John's prophecy.

Indeed, James's own interpretation of the Antichrist's identity in the *Fruitfull Meditation* bears a strong resemblance to the example of inference that Aristotle wrests from Aeschylus's *Oresteia*. As Aristotle writes, "In the *Choephoroe* [*Libation Bearers*] [Electra reasons,] 'Someone like me has come; but nobody is like me except Orestes; therefore he has come.'"[71] Similarly, James deduces that the Antichrist must be the pope since the combined attributes described in Revelation can fit only this figure. Just as James considered the Gunpowder Plot simultaneously an accident and an intentional act, he envisions the kings' conversion from two seemingly incompatible perspectives. In both cases, however, God's intrusion on the scene marks a certain timing of the event; the discovery of the Gunpowder Plot occurred just in time, and the moment of recognition achieved through understanding the divine word should happen "in the time appointed by God." Although for kings to "execute [God's] Iudgements,"[72] as James believes they should, each must first be converted by his Word,[73] God pro-

---

69. Aristotle, *The Poetics,* trans. Stephen Halliwell (Cambridge: Harvard University Press, 1991), 57–58.

70. Aristotle, *Poetics,* trans. Halliwell, 60–64.

71. Aristotle, *Poetics,* trans. Halliwell, 61–62.

72. James, *Paraphrase,* 289.

73. This procedure may be more thoroughly described in the Bishop of Winton's preface to the collected *Workes.* In his preface to the volume of James's complete works in which the *Paraphrase* was finally published, the bishop reaffirmed the king's authority to pronounce definitively upon the Book of Revelation; as he maintains:

> Yet this I thinke, I may safely say; That Kings have a kinde of interest in that Booke beyond any other: for as the execution of the most part of the Prophecies of that Booke is committed unto them; So it may be, that the Interpretation of it, may more happily be made by them: And since they are the principall Instruments, that God hath described in that Booke to destroy the Kingdome of Antichrist, to consume his State and Citie; I see not, but it may stand with the Wisedome of God, to inspire their hearts to expound it; into whose

vides the concurrence between the generic progress of Revelation and the time of empirical history. While the *deus ex machina* may be unnecessary within the confines of Aristotelian drama, he remains crucial in connecting the prophetic scene with earthly events.

James's own act of recognition commences when he identifies himself with John in the *Paraphrase*. Rather than explicating Revelation from a distance, he adopts the first-person form, emulating John's persona.[74] This gesture serves two related purposes, both linking James to the historical unfolding of Revelation and particularizing the prophecy. Just as Christ, in becoming embodied, reconciled the course of human history with a divinely plotted sequence of events, James, in identifying himself as earthly king with the material in John's heavenly vision, operates inversely, and urges the human consummation of a divine telos. The recognition James prepares by speaking in the first person in his *Paraphrase* is that of a worldly agent who divines within scripture an outline of his historical situation.

In a few brief comments, James also illuminates another reason for employing the first person: it limits the number of interpretations that can be provided. James claims that this choice is simply pragmatic, and intended "for the making of the Discourse more short and facile"; as he adds, "Although through speaking in his person, I am onely bounded and limitted to use one, and not diuers interpretations, of euery severall place; yet I condemne not others, but rather allow them to interpret it diversly."[75] While James's explanation is plausible, the use of a single gloss on Revelation may also appear important for his larger purpose—preparing to apply the prophecy to his own historical period. Although several interpretations of the allegory may subsist simultaneously before the prophecy is fulfilled, its historical realization will limit those possibilities. Thus James anticipates this moment by providing his own restrictions in advance. Furthermore, by speaking as John, James positions himself on the other side of the history that the prophet described; in other words, James intends to fulfill what John foresaw.

It should not be surprising, then, that the rhetoric of the *Paraphrase* at numerous points prefigures that of James's speech following the discovery of the Gunpowder Plot. Although still glossing the text of Revelation, James in

---

handes hee hath put it to execute, until the Lord shall consume both him and it with the Spirit of his mouth, and shall abolish it with the brightnesse of his coming.

Bishop of Winton, Preface, in *Workes.*

74. The unusual nature of James's stance is confirmed by the fact that none of the other commentators discussed employed the first person in explicating the text.

75. James, *Paraphrase*, 2.

these passages often adds comments designed to reinforce certain aspects of the prophecy to which he subsequently returns. His emphasis on the deceitfulness the Antichrist employs in waging war against the faithful becomes identified not only with Catholic equivocation but also with the method of the Gunpowder Plot itself. Likewise, the vision of a "generall destruction" from which God, through his "mercie," excepts the elect is first articulated in the *Paraphrase* before being enunciated in the Gunpowder Plot speech. Even the language of revenge—being "measured with the same measure wherewith they thought to measure us"—is repeated several times throughout James's discussions of Revelation. Finally, he articulates the prospect of a new Jerusalem in which kings—as the elect—will rule alongside God, which seems to anticipate the terms of salvation he envisions as ensuing after the Gunpowder Plot.

In *Revelation*, John asserts several times that Satan will resort to an emissary who misleads (*planaô*) by false miracles (13:14; 19:20).[76] Picking up this concept of deceitfulness, James substantially expands it to encompass, by implication, both the equivocation of Jesuits and the nature of papists' attack at Armageddon. Following the discovery of the plot, Catholic linguistic practices and the undermining activities of the Powder Men were often assimilated as two manifestations of the same dire propensities. Both also partook of a dramatic quality, the

---

76. The duplicitous character of the Antichrist is already embedded within the writings of Paul. In a passage that Giorgio Agamben has discussed in *The Time That Remains*, putting Paul in conversation with Carl Schmitt, the apostle declares: "Let no man deceive [*exapatêsêi*] you by any means: for *that day shall not come*, except there come a falling away first, and that man of sin [*tês anomias*] be revealed, the son of perdition. . . . And now ye know what with-holdeth [*to katechon*] that he might be revealed [*apokaluphthênai*] in his time. For the mystery of iniquity [*mustêrion tês anomias*] doth already work: only he who now letteth [*ho katechôn*] will let, until he be taken out of the way" (2 Thessalonians 3–7).

The problem with this passage lies in the relationship between the "man of sin," or, more literally, the man without law, and the one who holds back—the *katechon*. Interpreting them as separate, Schmitt identified the delay of the *katechon* with "Christian Empire" itself; according to this reading, "'Empire' signifies . . . the historical power that succeeds in restraining the advent of the Antichrist and the end of the current era." Quoted in Giorgio Agamben, *Le temps qui reste: Un commentaire de l'Épître aux Romains*, trans. Judith Revel (Paris: Bibliothèque Rivages, 2000), 173; translations are my own. As Agamben extrapolates from a similar take on the passage, which simply replaces empire with God himself, "In a certain sense, every theory of the State—including that of Hobbes—which sees in it a power destined to prevent or delay the catastrophe could be considered a secularization of this interpretation of 2 Thess. 2." (173–74). James himself reads 2 Thessalonians as an encapsulation of what John later would elaborate, stating that "*S. Paul* in the 2. to the *Thessalonians* doeth utter more clearly that which *Saint Iohn* speaketh more mystically of the *Antichrist*." James, *Paraphrase*, 308. As already observed, however, James's understanding of political post-history contravenes Schmitt's assumption that a properly Christian empire can be constituted only on the understanding that it holds back the return of the Antichrist rather than taking place subsequent to his defeat.

plot in its exceptional nature, outside of conventional genres, and equivocation in its similarity to the speech of the hypocrite, or actor.[77] The practice of equivocation, a manner of responding to interrogation designed to thwart questioners while preserving the answerer from the sin of lying, had been employed—at papal encouragement—to deal with the English ban against priests. [78]

During the second Gunpowder Plot trial, that of Father Henry Garnet, Coke had introduced into evidence *A Treatise of Equivocation*, or *A Treatise against Lying and Fraudulent Dissimulation*, which Garnet possessed, and had in fact— unbeknownst to Coke—written.[79] Coke took ownership of the text as a clear sign of guilt. In subsequently justifying the Oath of Allegiance, James not only invoked the general horror of the Gunpowder Plot but played as well upon the furor over equivocation—and in particular "mental reservation," considered the most dangerous of its varieties.[80] Mental reservation, since it allowed an individual to modify substantially—or even to negate—an uttered statement by inwardly appending the true meaning, made the speaker's intention impenetrable. Indeed, although the oath was purportedly intended to establish the subject's allegiance to the temporal sovereign, despite any papistical injunctions to the contrary, it can be read as a vow designed to undermine equivocation as such. The instability that characterized equivocating language was, in a sense, to be exorcised by the constancy of an oath. Rather than basing allegiance simply on the contractual nature of its words, however, the oath reinforced the division between intention and speech act by insisting on their conformity and mandating that the subject "sweare from [the] heart." It then concluded by explicitly rejecting equivocation with the words "All these things I doe planely and sincerely acknowledge and sweare, according to these expresse words by mee spoken, and according to the plaine and common sense and understanding of the same words, without any Equiuocation, or mentall euasion, or secret reseruation whatsoeuer."[81] At this moment, as the oath asks the subject to forswear plotting and the hypocrisy of an

---

77. In the *Fruitfull Meditation*, James explicitly conjoins and contrasts the "hypocrites," or Catholics, and the open enemies of the church—presumably the Turks. As he states: "In two sorts of men chiefly Satan shall utter himselfe, *to wit*, hypocrites, and auowed or open enemies to God. It is said then that Satan shall in the latter times rule a new ouer the world, who shall stirre up the nations under the banners of these two enemies to God, the hypocriticall and open, to spread themselues in great multitudes upon the earth." James, *Fruitfull Meditation*, 75.

78. See 27 Eliz. I, cap. 2 (1585).

79. Janet E. Halley, "Equivocation and the Legal Conflict over Religious Identity in Early Modern England," *Yale Journal of Law and the Humanities* 3 (1991): 33–34.

80. James VI and I, *Triplici Nodo*, in *Political Writings*, 105, 109.

81. James, *Triplici Nodo*, 89.

actor's speech, equivocation and treason have become allied. If the Gunpowder Plot is envisioned as a crime of intention—which, in its purity, will always remain secret—equivocation, which ensures that impenetrability, becomes the principal enemy. James himself, however, in contrast to Coke, places less emphasis on linguistic than on violent manifestations of deceit.

In his *Paraphrase*, James already considers Catholics duplicitous, and suggests something akin to equivocation as one manifestation of this propensity. Speaking of the "Grashoppers," whom he views as the religious agents of the pope,[82] he glosses, "And their faces were like the faces of men, and the faces of men signifie reason, as man is a reasonable creature: the likenesse then of their faces unto men, signifies that they shall, by curious arguments, pretend reason to maintaine their false doctrine, but it shall be but a counterfait resembling of reason indeed, euen as their crownes are like unto gold, but are not gold indeed."[83] Although the false reasoning James describes resonates with sophistry more than equivocation, it represents an analogous manipulation of language. By excoriating a similar falsity in Cardinal Bellarmine's writings on the subject, the *Premonition* justifies James's initial *Apology* for the oath; as he claims, "Fearing that by their untrew calumnies and Sophistrie the hearts of a number of the most simple and ignorant of my people should bee misse-led, under that faire and deceitfull cloake of Conscience; I thought good to set foorth an *Apologie* for the said Oath."[84] Sophistry thus emerges as the second order of equivocation—as a defense against the oath's attack.

James invokes the deceitfulness of Satan and his minions more insistently when he describes the scene of "Armageddon." While explaining, in the dedication, the alternative valences that his unitary interpretation will ignore, James focuses on this proper name and endows it with a narrative significance through providing several possible etymologies. As he explains, the Hebrew word could designate either "destruction by waters" or destruction on the hill of Mageddon, but James himself instead opts for the reading "destruction by deceit." In thus particularizing his interpretation of the word, James laid the groundwork for a historical episode of the Gunpowder Plot variety; at the same time illuminating how his etymology corresponds with John's own descriptions and mapping out a future drama of Armageddon, James writes that his reading "may very well agree

---

82. James, *Paraphrase*, 26–27. A passage on the "frogges" sent out by the pope, whom James equates with Jesuits, suggests that the "Grashoppers" are also to be similarly interpreted (52).

83. James, *Paraphrase*, 26.

84. James, *Premonition*, 292.

with the History, because [Armageddon] is the name of the place, saith Iohn, where the wicked being assembled together by the alluring and deceipt of Satan, and his three spirits of Diuels to make warre with the faithfull, were all destroyed by God, and so their destruction came, and was procured by deceipt."[85]

James subsequently elaborates upon this destruction by deceit and asserts that those kings and nations assembled to battle against the true church will be decimated. According to this account, the allies of Satan, not the faithful, are identified with the deceived. By deceit, the "frogges," or Jesuits, gather kings and countries together for the supposed destruction of their enemy—the true church—but really for their own destruction. The ultimate deceitfulness of this deceit, then, is that it works against friends rather than enemies. This scene of kings collected against the faithful in one respect recalls the Armada, but the idea of a deceitful destruction wrought by the Jesuits provided a foundation for James's reception of the Gunpowder Plot as well. The secrecy of the plotters' pursuits, however, becomes the forerunner of their own, rather than kings', destruction.

When interpreting the descriptions of Satan's demise—including Armageddon—that recur throughout Revelation, James reiterates the generality of this destruction and explains that the elect are saved only through a structure of exception. The elect themselves he identifies as those whose names have been written in the Book of Life, a book that remains closed to the uninitiated; as he elaborates, impersonating John quoting God, "I will also giue him a *White stone*, or a Marke of his election and righteousnesse through imputation, and in it a New name written, *to wit*, his name shall be written up in the *Booke of life*, which no man knoweth but he who receiues it; for no other may know the certaintie of ones Election, but onely he who is elected."[86] Election thus constitutes the secret of a personal salvation determined in advance but only privately known.

Since election is never mentioned in Revelation itself, and its temporality appears to conflict with the admonitory tone of John's prophecy, which seems in several places to urge reform, James is obliged to reconcile the two. In doing so, he claims that the purpose of John's warning is to make "inexcusable" those who fail to listen—even though they may be destined to do so. Whereas some are fated for a conversion—like the kings to whom James's own warning, or *Premonition*, is directed—others will never be swayed from pursuit of their duplicitous path. As James asserts at the conclusion of the *Paraphrase*—speaking for an angel rather

85. James, *Paraphrase*, 3.
86. James, *Paraphrase*, 10.

than God—"Despaire thou not of the effect of this Prophecie, although it prof-
ite nothing the wicked, but to make them the more inexcusable: For God hath
fore-signified, that he who doeth harme, notwithstanding this Prophecie shall
yet continue his wrongs."[87]

By contrast, the elect benefit not from their own works but from the
mercy, or pardoning, of God. This mercy is granted to those who have faith—
a Reformation doctrine that James at several points attempts to reconcile with
Revelation's references to works. He rationalizes these allusions when discussing
the Last Judgment by claiming that "as God is a Spirit, so iudgeth he the thoughts
of man, and so by faith onely iustifies him, which notwithstanding is done
according to his workes, because they, as the fruits of faith, cannot be separated
from it, and beare witnesse of the same to men in the earth." Emphasizing intentionality over acts, James reinforces the importance of the former even independently of the latter. James, again in the voice of God, furthermore explains
how salvation by faith occurs through a gift outside any economy of exchange:
"I shall giue to him that thirsteth, of the fountaine of water of life, freely, or for
nothing, *to wit*, he will grant saluation to all them who cal upon him for it, and
that for nothing; for it cometh of his free mercie, and not of any merit in us." This
exceptional mercy is conferred upon those marked as elect several times during
the course of Revelation, including and culminating with the Last Judgment.
Describing this final divine sorting, James writes that "the day of Iudgement was
come, wherein should that destruction ensue . . . which should ouerwhelme all
sorts of men, excepting always these that were marked, who were sundry times
excepted before, as ye heard."[88]

Election involves the political as well as the religious sphere. As the *Paraphrase*
and James's other texts on Revelation demonstrate, his concept of divine right
sovereignty not only confers religious legitimacy on the king but also accords him
a political place within the present and future churches. In addition to deeming
Revelation specially addressed to kings, he envisions a royal future for them, as
the elect. Whereas the papacy represents—through its "civill gouernment"—the
tyrannical "Empire" of a new Babylon, the elect reign first during the thousand-
year period of peace and, second, at the time of the Last Judgment. According to
James's description of the first group—those who were martyred—they "reigne
ouer the earth, and by their Martyrdome be Iudges theof; for it is called Christs
reigning and the Saints upon the earth, when his word, and trew professours

---

87. James, *Paraphrase*, 71.
88. James, *Paraphrase*, 66, 67, 62.

thereof, shine visibly therein." This equation of rulers with judges recalls James's claims to judicial supremacy in his more exclusively political writings. The second group assume their place as kings when, at the end of history, a "new Ierusalem" descends from the clouds to earth, the "bride" of Christ, in a scene that James describes with masque-like imagery. Once this occurs, "the Gentiles which are saued, shall walke in that light, and the kings of the earth shall bring their glory unto that citie; for all the faithfull kings shall resigne all their worldly glory in that citie, and receiue a new and incorruptible glory from the Lambe, who is the light thereof." Both "resigning" in the sense of abandoning and in the sense of resignifying, these elect kings continue in their anointed role, reigning "kings . . . for euer" rather than for a brief stint on earth. Unharmed by the fire that, instead of consuming, "renews" them, these kings—and their status as judges and execu- tors—are instead rendered eternal.[89]

Although destruction is general, sparing solely the elect, it is often accom- plished according to a logic of revenge, by figures who, despite being agents of God's will, remain themselves impure. As in Spenser's *Faerie Queene*, those who combat sin are tarnished by their very involvement with it. At several points, James describes how God uses a "hand" or—even more remotely—an "instru- ment" to accomplish justice through revenge; treating the rise of the papacy, James writes that "God shall iustly by the meanes of this false Church, as his instrument of reuenge, send a strong illusion and deceit, with great efficacie of miracles and wonders."[90] The operations of this *lex talionis* are often depicted in the terms of measurement that characterize both Shakespeare's *Measure for Measure* and James's own speech on the Gunpowder Plot. At one point in the *Paraphrase*, James adds to the otherwise fairly accurate translation "He who hath an eare, let him heare and take heede unto this sentence that followeth, *to wit*, If any man leade in captiuitie, in captiuitie shall he be led againe."[91] He appends to these phrases the conclusion "Then since ye are assured, that God in his good time shall iustly mete to their tyrannie, the same measure that they shall mete to his Church, let not your hearts in your affliction, through despaire of Gods reuenge, (because of his long suffering) swarue from the bold and plaine profess- ing of his trueth; for in this shall the patience and constant faith of the Saints or the chosen, be tried."[92] Rather than wreaking revenge themselves, the elect must

---

89. James, *Paraphrase*, 55, 64, 66–67, 69, 66.
90. James, *Paraphrase*, 42.
91. James, *Paraphrase*, 41, 13:9–10.
92. James, *Paraphrase*, 41.

allow the *lex talionis* to be carried out independently of them, awaiting salvation with perseverance despite any delay.

A Pattern for Pardoning (Tragicomedy II)

While James's own work on Revelation provided one model of tragicomedy, that which he largely followed in responding to the Gunpowder Plot, another had recently been proposed to him in the form of *Measure for Measure*. Indeed, James had seen Shakespeare's play on December 26, 1604, less than a year prior to the discovery of the Powder Men's scheme.[93] Critical attention has not focused on this circumstance, partly because the emphasis of law and literature scholarship has fallen largely on the reception of legal institutions within fictional forms rather than on the impact that works like plays generate in the political arena. Thus, although *Basilikon Doron* has often been read as an intertext of *Measure for Measure*, as discussed in chapter 1, and *Macbeth* has been mined for echoes of equivocation and other Gunpowder Plot motifs,[94] *Measure for Measure* itself has not generally been considered in terms of its influence on James.[95] Although James did not himself apply the recommendations of *Measure for Measure* to the revolutionary situation with which he was confronted, he could have—and would have benefited from doing so. Nor did *Measure for Measure* simply provide an ideal to which James could aspire—such as that of exemplifying the just ruler; instead, it suggested a generic and, specifically, tragicomic model for the monarchical sovereign. The complicated relationship that Shakespeare's play maintains with James's endeavors—both incorporating allusions to the king's writings and, in turn, advising him—should be viewed not as exceptional but as characteristic of an ongoing dialogue between the state and the stage.

Had James I been an attentive spectator of the play, he might have discovered a number of discrepancies between the version of tragicomedy presented

---

93. Alvin Kernan, *Shakespeare, the King's Playwright: Theater in the Stuart Court, 1603–1613* (New Haven: Yale University Press, 1995), 53.

94. For example, Gary Wills details how Shakespeare's drama fits into a group of "Gunpowder plays" which, performed in 1606, treated the events of the prior year and their aftermath. Characterizing these works, he states that they generally "deal with the apocalyptic destruction of a kingdom (attempted or accomplished), with convulsions brought about by secret 'mining' (undermining), plots, and equivocation. And witches are active in this process." Gary Wills, *Witches and Jesuits: Shakespeare's* Macbeth (New York: Oxford University Press, 1995), 9.

95. Work like Alvin Kernan's *Shakespeare, the King's Playwright* has, however, begun to remedy this deficiency.

by *Measure for Measure* and his personal approach. Listening with a careful ear, he would have heard the rhetoric of his own writings in the Duke's assertion—ventriloquizing the mercy of the law—"An Angelo for Claudio; death for death./ Haste still pays haste, and leisure answers leisure;/ Like doth quit like, and Measure still for Measure" (5.1.407–9). When that statement finds itself ironized by the Duke's subsequent actions, James might likewise have registered in the conclusion a critique of the revenge logic that both he himself and the Duke had voiced. Whereas James emphasized the apocalyptic teleology of his own salvation, Shakespeare's play remained more faithful to Bodin by demonstrating the Duke's failure to be divine. In accordance with this disparity, James, on the one hand, envisioned a comic, *deus ex machina* conclusion for himself and his allies, while retaining the structure of revenge tragedy for the associates of the Antichrist; Shakespeare, on the other hand, suggested how such tragedy could be eliminated from the state. Likewise, James again established the reference of the laws by proposing that Parliament—the primary legislative body—judge the conspirators, while *Measure for Measure* ensured the autonomy of reinstituted statutes by having the Duke pardon, thereby separating the laws from his sovereign judgment and executive power.

As a reader of Bodin and a not disinterested observer of the Duke's fluctuating reputation, James would also have noted the second function of the play's final pardons—that of restoring the sovereign's "Dignity" and honor. Although *Measure for Measure* detaches the laws from dependence on the sovereign and the particularity of an individual case, it simultaneously allows the Duke to overcome the threat of revolution and ensure his majesty by pardoning. Unlike James, Shakespeare refused to again assimilate lawgiving, judgment, and execution simply by proposing that they be situated in another body. Had James adopted Shakespeare's model instead of imaginatively displacing judgment onto Parliament, the king might have succeeded in shoring up his sovereignty. Interrupting the cycles of revenge and revolution, he would have generated both a discontinuity within the state and a chance to reform and reformulate it. In its Shakespearean incarnation, tragicomedy names this opportunity.

3

NON-SOVEREIGN FORGIVENESS /
Mercy among Equals in *The Laws of Candy*

The Shakespearean version of the theater of pardoning both permits the law to achieve a degree of autonomy from the sovereign and serves to reestablish the dignity of that sovereign. Several plays from the subsequent period, toward the end of King James I's reign, reject Shakespeare's version of tragicomedy as well as that of James himself and instead begin to reimagine pardoning as dissociated from monarchical sovereignty in the face of increasingly vivid depictions of the near demise of the state. These plays were composed at the same time that the genre of theaters of pardoning began to become more prevalent, around the end of James's reign and the beginning of his son's (Appendix A). Their significance lies not so much in their impact on contemporary audiences as in their efforts to envision alternatives to a linkage between pardoning and sovereignty, efforts that drew upon ancient political thought—including Plato's late writings and the Stoic tradition—circulating in their intellectual context. Although these attempts were short-lived, they demonstrate the contingency of the path that led from Shakespeare and James to later conceptual links between sovereignty and the pardon power.

One of these tragicomedies is *The Laws of Candy*, produced sometime between 1619 and 1623. Initially included in the first Beaumont and Fletcher folio in 1647, *The Laws of Candy* has been exposed to much subsequent debate on the subject of its authorship, and the play is now generally acknowledged to be either principally or partially written by John Ford, probably along with Philip Massinger.[1]

---

1. E. H. C. Oliphant, *The Plays of Beaumont and Fletcher: An Attempt to Determine Their Respective Shares and the Shares of Others* (New Haven: Yale University Press, 1927), 474–76; H. Dugdale Sykes, Review, *The Review of English Studies* 4, no. 16 (1928): 460–61. More recently, Brian Vickers has attributed the play to both Ford and Massinger, proposing the latter as the principal collaborator. *The Collected Works of John Ford*, vol. 2, ed. Brian Vickers (Oxford: Oxford University Press, 2017), 76–134.

Ford's involvement is significant, given his association with early modern common law through his long residence at the Middle Temple.[2] Although the extent to which Ford actually studied law rather than taking advantage of his location to court patrons for his poetry remains unclear, it is plausible that his interactions with the lawyers in training of the Inns of Court exerted an influence on his intellectual development. Certainly Plato's *Laws*—a text that legal writers of the early seventeenth century referenced extensively—found its way explicitly into his 1620 tract *A Line of Life* and, this chapter argues, implicitly into *The Laws of Candy*.

In *The Laws of Candy*, Antinous, a Cretan soldier returning victorious from battle against Venice, obtains the chief honor for military victory from the Senate, thereby outraging his father, Cassilane, the general of Crete, who had also laid claim to this title. As a result, Cassilane withdraws with his daughter Annophil and ultimately tries to wreak his revenge on Antinous through accusing him of ingratitude, an offense punishable by death according to one of the long-standing laws of the island. A love plot involving the princess Erota drives some complexities of the plot, and two foreigners play crucial roles, Gonzalo, described as "an ambitious Politick Lord of Venice," and Fernando, a Venetian captain whom Antinous had captured.[3]

At first blush, *The Laws of Candy* might seem to follow the pattern—established by King James himself in the aftermath of the Gunpowder Plot—of displacing sovereignty onto a legislative body, in this case the Senate of Candy (Crete). Yet in *The Laws of Candy*, the Senate itself is deprived of the ultimate power of restoring the state in the aftermath of successive acts of revenge that nearly culminate in the overturning of the polity. Instead, the laws furnish the opening for a foreigner to orchestrate a series of grants of forgiveness that establish the state anew. The laws here are fully independent and operate in conjunction with a kind of pardoning given between individuals rather than originating in sovereignty. This chapter first outlines the plot of *The Laws of Candy*, then demonstrates the significance of Shakespeare's plays, the context of the revival of justice upon petition to the House of Lords, and, most importantly, Plato's *Laws*, to understanding the political and generic interventions of the play.

---

2. Gilles Monsarrat, "John Ford: The Early Years (1586–1620)," in *The Collected Works of John Ford*, vol. 1, ed. Gilles Monsarrat, Brian Vickers, and R. J. C. Watt (Oxford: Oxford University Press, 2012), 12–38.

3. John Ford (with Philip Massinger?), *The Laws of Candy*, in *The Collected Works of John Ford*, vol. 3, ed. Brian Vickers (Oxford: Oxford University Press, 2017), 1–132; hereafter cited parenthetically.

Non-Sovereign Forgiveness

One royal figure, the princess "Erota" (beloved), appears in *The Laws of Candy*, yet her authority seems more romantic than political. Her brother, who had previously ruled Crete, here called Candy, died before the beginning of the action, leaving "a child our Prince," a child not listed as a character and alluded to only briefly (1.1.18; 4.1.175–77). Instead of a monarch, a Senate governs Crete. The play does not suggest, however, that this Senate instituted the laws at issue in the plot; instead these appear to date back to time immemorial, or at least to the moment of the "elder *Cretans*" (1.1.63). Within the confines of the play, however, the Senate *is* responsible for issuing judgment in a number of instances; individuals are given the power to hale one another into the Senate for verdict and condemnation.

In the first act, we are apprised both of the compelling power of the princess, Erota, who holds men in thrall, and who "can by no Character be well exprest,/ But in her onlie name, the prow'd *Erota*" (1.1.7–8), and of two laws for which Crete is renowned, that of gratitude and that of reward for the individual who, by popular acclaim, is recognized as the foremost warrior on the battlefield (1.1.47–71). As Gaspero, the secretary of state, explains, insisting that the Senate must be grateful to the Venetian Gonzalo, despite his status as a foreigner, "The Senate should be thankfull, otherwise,/ They should annihilate one of those Laws,/ For which this Kingdome is throughout the world/ Unfellowed, and admired" (1.1.47–50). Rather than suggesting that the Senate can repeal laws of its own accord or stem their application, Gaspero indicates that the Senate can only either acknowledge and honor or annihilate them. The persistence of these Cretan laws despite—or on account of—their archaic origins may have recalled English common law itself to contemporary audiences.[4]

Describing the two laws, Gaspero states first, "Who ere he be that can detect apparently/ Another of ingratitude, for any/ Received Benefit, the Plaintiffe may/ Require the offender's life, unless he please/ Freely and willingly to grant remission" (1.1.53–57). This law not only provides for punishment but also specifies the mechanism for pardoning, making remission available only by the willing grant of the one offended. It affects citizens and non-citizens alike, for "the Law/ Permits a like equalitie to Aliens,/ As to a home-borne Patriot" (1.1.59–61). Like the Due Process or Equal Protection Clauses of the Fourteenth Amendment of

---

4. Other language within the play conjures up the common law as well. A number of characters speak of "presidents," or precedents, and one suggests the combination of Chancery and common law jurisdictions by stating, "My case observes/ Both equity, and presidents" (1.2.73–74).

the United States Constitution, the first law appears to be open to all *persons*, rather than only citizens or subjects. As Gaspero explains the second law,

> The elder *Cretans* flourished many years,
> In War, in Peace, unparalel'd, and they
> (To spurre heroicke spirits on to vertue)
> Enacted that what man so ere he were,
> Did noblest in the field against his enemie,
> So by the generall voice approv'd, and knowne,
> Might at his home-return, make his demand
> For satisfaction, and reward. (1.1.63–70)

Only one individual may claim this reward, and, according to the established procedures,

> where the Souldiers do not all consent,
> The parties in contention, are refer'd
> To plead before the Senate; and from them,
> Upon an open audience, to be judg'd
> The Chiefe, and then to make demands. (1.1.85–89)

By its very nature, this law seems restricted to citizens or subjects, those who form the members of the domestic polity and hence would wage war on its behalf. The default under this law is for such an individual to be honored through democratic acclamation, but if faction or other discord arises among the soldiers, the Senate is appointed judge in the cause. In both of these contexts, the Senate is represented as hardly able to abrogate the laws, incapable of independently enforcing them, and charged with judging only the cases brought before it.

The two laws of Candy come into conflict, of course, during the play. The nature of this conflict derives, as Eugene Waith has demonstrated, from Seneca's *Controversiae*, one of which pits father against son in a contest for a military reward, and others of which insist on the enforcement of gratitude.[5] Although both laws possess equal authority in Candy, their grounds, when viewed from an external perspective, diverge. The law of gratitude, which extends equally to citizen/subject and alien, constitutes a law of relation between individuals; it is a law that Thomas Hobbes would, later in the century, include among his laws of

---

5. Eugene Waith, "John Fletcher and the Art of Declamation," *PMLA* 66, no. 2 (March 1951): 228–29; Seneca, *Controversiae*, in *Declamations* vol. 2, trans. M. Winterbottom (Cambridge: Harvard University Press, 1974), 10.2, 388–407.

nature rather than of civil society.[6] The law of military honor is instead one of the most nationalistic, conceptually reserved for the citizen/subject, and awarded by domestic and proto-political processes. As the play unfolds, both laws are subject to implicit critique, but the latter falls further from favor during the play.

As noted earlier, it seems at the outset that a battle has just ended between Crete and Venice, with Crete claiming the victory. An older general, Cassilane, and his son, Antinous ("contrary in mind"), both claim the reward of honor, and because each possesses supporters within the army, they require the Senate to arbitrate the disagreement. The operations of the Senate, as well as the arguments of the parties, are represented as customary, and Antinous refers to the notion of precedent. When Gonzalo wishes to speak, he emphasizes the Senate's traditions as well as his own foreign origins, inquiring, "With reverence to the Senate, is it lawfull,/ Without your Custome's breach, to say a word?" (1.2.217–18). Antinous himself likewise explains to his father and to the Senate, "My case observes/ Both equity and presidents; for sir,/ That very day whereon you got your Fame,/ You took it from some other, who was then/ Chiefe in repute" (1.2.73–77). Although using the language of precedent, Antinous is here referring to paradigms of succession similar to the one he has generated in supplanting his father. Antinous also affirms that, were his father not already renowned for his achievements on the battlefield, he himself "would undertake/ Alone, without the help of Art, or Character,/ But only to recount your deeds in Armes,/ And you should ever then be fam'd a president/ Of living victory" (1.2.35–39). The story, like a legal case, creates its own paradigm, or precedent, against which future cases of alleged valor may be measured.

Partly, it seems, because Antinous managed to capture the son of the last Duke of Venice, Fernando, and partly because the soldiers' acclamation falls somewhat more on Antinous's side, the Senate prefers him to Cassilane. Rather

---

6. Gordon Schochet treats Hobbes's account of this law of gratitude—the fourth law of nature—in "Intending (Political) Obligation: Hobbes and the Voluntary Basis of Society," in *Thomas Hobbes and Political Theory*, ed. Mary G. Dietz (Lawrence: University Press of Kansas, 1990), 61. It is, for Hobbes, associated with the commitment to a conquering sovereign, or a "sovereign by acquisition," because the subject owes gratitude to the sovereign for sparing his life. Schochet, "Intending (Political) Obligation," 60–61.

The motif of gratitude appears frequently and with great emphasis in Massinger's plays as well, including *The Bondman*, discussed in chapter 4. Robert Turner has read Massinger's repetition of that note in light of the centrality of patronage to his work and also linked the theme of gratitude with the genre of tragicomedy. Robert Turner, "Giving and Taking in Massinger's Tragicomedies," *Studies in English Literature, 1500–1900* 35, no. 2 (Spring 1995): 367–70. According to Turner, "As a genre inclined to generate admiration and praise, tragicomedy could . . . be suitable to the activities embodying generosity and gratitude since by definition these show characters acting at their best" (369).

than demanding some form of compensation for himself, Antinous instead asks the Senate to erect a statue to his father, which would constitute a "Monument and Trophy of his victories,/ With this Inscription to succeeding ages,/ *Great Cassilane, Patron of Candy's Peace,/ Perpetual Triumpher*" (1.2.292–95). This request, which Antinous alleges "was but onely to inforce/ The Senates gratitude" (1.2.322–24), does not have the effect of appeasing Cassilane; to the contrary, Cassilane is further infuriated, claiming that Antinous wishes to contribute to his disgrace by ensuring that, whenever future generations would mention Cassilane, they would also acknowledge "how [he] by [Antinous] was master'd" (1.2.329). As a result, Cassilane disowns Antinous, announcing, "Thou art no child of mine: thee and thy bloud,/ Here in the Capitoll, before the Senate,/ I utterly renounce" (1.2.334–36). Devastated, Antinous explains his plan to do his utmost to restore himself in his father's eyes and, if that fails, to exile himself to Malta (1.2.349–61). Antinous's supposed affront to his father's honor furnishes the engine for a strand of the plot that initially appears to operate according to the logic of revenge.

A second strand of the plot circulates around Erota, who is represented as enforcing a tyrannical love, the only relief from which would be her exercise of her seemingly sovereign mercy; the primary figure of devotion, Philander ("love for people"), the Prince of Cyprus, implores Erota, "If I offend with too much loving you,/ It is a fault that I must still commit,/ To make your mercy shine the more on me" (2.1.53–55). Gonzalo, the sinister and "politick" individual from Venice, rapidly enters into competition for Erota's hand, urging his birth but also, more important, his wealth as reasons why Erota herself should wish the alliance. Erota's desire is, however, instead sparked by the dejected Antinous, whom she first attempts to command then ultimately bargains with by promising to pay off his now destitute father's enormous debt to Gonzalo without allowing Cassilane to know his son is behind this transaction. Erota's consideration for this apparent contract is Antinous's own person, which he submits to her as the most valuable thing in her eyes that he can exchange.

Erota's companion Annophil is Cassilane's daughter and Antinous's sister. When Cassilane appears in Erota's presence, lamenting his son's treachery and his own penury, he seeks to bring Annophil with him to a solitary retreat; as he requests,

> Come *Annophill*,
> (My joy in this world) thou shalt live with me,
> Retired in some sollitarie nook,
> The comfort of my age; my dayes are short,

> And ought to be well spent, and I desire
> No other witnesse of them but thy selfe,
> And good *Arcanes*. (2.1.277–83)

When Annophil consents, they depart.

At the center of the play, act 3 begins with a revelation: Gonzalo, seemingly the friend of Crete, and Cassilane's creditor for untold sums, reveals to Fernando, his captured countryman, that he has in fact been plotting against Crete the entire time. Crete's military victory has, Gonzalo insists, sealed its overall defeat:

> One dayes conquest hath undone them,
> And sold them to their vassalage; for what
> Have I else toyl'd my brains, profusely emptied
> My moneyes, but to make them slaves to *Venice*,
> That so in case the sword did lose his edge,
> Then Art might sharpen hers? (3.1.3–8)

Under this account, military victory alone is not enough to secure the state, and in fact may even undermine it. Perhaps forewarned by the description "politick Lord," the reader is now alerted to Gonzalo's apparent status as enemy alien.

The means by which Gonzalo believes he has accomplished the feat of "undoing" Crete are twofold; first, he himself engineered the conflict between Cassilane and Antinous over who would be counted the military victor, and second, he indebted Cassilane to him "when *Cassilane* crav'd from the common treasure/ Pay for his Souldiers," to such an extent that Cassilane will be bankrupted (3.1.26–27). The former act—that of generating faction—verges on the instigation of civil war. The latter entails fomenting political strife through economic means; although the debt is personal to Cassilane, the state itself will be threatened when it is called.

We further discern that Gonzalo's ultimate goal involves marrying Erota in order to become king of Crete as well as Duke of Venice. The suggestion is not, however, that Erota herself will independently become sovereign, but rather that by acting in conjunction, they can usurp the government and transform it into a monarchy; as Gonzalo explains to Erota in attempting to persuade her to further his plot: "I meane/ To make you Empresse of my earthly fortunes,/ Regent of my desires, for did ye covet/ To be a reall Queene, I could advance you. . . . [W]hat if/ I set the Crowne of *Candy* on your head?" (4.1.160–74). Through the instruments of civil war and financial ruin, Gonzalo thus hopes to usurp the state and transform its mode of governance.

Gonzalo's plot is, fortunately, made known to Erota and the Senate by the prisoner Fernando, whom Cassilane had agreed to keep for the Senate at his own home. Fernando's sojourn with Cassilane provokes discussion of hospitality, which, in the Greek tradition of *xenia*, appeared also to be governed by laws; as Cassilane states (although not in relation to Fernando), "I dare not any way infringe the Lawes/ Of hospitality" (3.2.159–60). The play's treatment of hospitality complicates the distinction between personal and political; although Fernando is a political enemy, and a prisoner, he is simultaneously an object of the exercise of personal hospitality. It is not entirely to requite hospitality but rather to pursue Annophil, Cassilane's daughter, however, that Fernando reveals what he knows in a letter explaining that, in Annophil's words, "false *Gonzalo*, not intending more/ The utter ruine of our house, than generally/ *Candie's* Confusion" (4.1.86–88), is plotting treachery.

Freeing Crete of Gonzalo's influence is not quite as simple, though, as revealing his plot. As already noted, Cassilane is indebted to Gonzalo, a personal debt that parallels the financial obligation that Crete itself supposedly bears to Venice. Toward the end of act 4, the scene shifts to Cassilane, who is in the midst of recounting to his friend Arcanes the origins of this civil obligation:

> I'le tell thee how: *Baldwin* the Emperour,
> Pretending title, more through tyranny,
> Than right of conquest, or descent, usurp'd
> The stile of Lord o're all the *Grecian* Islands,
> And under colour of an amity
> With *Creet*, prefer'd the Marquess *Mountferato*
> To be our Governor; the *Cretians* vex'd
> By the ambitious *Turkes*, in hope of aide
> From the Emperour, received for Generall,
> This *Mountferato*; he (the wars appeased)
> Plots with the state of *Venice*, and takes money
> Of them for *Candy*: they paid well, he steales
> Away in secret; since which time, that right
> The state of *Venice* claimes o're *Candy*, is
> By purchase, not inheritance, or Conquest;
> And hence growes all our quarrel. (4.2.17–32)

It is at this point that we discover the genesis of the battle the end of which marked the commencement of the play; this struggle emanated from Venice's claim of dominion over Crete, a claim based not in the two means of acquisition recognized as legitimate in the seventeenth century, those of conquest and descent,[7] but instead in debt and financial obligation. Thus, not only will Cassilane's personal indebtedness to Gonzalo affect the viability of the state, but it also parallels Crete's larger fiscal obligation to Venice. Like the correspondence between the personal and political friend, the implications of debt are similar for the individual and the state.

In exchange for agreeing to subject himself to her romantic wishes, Antinous extracts a promise from Erota to pay off Cassilane's debt to Gonzalo without revealing that Antinous himself is behind the scheme. Even this well-intentioned plot miscarries, however, when Erota violates her vow and asks Cassilane to pardon his son out of gratitude to her; as Erota explains her action, "For requitall [of her investment], [I] only made my suite,/ That he would please to new receive his son/ Into his favour, for whose love I told him/ I had been still so friendly" (5.1.147–50). What results is nearly the demise of the state; in act 5, a series of individuals accuse each other before the Senate of ingratitude and seek the penalty of death, each new person accusing the prior accuser until the Senate itself is accused by Annophil. The chain commences with Cassilane, who urges an action of ingratitude against his son; Erota then follows suit, asking that Cassilane be condemned; Antinous returns the favor, accusing Erota; and finally, breaking the sequence, Annophil brings a charge against the Senate, claiming that it has been "unthankfull" to her father, and "crav[ing]/ The rigor of the Law against you all" (5.1.280–81). The scene appears to be one of revenge, where each successive individual "strikes home" against another, but by means of an accusation rather than a sword.

The Senate then becomes a judge in its own case, a position that had been anathema since at least Sir Edward Coke's report in *Bonham's Case* (1610), and, in doing so, condemns itself. The senator Possenne declares, "Though our ignorance/ Of *Cassilanes* engagements might asswage/ Severity of justice, yet to shew/ How no excuse should smooth a breach of Law,/ I yield me to the triall of it," to which his colleague Porphycio adds, "So must I" (5.1.285–89). Although this self-condemnation might seem a departure from the prior proceedings, it is in fact in keeping with the earlier accusations and convictions, which generally occur by confessions or guilty pleas that the Senate is bound to accept. Thus, after Antinous insists on pronouncing his own guilt, Possenne states, "You have doom'd your selfe,/ We cannot quit you now" (5.1.133–34). The Senate itself is

---

7. Hobbes, writing later in the century, analyzes three modes of obtaining sovereignty, those of acquisition or conquest, "dominion paternall," or descent, and institution, or social contract. Schochet, "Intending (Political) Obligation," 60–66.

incapable of issuing pardons when others have been injured and is restricted instead to confirming judgments made between the parties.

This situation is, in a sense, fitting, because the law being implemented, that of gratitude, could hardly be construed a civil law, but rather seems akin to a law of nature, as it would be conceived by Hobbes, or to an ethical principle. To the extent that it is an ethical principle, it should be recognized by each individual in lateral relations between them rather than being enforced by the state. The Senate's inability to pardon is connected with the relational nature of the law, as well as that of forgiveness. As many writers emphasize, the only person entitled to forgive is the one who has himself or herself been wronged. Although, as discussed in the Postlude, Kant would have allowed the sovereign too to forgive in certain instances, he insisted as well that such an act represented the greatest display of the sovereign's injustice.

One might think at this point that the tragic end had arrived, with the state on the verge of dissolution and Gonzalo still at large. Instead, however, an alternative manifests itself in the idea that Philander, the Prince of Cyprus who had haplessly loved Erota, must, at the behest of the Senate, serve as the "moderator in this difference" (5.1.291). Elaborating upon the "scene of miserie" that Cassilane has generated, Philander reproaches him and rehearses the curses that posterity will heap upon his memory (5.1.293–303). Ultimately Cassilane relents, not only forgiving Antinous—which has the effect, under the law, of freeing the latter ("'Tis the Law,/ That if the party who complains, remit/ The offender, he is freed" [5.1.318–20])—but also asking his own forgiveness in turn, although of his son rather than Erota, the one responsible for condemning him (5.1.330). The chain of vengeance is then repeated in a chain of forgiveness until Philander proclaims, "Then with consent/ Be reconcil'd on all sides" (5.1.337–38).

With this ending, Philander's name takes on a new significance; previously simply revealing him to be a besotted lover, it now indicates his status as a lover of mankind in its entirety. The state then is new begotten just as Antinous tells his father that he "new beget[s]" him with forgiveness. The basis for this renewed state is consent *between* citizens rather than a hierarchical structure of obligation. The exchange of forgiveness, like an exchange of gifts, binds individuals to each other in a condition of equality. As a foreigner, Philander, the *deus ex machina* who engineers the reconciliation, remains an outsider to the state, but at the same time underwrites its reconstruction, just as the founding moment can never be itself comprehended within what is founded. Although Erota accepts Philander in the end, it is in a changed capacity, her overweening pride tamed, as she herself admits. For the enemy alien Gonzalo is thus substituted the friendly stranger Philander, a foreigner within the state who will support it rather than undermine its very existence.

The first act of this newly founded state is then to engage in an exemplary display of justice, the trial of Gonzalo himself, as a traitor who plotted "treason to the peace and state of *Candy*" as well as (we discover belatedly) "treason to the State of *Venice*" (5.1.348–52). Although we learn that the alternatives Gonzalo faces are to be "sentence[d] . . . as he deserves/ Here, or . . . sen[t] . . . like a slave to *Venice*" (5.1.370–72), we are never informed of his ultimate fate; instead, he is simply escorted off the stage. It is at this point that the dichotomies previously undermined between friend and enemy are reasserted as the formative act of the reconstructed state.

The reversal from tragedy to tragicomedy here occurs not through the auspices of a god's intervention but instead through the activity of a foreigner, an outsider to the power structure of the state. Unlike a sovereign pardon provided from above, the forgivenesses in the play are exchanged between individuals, through a mutual consent that may represent a nascent form of social contract. By the end, the language of tyranny, which is deployed to characterize both Erota and Cassilane throughout the play, has been replaced with an emphasis on equality and on lateral relations among the characters. Faced with the generalization of revenge into the threat of civil war or revolutionary violence, the play presents as its solution a non-sovereign version of forgiveness.

Modifying Shakespeare

The play's version of tragicomedy differs significantly from that which emerged from *Measure for Measure* in chapter 1. Yet a number of passages in *The Laws of Candy* owe a debt to Shakespeare, and certain features of the plot recall his plays as well. The play's handling of its two principal Shakespearean intertexts, *Merchant of Venice* and *Measure for Measure*, holds important implications for its treatments of debt and law as well as its genre.[8]

The plot of *The Laws of Candy* bears some resemblances to that of *Merchant of Venice*. Erota is no Portia, but her position at the commencement of the play is somewhat similar to Portia's, although through her own volition rather than something akin to the casket test imposed by Portia's father.[9] Like Portia, Erota seems destined to reject all suitors, even the most highly placed, and international

---

8. Cassilane's character as well as his allegiance to his daughter Annophil are potentially reminiscent of *King Lear*, but the parallels with that play are not particularly striking.

9. William Shakespeare, *The Merchant of Venice*, ed. John Russell Brown, 2nd ser. (London: Arden Shakespeare, 1985), 1.2.27–32; hereafter cited parenthetically.

conquests whom she disdains surround her (*Merchant* 1.2.32–107). Similarly, once her affections are engaged to Antinous, Erota is willing to provide his father with financial backing in the face of his disastrous debt to Gonzalo, just as Portia was eager to fund the amount Antonio owed to Shylock, telling Bassanio, "Pay him six thousand, and deface the bond:/ Double six thousand, and then treble that,/ Before a friend of this description/ Shall lose a hair through Bassanio's fault" (*Merchant* 3.2.298–301). Finally, as Portia had argued before the Duke of Venice on behalf of Antonio, and insisted that Shylock be condemned to death absent the Duke's exercise of mercy (*Merchant* 4.1.342–59), Erota appears before the Senate and urges the demise of Cassilane, partly, it seems, in order to save Antinous. Both Portia and Erota call down the rigor of the law to effectuate their aims after their pleas for mercy prove of no avail. More generally, if Antonio's bond constitutes a crucial engine of the plot of *Merchant*, political as well as personal debts form the subject of *The Laws of Candy*, and indebtedness seems, from the vantage point of the play, a principal cause of civil and international unrest. Gonzalo is, in the end, treated similarly to Shylock, also labeled an "alien" (*Merchant* 4.1.345), and although not clearly condemned to death or to a return to Venice, is definitively expelled from participation in the state. We might wonder, therefore, whether the foundational place of the alien Philander at the reformation of the state is further underwritten by the prior exclusion of another form of alien, as the play returns to an unexamined dichotomy between alien friend and enemy alien.

The multiple allusions to *Merchant* in *The Laws of Candy* raise a question about the difference between the genres of the two plays and the distinction, more generally, between theaters of pardoning, on the one hand, and other forms of comedy, problem plays, or even tragicomedies, on the other hand. From one vantage point, *Merchant* could itself be seen as representing a theater of pardoning. Certainly the trial scene has famously engaged critics with its juxtaposition of mercy and justice, and the Duke pardons Shylock his life "before," the Duke tells him, "thou ask it" (4.1.364), although on the highly coercive conditions of forfeiting his property and converting to Christianity.[10] Yet the trial scene takes

---

10. The bibliography on the legal dimensions of *Merchant* and their intersection with debates about the relationship between the letter and spirit of the law, as well as positive law and equity, is vast. Some of the most prominent contributions include Quentin Skinner, "Why Shylock Loses His Case: Judicial Rhetoric in *The Merchant of Venice*," in *The Oxford Handbook of English Law and Literature, 1500–1700*, ed. Lorna Hutson (Oxford: Oxford University Press, 2017), 97–120; Richard Posner, "Law and Commerce in *The Merchant of Venice*," in *Shakespeare and the Law: A Conversation among Disciplines and Professions*, ed. Bradin Cormack, Martha Nussbaum, and Richard Strier (Chicago: University of Chicago Press, 2013), 147–55; Maxine MacKay, "*The Merchant of Venice*: A Reflection

place at the end of act 4 rather than the conclusion of the play as a whole. Indeed, the final act is preoccupied with a theme much more typical of Shakespearean comedies, such as *All's Well That Ends Well*—that of the recognition of a ring and settlement of conflicting claims to and about it through marriage or the reaffirmation thereof accompanied by the unraveling of disguises. Putting the space of an act between the trial scene and the end of the play allows *Merchant* to leave the audience with the impression that it has witnessed a comedy, despite Shylock's plight.

In theaters of pardoning, a final comic settlement is also often telegraphed, but abruptly and without a full development, in immediate proximity to the pardon that furnishes the play with its tragicomic conclusion. Hence in *Measure for Measure*, the Duke's proposal to Isabella follows hot on the heels of the series of pardons, and the episode is so abrupt that she never even responds. The plays that this book designates theaters of pardoning eschew development within the action of the comic implications of their conclusions and instead thrust contemplation of the sudden reversal that has just occurred and its consequences back onto the audience. While the pardons ensure non-tragic endings, the plays leave their spectators thinking about these pardons' broader implications for the world of the drama as well as for the audience members' own spheres beyond the stage.

At several moments, *The Laws of Candy* recalls *Measure for Measure* in a manner more textually specific than it does *Merchant*.[11] Antinous, in particular, seems to ventriloquize Angelo during the scene of successive accusations of ingratitude before the Senate of Crete. Echoing Angelo when he avers to the Duke, "I should be guiltier than my guiltiness,/ To think I can be undiscernible. . . . Then, good prince,/ No longer session hold upon my shame,/ But let my trial be mine own confession:/ Immediate sentence then and sequent death/ Is all the grace I beg" (*Measure* 5.1.413–21), Antinous accepts his father's accusation, stating, "'Tis all true,/ Nor hath my much wrong'd father limn'd my faults/ In colours halfe so black, as in themselves,/ My guilt hath dyed them: were there

of the Early Conflicts between Courts of Law and Courts of Equity," *Shakespeare Quarterly* 15, no. 4 (1964): 371–75; and Barbara K. Lewalski, "Biblical Allusion and Allegory in *The Merchant of Venice*," *Shakespeare Quarterly* 13, no. 3 (1962): 327–43.

11. There is a passage where the language of *The Laws of Candy* does conjure one of Shylock's speeches in *Merchant*. When asking the Senate for judgment, Cassilane demands, "If your Law be law,/ And you the Ministers of justice; then/ Think of this strange ingratitude in him [Antinous]" (5.1.113–15). Shylock had similarly told the Duke of Venice, in the trial scene, "If you deny me, fie upon your law!/ There is no force in the decrees of Venice:/ I stand for judgment,—answer, shall I have it?" (4.1.101–3).

mercy left,/ Yet mine own shame would be my Executioner:/ Lords, I am guilty" (5.1.116–21).

Subsequently addressing Philander's plea against his accusation of Erota, Antinous deploys language similar to that which Angelo had used earlier in *Measure for Measure*. When Isabella asked Angelo to remit her brother's punishment in act 2, he insisted, "It is the law, not I, condemn your brother" (2.2.80). Reformulating this phrasing, Antinous claims that "[Erota] is bloudy minded,/ And turnes the justice of the Law to rigor:/ It is her cruelties, not I accuse her" (5.1.199–201). By invoking the specter of Angelo, Antinous suggests an automatic application of the law, one unmediated by legal institutions or methods of proof. This vision resembles, indeed, a regime of revenge more than one of law. Once accused, an individual accepts culpability as if already dealt a mortal wound.

The references to *Measure for Measure* in *The Laws of Candy* invite the reader and audience to contemplate what kind of tragicomedy they are witnessing. Examining only the contexts in which suggestions of *Measure* appear might lead an observer to conclude that the play simply rehearses the undoing of revenge by forgiveness; by seeking revenge, a number of individuals together come close to destroying the entire populace of the state. As Erota observes about Cassilane's action of bringing his cause of ingratitude before the Senate, "Then he/ As void of gratitude, as all good nature,/ Distracted like a mad man, poasted hether/ To pull this vengeance on himselfe, and us" (5.1.150–53). The successive acts of forgiveness, each delivered by an individual rather than the state itself, would support this reading.

What is missing from this account, however, is the role of the Senate, Philander, and the law, as well as the completeness of the potential dissolution of the state. Although beginning on the intrafamilial level, revenge is rapidly generalized to constitute civic strife within the play, and Annophil's act of accusing the Senate itself seems a proto-revolutionary gesture. Furthermore, the intervention of Philander, the foreigner, represents a necessary catalyst for the subsequent acts of forgiveness. Without his attempt to reconcile the individuals within the state, the polity's self-destruction would have been complete. Seen in this light, the forgiveness between individuals does not simply represent a mirror image of revenge, but rather establishes the state on the basis of lateral instead of hierarchical relations, forming a ground for the constitution of Candy that emphasizes equality over tyranny. The forgiveness featured at the end of the play stands in contrast to the "mercy" that her lovers begged of Erota, a non-sovereign set of acts that places the reconstructed state on a new footing. In addition, the transformative possibility of individual forgiveness is secured by the law itself, which, from the commencement of the play, had specified that "free" and "willing" "remission" would undo the consequences of condemnation. Law hence undergirds the possibility of the non-sovereign forgiveness that emerges from *The Laws of Candy*.

Petitioning Parliament or the Senate

In the aftermath of the Gunpowder Plot, King James I had participated in shifting sovereignty to Parliament through imaginatively endowing that institution with the power of judgment, suggesting that Parliament should judge the conspirators. At the same time, one of James's spats with Coke involved the king's suggestion that he could judge in person. Both of these incidents indicate the link between judgment and sovereignty. That connection persists within *The Laws of Candy*, expressed through the language of petition. Although it is seemingly royal figures who are addressed in a petitionary manner in *The Laws of Candy*, the play treats these scenes skeptically and locates judgment more generally in the Senate.

The rhetoric of petition pervades *The Laws of Candy*, suggesting a suppliance befitting subjects to a sovereign. When first confronted with Gonzalo's romantic advances, Erota instructs her servant Mochingo to "tell him, if he have ought with us, let him/ Look lower, and give it in Petition" (2.1.112–13). Erota herself, in her attempt to woo Antinous, asks Philander to be an intermediary and informs him, "I that have lookt with scornefull eyes on thee,/ And other Princes mighty in their states,/ And in their friends as fortunate, have now prai'd,/ In a petitionary kind almost,/ This man, this wel-deserving man, (that I must say)/ To look upon this beauty" (3.3.70–75). Likewise, when conveying Antinous's letter of attempted reconciliation to his father, Decius, Cassilane's friend, observes, "'Tis a lowly/ Petition for your favor" (3.2.156–57).

In early modern England, petitions were commonly associated with pleas to the king for royal favor. As the *Oxford English Dictionary* elaborates upon this usage, a petition could consist in "a formal written request or supplication . . . for some favour, right, or mercy, or in respect of a particular cause," and was often addressed to the sovereign.[12] Shakespeare employs the term in this sense in *All's Well That Ends Well* when Helena response to the question "What's your will?" by saying, "That it will please you/ To give this poor petition to the king."[13] During

---

12. Krista Kesselring discusses sixteenth-century petitions for pardon in detail in *Mercy and Authority in the Tudor State* (Cambridge: Cambridge University Press, 2003), 91–135.

13. William Shakespeare, *All's Well That Ends Well*, ed. G. K. Hunter, 3rd ser. (London: Arden Shakespeare, 2006), 5.1.17–19; hereafter cited parenthetically.

the thirteenth century, petitions also began to be addressed to Parliament, as G. O. Sayles has described.[14]

Although "the private petitions presented to Parliament grew fewer and fewer in number" with the reign of King Edward III, and justice on petition to Parliament gradually fell into desuetude, the practice was resuscitated in 1621.[15] As James Hart explains in *Justice upon Petition: The House of Lords and the Reformation of Justice, 1621–1675*:

> The revival of the House of Lords judicature in the Parliament of 1621 began quietly and unobtrusively. Strictly speaking, the revival got underway on 3 March. The cause was a private one and the request for judicial assistance came, not from the Commons, but from the king. On that day James I forwarded to the Lords the petition of Edward Ewer asking that the record of Ewer's case in King's Bench be removed into the upper house for their review. The case signalled the revival of the Lords' appellate authority over the court of King's Bench—a jurisdiction long established but unused since 1589.[16]

While this account suggests an insouciance about the jurisdictional issues surrounding this revival of judicature, members of the House of Lords expressed concerns about its own and the House of Commons' capacity to judge on several occasions during 1621. In particular, they objected to the Commons' judgment

---

14. As Sayles writes:

> The king by reason of his office must do justice to all men, and happily the fountain of justice was inexhaustible. Therefore the writ system was supplemented by another form of action, action by plaint or petition, which allowed all who were wronged to bring complaints to the king's notice easily and without cost and expect to have them redressed.... [T]he presentation of written complaints to royal judges in royal courts was so well known and so well established that it was easy to extend the practice to Parliament, and very soon the intimate connection between Parliament and the redress of grievances had been created.

G. O. Sayles, *The Medieval Foundations of England*, 2nd ed. (London: Methuen & Co., 1950), 451–52.

15. Sayles, *Medieval Foundations*, 460.

16. James Hart, *Justice upon Petition: The House of Lords and the Reformation of Justice, 1621–1675* (London: Routledge, 1992), 15. Alan Cromartie similarly writes, "In 1621, without much fanfare, the House of Lords resumed its former practice of hearing court cases submitted by petition," noting that "at the same time, James permitted the revival of impeachment, the disused medieval procedure by which the Commons could mount a prosecution in front of a court consisting of the peers." Alan Cromartie, *The Constitutionalist Revolution: An Essay on the History of England, 1450–1642* (Cambridge: Cambridge University Press, 2006), 291.

against Edward Flood; in debating what measures to take, the Earl of Arundell opined, "I believe [the Commons] not to be a Courte of Recorde," and wished "to let them knowe that judicature belongs only unto us [the Lords]; they have encroached upon us; and knowe what satisfaccion they wyll gyve; for we are not satisfied with those presidents and reasons they have alledged."[17] They were similarly chary of King James's suggestion that he might judge if Lord Henry Yelverton had dishonored the king, as well as committing an offense cognizable by the House of Lords; as Warwicke maintained, "There is an ordinaunce, that whasoever is begun in this House shall be determined here." Finally, they examined various arguments and precedents to determine whether the House of Lords could adjudicate an appeal from a determination of the Lord Keeper in the case of Sir John Bourchier.[18] While discussion of the Ewer case may have been negligible, concerns about jurisdiction permeated the Lords' debates during that year.

Once it was again recognized as an available appellate tribunal, the House of Lords steadily increased in popularity among litigants during the following decades.[19] This shift of petitions from the king to the House of Lords echoes James I's insistence that Parliament judge the Gunpowder Plotters rather than that he himself pardon them. It represented, in other words, a recentering of judicial authority away from the king and toward Parliament.

This is, in a sense, precisely what seems to occur in *The Laws of Candy* as well. Although the exact date of the drama's composition remains uncertain, it could well have been written between 1621 and 1623, following the revival of petition in the House of Lords. At the commencement of the play, Erota is endowed with apparent sovereignty and represents the object of petition. By the end, however, she has been leveled to the position of citizen or subject, and the Senate instead has pride of place. More generally, the play stages two forms of tyranny, that of paternity and that of love, both of which it associates with the obligation of a subject to a monarch. Each of these is undercut by the conclusion of *The Laws of Candy*, in which equality instead represents the governing principle.

The two forms of tyranny depicted in *The Laws of Candy* possess parallels to the accounts of monarchical sovereignty circulating in seventeenth-century England, a polity that bears more analogies to the Crete of the play than simply

---

17. Samuel R. Gardiner, ed., *Lords' Debates in 1621* (London: Camden Society, 1870), 70 (Monday, May 7, 1621).

18. Gardiner, *Lords' Debates*, 56, 111–12; Jessie Stoddart, "Constitutional Crisis and the House of Lords, 1621–1629" (Ph.D. diss., UC Berkeley, 1966), 40–41.

19. Hart, *Justice upon Petition*, 16–18.

the fact that they are both islands. According to one version of the right of monarchs, the king acquired authority through analogy with the father, a postulate that Robert Filmer developed in both *Patriarcha* and other writings. As Filmer elaborated:

> Not only Adam but the succeeding patriarchs had, by right of fatherhood, royal authority over their children. . . . For as Adam was lord of his children, so his children under him had a command and power over their own children, but still with subordination to the first parent, who is lord paramount over his children's children to all generations, as being the grand-father of his people.
>
> I see not then how the children of Adam, or of any man else, can be free of subjection to their parents. And this subjection of children is the only fountain of all regal authority, by the ordination of God himself.[20]

Were the first father never to die, each new generation would still be held under his thrall, authority never renewed but instead remaining with the firstborn. This postulate Filmer connected with the work of, among others, Plato, who, he claims, "in his third book of *Laws* affirms that the true and first reason of authority is that the father and mother, and simply those that beget and engender, do command and rule over all their children."[21]

This notion of paternal rule possesses an obvious corollary in the despotic authority that Cassilane claims over his son. Like the Adam whom Filmer imagines, Cassilane insists that his son must never outgrow his pupilage and always remain in a condition of subservience. Such a situation Antinous himself associates with tyranny, proclaiming to Cassilane:

> For proof that I acknowledge you the Author
> Of giving me my birth, I have discharg'd
> A part of my obedience. But if now
> You should (as cruell fathers do) proclame
> Your right, and Tyrant-like usurp the glory
> Of my peculiar honours, not deriv'd
> From successary, but purchas'd with my bloud,
> Then I must stand first Champion for my selfe,
> Against all interposers. (1.2.15–23)

---

20. Robert Filmer, *Patriarcha*, in *Patriarcha and Other Writings*, ed. Johann P. Sommerville (Cambridge: Cambridge University Press, 1991), 6–7.

21. Robert Filmer, *Observations upon Aristotles Politiques*, in *Patriarcha and Other Writings*, 242.

Antinous alleges that he has fulfilled the requirement of filial obedience, but that his military honor, which accords him his proper dignity as a subject or citizen of the state, should be his own. Rather than remaining captured by the father's right, Antinous insists on his own autonomy. Cassilane, however, deems this an affront, and a kind of treason against himself.

In *The Laws of Candy* there also appears a romantic form of tyranny, one that plays upon another discourse of obligation that would become more prevalent during the reign of James I's son King Charles I. As Victoria Kahn has elaborated in *Wayward Contracts*, Charles deployed the rhetoric of romance in the service of generating loyal subjects. Here Erota, the character most represented as tyrannical, is female rather than male; this accords, however, with Rebecca Bushnell's account of the rhetoric of femininity surrounding the Renaissance conception of the tyrant in *Tragedies of Tyrants*. Erota's relation with her male admirers displays a tyranny of love that encourages her even to use a phrase reminiscent of Julius Caesar's "veni, vidi, vici" (I came, I saw, I conquered)—"I can, I do, I will"—in response to Philander's plea "O you cannot be/ So heavenly, and so absolute in all things,/ And yet retaine such cruell tyranny" (2.1.92–95). Erota similarly adjures Antinous to obey and subject himself to her as a corollary of his devotion to the state:

> *Erota*:
> Upon your Loyalty to the state and me,
> I doe command you Sir, not depart *Candy*:
> Am I not your Princesse?
>
> *Antinous*:
> You are a great Lady.
>
> *Erota*:
> Then shew your selfe a Servant and a Subject. (2.1.206–9)

By the end of the play, however, Erota has descended from this position of tyranny and has abjured her previous behavior. An early indication of her incipient transformation occurs when she changes her mind about whether to force Philander into petitioning Antinous on her behalf; she tells him, "Alas, it is a miserie I grieve/ To put you to, and I will suffer rather/ In his tyranny, than thou in mine" (3.3.111–14).

These personal forms of tyranny play out in the tyrannical heritage of Venice's claim over Crete. Indeed, the debt that Venice alleges Crete owes derives ultimately from the actions of "*Baldwin* the Emperour,/ Pretending title, more through tyranny/ Than right of conquest, or descent" (4.2.17–19). Venice's insistence on its right is thus an insistence on a position acquired not through the kinds of sovereignty acknowledged as legitimate in the seventeenth century, those of conquest or descent, but instead through tyranny.

By the conclusion of the play, however, Cassilane has asked and received forgiveness of Antinous, Erota has acknowledged her previous pride and accepted Philander on terms of equality, and Venice and Crete are friends rather than creditor and debtor. Moreover, although these figures of sovereign tyranny have been quelled, the Senate still remains, the main political organ of the polity. The shift from kingly to parliamentary control of petition is thus echoed in the play by a conversion from a tyrannical and monarchical to a senatorial vision of sovereignty. Just as sovereignty in England was becoming generalized, sovereignty in *The Laws of Candy* is recentered on the Senate instead of the tyrannical father or lover.

Platonic Precedents

The final and most crucial intertext, Plato's *Laws*, calls into question the centrality of sovereignty and suggests its displacement within *The Laws of Candy*. Plato's *Laws*, his last dialogue, and an attempt on the scale of the *Republic* to address the question of the constitution of the state, is set in Crete. The characters—Clinias, a Cretan; Megillus, a Spartan; and an anonymous Athenian—commence by discussing the origins of the laws, including who created them in the first place, a question they return to in several different forms and moments during the dialogue. At the outset, the Athenian inquires: "To whom is the merit of instituting your laws ascribed, gentlemen? To a god, or to some man?"[22] As is eventually revealed, Clinias and nine others have been commissioned to generate laws for a new Cretan colony, and the dialogue eventually turns toward the project of assisting him in doing so. The Athenian assumes the vantage point of wisdom, and the other participants in the dialogue are generally reduced to providing historical or factual information about their states and respective laws, or agreeing docilely to what the Athenian proposes.

The setting of *The Laws of Candy* itself suggests a parallel; the play, like the dialogue, takes place in Crete, and it concerns the application of laws of ancient origin. In referring to "laws" as its subject, the play's title may indicate its

---

22. Plato, *The Laws*, trans. A. E. Taylor, in *The Collected Dialogues of Plato*, ed. Edith Hamilton and Huntington Cairns (New York: Pantheon, 1963), 1226.

connection with Plato. Furthermore, representatives of three polities are present in *The Laws of Candy* as in Plato's dialogue—although *The Laws of Candy* includes individuals from Cyprus and Venice rather than Sparta and Athens. Analysis of *The Laws of Candy* in light of Plato's *Laws* further indicates the significant resonances between the themes of the two works.

A number of the arguments of the *Laws* find themselves reworked in *The Laws of Candy*. Although there is no direct evidence that Ford or his co-author deployed Plato in writing the play, there are strong circumstantial and textual clues pointing in this direction. In literary history, the influence of Plato has largely been examined in the context of the cults of Platonic love surrounding first King James I's wife, Queen Anne, and subsequently, and more prominently, King Charles I's wife, Henrietta Maria.[23] This focus has led to a neglect of the potential significance of Plato's political theory within the drama of the period. Although Debora Shuger treats the *Laws*—mediated through Martin Bucer's *De regno Christi*—as a significant backdrop for understanding *Measure for Measure*, even she "doubt[s] that the *Laws* was ever a well-known text."[24]

Plato's *Laws* was widely read and cited by lawyers, among others, during the early decades of the seventeenth century, as Richard Ross has noted, referring to "Plato's immensely influential *Laws*."[25] Compilations of ancient materials, such as *Polyanthea* and *Polyanthea Nova*, extensively quoted from the *Laws*, and Henry Finch, Francis Bacon, William Fulbeck, and Lodowick Lloyd, among others, referred at length to the dialogue. Many of these authors were concerned with the relationship among the laws of several jurisdictions, whether Chancery and common law, common and civil law, or religious and secular tribunals. For example, William Fulbeck's *A Parallele or Conference of the Civill Law, the Canon Law, and the Common Law of this Realme of England* (1601) and *The Second Part of the Paralelle* (1602) both adopted Plato's technique of staging a dialogue among those learned in the law of disparate jurisdictions (here dubbed "Nomomathes," "Canonologus," "Codignostes," and "Anglonomophilax") and

23. Elizabeth Jane Bellamy discusses both of these moments in her chapter on Plato in *The Oxford History of Classical Reception in English Literature*, vol. 2, 1558–1660, ed. Patrick Cheney and Philip Hardie (Oxford: Oxford University Press, 2015), 508–12, and a number of critics, including Erica Veevers and Karen Britland, have remarked on the Neoplatonic character of the drama and masques surrounding Henrietta Maria.

24. Debora K. Shuger, Political Theologies in Shakespeare's England: The Sacred and the State in Measure for Measure (New York: Palgrave, 2001), 11.

25. Richard Ross, "The Commoning of the Common Law: The Renaissance Debate over Printing English Law," *University of Pennsylvania Law Review* 146, no. 2 (January 1998): 359.

referred frequently to the work.[26] The *Laws* furnished a valuable precedent for the investigation and comparison of laws derived from disparate locales and the attempt to both reconcile the principles of these laws and generate a model for law going forward.

Even Ford himself, who may have been exposed to Plato more than his fellow playwrights through his residence at the Middle Temple, invoked Plato's *Laws* in his 1620 tract *A Line of Life*. Writing, "The best Law-makers amongst the Ancients, were so curious in their choice of men in Office in the Commonwealth, that precisely and peremptorily, they reputed that STATE plagued, whipped, tormented, wounded, yea wounded to death, where the subordinate Governours were not aswell unblemished in their lives and actions, as in their names and reputation," Ford invokes "Plato 3, 6, and 12 *de legibus*" in the printed text and "Plato 9, 6, and 12 *de legibus*" in the manuscript.[27]

Examining the contexts in which the *Laws* was conjured up within the period highlights certain topics of relevance to *The Laws of Candy*, particularly with regard to the status of law within a commonwealth, the relationship between war among and within states, the perils of too much ambition, the dangers of excess wealth, and the role of the family. Some of these concerns—such as the focus on wealth—echo the aspects of the Greek tradition in republican thought that Eric Nelson has recovered in conjunction with tracing the influence of the *Laws* among other texts, but others have been relatively neglected, including the significance of Plato's account of law for conceptions of sovereignty and the reception of his claims about war before Hobbes.[28]

As noted in chapter 1, Henry Finch's *Nomotexnia* cites Plato's *Laws* extensively when introducing positive law, maintaining, "Thus also *Plato* defines that which he is speaking of as *logismos*, the reasoning faculty, *hos genomênos* (he says), *dogma poleôs koinon nomos epônomastai*, the golden and sacred rule of reason which is called common law [marginal note: Plato lib. 1 de Legibus]."[29]

26. William Fulbeck, *A Parallele or Conference of the Civill Law, the Canon Law, and the Common Law of this Realme of England* (London: Adam Islip, 1601), and *The Second Part of the Parallele, or Conference of the Civil Law, the Canon Law, and the Common Law of this Realme of England* (London: Adam Islip, 1602). For a more detailed discussion of Fulbeck's background and significance, see Daniel R. Coquillette, *The Civilian Writers of Doctors' Commons, London: Three Centuries of Juristic Innovation in Comparative, Commercial, and International Law* (Berlin: Duncker and Humblot, 1988).

27. *Collected Works of John Ford*, 1:589, 636.

28. Eric Nelson, *The Greek Tradition in Republican Thought* (Cambridge: Cambridge University Press, 2004), 13, 115–17.

29. Henry Finch, *Nomotexnia; cestascavoir, un description del Common Leys dangleterre solonque les rules del Art* (London, 1613), 19 (chap. 6, "Del Leys Positif").

Finch claims that this passage demonstrates the co-origination of common and civil law and the roots of both in reason.

As Finch's invocation of the understanding of law itself in the *Laws* suggests, Plato's text was significant in the early seventeenth century partly because of its account of law's role within the polity. Although one of the concerns of the work is, as Ford's reference to "subordinate Governours" suggests, how to ensure the appropriate application of the laws once created, Plato's central premise remains an insistence on a government by law rather than its ministers, regardless of their excellence or mode of selection. Hence he writes:

> Those who are termed "magistrates" [*archontas*] I have now called "ministers" [*huperêtas*] of the laws, not for the sake of coining a new phrase, but in the belief that salvation, or ruin, for a State hangs upon nothing so much as this. For wherever in a State the law is subservient [*an archomenos*] and impotent, over that State I see ruin impending; but wherever the law is lord [*despotês*] over the magistrates, and the magistrates are servants [*douloi*] to the law, there I descry salvation and all the blessings that the gods bestow on States.[30]

Within the *Laws*, there is considerable discussion of the form of government, the Athenian insisting that the laws should establish an intermediate type of government between monarchy and democracy.[31] Nevertheless, the laws themselves are the crucial protagonists of and guides for the work.

Similarly, in *The Laws of Candy*, despite the prominence of the Senate, the laws themselves are the engines that set the plot in motion; they also provide for the possibility of its happy resolution through specifying that the free remission of a crime against the law of gratitude by the one offended can redeem that person from punishment. The laws—not the Senate—remain the crucial feature of the play, allowing for the efficacy of forgiveness between individuals and furnishing a framework for refounding the state. In this respect, they assume a quasi-constitutional function, assisting in dealing with contingencies and emergencies not anticipated in advance.

The specter of war looms throughout the *Laws* as the possible consequence of a failure of law. Under the heading "Bellum," *Polyanthea Nova* quotes a speech by Clinias early in book 1 that responds to the Athenian's inquiry as to the

---

30. Plato, *The Laws*, bks. 1–6, trans. R. G. Bury (Cambridge: Harvard University Press, 1926), 292–93.

31. Plato, *Laws*, trans. Bury, 222–25.

purpose of Crete's laws.[32] Clinias insists that they are best understood against the backdrop of the constant possibility of war:

> For . . . "peace," as the term is commonly employed, is nothing more than a name, the truth being that every State is, by a law of nature, engaged perpetually in an informal war with every other State. And if you look at the matter from this point of view you will find it practically true that our Cretan lawgiver ordained all our legal usages, both public and private, with an eye to war, and that he therefore charged us with the task of guarding our laws safely, in the conviction that without victory in war nothing else, whether possession or institution, is of the least value, but all the goods of the vanquished fall into the hands of the victors.[33]

As Richard Tuck has demonstrated, the resemblances here to Hobbes's account of a war of all against all—and ultimately Schmitt's thought—are not simply incidental. Tuck has traced a reference to the passage in Sir Francis Bacon's 1624 tract urging Charles I to resume war with Spain, developed during a period when Bacon and Hobbes were in significant contact, and posits the transmission of Plato's account to Hobbes through Bacon.[34]

The Hobbesian quality of Clinias's position is only further enhanced when the Athenian asks about the relationship of individuals to one another and, finally, of the person to himself. According to Clinias, an isomorphism exists among the levels of the individual, the interpersonal, and the political; as he states, "Humanity is in a condition of public war of every man against every man, and private war of each man with himself." Under this view, mastery is the goal, whether over self, family, or city. Later in the dialogue, the Athenian further develops the connection between the family and the polis, positing, on the example of the Cyclopses in the *Odyssey*, that the former constitutes the first society and forms the building blocks of the latter.[35]

---

32. Domenicus Mirabellius, *Polyanthea Nova*, ed. Josephus Langius (Lyon: Zetzner, 1604), 216.

33. Plato, *Laws*, trans. Bury, 6–7.

34. Richard Tuck, *The Rights of War and Peace: Political Thought and the International Order from Grotius to Kant* (Oxford: Oxford University Press, 2001), 126–27. Others have also argued for or assumed the connection. See Martin Bertman, "Hobbes' Science of Politics and Plato's *Laws*," *Independent Journal of Philosophy* 2 (1978): 49, 52; Karl Schuhmann, Piet Steenbakkers, and Cees Leijenhorst, "Hobbes and the Political Thought of Plato and Aristotle," in Karl Schuhmann, *Selected Papers on Renaissance Philosophy and on Thomas Hobbes* (Dordrecht: Springer, 2004), 191–218; Francis Cheneval, *The Government of the Peoples on the Idea and Principles of Multilateral Democracy* (New York: Palgrave Macmillan, 2011), 95.

35. Plato, *Laws*, trans. Taylor, 1228, 1275. This passage was later taken up by Robert Filmer in *Patriarcha*.

Rather than adopting Clinias's—and, ultimately, Hobbes's—position, however, the *Laws* as a whole sets up an alternative to the Hobbesian account. In critiquing Clinias's vision of the purpose of the laws, the Athenian builds from the bottom up. Taking the example of the family, he posits a relation of strife between brothers and a variety of solutions presented by an adjudicator; these range from killing the worse, to bringing them into submission, to a final suggestion, which the Athenian values most highly. As the Athenian indicates, "There might be still a third degree of merit in an adjudicator, if we could find one who would take in hand a family at variance with itself, reconcile its members for the future by his regulations, without the loss of a single life, and keep them on permanent amicable terms." This ideal of reconciliation the Athenian presents as "legislating with a view to the complete contrary of war."[36]

He then insists that faction, or civil war, remains more detrimental than external war, and that, to the extent that Crete's laws have regulated with a view to war, they have contemplated only the latter rather than the former;[37] even Crete's "magnificent eulogies" for its warriors exclusively concern international rather than domestic conflict. The Athenian's conclusion, which, of course, Clinias accepts, is that the lawgivers framed "their legislation . . . in the interest of virtue as a whole, not one fragment of it," that of prowess in war. The *Laws* thus simultaneously names faction, or civil war, as the worst form of conflict, and one neglected by Clinias's notion of success or honor in war. The ends of law should, for the Athenian, be reconciliation of the city-state's citizens and the attainment of virtue. Achieving moderation should also furnish a primary goal for the legislator.[38]

Carl Schmitt, significantly influenced by Hobbes, also drew upon Plato in *The Concept of the Political*, where he maintained that "the specific political distinction to which political actions and motives can be reduced is that between friend and enemy."[39] While *The Laws of Candy* harks back to the *Laws*, however, Schmitt instead returns to Plato's *Republic*, and the two works reach disparate conclusions. For Schmitt, the enemy is not defined as an economic foe—or

---

36. Plato, *Laws*, trans. Taylor, 1229.

37. Plato, *Laws*, trans. Taylor, 1231. This point is reinforced later in the *Laws* when the Athenian calls the "most fatal of disorders" of a society that of "distraction" (1328). He also indicates that "in all that concerns city and fellow citizens, the best man, and the best by far, is he who would prize before an Olympian victory or any triumph in war or peace, the credit of victory in service to the laws of his home, as one who has all his life been their true servant above all men" (1316).

38. Plato, *Laws*, trans Taylor, 1232, 1315.

39. Carl Schmitt, *The Concept of the Political*, trans. George Schwab (Chicago: University of Chicago Press, 1996), 26.

"competitor"—nor understood on the "societal-associational" level, nor, most important, identified as a "private adversary." As Schmitt articulates the concept:

> The enemy is not merely any competitor or just any partner of a conflict in general. He is also not the private adversary whom one hates. An enemy exists only when, at least potentially, one fighting collectivity of people confronts a similar collectivity. The enemy is solely the public enemy, because everything that has a relationship to such a collectivity of men, particularly to a whole nation, becomes public by virtue of such a relationship.[40]

The opposition between friend and enemy is, for Schmitt, constitutive of the political order, and the distinction must, he opines, be maintained; it is almost as essential, however, for him to disaggregate the personal from the political, and the moral from the political, separating out the private from the public friend.

Early in *The Concept of the Political*, Schmitt refers to Plato for support in differentiating between the public and the private enemy, yet he explains that the *Republic* views true war as possible only between Greeks and Barbarians, not among the city-states. According to Schmitt, "the thought expressed here is that a people cannot wage war against itself and a civil war is only a self-laceration and it does not signify that perhaps a new state or even a new people is being created." The language of self-laceration reappears a few pages later, when Schmitt explains the detrimental quality of civil as well as international war; for him, "war is armed combat between organized political entities; civil war is armed combat within an organized unit. A self-laceration endangers the survival of the latter." Thus Schmitt claims an importance for self-laceration, or civil war, which he reads Plato as denying. This is not insignificant, because for Schmitt, it is the possibility of war that constitutes the political sphere, as it does for Hobbes. As he explains: "The friend, enemy, and combat concepts receive their real meaning precisely because they refer to the real possibility of physical killing. War follows from enmity. War is the existential negation of the enemy."[41]

In *The Politics of Friendship*, Jacques Derrida undermined the antithesis of friend and enemy as well as the opposition between the personal and ethical, on the one hand, and the political, on the other, which Schmitt had attempted to establish. *The Laws of Candy*, taking up Plato's *Laws*, effects a similar critique of absolute distinctions, simultaneously positing both undermining and redemptive functions for aliens within the state. The figure of the alien is, for *The Laws*

---

40. Schmitt, *The Concept of the Political,* 27, 45, 28.
41. Schmitt, *The Concept of the Political,* 29, 32, 33.

of Candy, that of someone who might be a valued guest and friend as well as an enemy or prisoner, and of someone who could constitute a powerful ally rather than a formidable opponent. At the same time, however, the state is refounded in light of a formative exclusion, which reinscribes the friend-enemy distinction.

Here, as in some of the instances Bonnie Honig treats in *Democracy and the Foreigner*, "foreignness operates as an agent of (re)founding."[42] The figure of the foreigner solves some of the problems of foundation: "A foreign-founder's foreignness secures for him the distance and impartiality needed to animate and guarantee a General Will that can neither animate nor guarantee itself. Moreover, because he is not one of the people, his lawgiving does not disturb the equality of the people before the law. And, finally, his foreignness may well add to his charms and enhance his leadership. No known genealogy demystifies his charismatic authority." Nevertheless, the persistence of the foreign founder within the instituted state may occasion difficulties; hence, sometimes "the foreign-founder must leave after the work of founding is done."[43] Similarly, the ending of *The Laws of Candy* does not unambivalently embrace the foreigner. Rather than insist that the same foreigner who helped to reconstitute the state depart at the end of the play, however, *The Laws of Candy* splits the alien in two, embracing one and rejecting the other.

Likewise, in contrast to Schmitt's account, one of the principal causes of dissension within the state, the Athenian claims in the *Laws*, consists in inequality of resources. The best society—although one he acknowledges is not practicable—is one in which ownership is eliminated, and "friends' property is indeed common property." Because it will be impossible for any state to ensure that "all settlers . . . enter . . . with equal means of every kind," the Athenian sets out an arrangement for a second-best economic order. Even within this less than perfect polity, to avoid distraction or faction, "there must be no place for penury in any section of the population, nor yet for opulence, as both breed either consequence."[44] Unlike Schmitt, the *Laws* thus accords economic disparity a significant role in occasioning internal conflict and suggests methods of enhancing equality.

In keeping with this concern about excessive accumulations of wealth, *Polyanthea Nova* cites passages from the *Laws* several times under the heading of "pecunia," or money. One of the sections referenced occurs very close to the passages pertaining to economic equality and specifies that "money is to be held in honour last or third; the highest interests being those of the soul, and in the

---

42. Bonnie Honig, *Democracy and the Foreigner* (Princeton: Princeton University Press, 2001), 3.
43. Honig, *Democracy and the Foreigner*, 21, 15.
44. Plato, *Laws*, trans. Taylor, 1324, 1328–29.

second class are to be ranked those of the body. This is the true order of legislation, which would be inverted by placing health before temperance, and wealth before health."[45]

In *The Laws of Candy*, money also furnishes an engine of conflict on several levels. The reason why Gonzalo has acquired power over Cassilane stems from the former's act of paying for Cassilane's soldiers' salaries. As Gonzalo recounts, "When *Cassilane* crav'd from the common treasure/ Pay for his Souldiers, I strook home, and lent him/ An hundred thousand Duckets" (3.1.26–28). The implication here seems to be that the Senate should have stepped in to finance ongoing military endeavors but instead allowed Gonzalo to intervene. The prospect of Cassilane's ensuing bankruptcy generates the threat not only of the "utter ruine of [his] house" but also "generally/ *Candie's* confusion" (4.1.87–88). On the broader historical time horizon and the level of city-states, debt also fuels animosity, as when earlier, Marquesse Mountferato had taken money from Venice for Crete then absconded, leaving the island indebted (4.2.17–32). After describing this situation, Cassilane states, "Money . . ./ Is now a God on earth: it cracks virginities,/ And turns a Christian, Turke;/ Bribes justice, cut-throats honour, does what not!" (4.2.34–37).

Another source of division that early seventeenth-century critics found described in the *Laws* consisted in the quality of "ambition," which took on a particular political dimension. As Lodowick Lloyd opined in *A Briefe Conference of Divers Lawes: Divided into certaine Regiments*:

> The states of Princes and countries are ever in most danger, where ambitious men be, who fearing nothing at all secretly to speake against Princes and Magistrates ambitiously, whose ambitious nature seekes not onely to rule and raigne, but also to practice (without feare) through pollicie, to undermine states, and to overthrowe their country through ambition. . . . Of these men *Plato* saith: *Siquis privatim sine publico scitu, pacem bellumve fecerit, capitale esto* [marginal note: Plato de leg. lib. 12].[46]

The broader passage from the *Laws* returns to the friend-enemy distinction and insists, contra Schmitt, that "everyone shall regard the friend or enemy of the State as his own personal friend or enemy; and if anyone makes peace or war with any parties privately and without public consent, in his case also the penalty shall be death."[47]

---

45. Mirabellius, *Polyanthea Nova*, 882, quoting Plato, *Laws*, (5.744A).

46. Lodowick Lloyd, *A Briefe Conference of Divers Lawes: Divided into certaine Regiments* (London: T. Creede, 1602), 125.

47. Plato, *Laws*, bks. 7–12, trans. R. G. Bury (Cambridge: Harvard University Press, 1926), 520–21.

Finally, in accord with this suggestion of parallels among the individual, the family, and society, the Athenian indicates in the *Laws*—as Filmer takes up—that one of the legislator's chief concerns should be prescribing family law. Rather than being constructed only for public purposes, the best law must include "compulsion in private affairs." Among the areas of private life to be regulated are included, in addition to marriage, the disinheritance of a child. Although disinheritance will carry with it, for the Athenian, exile as well, he prescribes public legal procedures that will render such action extremely difficult for a father to carry out.[48] In the dialogue, the public and the private are thus rendered indistinct, so that the law concerns itself with family life, and family life itself carries implications for the state.

The theme of ambition appears at the outset of *The Laws of Candy* when Gonzalo is designated "an ambitious Politick Lord of Venice" in the list of characters. His efforts at engaging in policy to undermine the state are highlighted throughout, and his ambition ranges to destroying the governments of both Crete and Venice. A kind of mirror image to Fernando, who bases political reconciliation on personal amity, he feigns friendship in order to wreak civil unrest and estrangement between states.

The Laws of Candy likewise focuses on the ways in which Crete's law of military reward may sow internal dissension, either within the family, or within the polity, or both. It is, indeed, as Gonzalo observes, the very fact of military victory against Venice, and the consequent glory of one individual—Antinous—over others, including his father, that plunges Crete into a condition of internal distraction. As Plato insists in the *Laws*, the state itself *is* concerned with Cassilane's act of disowning Antinous, because this act of intrafamilial violence nearly leads to the dissolution of the polity itself, in the form of the successive pleas of ingratitude before the Senate in the final act.

Finally, the role of the alien in *The Laws of Candy* follows Plato in honoring the laws of hospitality yet also goes beyond the dictates of the *Laws*. Whereas Plato had insisted that the enemy of the state functioned also as a personal enemy, personal friendship is transformed into political alliance by the conclusion of *The Laws of Candy*. When Erota renounces her desire for Antinous, Philander, the Prince of Cyprus, designates him "my deserving friend" (5.1.400), while the Venetian prisoner Fernando and Cassilane establish a relation of friendship as well. The last line of the play affirms the conversion of this relation between individuals into a political alliance as well, with "*Venice* vow'd a worthy friend" (5.1.414).

---

48. Plato, *Laws*, trans. Taylor, 1356, 1480.

These three contexts—of Shakespeare, petition, and Plato—provide indications both of the conceptual structure of *The Laws of Candy* and of its political implications. The play's dialogue with *Merchant* and *Measure for Measure* suggests that its form of tragicomedy involves not simply undoing the effects of revenge but rather reconciling a state undermined by civil war or proto-revolutionary violence. In the play, sovereignty is removed from the figure of the tyrannical monarch and placed provisionally with the Senate, just as petitions shifted back in England from being directed primarily to the king to addressing the House of Lords. Sovereignty itself, however, is displaced by law, on the one hand, and individual forgiveness, on the other. Reading *The Laws of Candy* against the backdrop of Plato's *Laws* suggests the priority of law itself over sovereign, and the law of gratitude allows for the construction of a new basis of authority for the state through the reconciliatory intervention of the alien Philander at the end of the play and the mutual consent of individuals with each other.

The Laws of Candy presents a picture of a political arena that has transformed since Shakespeare and that has refused to internalize James I's vision of the divine right of kings. Inherited laws trump sovereignty, and these laws are applied to individuals by one another; their strictures can likewise be avoided not by a sovereign pardon but instead by multiple individual acts of forgiveness. Prefiguring Immanuel Kant's discussion of the situation in which the entire state risks dissolution because too many have participated in civil unrest, the play condemns then forgives all of its protagonists, suggesting the establishment of a new and more equal polity, one constructed out of non-sovereign forgiveness rather than the sovereign pardon. By the end of the play, rule has been generalized and is itself grounded in the act of an alien.

The play also generates an alternative to Schmitt's—and earlier Hobbes's—readings of Plato. Unlike in Schmitt, economic factors play a crucial role in *The Laws of Candy*, and debt of both a personal and political nature threatens the integrity of the state. Faction too, and the possibility of civil war, are specters haunting the political sphere, but, far from contradicting Plato on this point, *The Laws of Candy* has internalized one of the central concerns of Plato's own *Laws*. Likewise, the conclusion of the play postulates a potential ground of peace, rather than war, for the political, following again Plato's critique of the justifications for law proffered by some of the protagonists of his dialogue. Finally, the forgiveness provided within the play resists Schmitt's understanding of the sovereign decision and instead represents a relational act between equals. The *deus ex machina* is not a god but a foreigner, and his intervention establishes the state on a footing of non-sovereign connections.

As strife percolated between king and Parliament, drama like *The Laws of Candy* imagined both resolutions to revolutionary violence and alterations in the nature and place of sovereignty itself. If *The Laws of Candy* suggested a connection between seeking peace and basing the polity on law as well as individuals' non-sovereign acts, Philip Massinger's play *The Bondman*, probably written only a little later, likewise shifted focus away from sovereignty by insisting instead on certain principles for the proper construction of the state, whether monarchical or republican. Emphasizing not a kind of exceptional mercy that would put legality to one side but instead a clemency lying at the heart of the laws, *The Bondman* places priority upon the survival of the polity over alteration in its form of government. At the same time, however, it suggests that failures of citizenship or radical inequality among individuals may prove fatal to the success of the state.

4

FROM SOVEREIGNTY TO THE STATE / The Tragicomic Clemency of Massinger's *The Bondman*

The reception of *The Bondman*, Philip Massinger's 1623 tragicomedy, presents something of a puzzle: Why did audiences from Prince Charles, to republicans resisting the possibility of Charles II's return, to the spectators of the Restoration all respond to the play enthusiastically despite their disparate political vantage points? Annabel Patterson posits that the tragicomic structure of the play permitted Massinger to caution James I of the possibility of his subjects' resistance while simultaneously supporting his entrance into war upon the failure of the match between his son Charles and the Spanish infanta.[1] Under this account, tragicomic form enables *The Bondman* to represent radical eventualities by dispelling disaster at the end. Yet this explanation contrasts the realities of politics

---

1. Annabel Patterson, *Censorship and Interpretation: The Conditions of Writing and Reading in Early Modern England* (Madison: University of Wisconsin Press, 1984), 92–93. Political interpretations of *The Bondman* have proliferated since Samuel R. Gardiner's topical interpretation of the play in "The Political Element in Massinger," *Contemporary Review* 28 (1876): 495–507. These have diverged not only in their assessments of Massinger's relative support for monarchy and republicanism but also in their evaluation of whether Massinger's plays were more preoccupied with specific historical events and controversies or with political theory. For instance, Jerzy Limon argued in *Dangerous Matter: English Drama and Politics, 1623/24* (Cambridge: Cambridge University Press, 1986) that *The Bondman*, along with several other nearly contemporaneous plays, formed part of a propaganda campaign organized by Prince Charles and his favorite, the Duke of Buckingham. While acknowledging that Massinger's "plays exhibit an unflagging interest in general political theory," Allen Gross contended, by contrast, that Massinger's writings, including *The Bondman*, are not "full of specific references to contemporary politics." Allen Gross, "Contemporary Politics in Massinger," *Studies in English Literature, 1500–1900* 6, no. 2 (Spring 1966): 279, 290. More recently, Thomas Fulton has read *The Bondman* as indebted to imported Dutch republicanism. In doing so, he has concluded that Massinger demonstrates how "absolute rule promotes a corrupt, parasitic aristocracy whose self-indulgence causes them to put themselves before their country. Conversely, a more constitutional form, whether a republic, a mixed government, or a more securely parliamentarian monarchy, promotes a stronger, less self-serving citizenship." Thomas Fulton, "'The True and Naturall Constitution of that Mixed Government': Massinger's *The Bondman* and the Influence of Dutch Republicanism." *Studies in Philology* 99 (2002): 177.

too starkly with the fiction of the play. As Patterson writes, "The play's tragicomic structure averts the fulfillment of [the] 'if,' as later Stuart history could not."[2] *The Bondman* may not, however, simply outline disparate potential political avenues that it fails to fully follow but, in fact, suggest an alternative form of politics itself correlated with a tragicomic vision. According to this reading, the particular kind of tragicomedy employed both furnishes a positive model for a possible state and allows seemingly incompatible constituencies to welcome the play with open arms.

As with many of Massinger's works, the language of *The Bondman* resonates with the echoes of Senecan Stoicism. From the representation of the Corinthian general Timoleon as a kind of Stoic sage to the deployment of the rhetoric of slavery in relation not only to physical servitude but also to the overwhelming quality of the passions, the play continually invokes commonplaces of Stoicism. The allusion most salient to its genre may be the first, in the dedicatory poem to Philip, Earl of Montgomery, where Massinger lauds "the clemencie of [Philip's] Heroick disposition."[3] This clemency, which would allow the play to find "though perhaps not a welcome entertainment, yet at the worst a gracious pardon,"[4] recalls Lucius Annaeus Seneca's treatise *De Clementia*, a defense of clemency addressed to his pupil the emperor Nero.[5] Although a number of commentators have observed Massinger's debt to Stoic thought, even Benjamin Townley Spencer's detailed analysis of the connections between Seneca's writings and *The Bondman* in his 1932 edition of the play mentions *De Clementia* only once in passing.[6]

For Seneca, clemency (*clementia*), a capacity for transcending particular grievances for the benefit of the whole, is a quality preeminently to be desired in a ruler, and should not be confused with pity (*misericordia*), an undesirable affective state derived from witnessing suffering. The opposite of clemency consists not in severity (*severitas*) but rather in cruelty (*crudelitas*). Furthermore, pardoning (*venia*) does not always accompany clemency, because such pardoning might itself commit an injustice. Substituting clemency for pity allows for the undoing of tragedy by tragicomedy, yet within such tragicomedy, pardoning

2. Patterson, *Censorship and Interpretation*, 93.

3. Philip Massinger, *The Bondman: An Antient Storie*, ed. Benjamin Townley Spencer (Princeton: Princeton University Press, 1932), "Dedicatory Epistle."

4. Massinger, *The Bondman*, "Dedicatory Epistle."

5. Lucius Annaeus Seneca, "De Clementia," in *Moral Essays*, vol. 1, trans. John W. Basore (Cambridge, MA: Harvard University Press, 1928), 356–449.

6. Massinger, *The Bondman*, 20, 43–65, 182–84, 209–10, 211, 221–22, 223–25, 230–33, 237, 248–49.

will occur only for the good of the commonwealth rather than out of an effort to remit a particular person's punishment. The Stoic tragicomedy of *The Bondman*, putting clemency into service of the play, emphasizes the general good of the state over the life of the condemned individual.

In Massinger's Stoic tragicomedy, this general welfare of the state becomes disconnected from any particular form of rule. The multiplicity of eager audiences for *The Bondman* attests that the play provides fodder for conceiving of either monarchy or republicanism as a viable mode of organizing government. As long as those directing the state possess the appropriate qualities of reason and self-restraint and place priority on the interests of the commonwealth rather than their personal gain, *The Bondman* suggests, the polity may thrive. As Reid Barbour has shown in *English Epicures and Stoics*, Stoicism not only furnished ammunition for the republican opposition to King Charles I but also was affirmed by the monarch himself.[7] Specifically with respect to Massinger's *Believe as You List*, Barbour observes that "among the political and topical complexities of Massinger's play, Stoicism is the philosophy that, as Bacon feared, aims to trouble ancient states, but the fortitude of the hero inspired by the sage in the desert supports the moral legitimacy of kings over the imperial drive of a republic."[8] Within either a republic or a monarchy, however, Stoicism treats inequality—which may rapidly devolve into cruelty—with suspicion. Clemency furnishes the antithesis to such cruelty, and it secures the state against the enemies within—enemies far more potent than foreign foes. The expansiveness of clemency furnishes a mechanism for generalizing pardon in transmuted form, one that would be raised and revisited from the late Jacobean moment through the Restoration.

Stoic Tragicomedy

The two books of *De Clementia* were among the first of Seneca's works to be revived in western Europe, and they were widely received during the medieval period and the Renaissance, possibly furnishing the foil for the political theory of Niccolò Machiavelli's *The Prince*, as Peter Stacey has persuasively argued in

---

7. Reid Barbour, *English Epicures and Stoics: Ancient Legacies in Early Stuart Culture* (Amherst: University of Massachusetts Press, 1998), 145.

8. Barbour, *English Epicures and Stoics*, 192.

Roman Monarchy and the Renaissance Prince.[9] *De Clementia* also provided fodder for one of John Calvin's earliest endeavors, a commentary on Seneca's text published in 1532. Furthermore, the essay was included in the 1614 and 1620 editions of Thomas Lodge's translation, *The workes of Lucius Annaeus Seneca, both moral and naturall.*[10] Seneca represents *De Clementia* as not simply aimed at instructing its addressee, the emperor Nero, but itself generated in response to Nero's own prior action, his display of reluctance in signing the death warrant of two condemned thieves.[11] Furnishing an early example of the genre of the mirror of kings, Seneca endeavors to "shew thee [Nero] to thy selfe, in such sort, as thou mayest receive a perfite contentment thereby," presenting a picture of Nero that will itself encourage the emperor to continue along the path of clemency.[12] Taking up this task, Seneca both elaborates on the value of clemency and provides a conception of its scope that contrasts with customary understandings.

As a kind of manual for princes along the lines that Peter Stacey has delineated, *De Clementia* supplies the contours of a political theory. As an attempt to reposition clemency in relation to pity and cruelty, it alters an Aristotelian theory of tragedy. Writing in the aftermath of the Roman revolution and the demise of the Roman Republic, Seneca justifies the power of the emperor on the basis of his virtue, which is "ground[ed] upon a strictly Stoic notion of reason." The emperor thus becomes a kind of Stoic sage. As such, he can save from itself the otherwise factionalized people—a people that, through civil strife, "had become merely a multitude" and "had lost its *virtus* [virtue], its *ratio* [reason], to such a degree that it appears to have become nothing better than an irrational animal requiring forceful restraint." Only through the intervention of the emperor, who will "always ensure that the *bonum commune* [common good] and never a partisan interest is upheld by his government," may freedom be restored and Rome itself become the "Stoic cosmic city."[13] Clemency is the foremost characteristic of this

---

9. Peter Stacey, *Roman Monarchy and the Renaissance Prince* (Cambridge: Cambridge University Press, 2007), 81.

10. Lucius Annaeus Seneca, *The Workes of Lucius Annaeus Seneca newly inlarged and corrected by Thomas Lodge D.M.P.* (London: William Stansby, 1614); hereafter *Workes*. As J. H. M. Salmon has claimed, Lodge's 1614 translation "is in many ways a monument to the Jacobean Neostoic cult." J. H. M. Salmon, "Stoicism and the Roman Example: Seneca and Tacitus in Jacobean England," *Journal of the History of Ideas* 50, no. 2 (April–June 1989): 199. It was based on the 1605 Latin edition prepared by Justus Lipsius. Salmon, "Stoicism and the Roman Example," 200. English quotations from Seneca in the text are generally taken from the 1614 edition of Lodge's translation.

11. *Workes*, 605.

12. *Workes*, 583; Stacey, *Roman Monarchy and the Renaissance Prince*, 4–5, 37.

13. Stacey, *Roman Monarchy and the Renaissance Prince*, 31, 33, 47.

virtuous emperor, the capacity that allows him to prioritize the general welfare over individual interests.

The critique of an Aristotelian version of tragedy remains somewhat more implicit in *De Clementia*. Scholars have long debated the compatibility of Seneca's philosophical writings with his tragedies, some contending that the violence and passion of his plays conflict with the Stoic effort to conquer the emotions, and others discerning more complex connections between the feelings generated in the spectator and the appropriate attitude of the proper Stoic individual.[14] Kathy Eden provided a suggestive account of the relation between a Senecan and an Aristotelian conception of the role of emotions in tragic and legal judgments in *Poetic and Legal Fiction in the Aristotelian Tradition*, but refrained from fully elaborating its implications. According to Eden, who cites *De Clementia* for the distinctions she draws:

> Seneca . . . rejects [the Aristotelian] view of the passions; and this rejection includes fear and pity—the two emotions associated with tragedy. The Stoics, including Seneca, define fear as the opposite of courage, and so its eradication needs little additional justification. Pity, however, describes a more complex response, including elements of human sympathy and fairness, which the Stoics would preserve. Seneca, consequently, differentiates two concepts inseparable in the Aristotelian *eleos*: *misericordia* and *clementia*. The first is characteristic of the feeble-minded and women; the second befits kings.[15]

Although fear can be rejected outright, pity must be treated more circumspectly; while *misericordia*—the translation of Aristotle's *eleos*, or pity, in Latin editions of the *Poetics*—is to be avoided, *clementia* must not be dispensed with at the

---

14. Gregory Staley has attempted to elaborate a Senecan theory of tragedy that would account for both the explicitly philosophical writings and the plays, claiming:

> The Stoics accepted the Platonic notion that tragedy is an image of the passionate soul; they did not, however, find harm in the experience. Influenced by Aristotle's *Rhetoric*, the Stoics interpreted emotion as a cognitive and persuasive process in which judgment follows and is influenced by our preliminary and unavoidable emotional responses to powerful impressions. . . . The vividness of tragedy's images may arouse our emotions, but these are only preliminary and involuntary; we can in the end judge their truth value.

Gregory Staley, *Seneca and the Idea of Tragedy* (Oxford: Oxford University Press, 2010), 94–95. Notable works on the other side include Charles Segal, *Language and Desire in Seneca's* Phaedra (Princeton: Princeton University Press, 1986); and Alessandro Schiesaro, *The Passions in Play:* Thyestes *and the Dynamics of Senecan Drama* (Cambridge: Cambridge University Press, 2003).

15. Kathy Eden, *Poetic and Legal Fiction in the Aristotelian Tradition* (Princeton: Princeton University Press, 1986), 101.

same time. Putting to one side the question of whether Seneca's own tragedies accomplish this end, it is possible to derive an emendation of Aristotle from Seneca's treatment of clemency. This revised Aristotelian frame may, however, conduce more to tragicomedy than to tragedy.

In order to explicate the appropriate parameters of clemency, Seneca refutes what he deems a number of misinterpretations. At first, he explains why, contrary to certain claims about it, clemency does not "embold[en] those men that are most wicked."[16] Since it must be exercised only in moderation, clemency fails to occasion such a perverse result; furthermore, because of circumstantial misfortunes, even the innocent may have need for the employment of clemency. Later, in the second book, where he defines clemency, Seneca counterposes it with cruelty, which he associates with seeking revenge. Those are "cruell, who . . . keepe no measure. . . . We may . . . say this crueltie is an inclination of the minde unto most grievous punishments." Clemency instead imports "a moderation of the minde, that restraineth the power which man hath to revenge himself."[17] Cruelty and clemency hence stand in opposite relations to revenge, the former carrying revenge to its utmost limits and the latter avoiding absorption in the cycle of revenge and its concomitant passions.

If clemency is juxtaposed with cruelty at one extreme, it is opposed to mercy at the other. Whereas mercy focuses on the object of suffering and involves a disruption of the observer's tranquility through the experience of a sympathetic pain, clemency remains a rational practice. As Seneca writes, "A wise man is not mooved with sadness for an others misery, because hee is exempt from miserie; but otherwise, he will willingly and with a ioyfull heart, do all that which the merciful would doe against their wills."[18]

Between cruelty and mercy, two responses to tragedy seem to be ruled out: exulting in the extremities of an excessive revenge and experiencing the pity (*misericordia*) that Aristotle associates with the proper tragic catharsis. Seneca's subsequent contrast likewise suggests a modification of tragicomedy. If tragicomedies like *Measure for Measure* depend for the undoing of disaster on a series of final pardons, an alternative ending must be found to satisfy Seneca. According to the philosopher's claim, "a wise man ought not to give [pardon]."[19] Whereas pardoning remits deserved punishment, clemency allows for a

---

16. *Workes*, 584.
17. *Workes*, 584, 585, 606.
18. *Workes*, 607.
19. *Workes*, 608. The terms *ignorare* and *venia* are both used for pardoning in this passage.

mitigation of the consequences of crime. Whereas the one pardoning admits that he should not have condemned in the first place, the individual displaying clemency "counsaileth" and "correcteth" and "doth as much as if he pardoned." Whereas the objects of pardoning may simply return to their course of crime, clemency aims to reform them: "A wise man will forgive many things, and save many that are scarcely wise, yet such as may become capable. Hee will imitate good husbandmen, who not onely cherish straight and tall trees, but applieth under-props likewise to uphold those which are made crooked by some accident. . . . [A] wise man shall see how hee ought to entertaine every nature, and by what meanes those that are depraved, may be strengthened and straightned."[20]

Under the 1614 translation, clemency appears in the guise of equity, as opposed to the established custom of the common law, so that "clemencie hath free will, shee iudgeth not according to use and custome, but according to equitie and right." The examples that Seneca furnishes also fit with early modern understandings of equity, involving an assessment of the intention or lack thereof of an actor and the possibility that the person might reform. As Seneca writes: "He will be contented to admonish some without chastising them, considering that they are old enough to amend. Hee will dismisse an other in safetie, although he be apparently guiltie, because he hath beene deceived, and fell into the offence being drowned in wine. He will dismisse his enemies in safetie, and sometimes with commendations, if they have undertaken Warre upon honest grounds, as for their faith, confederate or libertie."[21] These instances of individuals whose youth suggests their malleability in the direction of good, people who have erred seemingly without conscious awareness of criminality, and opponents who have waged war in support of their liberty, religion, or allies all indicate an equitable inquiry into the character of the accused and his motives.

Seneca's explanation in the first book of *De Clementia* of the reasons why the wise man, and in particular the wise ruler, should display clemency helps to illuminate what Stoic tragicomedy might entail. The principal grounds for clemency in a ruler who wishes to avoid tyranny are twofold: first, it helps to secure the peace of the state, and second, it emanates from the proper consideration of the entire commonwealth as naturally connected to its ruler, in the same way that the body is linked to the soul. It is, Seneca claims, Nero's clemency that lies behind his subjects' belief that they possess "an excellent forme of publique governement, which containeth all that which is requisite to establish a perfect

---

20. *Workes*, 608, 609.
21. *Workes*, 609.

libertie." When excessive fear is inflicted on the subjects of a tyrant, they are more likely to rebel, while the clemency of the wise prince quells unrest among his subjects: "A moderate feare restraineth mens minds, but a continuall violence, and such as is raised even unto the brimme, awakeneth and emboldneth those that are deepest asleep and giveth them courage to hazard all." Instead, the philosophically informed ruler should mete out chastisement in the same measure as a father, keeping in mind the goal of reformation rather than allowing himself more extreme responses to transgression.[22]

Before arriving at this analogy between the emperor and the father, however, Seneca develops in more detail a metaphor depicting the ruler as the soul of the commonwealth. This soul must make every effort to preserve the body with which it is linked—the corporate body composed of the emperor's subjects. The prince's clemency is, under this account, even more crucial than that of any commoner, partly because it emanates from a desire for self-preservation, and partly because the clemency of the ruler can be exercised on a greater stage than that of the subject. According to Seneca:

> As we may truly conclude, . . . thou are the soule of the Common-wealth, and shee the bodie; Thou seest, as I thinke, how necessary Clemencie is: for thou seemest to spare thy selfe when thou sparest others. Thou oughtest therefore to beare with evill subjects, no otherwise then thou wouldest doe with languishing members and if sometimes there be neede of bloud-letting, take heed lest the veine be opened more largely then the sickenesse requireth. Clemency therefore, as I said, is agreeable unto all mens nature, but especially it best befitteth Princes, because in them she findeth more people to preserve, and a greater matter wherein to shew herselfe. For how little hurteth a private cruelty? But Princes displeasure is a warre.[23]

The emphasis on the ruler's clemency as a form of self-preservation in this passage recalls the primacy placed more generally on self-preservation within the Stoic system. The Stoic conception of *oikeiosis*, or "orientation," renders self-preservation "the basic desire or drive in all animals (including human beings)."[24] As Diogenes Laertius observes, "An animal's first impulse, say the Stoics, is to self-preservation, because Nature from the outset endears it (*oikeiouses*) to itself, as Chrysippus affirms in the first book of his work *On Ends*; his own words are,

---

22. *Workes*, 585, 593, 595.
23. *Workes*, 587.
24. John Sellars, *Stoicism* (Berkeley: University of California Press, 2006), 108.

'The dearest thing (*proton oikeion*) to every animal is its own constitution and its consciousness thereof.'"[25] The self-preservation of the subjects in Seneca's account merges seamlessly with the self-preservation of the prince.

The nature of a Senecan Stoic version of tragicomedy as well as of the state begins to emerge here. Rather than involving a series of individual pardons at the end of the play, ones that might either acknowledge a prior injustice or exempt from punishment those who otherwise deserve it, this kind of political tragicomedy would entail preservation of the body politic through enlargement of the sovereign's compass of concern. It might also entail invocation of the specter of cruelty in order to expunge it from the commonwealth.

The form of rule derived from *clementia* stands in contrast with a conception of the sovereign or the pardon as exception, along the lines described theoretically by Giorgio Agamben and Jacques Derrida. Philip Lorenz's careful readings in *The Tears of Sovereignty* have teased out the operations of sovereignty as exception in early modern drama as well, including works such as Lope de Vega's *Fuenteovejuna*. In the context of that play, Lorenz suggests that "because the entire village, collectively, defies sovereignty's attempt to subject the event to a legal decision, the Catholic Kings are *forced* to pardon them. Sovereignty's desire to make of the village an *example* is forced to settle for an *exception* instead."[26]

One particular form of cruelty with which Seneca appears concerned and which he analogizes with the tyrant's treatment of his subjects is the master's abuse of a slave. Even with regard to slaves, Seneca insists, justice applies, and a form of natural right pushes back against legal authority:

> It is an honour to know how to commaund a mans servants modestly, and in our slave wee are to thinke not how much punishment he may endure and we inflict upon him without reproofe, but what the nature of right and justice will permit thee: which commandeth us to spare our Captives and such whom we have bought to be our bond-slaves. . . . Although wee have authoritie to doe what wee list with our slaves, there is somewhat which the common right of living Creatures permitteth us not to execute upon a man, because he is of the same nature that thou art.[27]

---

25. Quoted in Sellars, *Stoicism*, 107–8.
26. Philip Lorenz, *The Tears of Sovereignty: Perspectives of Power in Renaissance Drama* (New York: Fordham University Press, 2013), 147. The passage continues on to complicate whether *Fuenteovejuna* actually functions as an example or exception, but the excerpt quoted here highlights the potential of the pardon to form a kind of exception. If here a pardon represents an exception from sovereignty, it may in other circumstances also serve as an exceptional reinforcement of sovereignty.
27. *Workes*, 597.

The natural equality among all human beings limits the extent to which the constructed relation of master and servant or slave permits the exercise of force. The servant or slave must be spared rather than scourged in the interests of humanity.

Seneca elaborates that the same principle applies with regard to the emperor's treatment of his subjects. Comparing the empire with the household, he writes, "How much more just is it for thee not to abuse men free, ingenious, and honest, as thy bond men, but to entertaine them, for such as are under thy government to defend them as thy subjects, and not to afflict them as thy slaves." Cruelty, in particular, serves to undermine respect for either the master or the prince: "Even as cruell Masters are pointed at thorow the whole Citie, and are reputed both hatefull and detestable: so the cruell demencie of Princes, who have contracted infamie and hatred against them selves, are inregistred in Histories to bee a hatred to posteritie."[28] Just as the master must eschew cruelty and instead adopt an attitude of clemency, so must the ruler in dealing with his subjects.

Clemency is also connected terminologically with the release from bondage early in Seneca's treatise. In the passage of *De Clementia* announcing its sections, a passage that mystified Calvin,[29] Seneca proclaimed: "Here I shall divide this subject as a whole into three parts. The first will treat of manumission [*manumissio*]; the second will aim to show the nature and aspect of clemency."[30] The invocation of "manumission" here, about which Calvin expressed confusion, must also have puzzled Lodge, as he simply stated, "The first [part] shall serve for a Preface or Induction."[31] Seneca appears, however, to

---

28. *Workes*, 597.

29. As Calvin wrote:

> Here Seneca gives the division of his work, but I cannot say I have quite understood it yet. I prefer a man to be a teacher of real frankness rather than delude his reader with frivolous subtleties. For he does not set forth his subject matter in the order he proposes. Nor is it apparent what he means by the word MANUMISSION in the first part. The blame for this is to be ascribed not so much to us as perhaps to the author himself.

John Calvin, *Calvin's Commentary on Seneca's* De Clementia, ed. Ford Lewis Battles and André Malan Hugo (Leiden: E.J. Brill, 1969), 79.

30. *Workes*, 77.

31. The introduction to *De Clementia*—taken from Justus Lipsius's 1605 edition of Seneca's works, on which Lodge's translation is based—does devote more attention to the term, but, rather than reading "manumission," substitutes for it "manuduction," or "the act of directing or guiding" (*Workes*, 582). This substitution follows Lipsius's own introduction, which reads "*unum Manuductionis*." Lucius Annaeus Seneca, *Annaei Senecae Philosophi Opera, Quae Existant Omnia*, ed. Justus Lipsius (Antwerp: Plantin-Moretus, 1605), 187. Although Lipsius keeps *manumissio* in Seneca's text, his note on the term suggests that he deems it a corruption of *manuductio*. *Annaei Senecae Philosophi*

be using "manumission" as a synonym for an act of clemency, linking the grant of freedom in situations of servitude with the ruler's capacity for behaving expansively toward his subjects.

A passage from another of Seneca's essays, included in the 1614 edition, *Of Benefits*, dramatizes one possible set of interplays among manumission, bondage, and cruelty. Recounting a story from Claudius Quadrigarius's *Chronickes*, Seneca elaborates how two slaves staged an elaborate scene of deception in the midst of war in order to save their mistress. To convince the enemies who had conquered the city of Grumentum that they had greater entitlement to vengeance on their mistress than those who had taken the city, these slaves decided to pretend that she had treated them with cruelty. Hence, when "the victorious enemie ranged and reveled everie where, these two slaves (who knew all the by-waies) were the first that set forward to make bootie of the house wherein they had served. And having surprised their Mistris, they rudely drove her before them: And being demanded what woman shee was: they answered that it was their Mistris, who had in times past most cruelly handled them, and that they dragged her out, to bring her to her death."[32] Instead, they hid her to provide protection. Subsequently, "when the Roman Souldiers were satisfied with pillage, and reduced to their former discipline and manners, these slaves likewise returned to their former servitude, and gave their Mistresse her wonted libertie." Rather than simply reinstating the earlier hierarchy, however, their mistress "presently set them both at libertie." Significantly, Seneca adds that she "was not ashamed to receive her life at their handes, over whom shee had absolute power both of life and death."[33] The absolute power of the master over the slave itself exists within a framework of time and contingency. Far from a static state, the relation of master and slave may be rapidly reversed by the intrusion of an invading army or by other political upheavals. At these moments, the cruelty or lack thereof of the master may affect his or her fate at the hands of a bondman. Likewise, the slave's own display of clemency allows for his subsequent manumission by the mistress. The grant of life or freedom to another person remains the opposite of cruelty, whether performed by a master or a slave.

Opera, 189. This further indicates the perplexity that Seneca's use of *manumissio* occasioned for early modern editors of his work. Lipsius's work on Seneca is discussed in Jan Papy, "Erasmus's and Lipsius's Editions of Seneca: A 'Complementary Project'?," *Erasmus of Rotterdam Society Yearbook* 22 (2002): 10–36.

32. *Workes,* 53.
33. *Workes,* 54.

Putting Clemency into Practice

The episode from *Of Benefits* presages some of the plot components of *The Bondman*, the main textual sources of which are generally acknowledged to be Plutarch's lives of Timoleon and Dion, one of the *Controversiae* of Seneca the Elder, Diodorus Siculus's account of the Servile Wars in Sicily, and a story from Justin's *Epitome of the Philippic History of Pompeius Trogus.*[34] The Senecan components of *The Bondman* become evident, however, only from detailed analysis of the play's construction, which emphasizes the links between personal and political servitude, the connection between the regulation of the emotions and proper rule, and the differences among clemency, cruelty, and pity.

At the outset, Syracuse finds itself in danger of being captured by Carthage. Because the inhabitants of Syracuse have become used to a life of affluence and leisure, they lack a sufficiently capable general to defend the island and its "liberties" against the foreign fleet.[35] Instead, the Senate has to resort to Timoleon, lent from Corinth, as its leader; by waging war on behalf of the Syracusans, Timoleon is defending Greece in its entirety against empire, since Carthage "will not end, till *Greece*/ Acknowledge her their Soveraigne" (1.1.62–63). Even after the Senate has chosen Timoleon "with a generall suffrage" (1.3.82) and extolled his excellence, he has difficulty raising resources for his expedition, as the "free Lords" of Syracuse (1.1.61) remain miserly about their money. Timoleon expostulates with them, "Doe you prize your mucke/ Aboue your liberties? and rather choose/ To be made Bondmen, then to part with that/ To which already you are slaues?" (1.3.231–34).

Only when the virtuous Cleora, the daughter of the Praetor of Syracuse, Archidamus, intervenes and gives away her jewels are the remainder of the citizenry shamed into following suit and funding Timoleon's enterprise. Even at this point, the Syracusans contemplate sending hired men and slaves into battle instead of waging war themselves. Again Cleora addresses the assembly, proclaiming that the rewards of battle should not be reaped by slaves:

> Are you men? . . .
> Yet now your Countries libertie's at the stake,
> Honour, and glorious tryumph, made the garland
> For such as dare deserve them; a rich Feast

---

34. Philip Edwards emphasizes the *controversiae* in "The Sources of Massinger's *The Bondman*," while Spencer focuses on the other three sources. Philip Edwards, "The Sources of Massinger's *The Bondman*," *Review of English Studies* 15, no. 57 (1964): 21–26. As noted earlier, Spencer's edition also indicated several passages in which the play echoes Senecan Stoicism and, in particular, *Of Benefits.*

35. Massinger, *The Bondman*, 1.3.9; hereafter cited parenthetically in the text by act, scene, and line.

Prepar'd by Victory of immortall viands,
Not for base men, but such as with their Swords
Dare force admittance, and will be her Guests,
And can you coldly suffer such rewards
To be propos'd, to Labourers and Slaues?
While you that are borne Noble (to whom these
Valued at their best rate, are next to Horses,
Or other Beasts of carriage) cry ayme,
Like idle lookers on, till their proud worth
Make them become your masters? (1.3.326–41)

Her words seem to persuade at least some reluctant men to enter Timoleon's forces.

One particular family exemplifies the internal problems that have beset Syracuse. Cleon, described as "a fat impotent Lord" in the cast of characters, is married to Corisca, who takes every opportunity to engage in infidelity, including with Cleon's son Asotus, nominally a suitor of Cleora. Although Cleon gives up some of his vast wealth for the expedition against Carthage, he and Asotus refuse to participate in the war, and both Asotus and Corisca cruelly abuse their bondmen. Cleon is represented as himself a slave to his money, Corisca to her passions, and Asotus to the possibility of lording it over his own slaves.

One passage links Asotus's cowardice with his cruelty to his slave Gracculo. Although Asotus himself has abdicated all honorable functions of a citizen, he desires to become ruler in the household kingdom. Having been compared by others to various weak or ignominious animals, like a sheep or—as his very name suggests—an ass, Asotus instead tries to emulate a more noble beast, the lion, by beating Gracculo while denominating him a dog:

Asotus: You slaue, you Dogge, downe Curre.
Gracc.: Hold, good young Master.
For pitties sake.
Asotus: Now am I in my kingdome.
Who saies I am not valiant? I begin
To frowne againe, quake villaine.
Gracc.: So I doe, Sir,
Your lookes are Agues to me.
Asotus: Are they so Sir?
'Slight, if I had them at this bey, that flout me,
And say I looke like a sheepe, and an Asse, I would make 'em

Feele, that I am a Lyon.
Gracc.: Doe not rore, Sir,
As you are a valiant beast: but doe you know
Why you use me thus?
Asotus: I'le beat thee a little more,
Then study for a reason, O I haue it,
One brake a iest on me, and then I swore
Because I durst not strike him, when I came home
That I would breake thy head.
Gracc.: Plague on his mirth,
I am sure I mourne for't. . . .
I am bruised to ielly; better be a dogge,
Then a slaue to a Foole or Coward.
Asotus: Heere's my Mother,
Shee is chastising too: How braue we liue!
That haue our slaues to beat, to keep us in breath,
When we want exercise. (2.2.1–25)

While Asotus begins by attempting to render Gracculo bestial by calling him "dogge," Gracculo soon laments that even a dog is better off than one enslaved to such a master. This master too finds himself more animal than man—either a lion in his own imagination, or a sheep or an ass according to the perception of others. For both the master and the slave, retaining humanity proves difficult. Reason itself is in abeyance. It becomes evident that Asotus's actions stem from displaced revenge rather than rational motivation when he cannot immediately answer Gracculo's question "doe you know/ Why you use me thus?" This language of use pervades the play, often designating forms of abuse and pertaining to the use of self as well as others. Those who are instrumentalized—either by their own perverse passions or through the will of others—frequently lose their humanity in the process.

The political plot of the play is accompanied from the beginning by a second strain of romance. The audience discovers in the first scene that Leosthenes is a suitor for Cleora's hand in marriage. A friend of Cleora's brother Timagoras, Leosthenes appears to have won his beloved's affections but still remains unsure how her father, Archidamus, is disposed toward him. At the same time, it transpires that a noble Theban, Pisander— whose advances toward Cleora Timagoras had encouraged Archidamus to reject—has returned to Syracuse, and even to Archidamus's own household, disguised as the slave Marullo. As we discover later, Pisander had initially come to Syracuse to avenge Leosthenes's infidelity to Pisander's own sister Statilia—also disguised as a slave under the name of Timandra—but in the process, had become enamored of Cleora.

Two developments over the course of the drama succeed in wresting Cleora's love from Leosthenes and transferring it to Pisander; the first is the confirmation of the unchecked quality of Leosthenes's passions and the second is Pisander's demonstration of the opposite characteristic, temperance. Almost as soon as his character is introduced, Leosthenes is associated with jealousy; Timagoras implores him, "Prethee doe not nourish/ These jealous thoughts" (1.1.24–25). Despite this warning, Leosthenes's jealousy causes him to express distrust to Cleora about how she will conduct herself during his absence. Subsequently, despite the fact that Cleora has bound her eyes against other sights and refrained from speaking the entire time he was away, Leosthenes, returning victorious from battle, still believes that she may have been possessed in some way by another. It is this jealousy that Cleora fears would make Leosthenes "tyrannize" if he "stood possess'd of/ That [i.e., Cleora herself], which is [his] only in expectation" (3.3.180–81).

The motivation for Leosthenes's fears when he arrives back in Syracuse is a slave rebellion that Pisander/Marullo had instigated during the absence of the citizens who left the city to fight against Carthage. Pisander employs three rationales to justify the revolt, one primarily personal, the second largely political, and the third somewhat metatheatrical. First, by taking over the city, Pisander attempts to gain closer access to Cleora; as he reveals after the rebellion has failed, "had [the bondmen] stood firme,/ I could have bought *Cleoras* free consent,/ With the safetie of her Fathers life, and Brothers" (4.3.6–8). Whether such consent under conditions of conquest could actually be considered free is a separate question, but Pisander appears to believe that it would be, as his sister Statilia's right to Leosthenes, which he insists upon upholding, stems from a similar circumstance. As Pisander later admonishes Leosthenes, "This is shee/ To whom thou wert contracted: this the Lady,/ That when thou wert my prisoner fairely taken/ In the *Spartan* warre, that beg'd thy libertie,/ And with it gaue her selfe to thee ungratefull" (5.3.179–83).

At the same time, Pisander adduces a second reason for inciting the bondmen to action, both in addressing them and in subsequently justifying the incident to Archidamus and the other rulers of the city. Recalling scenes like Asotus's abuse of Gracculo, he explains that the improper control of the household, like the political mismanagement of the city, has led the slaves not merely to be treated as inhuman but even to be dealt with more cruelly than animals. Whereas the model of the commonwealth could in a prior age be traced from the well-governed household, the abusive behavior of the Syracusan citizens has disrupted the analogy. As Pisander/Marullo states to the leaders of Syracuse when speaking not for himself but "for all":

> Your tyranny
> Drew us from our obedience. Happy those times,
> When Lords were styl'd fathers of Families,
> And not imperious Masters; when they numbred
> Their seruants almost equall with their Sonnes,
> Or one degree beneath them; when their labours
> Were cherish'd, and rewarded, and a period
> Set to their sufferings; when they did not presse
> Their duties, or their wills beyond the power
> And strength of the performance; all things order'd
> With such decorum, as wise Law-makers,
> From each well-gouern'd priuate house deriu'd
> The perfect model of a Common-wealth;
> Humanity then lodg'd in the hearts of men,
> And thankfull Masters carefully prouided
> For Creatures wanting reason. The noble horse
> That in his fiery youth from his wide nostrells,
> Neigh'd courage to his Rider, and brake through
> Groues of opposed Pikes, bearing his Lord
> Safe to triumphant victory, old or wounded,
> Was set at libertie, and freed from seruice.
> The Athenian Mules, that from the Quarrie drew
> Marble, hew'd for the Temples of the gods,
> The great worke ended, were dismiss'd, and fed
> At the publique cost; nay, faithfull dogs haue found
> Their Sepulchres; but man to man, more cruell,
> Appoints no end to the sufferings of his slaue;
> Since pride stept in and ryot, and o'return'd
> This goodly frame of Concord, teaching Masters
> To glory in the abuse of such, as are
> Brought under their command; who grown unusefull,
> Are lesse esteem'd than beasts; this you haue practis'd,
> Practise'd on us with rigor; this hath force'd us,
> To shake our heauy yokes off. (4.2.52–85)

Under Pisander/Marullo's account, the use of the bondmen, unlike even the treatment of working animals, has devolved into abuse, and cruelty has usurped any other possible relation between master and slave in Syracuse. Although he associates the bondmen with "creatures wanting reason," Pisander/Marullo insists that "humanity" cannot justify the treatment they have of late received and would instead produce at least some reward other than cruelty for enduring service.

To the bondmen themselves, he likewise adduces moral and political rather than self-interested reasons for the rebellion. In urging them to take action, however, Pisander/Marullo emphasizes absolute equality among men more than the Syracusans' tyrannous overstepping of masters' proper roles. He opines:

> Equall nature fashion'd us
> All in one molde: The Beare serues not the Beare,
> Nor the Wolfe, the Wolfe; 'twas ods of strength in tyrants,
> That pluck'd the first linke from the Golden chayne
> With which that thing of things bound in the world.
> Why then, since we are taught, by their examples,
> To loue our Libertie, if not Command,
> Should the strong serue the weake, the faire deform'd ones?
> Or such as know the cause of things, pay tribute
> To ignorant fools? All's but the outward gloss
> And politicke forme, that does distinguish us. (2.3.32–42)

Invoking the Stoic conception of the golden age, Pisander/Marullo recommends following the model of equal freedom found among animals rather than consenting to the inequality of the contemporary human political order.[36]

The bondmen are, however, not represented as fully capable of assuming the liberty that Pisander/Marullo has encouraged. Rather than allowing them to derive inspiration for the rebellion from reason, Pisander must instead ply them with alcohol, urging them to imbibe "strong, lusty wine: drinke deepe, this juyce will make us/ As free as our Lords" (2.3.10–11). Upon the success of the revolt, order also rapidly dissolves among the slaves, who in a drunken bout fight about sexual access to Olimpia, a former mistress who has now married the man who was earlier her slave. When Pisander/Marullo inquires, "Quarrell among your selues?," one of the bondmen answers, "Yes, in our Wine, Sir,/ And for our

---

36. See Massinger, *The Bondman*, 209–10.

Wenches" (3.3.128–29). Finally, they are easily overthrown again by the return-ing army once the Syracusans decide to treat them not as equal enemies but as "wilde beasts" and proceed to menace them with whips (4.2.113).

Before the bondmen have been subdued, however, they succeed in demon-strating to Cleon, Corisca, and Asotus how the latter have failed to maintain a well-governed household. Treating these previously tyrannous individuals in the same fashion in which they themselves had previously acted, their former slaves extract from them verbal recognition of their earlier errors. Hence Corisca asks, "Whom can we accuse/ But our selues for what we suffer?" (3.3.57–58), and Asotus admits: "I am punish'd,/ For seeking to Cuckold mine owne naturall Father./ Had I beene gelded then, or us'd my selfe/ Like a man: I had not beene transfor'd, and forc'd/ To play an ore-growne Ape" (3.3.81–85). At the same time that he was mistreating his bondman, Asotus had failed to "use" even himself like a man; his more visibly animalian role under Gracculo's management simply embodies his moral inhumanity. Not only are the bondmen quelled by being confronted as wild beasts, but also the citizens of Syracuse themselves have dem-onstrated an inability to fulfill the demands of living as men and women.

Pisander/Marullo's own conduct during the rebellion is exemplary, the sec-ond development that endears him to Cleora. Although he has instigated the uprising in part to gain access to Cleora, he refrains from inflicting unwanted advances upon her and even allows her to preserve the silence she had promised to Leosthenes before he departed. As Pisander/Marullo tells Cleora, "I doe deny you to my selfe, to giue you/ A pure unspotted present to my riuall" (3.2.100–101). Using gestures rather than words, Cleora signs her gratitude. To Archidamus and others, Pisander/Marullo's forbearance at this moment seems more the stuff of fable than reality, although its truth is borne out by inquiry. Timoleon himself exclaims,

> Tis wondrous strange! nor can it fall within
> The reach of my beliefe, a slaue should be
> The owner of a temperance, which this age
> Can hardly paralell in free-borne Lords,
> Or Kings proud of their purple. (5.3.1–5)

The third reason why Pisander provoked the slave revolt is necessarily dis-closed only retrospectively, when the Syracusans have regained control over their city and he has revealed his true identity. At this point, Pisander insists that he discovered the bondmen inclined toward rebellion because of the ill-treatment they had received and that he decided to stage a demonstration for the Syracusans of the disaster that might ensue if they failed to alter their attitude toward their slaves. As Pisander claims: "I found their natures apt to mutinie/ From your too cruell usage; and made triall/ How farre they might be wrought on; to instruct you/ To looke with more preuention, and care/ To what they may hereafter undertake/ Upon the like occasions. The hurt's little/ They haue committed, nor was euer cure/ But with some paine effected" (5.3.220–27). Employing the language of therapy, Pisander explains the aim of the revolt along the lines of didactic tragicomedy. By directing a display of what the Syracusans' bondmen might do under controlled circumstances, Pisander both alerts the citizens to the internal danger besetting their state and prevents true calamity from befalling them. His tragicomedy is aimed at showing the ills that result from cruelty and thereby deterring such behavior in future.

The play raises several possible methods of responding to the revolution once the Praetor Archidamus and the other citizens of Syracuse have been restored to their places in the city. Four principal strategies emerge. The first two rely, from a Stoic perspective, excessively on emotional reactions to the situation, whether vengeful or compassionate. Indeed, as Martha Nussbaum has pointed out in *Upheavals of Thought*, a Stoic objection to the exercise of compassion rests on the ease with which this disposition can lapse into its opposite, revenge. The third and fourth mechanisms emphasize the recovery of the state and rely less on personal sentiment and more on the application of general political and legal principles, although ones that may be flexible enough to take into account the particularities of the individual case.

Leosthenes, spurred on by jealousy and joined by Timagoras, presents the most savage mechanism for dealing with the revolutionary episode, relying on the deployment of force. Having spied on a dialogue between Cleora and Pisander/ Marullo that they incorrectly interpret in a dishonorable light, Leosthenes and Timagoras attempt to kill Marullo and seize possession of Cleora. The scene unfolds as follows:

> *Timagoras.* The base villaine (Marullo)
> Shall neuer liue to heare it. *Enter Archidamus, Diphilus, and Officers.*
> *Cleora.* Murther, helpe,
> Through me you shall passe to him.
> *Archid.* What's the matter?
> On whom is your Sword drawne? are you a iudge?
> Or else ambitious of the hangmans office
> Before it be design'd you? you are bold too,

Unhand my daughter.

Leost. Shee's my valours prize.

Archid. With her consent, not otherwise. You may urge

Your title in the Court; if it proue good,

Possesse her freely: Guard him safely off too. (5.2.78–87)

Only the sudden arrival of Archidamus and the authorities thwarts Timagoras's attempt to kill Marullo and Leosthenes's effort to carry off Cleora without any public determination of the legitimacy of either the execution or the marriage. The play's judgment on this rash approach seems akin to that of Pisander/Marullo, who states, "Hee's more a slaue, then Fortune,/ Or Miserie can make me, that insults/ Upon unweapon'd Innocence" (4.4.59–61).

Similarly relying on sentiment, Cleora's solution adopts the extreme opposite to Timagoras's and Leosthenes's. After Pisander/Marullo's woes have been recounted to Cleora, she is viscerally moved to compassion and implores her father to treat him with mercy. Visiting the imprisoned Pisander/Marullo, who kneels before her, Cleora insists:

Cleora. Rise. I am flesh and blod,

And doe partake thy tortures.

Pisander. Can it bee?

That charity should perswade you to discend

So farre from your owne height, as to vouchsafe

To looke upon my sufferings? How I blesse

My fetters now, and stand ingag'd to Fortune

For my captiuity, no, my freedome rather!

For who dares thinke that place a Prison, which

You sanctifie with your presence? Or belieue,

Sorrow has power to use her sting on him,

That is in your compassion arm'd, and made

Impregnable? (5.2.9–19)

Cleora's response to Pisander/Marullo's suffering is one of identification, whereby she too experiences his misery through her charity and compassion. As a result of her sympathy with the bondman, Cleora advocates for him with Archidamus, requesting that the seeming order of Archidamus's own household on his return "moue you/ To pitty poor *Marullo*" (5.1.14–15).

Rather than adopting Cleora's compassion in its entirety, however, Archidamus replies with a more politically oriented account of how the polity should be restored. According to Archidamus, "'Tis my purpose/ To doe him [Marullo] all the good I can," to which Cleora responds, "But his offence being against the State,/ Must have a publique triall" (5.1.15–17). Just as Archidamus upheld the rule of law against the summary execution intended by Timagoras and Leosthenes, he insists that Pisander/Marullo himself must be judged in public rather than excused in private. Nor does Archidamus put himself in charge of the proceedings. Instead, Timoleon, having successfully led the Syracusan army, also administers justice within the state. A stranger to the city, he is better situated to render an impartial judgment when the internal conflict of civil strife is concerned.

Although Archidamus initially pleads with Timoleon to give Marullo an "aequall hearing" (5.3.10) despite his status as slave, this request comes to seem almost superfluous when Timoleon presents his conception of a just proceeding. Addressing the still disguised Marullo, Timoleon instructs, "Nor be thou daunter (howsoe're thy fortune,/ Has mark'd thee out a slaue) to speake thy merits;/ For vertue though in rags may challenge more,/ Then vice set off with all the trimme of greatnesse" (5.3.37–41). At this point, Pisander/Marullo himself acknowledges Timoleon's suitability for his position: "I had rather fall under so iust a iudge,/ Than be acquitted by a man corrupt/ And partiall in his censure" (5.3.42–44). From the beginning of the proceeding, however, indications abound that the justice of Timoleon's judgment will not exclude clemency. When Timoleon explains the order of the trials, in which "The right of this faire virgin first determin'd,/ Your Bond-men shall be censur'd" (5.3.29–30), Cleon quickly adds, "With all rigour,/ We doe expect" (5.3.30–31), but his wife, Corisca, insists, "Temper'd, I say, with mercie" (5.3.30). At the moment when Timoleon turns to judging the rebellious bondmen, he himself reiterates this conjunction, stating, "And though you haue giu'n me power, I doe intreate/ Such as haue undergone their insolence,/ It may not be offensiue though I studie/ Pitty more then reuenge" (5.3.234–37).[37] Timoleon's mode of judgment hence involves the equal public hearing of even seemingly unequal parties and the incorporation of clemency into the heart of judgment.

An alternative but similarly political solution is proposed by Pisander/ Marullo upon the return of the Syracusan army to the city; this outcome is never implemented, but could linger in the imagination of the audience as another mechanism for restoring civil order. Emphasizing freedom rather than simply

---

37. As this passage demonstrates, the text of *The Bondman* is not always precise in distinguishing between pity on the one hand and clemency on the other. Despite the conflation of terminology, however, one can trace the distinctions between the concepts through attention to the contexts in which the particular words are used. In this instance, for example, the kind of pity Timoleon employs resembles clemency more than compassion.

a return to a reformed version of the earlier system, Pisander's solution invokes the possibility of a "generall pardon" of the kind often provided by English kings on their coronation and sometimes passed by Parliament subsequently during a reign.[38] Hence Pisander demands

> A generall pardon, first, for all offences
> Committed in your absence. Libertie,
> To all such, as desire to make returne
> Into their countries; and to those that stay,
> A competence of land freely allotted
> To each mans proper use; no Lord acknowledg'd.
> Lastly, with your consent, to choose them wiues
> Out of your Families. (3.2.93–100)

According to this vision, the former bondmen would either be released from obligation to Syracuse or rendered citizens, endowed with the land and families that would make them equal with the existing members of the polity. The "generall pardon" requested would cover both all participants in the rebellion and all of their actions during the designated period rather than specifically singling out certain individuals or deeds for forgiveness or censure. The significance of the concessions that this version of transitional justice would require, however, and the severity of the societal reordering that it would ensure is demonstrated by Archidamus's response. As Archidamus replies, "*Carthage*, though victorious,/ Could not haue forc'd more from us" (3.2.100–101). The suggestion here is that civil strife could lead to an even more significant overturning of the structure of the polity than foreign conquest. The slave rebellion resulting from the mismanagement of domestic affairs might fundamentally alter the form of government to a greater degree than becoming part of the Carthaginian empire.

Although Pisander refrains from mentioning the possible reputational effects of this "generall pardon," the bondmen themselves prove concerned with the popular representation of their actions, a concern that implicates the dramatization furnished by Massinger's own play. Their invocation of metatheater resonates with

---

38. As Cynthia Herrup explains in "Negotiating Grace," which treats the relative dearth of parliamentary general pardons under James I and their complete absence under Charles I, the phrase "general pardon" could designate either "pardons of grace," which "originated in a sovereign's 'special grace,' 'certain knowledge' and 'will,'" or "parliamentary pardons," or "even any especially generous special pardon." Cynthia Herrup, "Negotiating Grace," in *Politics, Religion and Popularity in Early Stuart Britain: Essays in Honor of Conrad Russell*, ed. Thomas Cogswell, Richard Cust, and Peter Lake (Cambridge: Cambridge University Press, 2002), 127 and n. 10.

Pisander's third justification for the rebellion itself, that of displaying potential disaster to the citizens while simultaneously averting fatal consequences. When the slaves still believe that they will be condemned to death, Gracculo, as their spokesman, implores Timoleon only that "we may not twice be executed," meaning "at the Gallowes first, and after in a Ballad/ Sung to some villainous tune" (5.3.244, 245–46). Indeed, instead of having his revolutionary exploits recounted, Gracculo would like to be known as the one who encouraged the state to ban speaking about such things. As he continues, "Let the State take order/ For the redresse of this abuse, recording/ 'Twas done by my aduice, and for my part/ I'le cut as cleane a caper from the Ladder,/ As euer merry Greeke did" (5.3.252–56).

While hardly prescient enough to foresee the deployment of acts of oblivion during the Interregnum and on the restoration of King Charles II, Gracculo encourages a measure that would similarly erase the memory of the revolutionary activity even though, in his version, punishment rather than pardoning would furnish a prerequisite for such erasure. Were Massinger's own play more condemning of the bondmen, *The Bondman* itself could be taken to execute the rebels' character even though Timoleon pardoned their lives. The play, however, notably abstains from heaping abuse on the slaves of Syracuse and instead leaves open several possible interpretations of their actions, including one in which they are simply attempting to obtain a just equality among men.

The analogies between the plot of *The Bondman* and the example of the slaves who preserved their mistress in *Of Benefits* should now have become clearer. Like these slaves, Pisander/Marullo, amidst the tumult of the rebellion, ensured the preservation of Cleora's life and virtue. Whereas the slaves from *Of Benefits* adduced their mistress's cruelty as a pretended excuse for killing her, Massinger's bondmen can invoke the actual cruelty of their masters as a justification for their rebellion and their abuse of individuals like Corisca and Asotus during their brief ascendancy. The unnamed mistress in *Of Benefits* displays a gratitude like that of Cleora, unchecked by the fact that those preserving her life were individuals over whom she herself had previously possessed the power of life and death. Yet whereas manumission alone is the result of the service of the slaves in *Of Benefits*, Pisander actually succeeds in marrying Cleora at the end of *The Bondman*. The most significant difference between Seneca's example and Massinger's story consists in Pisander/Marullo's role in instigating the bondmen's rebellion, a role that renders him somewhat more implicated than his earlier counterparts in Cleora's temporary misfortunes. Nevertheless, his third reason for urging the bondmen on—that they would otherwise have undertaken similar actions at an even less propitious moment when Pisander/Marullo was not on hand to regulate their conduct—somewhat reduces the discrepancy between the two stories. If Seneca's slaves engaged in a ruse to protect their mistress, Pisander/Marullo's entanglement in the rebellion can be seen as an even more sophisticated feint ultimately designed to protect Syracuse from its self-inflicted ills.

The tragicomic conclusion of *The Bondman* also follows the model of Stoic clemency rather than falling into the cruelty of revenge, as Leosthenes's intended resolution of the action would have done. At the same time, the play avoids another possible version of tragicomedy—that which Cleora seems to propound. Although Cleora in many ways endorses Stoic principles, her quite visceral displays of fellow feeling for Pisander/Marullo controvert Seneca's claims about the importance of restraining oneself from feeling sorrow at the same time one is treating other men with clemency. In addition, because, as Archidamus points out, Cleora's pleas for mercy disregard the state's interest in Pisander/Marullo's crime, following her desired approach would lead to neglect of that very public sphere that Cleora herself had, at the commencement of the play, urged the Syracusans to consider. A tragicomedy in which mercy rather than justice dominated the scene would fail to fulfill the Stoic injunction to consider the general good of the state and its self-preservation rather than the particular plight of any one individual. Timoleon thus implements a form of justice that incorporates clemency within itself but does not fall prey to excessive pity.

At the same time, Pisander/Marullo's suggestion of a form of transitional justice—one ignored entirely by the conclusion of the play—likewise considers the good of the polity and simultaneously renders it more egalitarian. Given Stoic thought about the relationship between freedom and merit, and the necessary moral enslavement of all those subject to the passions, it might seem that the equality Pisander/Marullo espouses could be accomplished within Stoicism only if all individuals had demonstrated their virtue. Under this account, the bondmen's general drunkenness during the period of the rebellion would controvert their capacity to become equal members of the city once Syracuse was restored to order. Nevertheless, the possibility would remain that, if their virtue could be demonstrated, the bondmen might still achieve an equal position within the polity.

The first two suggested resolutions of the play—Leosthenes's and Cleora's—would both violate Stoic principles by involving an excess of emotional involvement, although Leosthenes emphasizes revenge and Cleora pity. The third and fourth potential endings—that advocated by Archidamus and the one suggested by Pisander/Marullo prior to the recapture of Syracuse—would both accord with Senecan Stoicism, but the fourth proves impracticable within the confines of the play's political reality. The outcome actually chosen integrates clemency into the state, representing the reconciliation of mercy with the rule of law, a reconciliation that bears a substantial resemblance to the incorporation of equity within the early modern English state.

From Sovereignty to the State

Taking its cue from Seneca's defense of monarchical rule in *De Clementia*—a defense based not in a theory of the ideal state but in the incapacity of the multitude to benefit from the political freedom of a republic—*The Bondman* thus focuses less on the form of government than on the mechanisms for maintaining peace and enhancing the general welfare. Suggesting the ills of both tyranny and the mob, Massinger's play stages the virtues of a particular kind of rule, one characterized by clemency and equity, as opposed to the regimes of either absolute mercy or cruelty. The alternative to this solution is presented not as another form of government but instead as the very undoing of the state through its descent into civil war. The centuries-long disagreement about the play's political meaning stems from misrecognition of the nature of its political intervention. Rather than siding with particular political figures of the time, or encouraging nascent republicanism, *The Bondman* suggests the mechanisms for avoiding civil conflict and the advantages of doing so. The seventeenth-century contexts of its reception can, furthermore, be read as responding to this dimension of the play.

We know from Sir Henry Herbert's records that *The Bondman* was performed in 1623 before then Prince Charles. As Herbert wrote on December 27, 1623, "Upon St. John's night, the prince only being there, The Bondman, by the queen [of Bohemia's] company [was performed]. Att Whitehall."[39] As we will see in chapter 5, once crowned, King Charles I was a vehement advocate for a particular device of transitional justice, the Act of Oblivion, which went beyond a general pardon to insist on erasing the memory of rebellious deeds. Pisander's recommendation of a general pardon accompanied by the grant of property rights, combined with the bondmen's own request that their deeds not be rehearsed in literary fashion, seems to presage the idea of oblivion.[40]

---

39. J. Q. Adams, *The Dramatic Records of Sir Henry Herbert, Master of the Revels, 1623–1673* (New Haven: Yale University Press, 1917), 51.

40. David Norbrook has suggested that, in fact, the Act of Oblivion did suppress awareness of the republican writers and lines of thought that characterized the period between 1627 and 1660. David Norbrook, *Writing the English Republic: Poetry, Rhetoric and Politics, 1627–1660* (Cambridge: Cambridge University Press, 2000), 1–22.

Only a little more than a year after the staging of *The Bondman*, a conception of oblivion entered into the Lord Keeper's speech to Parliament on behalf of King James, one associated with civil war among the Greeks. Responding to an invocation of earlier conflicts between Parliament and the king, the Lord Keeper insisted:

> *Lex oblivionis* is the best; let the Memory of these Abortions be buried in the River *Lethe*, never to be remembered. I will put you in Mind of a Story, which *Tully* relateth out of *Thucydides*: The *Thebans*, having overcome the *Lacedemonians*, in Memory thereof erected a Brazen Trophy, whereof a Complaint was made (*eo quod aeternum*) before the Common Council of the *Amphictyons*, that, by that Trophy, the Memory of their Discord was made eternal. And their Judgement was, That it should be demolished, because it was not fitting that any Record should be of Discord between *Greek* and *Greek*.[41]

Although the Lord Keeper's reference is to Cicero and Thucydides,[42] resonances also echo with the setting of *The Bondman*, and the support of Cyprus for Syracuse against the Carthaginians, as well as the play's suggestion that the bondmen's actions be forgotten. The passage likewise conjures the image of the monument to his own prowess that Cassilanes, the irate father in *The Laws of Candy*, objected to his son's erecting because it would demonstrate that son's greater honor in perpetuity. The appropriate resolution of civil conflict here is conceived to be erasure of the underlying events.

While *The Bondman* was performed during the Interregnum, on the eve of the Restoration, to stir republican sentiment, as Thomas Fulton has discussed,[43] it was also revived early and often on the restoration of King Charles II. In 1660, "one of the first plays acted was Massinger's *Bondman*, in which Thomas Betterton won high applause as Pisander. . . . The presumption is that *The Bondman* was performed a number of times during the summer and fall of 1660, but specific information is lacking."[44] *The Bondman* appears to have been Samuel Pepys's favorite play as well; not only did he see it on a number of occasions, but

---

41. Speech of the Lord Keeper, February 21, 1624, in *Journal of the House of Lords*, vol. 3, *1620–1628* (1767–1830), 210–13.

42. The particular story at issue derives from book 2 of Cicero's *De Inventione*.

43. Fulton, "'The True and Naturall Constitution,'" 152–53.

44. James G. McManaway, "Philip Massinger and the Restoration Drama," *ELH* 1, no. 3 (December 1934): 282.

also he claimed to have read the work and liked it more each time.[45] Pepys's affinity for Betterton can explain only part of his reaction, as it does not account for Pepys's eagerness to peruse the text as well as to see the play performed. Although any conclusions about the source of Pepys's and other Restoration theatergoers' interest in the play must remain speculative, *The Bondman*'s insistence on clemency may well have resonated with a public that had recently benefited from the Act of Oblivion passed by Parliament immediately upon Charles II's restoration.

Tragicomedy, Republicanism, and Reason of State

Several tragicomedies staged toward the end of King James's reign, shortly before his ill-fated son Charles's ascension to the throne, began to imagine revolution through representing forms of civil conflict. Refusing to place these imagined episodes within a framework of revenge and consequently wreaking retribution—as King James himself had insisted on doing with the Gunpowder Plot—these plays instead suggest that the occasion of the near dissolution of the state could furnish an opening for rethinking politics. Chapter 3 and the present chapter have focused on two such works in particular. Although other plays of the period—including parts of the extensive Beaumont and Fletcher canon and a number of Massinger's dramatic interventions—address similar issues, *The Laws of Candy* and *The Bondman* more vividly present the possibility of disaster and crystallize how variants on pardoning could contribute to reformulating the state. *The Laws of Candy* responds to the prospect of the polity's demise by constructing it anew not through a sovereign act of authority but instead through connections built laterally between citizens and predicated on interpersonal forgiveness, a form of forgiveness for which the law of Crete itself furnishes an opening. *The Bondman* presents a slave rebellion as an opportunity for placing at the heart of the state a Stoic conception of clemency that emphasizes the general welfare over particular factions or individual interests.

At the same time that they conjure up an increasingly tangible threat of revolution and suggest mechanisms for averting or responding to it, these plays modify the form of tragicomedy, moving away from the kind of theaters of pardoning exemplified by *Measure for Measure*. In Shakespeare's play, as we saw in chapter 1, a series of final pardons both secured the applicability of the laws going

---

45. Martin Garrett, ed., *Massinger: The Critical Heritage* (London: Routledge, 1991), 11–12, 77–80.

forward and reaffirmed the Duke's sovereignty. In *The Laws of Candy*, official pardons are put to one side, and the interpersonal forgiveness of one individual by another replaces the sovereign display of majesty that accompanied Duke Vincentio's exercise of the pardon power. Influenced by Seneca's *De Clementia*, *The Bondman* too refuses to stage the conventional tragicomic pardon, but for different reasons. Insisting on clemency without concomitant sympathy, *The Bondman* depicts a version of mercy that retains profound respect for the laws; clemency is exercised to preserve the well-being of the state as a whole and spares only those who may still be redeemed or whose motives an equitable approach might regard as permissible. In each case, the final pardons that characterize many earlier tragicomedies are transmuted. Rather than assuming a political form in the first place, pardoning is shifted into the ethical register of forgiveness or clemency; although ethical acts or states, however, forgiveness and clemency turn out, in the two plays, to possess profound implications for politics.

In the course of constructing political representations and modifying tragicomic conventions of genre, *The Laws of Candy* and *The Bondman* cover other common ground. Both return to Greece, and to ancient philosophy—rather than to ancient drama, like *Measure for Measure*—for political insight. Each alludes to the disastrous consequences of civil war, represented by the conflict between Greek and Greek, although *The Bondman* emphasizes more than *The Laws of Candy* the possibility of another form of internal strife, that between citizens and subordinated outsiders. The two plays likewise see in the foreigner not simply a threat but rather the potential salvation of the commonwealth. Both also emphasize the extent to which economic problems, whether excessive indebtedness or distributional inequality, can contribute to the polity's demise. And each is derived to some degree from Seneca the Elder's *Controversiae*, part of the rhetorical influence that Neil Rhodes has deemed central to what has been called the Shakespearean "problem play"—including *Measure for Measure* and *The Merchant of Venice*—and that lent the genre its moral ambiguity.[46]

Some of these resemblances between the plays are linked with the republicanism that had been circulating at least in a subterranean fashion since the

---

46. Neil Rhodes, "The Controversial Plot: Declamation and the Concept of the Problem Play," *Modern Language Review* 95, no. 3 (July 2000): 609–22. Eugene Waith explored the significance of the *controversiae* to Massinger in particular, explaining how the form of the declamation changed "when political freedom came to an end in Augustan Rome" and "all pretense of verisimilitude was dropped, and the popular cases took off from imaginary laws and fantastic complications." Eugene Waith, "Controversia in the English Drama: Medwall and Massinger," *PMLA* 68, no. 1 (March 1953): 288. The fantastic quality of the laws forming the subjects of the *controversiae* lent them particular suitability for dramatic reinterpretation.

Elizabethan period. As Markku Peltonen and David Norbrook have convincingly shown, the conventional view that the vocabulary of republicanism emerged only during the 1650s is flawed; instead, republican themes continued to be played in the background during the late sixteenth and early seventeenth centuries. These were often associated with the classical humanist tradition, including ancient works of philosophy and history.[47] Thomas Hobbes even partly attributed the English Revolution to the republicanism arising from improvident reading of these kinds of materials. As he wrote in *Leviathan*, "As to Rebellion in particular against Monarchy; one of the most frequent causes of it, is the Reading of the books of Policy, and Histories of the antient Greeks, and Romans."[48] In addition to sharing a set of references similar to those of the plays discussed in this chapter, early seventeenth-century republicanism touched upon similar motifs, including the qualities of the virtuous citizen, the "benefits of the *vita activa*," and the dangers of corruption within the commonwealth.[49]

Nevertheless, republicanism is not the only note struck by these plays. As Peltonen himself acknowledges, within the Jacobean period, "several English writers were also disposed to come to terms with the new arguments of reason of state,"[50] arguments that emphasized the role of necessity in politics and the distinctions between individual and political morality. Addressing the Italian scene, Maurizio Viroli has shown how, by the end of the sixteenth century, "the language of politics as civil philosophy gave way gradually to the conception of politics as reason of state," emphasizing "the art of preserving a man or group's power."[51] Although Giovanni Botero's *Della ragion di stato* only explicitly outlined the theory of reason of state in 1589, over a decade later than Bodin's *Six*

---

47. Markku Peltonen, *Classical Humanism and Republicanism in English Political Thought, 1570–1640* (Cambridge: Cambridge University Press, 1995), 2, 7; Norbrook, *Writing the English Republic*, 1–139.

48. Thomas Hobbes, *Leviathan*, ed. Richard Tuck (Cambridge: Cambridge University Press, 1991), 225–26.

49. Peltonen, *Classical Humanism*, 15, 20.

50. Peltonen, *Classical Humanism*, 156.

51. Maurizio Viroli, *From Politics to Reason of State: The Acquisition and Transformation of the Language of Politics, 1250–1600* (Cambridge: Cambridge University Press, 1992), 238. According to Giovanni Botero's early definition:

> State is a stable rule over a people and Reason of State is the knowledge of the means by which such a dominion may be founded, preserved and extended. Yet, although in the widest sense the term includes all these, it is concerned most nearly with preservation, and more nearly with extension than with foundation; for Reason of State assumes a ruler and a State (the one as artificer, the other as his material) whereas they are not assumed— indeed they are preceded—by foundation entirely and in part by extension. But the art of foundation and of extension is the same because the beginnings and the continuations are of the same nature. And although all that is done to these purposes is said to be done

Livres de la République, Bodin's work exerted a considerable influence on Botero, and some have seen Bodin's conception of sovereignty as isomorphic with reason of state itself.[52] By incorporating some of Bodin's logic into his techniques of rule, James I thereby introduced an element of reason of state into English politics, an element that combined in sometimes surprising ways with the components of republicanism.

Neither *The Laws of Candy* nor *The Bondman* presents an undiluted republicanism, but instead both take up the challenges reason of state attempted to address—challenges that had become more fully theorized in England during James's reign—from within the classical humanist tradition. In particular, they take seriously the problem that the reason of state tradition poses about the relationship between individual and political morality, but they attempt to solve that problem in a manner that sidesteps the tradition through recourse to ancient philosophy. As Carl Friedrich put the issue poignantly in his classic work *Constitutional Reason of State: The Survival of the Constitutional Order*:

> Only when there is a clash between the commands of an individual ethic of high normativity and the needs and requirements of organizations whose security and survival is at stake can the issue of reason of state become real. For reason of state is nothing but the doctrine that whatever is required to insure the survival of the state must be done by the individuals responsible for it, no matter how repugnant such an act may be to them in their private capacity as decent and moral men.[53]

Rather than accepting the inevitability of the disjunction between individual and political morality at the moment when the state is threatened, *The Laws of Candy* and *The Bondman* instead envision a means for restoring the state that emphasizes an ethical basis for political participation. In *The Laws of Candy*, individual forgiveness furnishes a prerequisite for preserving the polity, whereas in *The*

---

for Reasons of State, yet this is said rather of such actions as cannot be considered in the light of ordinary reason.

Giovanni Botero, *The Reason of State*, trans. P. J. Waley and D. P. Waley (London: Routledge, 1956), 3. Preservation of the state rather than its foundation hence becomes the preoccupation of reason of state.

52. For example, Harvey Mansfield remarks that Bodin's "sovereignty was little different in effect from what came to be called, soon after Bodin, reason of state." Harvey Mansfield, *Taming the Prince: The Ambivalence of Modern Executive Power* (Baltimore: Johns Hopkins University Press, 1993), 158. See also Botero, *The Reason of State*, ix.

53. Carl Friedrich, *Constitutional Reason of State: The Survival of the Constitutional Order* (Providence: Brown University Press, 1957), 4–5.

Bondman, the Stoic character trait of clemency must accompany the proper exercise of rule. Despite deploying some of the more conventional tropes of republicanism, these plays represent an innovation within the tradition in that they take seriously the issues that reason of state theories had recently brought to the fore.

Furthermore, the historical moment of both plays, written and first performed late in James's reign, occasioned new reasons for political anxiety. Debates have long raged among historians about the extent to which early Stuart constitutional disputes provided a prelude to the Civil War, or whether the causes of the mid-century Revolution were more immediate.[54] Although no consensus has been reached on the issue, at least some have again returned to James's reign for indications of brewing unrest.[55] James's conflicts with the common law judges had come to a head in 1616 with the removal of Sir Edward Coke, and James failed to call a Parliament between 1614 and 1621. When Parliament again found itself in session, harmony did not ensue; the 1621 Parliament had a disastrous ending, involving an ill-fated petition to the king asking for war with Spain and a Protestant marriage for Charles and was analyzed by one commentator as "a study in constitutional conflict."[56] Without adopting the overly teleological trajectory of Whig history, it is possible to diagnose in these Jacobean events a cause for anxieties about civil conflict sufficient to spawn dramatic stagings of a revolutionary threat.

While responding to the surrounding political climate and to the various domestic and international tensions of the late Jacobean period, including the

---

54. Peter Gaunt offers a useful account of the various historiographic traditions in the prefatory material to part two of Peter Gaunt, ed., *The English Civil War: The Essential Readings* (Oxford: Blackwell, 2000), 34–58. As he discusses, the Whig accounts of S. R. Gardiner and C. H. Firth insisted on interpreting the Civil War as one stage of a long transition toward freedom within the English tradition. Hence, "for many Whig historians, England embarked on the high road to civil war in the early seventeenth century, with the political and constitutional clashes between James I and his parliaments, a conflict which intensified under his successor and eventually led to breakdown and war." Gaunt, *The English Civil War*, 36. Revisionist historians like Conrad Russell instead deemed these conflicts of a more minor variety, including between local interests and governmental policy; as Mark Kennedy has put it, "One of the hallmarks of revisionism has been its emphasis on the immediate context of events and a corresponding lack of interest in long-term developments." Gaunt, *The English Civil War*, 43. The revisionist account itself has, of course, met with counter-resistance, and a number of historians have argued that the 1620s were riven by deep divisions, including Thomas Cogswell, *The Blessed Revolution: English Politics and the Coming of War, 1621–4* (Cambridge: Cambridge University Press, 1989); and Michael Young, "Buckingham, War and Parliament: Revisionism Gone Too Far," *Parliamentary History* 4 (1985): 45–69. See Gaunt, *The English Civil War*, 42.

55. Gaunt, *The English Civil War*, 49.

56. Robert Zaller, *The Parliament of 1621: A Study in Constitutional Conflict* (Berkeley: University of California Press, 1971).

conflicts between king and Parliament, the plays considered here venture beyond simply indicating practical responses to the rising prospect of civil war. They rather take advantage of the chance provided by such a prospect to imagine modes of political relation transcending even those that would be realized by the English Revolution. Hence *The Laws of Candy* examines how forgiveness might work in the service of democracy in a manner that augurs not Oliver Cromwell but rather Hannah Arendt, and *The Bondman* raises—but does not fulfill—the possibility of a general pardon for slaves that would also allow for their economic and political integration into the community, a general pardon that foreshadows not only the Act of Oblivion that Parliament passed on the Restoration at the urging of King Charles II but also an as yet unachieved society of greater economic as well as status equality.

These tragicomedies participate in the seventeenth-century transformation of the pardon power from a monarchical gift to a legislative act by conjuring up increasingly revolutionary forms of violence and proposing solutions to restore the peace. At the same time, however, they do not simply embody a stage within the evolution of the pardon power. While the plays may point partly in the direction of Kant and Schmitt, they nevertheless furnish a set of alternative visions of political community, providing untapped alternatives to both liberal constitutionalism and the sovereign exception.

5

BETWEEN ROYAL PARDONS AND ACTS OF OBLIVION /
The Transitional Justice of Cosmo Manuche and James Compton, Earl of Northampton

Theaters of pardoning continued to be composed and performed during the 1630s and somewhat more sparsely in the 1640s. Following the closure of the theaters in 1642, fewer such works appeared until the aftermath of King Charles I's trial and execution in 1649. The 1650s witnessed the writing and circulation of several new installments in the theater of pardoning as well as the first publication of a number of earlier examples (Appendix A). While these were, like most tragicomedies of the Interregnum, royalist in bent, they tended, as Susan Wiseman has claimed of Protectorate tragicomedy generally, to furnish "a complex discursive space for debate within inevitably compromised royalisms against the unresolved context of the Commonwealth and Protectorate."[1] The effort to grapple with the contemporary scene from a royalist perspective led, on the one hand, to the imaginative reinvigoration of a sovereign pardon along the lines of *Measure for Measure* and, on the other, to attempts to consider the appropriate treatment of subordinates within the state as a matter of what would now be called transitional justice.[2]

---

1. Susan Wiseman, *Drama and Politics in the English Civil War* (Cambridge: Cambridge University Press, 1998), 190.

2. Although "transitional justice" is a phrase of recent origin, the concept has been used to speak about a number of historical episodes, from the Athenian amnesty of the fifth century BC onward. As Jon Elster has defined transitional justice, it involves "political decisions made in the immediate aftermath of [a regime] transition and directed towards individuals on the basis of what they did or what was done to them under the earlier regime." Jon Elster, "Coming to Terms with the Past: A Framework for the Study of Justice in the Transition to Democracy," *European Journal of Sociology* 29, no. 1 (May 1998): 14. He describes in more detail a number of the historical moments of transitional justice in *Closing the Books: Transitional Justice in Historical Perspective* (Cambridge: Cambridge University Press, 2004). Applying the concept within seventeenth-century England, David Dyzenhaus has argued that "Thomas Hobbes's *Leviathan* is a theory of transitional justice," asserting that "*Leviathan*, in my view, contains both significant instruction about how to achieve civic peace in the face of deep

This chapter focuses on the writings of two figures closely linked within this moment, the playwright Cosmo Manuche, an Italian of obscure background who used the designation "Major," perhaps signaling armed involvement in the royalist cause, and his patron, James Compton, the third Earl of Northampton, who also composed some dramatic works.[3] Although Manuche may have received compensation from Cromwell for spying in 1656, both Compton and Manuche largely remained loyal to Charles I's son, the exiled King Charles II; indeed, as Luke Beattie has observed, there may have been "no . . . major Royalist conspirator [other than Compton] writing plays concurrently with plotting."[4] A number of their writings remain in manuscript, including in a substantial collection rediscovered in 1977 at the library of Castle Ashby, the ancestral home of Compton's descendants.[5]

These materials include a tract titled "The Martird Monarch," completed shortly after Charles I's execution, and a couple of pages that Luke Beattie has dubbed a "Political Treatise" and situated between 1651 and 1652, both in James Compton's hand.[6] The brief and incomplete "Treatise," transcribed for the first time in Appendix B, tackles the problems of transitional justice posed by the English Revolution and the establishment of a new government and, in doing so, advocates for "an act of indemnitie, or of oblivion stille it what you please," a form of immunization from and forgetting of punishment that King Charles I himself had advocated.

Manuche's plays *The Just General*, from 1652, and *The Banish'd Shepherdess*, still in manuscript and dating from 1659 or 1660, demonstrate a similar concern for transitional justice; both depict worlds in which sovereignty is fragile, treachery is rife, and there remain questions about how to manage those who have been disloyal to the prior regime, either within the intermediate world of the play or once a restoration has occurred. At the same time, *The Just General* insists on maintaining the link between pardoning and royal sovereignty, although the

---

ideological division and an account of how to construct political and legal institutions in order to maintain that peace." David Dyzenhaus, "*Leviathan* as a Theory of Transitional Justice," in *NOMOS LI: Transitional Justice*, ed. Melissa S. Williams, Rosemary Nagy, and Jon Elster (New York: NYU Press, 2012), 180.

3. Dale Randall, *Winter Fruit: English Drama, 1642–1660* (Lexington: University Press of Kentucky, 1995), 346–47.

4. Luke Beattie, "Theatrical Potential in the Cavalier Plays of James Compton, Third Earl of Northampton," *Studies in Theatre and Performance*, 33, no. 1 (January 2014): 97.

5. For a comprehensive account of the Castle Ashby manuscripts and a discussion of their authorship, see Luke Beattie, "How Were the Anonymous Castle Ashby Play Manuscripts Created, and Why?" (Ph.D. diss., University of Exeter, 2011).

6. Beattie, "Castle Ashby Play Manuscripts," 129–30. The "Treatise" is available in manuscript at the British Library, BL MSADD60282.

pardon itself becomes unstable since grounded in the friable rock of the king's majesty.

These theaters of pardoning reveal the marks of their composition in a world where revolution has not just been figured and narrowly averted but where the state has instead already been overturned. *The Just General* and *The Banish'd Shepherdess* are concerned with members of the populace who are certainly not upright, and may be easily misled, but could also be reintegrated into the new state in a fairly straightforward fashion. Compton's "Treatise" contemplates an act of oblivion as the mechanism by which to accomplish this task, and, in doing so, articulates the virtues of such a device of transitional justice. In the remainder of this chapter, I first examine his treatment of oblivion in conjunction with the contexts for oblivion's historical emergence in domestic and international law, then turn to an analysis of Manuche's plays.

Genealogies of Oblivion

In mid-seventeenth-century England, the language of oblivion seemingly sprang from nowhere to become a prominent element of political discourse; it enjoyed a brief efflorescence through the late eighteenth century then rapidly disappeared as suddenly as it had emerged, giving way to the related and sometimes linked concept of amnesty. An investigation of the roots of the notion establishes four principal genealogies, several of which intersect. First, oblivion clauses entered modern treaty practice with the Treaty of Westphalia in 1648; some medieval treaties contained similar language and concepts, which scholars of international law have traced, but oblivion became a standard and routinized component only with the peace agreements of Osnabrück and Münster. Second, a reception of classical sources, including both accounts of the Athenian amnesty of 403 BC and—as Jessica Wolfe has demonstrated—Homer's *Odyssey*, brought to the fore the potential for the use of forgetting as a technique of recovery from conflict. Third, a set of sixteenth-century French edicts emerging out of the Wars of Religion and culminating in the 1598 Edict of Nantes generated substantial commentary lauding forgetting as a strategy for overcoming civil conflict. Finally, and probably most relevant to the political deployment of oblivion in mid-seventeenth-century England, Mary, Queen of Scots, King James I's mother, had passed an Act of Oblivion shortly after the conclusion of the Siege of Leith as an alternative to the Treaty of Edinburgh, which also contained a provision for oblivion, and which she refused to ratify. In this instance, the Act of Oblivion emanated from a similar treaty provision but furnished a precedent for Mary's descendants to deploy.

Heinhard Steiger has described the efflorescence of clauses of oblivion linked with amnesty in both the practice and theory of international law, explaining:

> Emer de Vattel (1714–67) and Immanuel Kant (1724–1804) had argued that amnesty was a necessary element in a peace agreement. The classic amnesty clause was linked with general oblivion. It dealt with damages, additional losses, etc., during the war, whoever the perpetrators were, the army or others, for whom the parties were responsible. . . . Peace came down to a new beginning. Old debts should not burden peace. Criminal proceedings were also excluded. Initially, this also meant reciprocal forgiveness. However, this aspect became obsolete as references to the question of responsibility for the war or for what happened during the war disappeared. . . . In the period considered here [after the Paris Peace Treaty of November 20, 1815], the general amnesty clauses disappeared from European peace treaties.[7]

Several accounts of the history of amnesty and oblivion in treaty provisions do not support the use of the actual term "oblivion" or its Latin equivalent *oblivio* within early medieval practice until the fourteenth century. A few annalists' accounts of treaties, however, refer to amnesty or oblivion in describing particular accords. Hence Norbert Ohler notes Otto von St. Blasien's account of a peace agreement in 1186 between the emperor Frederick and King William of Sicily, which describes an "amnestia, id est malorum oblivio . . . in eternum mansura."[8] Jörg Fisch, in his comprehensive *Krieg und Frieden im Friedensvertrag*, likewise observes that the Annals of Fulda represents that, in the Treaty of Tusey, "the King, who is the one who has been harmed, releases everything that was done between them (*dimittunt*), and also gives up what remains in memory (*cuncta recto oblivioni tradenda censentes*)."[9] Explaining that "this transformation is particularly surprising because otherwise at that time oblivion is not connected with treaties," Fisch posits that "one should conclude that the act of oblivion succeeded outside of the treaty mechanism, probably only orally."[10]

---

7. Heinhard Steiger, "Peace Treaties from Paris to Versailles," in *Peace Treaties and International Law in European History from the Late Middle Ages to World War One*, ed. Randall Lesaffer (Cambridge: Cambridge University Press, 2004): 84.

8. Norbert Ohler, "Krieg und Frieden am Ausgang des Mittelalters," in *Krieg und Frieden im Übergang vom Mittelalter zur Neuzeit* (Mainz: Philipp Von Zabern, 2000): 7; *Die Chronik des Otto von St. Blasien*, ed. Horst Kohl (Leipzig: Franz Dunder, 1881), 42.

9. Jörg Fisch, *Krieg und Frieden im Friedensvertrag* (Stuttgart: Klett-Cotta, 1979), 75.

10. Fisch, *Krieg und Frieden*, 75.

In the later Middle Ages, according to Fisch, the language of forgetting continues to be sparsely deployed, although it becomes somewhat more frequent in the fourteenth and especially the fifteenth centuries. Still, "the Latin noun *oblivio* is lacking" and "*amnestie* arises only once" in a translation of a 1348 treaty. Terms referring to the parties' putting behind them the memory of what is past diminish pronouncedly during the early part of the sixteenth century but then flourish from the mid-sixteenth century onward and become prominent in the early seventeenth century. Perhaps the earliest actual use of "oubly et amnestie," or "oblivion and amnesty," occurs in a treaty between the British and Dutch East India companies from 1619, a treaty derived from negotiations that King James I had pressed.[11] The first article of the treaty contains this language, according to Jean Dumont's *Corps Universel Diplomatique des Gens*; a contemporaneous English version refers to "forgetting and utter extinguishment."[12] King James's involvement in the treaty was possibly not a coincidence; as discussed later in this chapter, from the reign of his mother in Scotland, the Stuarts seem to have pressed for policies of oblivion. More broadly, Randall Lesaffer intriguingly connects the rise in provisions for forgetting in the sixteenth century with "the emergence of sovereign princes," which rendered obsolete the concept of just war, which had brought with it the assumption that "in a subsequent peace treaty, the responsibility for the war should be attributed to one of the treaty partners and a punishment should be imposed upon the unjust belligerent."[13]

In 1648, the Treaty of Westphalia, concluding the Thirty Years' War, prominently featured forgetting and oblivion—as well as amnesty—of whatever had been done since the commencement of hostilities.[14] With this agreement, an

---

11. *Calendar of State Papers, Domestic Series, of the Reign of James I: 1619–1623*, ed. Mary Anne Everett Green (London: Longman, Brown, 1858), 1 (January 8, 1619).

12. Fisch, *Krieg und Frieden*, 79, 93, 94.

13. Randall Lesaffer, "From Lodi to Westphalia," in *Peace Treaties and International Law in European History from the Late Middle Ages to World War One* (Cambridge: Cambridge University Press, 2004), 39.

14. The relevant section of the treaty states:

> That there shall be on the one side and the other a perpetual Oblivion, Amnesty, or Pardon of all that has been committed since the beginning of these Troubles, in what place, or what manner soever the Hostilitys have been practis'd, in such a manner, that no body, under any pretext whatsoever, shall practice any Acts of Hostility, entertain any Enmity, or cause any Trouble to each other; neither as to Persons, Effects and Securitys, neither of themselves or by others, neither privately nor openly, neither directly nor indirectly, neither under the colour of Right, nor by the way of Deed, either within or without the extent of the Empire, notwithstanding all Covenants made before to the contrary: That they shall not act, or permit to be acted, any wrong or injury to any whatsoever; but that all that has pass'd on the one side, and the other, as well before as during the War, in Words,

amnesty clause became a requisite component of international peace treaties and a subject of scholarly reflection by international lawyers.[15] Hence the German legal scholar Henricus Cocceius published a treatise in 1691 that deals extensively with amnesty, distinguishing between simple amnesties and those that also specified some form of restitution.[16] In this work, Cocceius also refers to ancient examples of amnesty, such as the Athenian amnesty of 403, in the wake of the restoration of democracy following the reign of the thirty tyrants after the Peloponnesian War.[17]

In addition to the possible influence of this Athenian precedent on early modern England—for which there is little direct evidence—the Homeric conception of *lêthê*, given as the Greek equivalent of "oblivion" in *Polyanthea Nova*, furnished an important conceptual frame from Erasmus onward, as Jessica Wolfe has demonstrated. Explaining that *lêthê* functions as a "salve for conflict" in the *Odyssey*, Wolfe traces Erasmus's debt to the Homeric vision of *lêthê* in his *Adages*, where he "identifies oblivion as a specifically Homeric antidote to conflict: both *Ne malorum memineris* [remember no wrongs] and *Malorum oblivio* [forgetting wrongs] cite lines from the *Iliad* that address the crucial role of forgetting as a means of establishing peace."[18] Philosopher Thomas Hobbes's translations of Homer late in his life likewise serve to connect the Homeric notion of *lêthê* with political forms of oblivion, as Wolfe also observes, commenting that in his "rearrangement of the *Odyssey*'s final lines" to state "And thus it was agreed that War should cease," Hobbes "confirms one of the central aims of his own political philosophy: the establishment of a covenant that ensures peace and harmony. The line thus comes to affirm his own hope for a 'pacified post–Civil War English society' achieved through an Act of Oblivion that resembles the truce established by Homer's Athena."[19]

In France, as noted earlier, responses to the Wars of Religion increasingly invoked forgetting during the later part of the sixteenth century, culminating in

---

Writings, and Outrageous Actions, in Violences, Hostilitys, Damages and Expences, without any respect to Persons or Things, shall be entirely abolish'd in such a manner that all that might be demanded of, or pretended to, by each other on that behalf, shall be bury'd in eternal Oblivion.

Treaty of Westphalia, accessed December 20, 2018, http://avalon.law.yale.edu/17th_century/westphal.asp.

15. Fisch, *Krieg und Frieden*, 96.

16. Henricus Cojjeius, *Disputatio Juris Gentium, de Postliminio in Pace, et Amnestia* (Frankfurt: Christopher Zeitler, 1691), 42–72.

17. Cojjeius, *Disputatio Juris Gentium*, 44.

18. Jessica Wolfe, *Homer and the Question of Strife from Erasmus to Hobbes* (Toronto: University of Toronto Press, 2015), 101.

19. Wolfe, *Homer*, 381.

the 1598 Edict of Nantes. As Andrea Frisch has elaborated in *Forgetting Differences*, theological divisions over the analogy between divine and sovereign forgiveness as well as resistance to the use of pardons as objects of exchange helped contribute to the replacement of pardoning by oblivion. Frisch's discussion of the significance of an increasing emphasis on oblivion for transformations in sovereignty in sixteenth-century France resonates with my argument in this book. As Frisch explains the effect of forgetting on royal sovereignty: "Unlike royal pardon . . ., which locate[s] political agency in the sovereign, the policy of *oubliance* places the burden of reconciliation on French subjects. The rejection of pardon underlines the fact that the law of oblivion was not merely a command on the part of the king to be followed by the people; it was a law to which the king himself was subject."[20] Although these efforts at forgetting spawned significant commentary, including the jurist Antoine Loisel's *De l'amnestie ou oubliance des maux* (1582), clear paths have not yet been established along which the idea of oblivion would have been transmitted from France to England.

More directly relevant to the context of early and mid-seventeenth-century England was the Act of Oblivion passed in 1563 by the ninth Parliament of Mary, Queen of Scots. This law arose out of the Reformation-related struggles among England, Scotland, and France, and represented an alternative to signing the Treaty of Edinburgh, which Mary—to the displeasure of Queen Elizabeth, whom the treaty recognized as the rightful sovereign of England— refused to do. The Act of Oblivion mandated, among other things, that "all deede . . . contrair the Lawes of this Realme" from March 6, 1550, until September 1, 1660,

> and the memorie therof with all actiones civill or criminall, that may result therethrow . . . be expired, buryed and extinct for ever: even as the same had never bene maid, done, counseled, thoucht, pretended, nor assisted to, swa that they, nor their aires, nor successoures may be indicted, persewed, summoned, accused, followed, or convened therefore civilie or criminallie, before her Hieness, or her Graces Successoures, nor three Estaites of Paliament, nor other Judge or judges criminall or Civill, Spirituall or Temporall quhat-sum-ever.[21]

---

20. Andrea Frisch, *Forgetting Differences: Tragedy, Historiography, and the French Wars of Religion* (Edinburgh: Edinburgh University Press, 2015), 41.

21. "The Act of Oblivioun" (June 4, 1563), in *The Acts of the Parliaments of Scotland*, ed. Thomas Thomson and Cosmo Innes, 2:535–36.

While requiring the legal and political expungement of the events leading up to the Treaty of Edinburgh, the Act of Oblivion managed to reassert Mary's sovereignty at the same time as permitting her to maintain silence on the question of who should succeed to the English crown.

It is perhaps not surprising, then, that Mary's grandson King Charles I of England would attempt to revive the politics of oblivion—although unsuccessfully in his case. Charles had begun to press such legislation in relation to the first Bishop's War with the Scots in 1639. This gesture would have followed the disarmament of the Scots and been accompanied by Charles's own participation in the Scots Parliament. Although the Scots agreed to cease their rebellion, when the subject of the Act of Oblivion arose in the Parliament, they resisted it and instead wished "to justifie themselves, and all their former proceedings, and urge an act of *Iustification* to be recorded in Parliament."[22] Following resumption of hostilities, the Scots (joined by the English Parliament) did eventually accept—and even solicit—another Act of Oblivion, one effect of which was to prevent Charles I from even mentioning it when responding to subsequent charges from Parliament.[23]

A number of subsequent assays at and failures to achieve acts of oblivion followed during the remainder of Charles I's reign. As a rule, the king would propose such an enactment, and parliamentary forces would express opposition to pardoning those who were in league with Charles himself or were already under parliamentary investigation.[24] The response that King Charles framed to

---

22. William Sanderson, *A Compleat History of the Life and Raigne of King Charles from His Cradle to His Grave* (London: Humphrey Moseley, 1658), 252, 254.

23. William Sanderson, in his history of Charles I's reign, reported the king's remarks: "As for the *Scots* Troubles, these unhappy Differences are wrapt up in perpetual silence by the Act of Oblivion passed in Parliaments of both Kingdoms, which stays him from any further Reply to revive the memory of these evils." Sanderson, *A Compleat History*, 503.

24. Sanderson's account demonstrates this dynamic. In 1644 King Charles declared that "for the total removing of all Fears and Iealousies, his Majestie is willing to agree, that upon the conclusion of Peace, there shall be a general Act of Oblivion and free Pardon past by Act of Parliament in both his Kingdoms respectively." Sanderson, *A Compleat History,* 857–58. Parliament then demanded in 1646 that certain people be excepted from the peace and from any Act of Oblivion. Parliament insisted "that these persons shall expect no pardon. In a word all the persons of Honour and Quality that have taken up Arms for the King in *England* or *Scotland*, (which because the Treaty took no effect is but frivolous to insert.) And all such others as being processed by the Estates for Treason shall be condemned before the Act of Oblivion be passed," and, furthermore, "that all Iudges, Officers, and Practicers of the Law, that have deserted the Parliament, be incapable of Office or Practice in the Law." Sanderson, *A Compleat History,* 917.

Charles again suggested the possibility of an Act of Oblivion in 1647, observing that "the Army (for the rest though necessary, yet I suppose are not difficult to content) ought (in my judgment) to enjoy the liberty of their consciences, have an Act of Oblivion or Indempnity (which should

one iteration of this objection summarized his general posture on the subject, which insisted upon both loyalty to his adherents and oblivion as a means of achieving a more lasting peace:

> This he [Charles I] well knoweth, That a general Act of Oblivion is the best bond of Peace; and that after intestine troubles, the wisdom of this and other Kingdoms hath usually and happily in all Ages granted general Pardons, whereby the numerous discontentments of Persons and Families otherwise exposed to ruin, might not become fuel to new disorders, or seeds to future troubles. His Majesty therefore desires, that his two Houses of Parliament would seriously descend into these considerations, and likewise tenderly look upon his condition herein, and the perpetual dishonour that must cleave to him, if he shall thus abandon so many persons of Condition and Fortune that have engaged themselves with and for him, out of a sense of duty, and propounds as a very acceptable testimony of their affection to him, that a general Act of Oblivion and free Pardon be forthwith passed by Act of Parliament.[25]

Although the Interregnum Parliament would eventually, after some delay, take this politic advice and pass a general pardon of its own, Charles's plea, when made, fell upon deaf ears, and he never received the advantage of such an act.[26]

The successive rejections of Charles's offers of and requests for oblivion did not, however, cause him to abandon belief in the power of pardoning, even beyond his own death. In his final letter to his already exiled son, Charles instructed the latter to follow his own course in preferring clemency and oblivion to revenge, for both religious and political reasons:

> Let then no passion betray you to any study of revenge upon those, whose own sin and folly will sufficiently punish them in due time. But as soon as the forked Arrow of Factions Emulations is drawn out, use

---

extend to all the rest of my Subjects)." Sanderson, *A Compleat History*, 1048. In 1648 he likewise urged "*that an Act of Amnestie or Oblivion be passed, the very means of all traverses which happened in the heat of War may be utterly deleted.* This Demand they liked not, but with cautely and limitations, by the benefit whereof the Parliament might persecute many of the Royallists." Sanderson, *A Compleat History*, 1096.

25. Sanderson, *A Compleat History*, 983–84.

26. Oliver Cromwell, "An Act of General Pardon and Oblivion," February 24, 1651 (London: John Field, 1651). The parliamentary pardon is discussed in *The Cavaliers Jubilee: Or, Long Look'd for Come at Last: viz. The Generall Pardon* (London: William Ley, 1652). The subtitle, "Long Look'd for Come at Last," indicates even the Interregnum Parliament's reluctance to pass a general pardon and the resultant delay.

all Princely Arts and Clemency to heal the Wounds; that the smart of the cure may not equall the anguish of the Hurt. I have offered Acts of Indemnity and Oblivion, to so great a Latitude, as may include all, that can but suspect themselves to be any way obnoxious to the Laws; and which might serve to exclude all future jealousies and insecurities. I would have you alwaies propense to the same way; when ever it shall be desired and accepted, let it be granted, not only as an Act of State Policy and necessity, but of Christian charity and choise. It is all I have now left me, a power to forgive those that have deprived me of all; and I thank God I have a heart to do it; and joy as much in this grace, which God hath given me, as in all my former enjoyments. . . . The more conscious you shall be to your own merits, upon your people; the more prone you will be to expect all Love and Loyalty from them; and to inflict no punishment upon them for former miscarriages: you will have more inward complacency in pardoning one, then in punishing a thousand.[27]

In exalting the power of pardoning to his son, Charles I wrote with more effect than in his entreaties to Parliament. Upon the Restoration of Charles II to the throne, an anonymous "Person of Quality" penned a *History of His Sacred Majesty Charles II* that elaborately sketched the new king's character for forgiveness. As the author insisted, "[Charles II's] very nature enclines him to a compassion. He pitties those that will not pitty themselves, and whilst they are conspiring his destruction, his prayers procure their safety. Nor can the utmost of their injuries provoke him to a retalliation. He hath learned not only of God, but of the King his father, to forgive his enemies." The writer, in adducing reasons for Charles's propensity for compassion, maintains that "[the king] knows that whilst he kills a Subject he weakens his kingdom. Rebels themselves may be found usefull; and though justice can not, yet his Majesties clemency will admit their pardon."[28]

At the time of the Restoration, Charles II had already indicated several times his preference for pardoning over punishment. In his 1651 *Declaration to All His Loving Subjects of the Kingdome of England and Dominion of Wales*, issued from his camp at Woodhouse, Charles declared that he wished "to evidence how fare we are from Revenge" by "Declar[ing] and Engag[ing] Our Selfe to give Our Consent to a full Act of Oblivion and Indempnity for the security of all Our Subjects of England, and Dominion of Wales, in their Persons, Freedomes, and

---

27. Sanderson, *Compleat History*, 1145–46.
28. John Dauncey (?), *The History of His Sacred Majesty Charles II* (London: James Davies, 1660), 228, 227.

Estates, for all things done by them relating to these Wars these seven yeeres past, and that they shall never be called in question by Us for any of them," excepting only Cromwell, and some others "who did Actually sit, and Vote in the Murther of Our Royall Father."[29] Charles had likewise promised passage of an Act of Oblivion to his British subjects when seeking restoration, and subsequently opined to Parliament that, in the absence of this promise, "neither I nor You had been now here."[30]

In the literary context, references to oblivion drew both upon the Homeric strand and on the Stuart strain. A particularly striking instance occurs in William Cartwright's *The Lady-Errant*, a royalist play of the 1630s, subsequently published in 1651, which Jane Farnsworth has identified as an astute commentary on King Charles I's policy of noninvolvement in the continental war with Spain.[31] At the end of that work, Demarchus, the king of Cyprus, who has been absent for most of the plot, proclaims:

> Hat only is between th'Ignoble, when
> The Good dissent, tis only difference,
> No malice; Vertue flames in both, and so
> Each must the other Love; their Discords are
> More blameless than th'Embraces of the Bad;
> 'Tis to stand off, rather than bear a Grudge.
> And if they fight, when e'r they do lay down
> Their Weapons, they lay down their Anger too.
> As we affect then to seem good, and are so,
> Let one Oblivion wrap up what hath past
> On either side.[32]

Under this account, one of the features distinguishing discord between "the good" and "the bad" consists in the ability to move forward after the resolution of strife rather than harboring continued animosity and the desire for further

---

29. King Charles II, *Declaration to All His Loving Subjects of the Kingdome of England and Dominion of Wales* (London: John Field, 1651).

30. King Charles II, *His Majesties Gracious Speech to the House of Peers, the 27th of July, 1660 concerning the Speedy Passing of the Bill of Indempnity & Oblivion* (London: Christopher Barker and John Bill, 1660), 4.

31. Jane Farnsworth, "Defending the King in Cartwright's 'The Lady-Errant' (1636–37)," *Studies in English Literature, 1500–1900* 42, no. 2 (Spring 2002): 381–98.

32. William Cartwright, *The Lady-Errant: A Tragi-Comedy*, in *The Plays and Poems of William Cartwright*, ed. G. Blakemore Evans (Madison: University of Wisconsin Press, 1951), 160.

revenge. Performing the role of the one who claims to be good hence requires the adoption of a strategy of forgetting wrongs committed.

It was within this context that James Compton, the third Earl of Northampton, composed a defense of a parliamentary Act of Oblivion, after the execution of Charles I in 1649 and presumably prior to the passage of such a parliamentary provision in 1651 (now 1652).[33] Despite his strong identification as a royalist, Compton's reasoning in the "Political Treatise" does not suggest an active effort to restore King Charles II. Instead, it accepts the current state of affairs and considers how to maximize the health of the state in light of contemporary realities. Hence he emphasizes the concerns of transitional justice with future welfare, the reintegration of dissidents, finality in the settlement of grievances, and the avoidance of continued hostilities.

Accepting parliamentary control, Compton begins from the position of "holding it for granted that those who inwardly repine must now outwardly submit." Despairing that his work could change people's minds with regard to their ultimate political position, he puts that effort to one side. He instead considers what "most for the future . . . may tend to the honor and wellfare of this nation," placing in the foreground not an attribution of responsibility for the preceding conflicts but rather an investigation of prospective benefits. As Compton emphasizes, this concern for future benefits should trump worries that royalists might gain too much from an indemnity or oblivion. Claiming, "Some may think this maxim rather propounded for the Cavaliers benefit than the States safety," he urges that "if with unpartiall eyes it has been looked into, it will be found much more tending to future tranquillitie of this commonwealth, then to their advantage, though bothe will reape much by it, the cavalier satisfaction and the commonwealth securitie." Under this view, supporters of the Revolution should suppress their desire to extract more from defenders of King Charles I and instead focus on preserving their new commonwealth.

For this reason, Compton maintains the importance of two kinds of legal regulation, one establishing limits on the punishment of royalists and the other prescribing penalties for continuing as an enemy of the state. These provisions in combination would create incentives for royalists to set aside their grievances and attempt to regroup as part of the new commonwealth. As Compton puts it, one "cause of the raising war or taking other waies to change a present forme of government, is when the rulers bind not themselves by some apparent act, from oppressing any they have promised to forgive, but that the delinquent is

---

33. British Library MS ADD60282. For the complete transcription, see Appendix B.

never sure after all composition, but still liable to all inconveniencies." Another consists in the absence of a "solid law . . . provided for the punishment of [open or secret enemies to the state], for their the hops of advantage may be vast, the danger small, and if it chance that suche treasons thrive not yet if such punishment be inflicted, though not greater than the offense deserves, yet not what the law in former times held forth, it shall be imputed for injustice and breed ill blood." Finally, Compton places priority throughout on averting further conflict, using phrases like "tending to the future tranquillitie," "reap[ing] . . . securitie," "the safety of the state," and "removing all possibilitie of danger from inbred commotions."

A comparison with a recent account of the goals of institutions charged with effectuating transitional justice is instructive. As Melissa Williams and Rosemary Nagy explain, these entities "are expected to deliver justice to the perpetrators of past wrongs, recognition and reparation to their victims, a truthful and common public narrative of past wrongdoing, and the conditions for lawful order and societal peace."[34] For Compton, attainment of a common narrative seems impossible; he focuses instead on setting limits to reparation and maintaining the conditions for lawful order and societal peace. While this emphasis could—as he himself acknowledges—seem biased in his own favor as a supporter of King Charles I, examination of the plays of his protégé Cosmo Manuche suggests a more complicated explanation, as Manuche approaches the imminent restoration of King Charles II to the throne with a similar set of priorities.

Sovereigns and Subordinates

Although they do not explicitly reference acts of oblivion, several of Manuche's plays present worlds in which the sovereign has slipped from his position of security and the focus is placed squarely on the behavior of subordinates, including both the question of how they should be judged and the issue of how they can be reintegrated into the commonwealth. In *The Just General*, published in 1652, shortly after Compton's manuscript was written, a sovereign clearly associated with King Charles II, and depicted as weak along a number of different dimensions, asserts his capacity to pardon and its meaning as a sign of his sovereignty, while at the same time relying on the prior expression of forgiveness

---

34. Melissa Williams and Rosemary Nagy, introduction to Williams, Nagy, and Elster, *NOMOS LI*, 5.

to the perpetrators by his subjects as an implicit source for his authority. By the time of *The Banish'd Shepherdess*, a play available only in manuscript, the rightful king is even more absent, and much of the action features his supporters' jests against the minions of the now fled masterminds of usurpation. It is precisely this class of followers whom the Act of Oblivion passed upon Charles II's restoration would have protected. Despite the royalist thrust of both of these plays, the king himself is of less concern than his unruly subjects.

The title of *The Just General* itself suggests the displacement of interest from the sovereign to his principal subordinate, the "just general" of the title. Set in Sicily, the play begins with the young King Amasius's deliberations about a letter sent to him from this general—aptly named Bellicosus—who "affirm[s]/ A Cessation Of Arms, on both sides,/ For these three moneths" and simultaneously advises Amasius to forswear his love for Aurelia, a woman of little means, on the grounds that it will displease his subjects.[35] Having been encouraged to put faith in Bellicosus by his deceased father—the resonances with Charles I and Charles II commencing early—Amasius vacillates between attempting to find the wisdom in the general's suggestion and distrusting his motives.

When Amasius discovers that Aurelia is nowhere to be found—on account of a plot driven by a "proud rich lady" named Artesia, of whom the general's son Delirus is enamored—Amasius immediately suspects the general and departs the city disguised as a friar to search everywhere for his beloved, hoping that she remains alive. In Amasius's absence, Bellicosus returns to the city and, despite actually being loyal to the young king, and after a series of delaying tactics fail, accepts the crown himself from the agitated multitude. In the meantime, King Amasius discovers Aurelia in a pastoral landscape in the guise of a shepherdess and is apprised of the plot that Artesia and Delirus had laid against her life.

One of the king's noble followers, Antonio, then returns to court, where Bellicosus is now in charge, to provoke an admission from Delirus. That accomplished, Bellicosus in shame and regret sentences both his son and Artesia to death. The pair in turn beg forgiveness of each other, then of the people, who give common voice to forgiveness in anticipation of the culprits' speedy execution. King Amasius finally returns and grants a pardon over Bellicosus's protests, then reveals the still living Aurelia.

Dale Randall has noted King Amasius's similarities to various historical figures, including the young King Charles II, who had only recently lost to

---

35. Cosmo Manuche, *The Just General: A Tragi-Comedy* (London: G. Bedell, 1652), 1.

Cromwell's New Model Army at Worcester, following which he fled.[36] The play jokes at several points about its topicality, as Amasius ponders: "Surely the Court is mercifully sparing in their/ Search of me; I hear no hew and cry sent after me./ (Though I have read t'has been a course, some/ Sawcy subjects have presumed to take in search of/ Their lost king.)," and Antonio notes, "It being now in fashion for Princes to make escapes in/ Womens habit."[37] Like that of Charles II, Amasius's sovereignty is precarious, and he is temporarily deposed, although the play anticipates his happy restoration.

While Amasius's departure from court has historical parallels, it also possesses metatheatrical implications, recalling the plot of *Measure for Measure*. Two differences from dramatic precedents like *Measure for Measure* are striking, though: first, the absence of the king does not merely suggest the possibility of revolution but actually precipitates a temporary change of ruler, and second, the law driving the plot in *Measure for Measure* and *The Laws of Candy* has disappeared, leaving only treachery and loyalty in its wake. Both of these changes situate *The Just General* firmly within the realm of transitional justice, where authority is not fixed nor law secure.

Various characters in *The Just General* remark disparagingly about "the multitude" and "that many headed beast (the commonwealth)," yet the play itself does not definitively dismiss the perspective of the populace. Considering Bellicosus's warning not to wed Aurelia, Amasius reflects "What appears just to us, not season'd/ To the palat of the giddy headed multitude,/ To them's unjust./ 'Tis not what we, but what they will that must," suggesting that even the king deems the views of his subjects weighty. He similarly requests the advice of his counselors, calling them "Landlords/ To the Commonwealth."[38]

Between the time when King Amasius departs at the beginning of act 3 and his return, a number of passages treat the fickle allegiance of the subjects of the realm. As one of Amasius's erstwhile attendants recounts:

> The common people ignorant of their
> Own safety (wedded to change) unanimously begin
> To call *Bellicosus* King; some crying up his
> Valour, and experience in the wars, some his
> Justice, all his honesty; whose loyall heart appears
> So far from coveting a crown, he seems much

---

36. Randall, *Winter Fruit*, 349–50.
37. Manuche, *The Just General*, 40, 46.
38. Manuche, *The Just General*, 2–3.

Troubled at the clamour. And should the King
His discontent detain him long from Court, 'tis
Thought the Generall must accept it, to appease
The Frantick multitude, who rashly may (should he
Refuse) elect more undeservedly.

Shortly thereafter, Bellicosus comes up with a delaying tactic, involving pretended letters from the absent king, in the hopes that "This/ The distracted people may (for a time)/ Appease." This strategy succeeds only temporarily, as the audience discovers in act 4 that Bellicosus has reluctantly accepted the throne. As the same attendant remarks, "I hope the rout's now pleas'd they have a King,/ Yet some cry'd out for none (the devil stop their wind-pipes)/ The General appeared much backward, in the judgment/ of the standers by, to accept the Government; yet Crowns/ Are things, seldom unwelcome come,/ How e'r with care maintain'd," to which another responds that "the General nothing acted/ Outwardly in show but what his loyal heart provok't him too,/ Nor could he with the safety of the Kingdom (as things/ Then stood) refuse to accept the Crown;/ For that besides the present danger might have ensu'd/ By the domestick rabble, had he refus'd."[39] Lest the audience miss the chronology, Aurelia's father's servant puts together the entire narrative, recounting it subsequently to the still disguised Amasius.

As the conspirator Artesia later also confirms, "The multitude with noise hath made their General King," a circumstance that leads her to put aside her prior jealousy of Aurelia and her aspiration to become Amasius's spouse in her stead and turn her affections to Delirus, who would now be in the royal line.[40] Just as the "common people" are "wedded to change," Artesia wishes to be wedded to sovereignty, upon whomever it sits.

Although the fickle character of the people is evident in these passages, a certain wisdom appears in the crowd's judgment, for Bellicosus's agreement to accept the crown leads Sicily's international enemies to be quelled. Likewise, once Amasius returns, they accept him as their king, confirming Bellicosus's surrender of the crown, crying, "Long live Amasius King of Sicily," as "*all kneele.*"[41] From the vantage point of preserving the state, the multitude's vacillations begin to display some logic.

---

39. Manuche, *The Just Generall*, 32–33, 47, 52. The term "rout" appears several times in the play, drawing on the now largely obsolete meaning of "a disreputable group of people; a violent or unlawful mob; a gang of criminals or ruffians; (also) a violent horde" (*OED* definition 3a).

40. Manuche, *The Just Generall*, 49.

41. Manuche, *The Just Generall*, 64.

The people also have a role in the play's final pardons. From early in the action, pardoning is figured in connection with sovereignty. When Delirus announces that King Amasius has left in the wake of Aurelia's disappearance and is chided by Artesia, he responds, "You almost stagger'd me, I know now/ 'Twas but in jest to try my temper,/ And I forgive it." Artesia replies: "Hah, hah! Forgive it? You are not my Ghostly—*Laughs*/ Father, 'Twas language might have become your/ King, but sounds to saucy for a subject."[42] The language of forgiveness here is coded as part of Catholic ritual or appropriate only for kings.

Amasius self-consciously takes up this latter usage at the end of the play when he, returning, halts the imminent executions of Artesia and Delirus. As he asserts, "I here/ Pronounce their pardons, which stands irrevocable,/ If I command in chief."[43] The finality of the pardon here depends on the prior existence of sovereignty. The statement thus suggests that calling into question the merits of Amasius's pardons would deny his supreme authority in the commonwealth. The "if" is significant: earlier exercises of pardoning may have confirmed sovereignty, but the premise of prior sovereignty itself was never so explicitly in question. The pardon here becomes a kind of challenge to the people to reject or affirm the restored king's sovereignty.

Yet it is significant that, prior to this pardon, the people as a whole, as well as Bellicosus, had expressed forgiveness—but not remission of punishment—for the perpetrators. Thus Bellicosus exclaims, "Ere you go, take with you my forgiveness, and with it,/ Both my blessings." After Delirus himself requests forgiveness, "All" then pronounce, "Our prayers, and tears speak for us, we both/ Forgive and pitty."[44] King Amasius hence extends his sovereign pardon in a context that has already been primed by popular forgiveness. Just as the multitude's dissent or approval swayed Bellicosus to temporarily accept the position of king and caused Amasius himself consternation with respect to marrying Aurelia at the beginning of the play, the pitying character of the people furnishes an implicit authorization for Amasius's pardon.

An exercise of the pardoning power furnishes a visible sign of Amasius's sovereignty, returning us in part to the world of *Measure for Measure*, but with the significant difference that the ground of sovereignty is tangibly shaking, and the sovereignty restored is one that remains contingent on popular will.

---

42. Manuche, *The Just General*, 29.
43. Manuche, *The Just General*, 65.
44. Manuche, *The Just General*, 63.

Furthermore, the Sicilian people are represented as at once erratic and canny about preserving their country.

By the time of *The Banish'd Shepherdess*, the "common people" have redeemed themselves and are represented as fully supporting their wronged prince's restoration, proclaiming him king through a "general acclamation" at the end of the play.[45] In this work, seemingly penned on the eve of the restoration of Charles II, the plot centers even more pronouncedly on subordinates than does that of *The Just General*. The shepherdess of the title, Corilliana, is mother to the exiled prince and attended by various other shepherdesses throughout a number of pastoral scenes. She awaits the restoration of her son, Charilaus, who remains absent for much of the action. Yet despite the name of the play, even Corilliana does not furnish its principal point of interest. Instead, one group of men designated "loyall subjects of Charilaus and soldiers of fortune" and another called "rebells and servants to the notorious traitors to Charilaus" generate a comic subplot that comes to dominate the story.

The Banish'd Shepherdess opens with a scene featuring the said loyal subjects, who discover that their rebellious counterparts are attempting to regroup in light of a change in political circumstance and are essaying "to make provision/ In case their politick masters are prone to flight." The loyal subjects then hide to witness subsequent dialogue among the subordinate rebels, whom we find were previously "great panders and petty traytors," disreputably employed in stealing and other minor or less minor misdeeds "before rebellion prosper'd." When the two groups meet, one of the rebels urges the others to cease their quarreling, avoid the "scorne, base pride/ And emulation" that had been the downfall of their masters, and instead unite against the "Common Enemie." They are, however, unable to achieve any form of collaboration, a failure represented as part of the reason for the lack of success of the revolution itself.

The problem posed by these servants of traitors becomes, early in the play, a difficulty identifiable as one of transitional justice. As a loyal subject inquires, partly rhetorically, "Dare you share with them [their masters] the spoile of their country,/ And not participate of their deserved punishments?" The same character castigates Lysander, a fellow traveler, for being "too mercifull [to the rebels]/ Which was a fault, I (hardly) can forgive." Responding, Lysander emphasizes that

---

45. All quotations from *The Banish'd Shepherdess* derive from my transcription of the play from the manuscript in Patrick Kennedy Canavan, "A Study of English Drama" (Ph.D. diss., University of Southern California, 1950); the play is also available in MS at the British and Huntington Libraries (BL, Add. MS60273; Huntington Library, MS EL 8395).

he has not exercised mercy but instead has a trick up his sleeve, and intends to play an extended joke at the rebels' expense. He does indeed carry out this plan for much of the play, arranging to steal money from the rebels and, finally, generating a scene of repentance through the appearance of a pretended goddess—in actuality one of Corilliana's attendants. The play thereby sets up questions about the fate of low-level perpetrators and suggests as a response a theatrical form of punishment that will render them ridiculous and potentially impoverished but otherwise relatively unharmed.

Transitional justice is not a consideration only for loyalists, however; the rebels also reflect on the consequences of a restoration for themselves. One, Lepidus, observes that "wee are contriving/ For a future livelihood, without regarding/ Our future safety" and expresses some brief compunction, noting that "wee have been egredious rogues/ And wee must suffer for it./ Plague of these revolutions of times." Another, Clinius, puts faith in Charilaus's reputation for mercy—calling to mind Charles II's commitment to acts of oblivion. As Clinius states:

> Wee must acknowledge wee are rogues,
> And by a seeming, humble confession, expect some mercy
> If the tyde doe turne.
> Our prince wee know (how ere wee have abus'd him)
> Is mercyfull, beyond, what wee ought to hope,
> We can deserve: should wee (miraculously) prove honist.
> Which ever will be thought, compulsion, not obedience,
> Wrought in us.

Although the rebels' compunction may be partly feigned, these passages give the sense that there is little difference for them between acting and being; the parts they play may soon define their new roles. Hence Lepidus can say plausibly late in the play of another rebel, "This wretch, will quite deceive my expectation/ And prove reall honest."

With respect to the anticipation of mercy, Corilliana herself as well as her daughter Corilla confirm the royal inclination toward forgiveness. After listening to a diatribe against the rebels from one of her shepherdesses, Corilliana exclaims, "Fye, fye. No more of this you're too uncharitable./ May heaven forgive their faults. Long may they live./ T'injoye those comforts I could (freely) give," to which Corilla rejoins: "Amen, say I. May all their ill deed be buried/ In their repentance. And happinesse/ Crowne all their future dayes." Corilla's reference to the burial of ill deeds recalls the language associated with oblivion, a context further reinforced by the appearance of Morpheus, bringing sleep to Corilliana and her attendants, followed by a vision of the restoration of Charilaus.

Despite expressing the suffering they have caused him and his compatriots, Charilaus similarly wishes of the rebels, "May their repentance divert heavens judgments/ It is a prayer, I would have all my faithfull/ Subjects learne." He likewise repeatedly refers to the virtues of charity. Nancy Klein Maguire has also noted that both Corilliana and Charilaus are represented as merciful but has attributed that depiction to Manuche's desire to "[allay] fears of a vengeful king" rather than to Charles II's own efforts to present himself in that guise.[46]

Ultimately *The Banish'd Shepherdess* suggests a particular form of transitional justice, one in which the subordinates allied with the king create a theatrical punishment for low-level perpetrators, but the royal family themselves resist implementing penalties and are instead responsible only for pardoning. The "scene of mirth" that Lysander put on at the rebels' expense culminates in a scene that only the loyal subjects and attendants of Corilliana know is theatrical rather than real, one in which the rebels are forced to plead for forgiveness and accept the penance assigned them by a pretended goddess. Notably, the shepherdesses refrain from telling Corilliana about the planned performance for fear that she will stop them from undertaking it out of her mercy.

The completion of the performance coincides with the news of Charilaus's restoration, at which point the play seems to forget about the erstwhile rebels. They do, however, reappear at the very end. Lysander, who had previously expended much of his energy in tormenting these opponents, now pleads for their pardons, which Corilliana—rather than Charilaus—grants, stating, "I freely doe forgive them," and urging: "May all the godds as freely pardon you/ As (here) I doe. Live, and be happy." Although Charilaus and Corilliana were conspicuously absent from the theatrical mocking of the rebels, that prior scene appears to have furnished the extent of punishment requisite for Corilliana's forgiveness to reintegrate them into the people of her son's state. Symbolic punishment here occurs but within the delimited space of a play within a play, and it has its definitive end before the close of Manuche's drama.

In Susan Wiseman's interpretation, "*The Banish'd Shepheardess* presents the situation in 1659 as fraught, with few clear boundaries between 'loyal' and 'disloyal.'"[47] While this chapter concurs with the diagnosis of the situation depicted as fraught, it argues that the location of complexity lies elsewhere than the boundary between loyal and disloyal. Instead, the play dramatizes the role of

---

46. Nancy Klein Maguire, *Regicide and Restoration: English Tragicomedy, 1660–1671* (Cambridge: Cambridge University Press, 1991), 45.

47. Wiseman, *Drama and Politics*, 208.

subordinates in ensuring the success or failure of a restoration and the crucial decisions involved in attempting to bring those who had previously been conspirators back into a common people.

From *The Just General* to *The Banish'd Shepherdess*, Manuche remained concerned with the dynamics of transitional justice, although in the latter context he focused more on ensuring sufficient but not excessive punishment for conspirators than he had in the earlier play. In each tragicomedy, the pardons granted by a restored sovereign appear to be predicated on a prior acceptance of forgiveness by the wronged subjects. Although pardoning remains an emanation of sovereignty, it is given successfully only when the subjects have also agreed. This context of authorization would prove important to the Act of Oblivion passed on King Charles II's restoration to the throne and Thomas Hobbes's treatment of it, the subjects of the next chapter.

6

PARDONING REVOLUTION /
The 1660 Act of Oblivion and Hobbes's
Recentering of Sovereignty

As is widely known, many of the writings of the philosopher Thomas Hobbes were inflected by his royalist leanings and a perspective that has sometimes been characterized as "authoritarian."[1] Despite these royalist tendencies, however, and his support for the restoration of Charles II to the English throne, Hobbes fundamentally altered the existing conception of sovereignty after the English Revolution in a way that would prove deleterious to the continued power of the monarch. If King James I had emphasized his capacity to judge over his ability to make and promulgate laws, Hobbes instead grounded sovereignty in lawgiving and envisioned the king's equitable power of judgment as derivative of this more fundamental mark of majesty. In doing so, Hobbes turned the conception of sovereignty toward the generality of lawgiving rather than the singularity of judgment, a displacement that paved the path for the transfer of sovereignty from king to Parliament. The Act of Oblivion passed by Parliament

---

1. Johann P. Sommerville, "Lofty Science and Local Politics," in *The Cambridge Companion to Hobbes*, ed. Tom Sorell (Cambridge: Cambridge University Press, 1996), 247–48. The exact nature of Hobbes's political commitments has been the subject of extensive debate and commentary, with some supporters of an authoritarian reading and others who maintain that Hobbes paved the way for either modern liberalism or democracy or both, perhaps even intentionally. Kinch Hoekstra furnishes a helpful survey of these positions in "A Lion in the House: Hobbes and Democracy," in *Rethinking the Foundations of Modern Political Thought*, ed. Annabel Brett and James Tully (Cambridge: Cambridge University Press, 2006). Most recently, in *The Sleeping Sovereign*, Richard Tuck has made a full-throated defense of the idea that Hobbes supported democratic sovereignty, although not the democratic administration of government. Nothing in the argument of this chapter presupposes an authoritarian account of Hobbes. However, the thrust does depart from Tuck's contentions in *The Sleeping Sovereign* insofar as he posits a division between the actual location of sovereignty and the implementing capacity of government. In this regard, I agree with Hoekstra's critique of Tuck's position based on the notion that "Hobbes argues that *de jure* sovereignty follows from *de facto* sovereignty, and not the other way around." Hoekstra, "A Lion in the House," 203; see also Kinch Hoekstra, "The *De Facto* Turn in Hobbes's Political Philosophy," in *Leviathan after 350 Years*, ed. Tom Sorell and Luc Foisneau (Oxford: Oxford University Press, 2004), 33–73.

after the Restoration, which Hobbes himself analyzed in his *Dialogue between a Philosopher and a Student of the Common Lawes*, provides a particularly striking example of how this transfer unfolded on a conceptual level; in this instance, something like the pardon, which represented the act of sovereignty most closely linked with the singularity of the monarch, was itself generalized and transferred to Parliament instead of being exercised exclusively by the king.

At the same time, Hobbes's theories were not expressed in terms of the political or dramatic paradigms through which conceptions of sovereignty had emerged during the first half of the seventeenth century in England. Instead, they posited a particular role for philosophy itself in providing a ground for the political sphere. As Quentin Skinner has observed, "It has been said, and rightly, that Hobbes was the first thinker to produce a comprehensive philosophical system in the English language."[2] Perhaps because of the political and legal disruption that the English Revolution represented, Hobbes sought a new foundation, one that emanated from philosophy. Whereas a jurist like Sir Edward Coke had been able to theorize the obligations of the common law and its relations to the sovereign from within the compass of law itself, Hobbes insisted on stepping outside and, like Socrates, addressing the law as a foreigner to it. For the first time in the English tradition, then, rather than being constituted through dramatic and political interventions, the law is examined from beyond its bounds, philosophy announcing and delimiting for law—and even for sovereignty—its proper place.

Although the philosophical account of sovereignty that Hobbes provided has enjoyed a substantial post-history in continental Europe, it nevertheless bears the traces of its English origins.[3] The oppositions between equity and common law, king and Parliament, and judging and lawgiving —all connected with a particular set of English legal and political institutions—pervade Hobbes's *Dialogue*. While his efforts to undermine and transmute these binaries enable Hobbes's theory to attain the abstraction of philosophy, the residues of their influence remain within his conception of sovereignty. On one reading, the *Dialogue* could be seen as representing Hobbes's efforts to enact his own oblivion on Sir Edward Coke and the body of early seventeenth-century English legal theory for

---

2. Quentin Skinner, *Reason and Rhetoric in the Philosophy of Thomas Hobbes* (Cambridge: Cambridge University Press, 1996), 436.

3. Deborah Baumgold has similarly argued that Hobbes's theory of politics "came to require" a "historical dimension" and "became less an explanation of the structure of sovereignty everywhere and always, and more a contingent account of the constitution of a particular nation-state." Deborah Baumgold, "When Hobbes Needed History," in *Hobbes and History* (London: Routledge, 2000), 26.

which his name stands. While Hobbes may have thereby succeeded in directing the attention of subsequent philosophy toward his own vision of sovereignty and away from its precursors, the oblivion was necessarily rendered incomplete by the *Dialogue*'s own indebtedness to its seventeenth-century English context. Names and details may have succumbed to amnesia, but certain patterns and paradigms still remain.

After briefly describing the historical significance of the Act of Oblivion and Hobbes's treatment of it, this chapter turns to Hobbes's deployment of the dialogue form, and his use of this philosophical genre to undermine the force of legal definitions established by tradition and instead posit reason and the authority of the king as their combined grounds.[4] The next section of the chapter examines the relationship between the English Court of Chancery and two versions of equity—one constituting equity as an exception, or a mitigation, of the common law, and the other insisting on equity as an aspect of the law itself. Invoking both of these conceptions at various points, Hobbes undermines the primacy of the common law and replaces it with a vision of equity based on the reason and authority of the sovereign. I then examine why, despite invoking equity, which had previously seemed tied to the discretionary capacity of the sovereign, and might be thought to support a Schmittian version of the sovereign as "he who decides on the exception,"[5] Hobbes appears to place priority on lawgiving rather than judgment. As the chapter finally argues, pardoning, which bears certain analogies to equity, falls victim, in Hobbes's account of the 1660 Act of Oblivion, to a similar generalization that renders it more akin to a law than an exception, and more a manifestation of Parliament's power than that of the king. The chapter concludes by outlining the historical moorings of Hobbes's account in the form of the prehistory and passage of the Act of Oblivion itself.

---

4. As Quentin Skinner explained in *Reason and Rhetoric in the Philosophy of Hobbes*, Hobbes's earlier works accord a greater power to reason alone than his post–Civil War writings. Skinner claims that "Hobbes's conception of civil science in *The Elements of Law* and *De Cive* is founded on the belief that scientific reasoning possesses an inherent power to persuade us of the truths it finds out. By contrast, *Leviathan* declares that the sciences are small power, and reverts to the typically humanist assumption that, if we are to succeed in persuading others to accept our arguments, we shall have to supplement the findings of reason with the moving force of eloquence." Skinner, *Reason and Rhetoric*, 426. Although the force discussed later in this chapter is that of the sovereign rather than eloquence per se, the invocation of force as well as reason in the *Dialogue* is similar to that which Skinner discusses.

5. Carl Schmitt, *Political Theology: Four Chapters on the Concept of Sovereignty*, trans. George Schwab (Chicago: University of Chicago Press, 2006), 5.

Hobbes, His *Dialogue*, and the Act of Oblivion: A Historical Concatenation

On August 29, 1660, following the newly restored King Charles II's repeated entreaties to Parliament, the Act of Oblivion he had proposed—or, more fully, "The Kings Majesties most Gracious, Free and General Pardon, Indempnity, and Oblivion"—became law. Thomas Hobbes would, in his posthumously published *Dialogue between a Philosopher and a Student of the Common Lawes of England* (1681), explain that "this word *Act of Oblivion* was never in our Law-Books before," and search as far back as ancient Athens for what he deemed the sole relevant historical precedent.[6] Hobbes's shock at this supposed innovation was, as chapter 5 demonstrated, rather unwarranted; in particular, Charles's father, the ill-fated Charles I, had made several assays in a similar direction as his prospects in the Civil War grew increasingly bleak, and Charles II himself had proposed the possibility of an Act of Oblivion in attempts to reach out to those he claimed as his British subjects from his exile in France. Furthermore, under Cromwell, the Interregnum Parliament itself had in fact passed such an act in 1652.

Earlier charters of pardon, coronation pardons, and parliamentary general pardons also bore a structural resemblance to the 1660 Act of Oblivion, yet the act did constitute an innovation on several fronts.[7] In passing the 1660 statute, Parliament became the first body to acknowledge the central problem of reestablishing a political order in the wake of failed revolution, that of the fate of those responsible for or complicit in the prior violent struggle or involved in

---

6. Thomas Hobbes, *A Dialogue between a Philosopher and a Student of the Common Lawes of England* (1681), ed. Joseph Cropsey (Chicago: University of Chicago Press, 1971), 157; hereafter *Dialogue*.

The early modern efflorescence of oblivion seems itself to have been forgotten by much recent political theory. For example, Giorgio Agamben has claimed that the Athenian strategy of amnesty, which he deems "not simply a forgetting or a repression of the past" but also "an exhortation not to make bad use of memory," is completely foreign to "what civil war seems to be for the moderns: namely, something that one must seek to render impossible at every cost, yet that must always be remembered through trials and legal persecutions." Giorgio Agamben, *Stasis: Civil War as a Political Paradigm*, trans. Nicholas Heron (Stanford: Stanford University Press, 2015), 16. Agamben's description fits the paradigm established in the wake of twentieth-century atrocities but neglects the earlier context of acts of amnesty and oblivion in the sixteenth through eighteenth centuries.

7. For a thorough discussion of the general pardon in the sixteenth century, see Krista Kesselring, *Mercy and Authority in the Tudor State* (Cambridge: Cambridge University Press, 2003), 56–90. Cynthia Herrup treats the early Stuarts' inheritance of the general pardon more specifically in "Negotiating Grace," in *Politics, Religion and Popularity in Early Stuart Britain: Essays in Honor of Conrad Russell*, ed. Thomas Cogswell, Richard Cust, and Peter Lake (Cambridge: Cambridge University Press, 2002), 124–42.

the interim regime. In today's parlance a concern of "transitional justice," as chapter 5 contends, this question of the treatment of perpetrators or revolutionaries emerged for twentieth-century theory in the work of Hannah Arendt, including both *Eichmann in Jerusalem* and *On Revolution*.[8] Staging exemplary justice upon those responsible for the temporary establishment represents one possible strategy—that adopted in the trial of Adolf Eichmann. In the context of the Act of Oblivion, however, although certain individuals were exempted from its compass precisely for the purpose of bringing them to justice, the most striking aspect of the law consisted not in its ability to generate a theatrical display but rather in its refusal to stage justice, a refusal that was general in nature and insisted that the deeds of the revolutionaries should be obliterated even from the theater of memory.

The structure of the Act of Oblivion thereby violated many of the central principles of pardoning itself—that pardoning not be general but rather be tailored to the circumstances of a particular case, resembling a judgment instead of a law; that it be granted by the one aggrieved, here the king, rather than by Parliament; and that it forgive but not forget. While retaining the strategic efficacy of a pardon, that of exalting the majesty of the king and avoiding further revolutionary violence, the Act of Oblivion that Charles II had labored to implement simultaneously suggested the force of the revolutionary position, and the reorientation of law away from the specificity of judgment and toward the generality of legislation. From this realignment, it was but a short step to the transfer of sovereignty from king to Parliament, and from monarchical to parliamentary supremacy.

The treatment of the king's legal authority in Hobbes's *Dialogue*, while nominally reinforcing monarchical power, nevertheless demonstrates the shift toward a legislative vision of the nature of sovereignty. The aims of the *Dialogue* are twofold: first, it works to undermine Sir Edward Coke's early seventeenth-century theory of the English legal system, which emphasized the role of judges and common lawyers as the guardians of the liberties of the subject, and instead posits a centralization of legal authority and force in the king; second, it tries to demonstrate the subordination of the common law to philosophy, or rather to establish philosophy as the only discipline that can illuminate the grounds and constitution of law.

---

8. According to Ruti Teitel, "the threshold dilemma of transitional justice is the problem of the rule of law in periods of radical political change. By their very definitions, these are often times of massive paradigm shifts in understandings of justice." Ruti Teitel, *Transitional Justice* (New York: Oxford University Press, 2000), 11.

Taking aim against the institutional conflicts between the courts of the common law and Chancery, the seat of equity, the Philosopher of the *Dialogue*—who adopts a seemingly Hobbesian position in opposing the ventriloquized version of Coke emanating from the Student of the Common Laws—insists that these controversies emerged out of a misconstruction of the sources and nature of legal authority. What generated the debate, he claims, is a set of definitional confusions that only a philosopher can resolve. It is through this assertion that philosophy alone can furnish the basis for evaluating claims about law that the Philosopher provides a vantage point from which to resolve the impasse in the controversy about the relative places of equity and law.

In contrast to Coke's emphasis on the primacy of the common law, the Philosopher maintains that, in advance of civil society, all law consists in the law of nature, which he also calls the law of reason, or equity.[9] In order to translate this primordial equity into what we might name positive law, and what the Philosopher denominates the realms of justice and civil law, it is necessary not only to add the force that sovereignty provides but also to establish the dictates of the law of reason—over which individual subjects might disagree—through assent to the king's interpretation of equity. The sovereign[10] thus provides, for the Philosopher, an epistemological grounding as well as a foundation for the

---

9. David Gauthier has also argued for a view of the laws of nature as "primarily rational precepts" in his essay "Hobbes: The Laws of Nature," *Pacific Philosophical Quarterly* 82 (February 2003): 258–84.

Treatments of Hobbes's use of equity have largely focused on the Aristotelian and natural law heritage of equity rather than the institutional dynamics of the relationship between common law and equity in seventeenth-century England. Even Larry May, who acknowledges the institutional understanding of equity as the jurisprudence of Chancery, neglects the significance of that historical background in "Hobbes on Equity and Justice," claiming that "the Lord Chancellor's Courts of Equity came to have such wide jurisdiction by the 17th century as to be virtually indistinguishable from the common law courts." Larry May, "Hobbes on Equity and Justice," in *Hobbes's "Science of Natural Justice*," ed. C. Walton and P. J. Johnson (Dordrecht: Martinus Nijhoff, 1987), 242. He thereby neglects the entire political controversy over the jurisdiction of these respective bodies. While noting the institutional role of Chancery as a court of equity, Dennis Klimchuk similarly disregards the political stakes of the division over the respective powers of the Chancery and common law courts. Dennis Klimchuk, "Hobbes on Equity," in *Hobbes and the Law*, ed. David Dyzenhaus and Thomas Poole (Cambridge: Cambridge University Press, 2012), 180–85.

In this regard, the burgeoning of work by literary scholars like Kathy Eden and Elliott Visconsi on the varieties of equity in early modern England has not yet been taken sufficiently into account by those assessing Hobbes's understanding of equity. Thomas Poole has, however, begun to fill in this gap by unpacking the importance for Hobbes of equity as "a particular court—Chancery— and a particular body of law that stemmed from it." Thomas Poole, "Hobbes on Law and Prerogative," in Dyzenhaus and Poole, *Hobbes and the Law*, 92.

10. Whereas, in *Leviathan*, Hobbes calls the king the "sovereign representative," the participants in the *Dialogue* speak simply in terms of sovereignty and "sovereign power."

authority of law. At the same time, the king is bound not by civil law but only by equity; despite guaranteeing the fulfillment of the covenant, he remains accountable only outside its scope, to God rather than to his subjects.

The *Dialogue* thereby seems to solve the early seventeenth-century problem of the relative places of common law and equity. But why revisit that controversy in retrospect? Was the *Dialogue* simply belated, or was its own force otherwise situated? The institutional conflict between law and equity had already, in one sense, been decided by King James I when he divested Coke of his role as chief justice of the Court of King's Bench as a result of Coke's continual attempts to restrict the jurisdiction of Chancery. It had been further flamed by proposals to abolish the Court of Chancery during the Interregnum, but with the abandonment of these efforts and some incremental reforms, it seemed as though institutional stasis had been achieved.[11] By the time of the Restoration, the more material debate—as a work like Hobbes's *Behemoth; or, the Long Parliament* attested—concerned the relative places of king and Parliament, and of the discretionary executive or judicial authority of the former as opposed to the legislative activity of the latter.

Bolstering the king's authority within this new order, Hobbes's *Dialogue* situates legislating rather than judging as the central legal act, of which others are simply derivative. Hobbes's *Leviathan* had already insisted on the difference in degree rather than kind of judging and legislating, and had criticized the notion that the two functions could be delegated to disparate bodies. The office of the sovereign representative should instead be unitary and exercise all of the powers incident to sovereignty. Placing priority upon legislation over judging carries implications for the *Dialogue*'s vision of equity. Equity, the primary valence of which had once entailed moderating the rigors of the law in a particular case through the exercise of a religiously informed conscience, and which in that incarnation bore some resemblance to pardoning, comes to assume the law-like aspect of a general rule and to designate the proper interpretation of a statutory directive. It is, then, hardly surprising that the Act of Oblivion itself would appear

---

11. The principal bill urging the restriction of Chancery's scope during this period consisted in "An Ordinance for the better Regulating and Limiting the Jurisdiction of the High Court of Chancery" (August 21, 1654), in *Acts and Ordinances of the Interregnum, 1642–1660*, ed. C. H. Firth and R. S. Rait for the Statute Law Committee, vol. 2 (Holmes Beach, FL: Wm. Gaunt, 1969), 940–67. A law proposing abolition of the Court of Chancery was also considered in Parliament. *Commons Journal* 7 (October 19, 1653): 336. Barbara Shapiro discusses several of the approaches to altering or eliminating Chancery in "Law Reform in Seventeenth-Century England," *American Journal of Legal History* 19 (1975): 282, 293.

not so much in the form of an exemplary pardon, along the lines of the one that Duke Vincentio performs in *Measure for Measure*, but rather as a legislative act.

Forgiveness and pardoning themselves represent, for Hobbes, not only pragmatic acts that the sovereign should undertake to ensure peace for the future, but also the sole means by which individuals may be released from the obligations they incur through entering into the social contract. Pardoning constitutes, therefore, the most crucial precondition for reestablishing a political order cleft by internal strife. Endowing the Act of Oblivion with the generality of a law and permitting Parliament to pass it thereby turned the focus of the Restoration toward Parliament at just the moment when King Charles II seemed to reaffirm the monarchy by assuming the royal mantle.

Philosophy, Authority, and the Common Law: Some Dialogues on Definition

Adoption of the dialogue form situates Hobbes's *Dialogue between a Philosopher and a Student of the Common Lawes of England*, as well as his *Behemoth; or, the Long Parliament*, within the philosophical tradition that commenced with Plato. At the same time, it performs an argument about the nature of proper discussions of law, an argument that entails a conception of the nature of law itself.

The effect of *Behemoth*'s dialogic construction is to provide a particular kind of account of the history of the English Revolution and Interregnum, one that demonstrates the strangeness of events through allowing character A to recount them in retrospect and character B to pose questions from the vantage point of reason accompanied by ignorance of the facts. Alluding to the perspective of one observing England from the world stage, A explains that "he that thence [from 1640 to 1660], as from the Devil's Mountain, should have looked upon the world and observed the actions of men, especially in England, might have had a prospect of all kinds of injustice, and of all kinds of folly, that the world could afford."[12] B, mentioning his youth, and consequent inability to occupy the place of a spectator during the course of the Revolution, then requests that A "set [him] . . . upon the same mountain, by the relation of the actions you then saw, and of their causes, pretensions, justice, order, artifice, and event." The logic undergirding history, as represented in A's account, thus finds itself, during the

---

12. Thomas Hobbes, *Behemoth; or, the Long Parliament* (1682), ed. Ferdinand Tönnies (Chicago: University of Chicago Press, 1990), 1; hereafter *Behemoth*.

course of *Behemoth*, called into question by B's queries. Rather than asking simply about the "facts," B emphasizes that he wishes to know "not so much of those actions that passed in the time of the late troubles, as of their causes, and of the councils and artifice by which they were brought to pass," analysis that he finds lacking in conventional histories of the period.[13] The result is a philosophical critique of the grounds for the sequence of events described.

Hobbes's *Dialogue* stages a similar critique of experience from the standpoint of philosophy, although here it is of Sir Edward Coke's claims for the ascendancy of legal knowledge acquired by accumulation rather than of the causes of historical occurrences. The Student of the Common Lawes continually articulates fragments from the writings of Sir Edward Coke, King James I's attorney general and subsequently chief justice of the Court of Common Pleas and then the King's Bench, which the Philosopher, whose persona one might identify with Hobbes himself, insists are philosophically unsound. As often occurs in the dialogue form, the questions that the Philosopher raises generally concern the definition of terms.[14] Because the Student, following Coke, has misconstrued the meaning of particular words, he has been led into philosophical error. The common law itself, as Coke promulgated it, consists solely in a subordinate version of philosophy, a circumstance that it is Coke's

---

13. *Behemoth*, 45.

14. Plato's dialogues exemplify the dialogue form's obsession with definition. In the *Cratylus*, Socrates draws out the relationship between names and their referents. In doing so, he introduces the figure of the "legislator," asserting that "not every man is able to give a name, but only a maker of names, and this is the legislator, who of all skilled artisans in the world is the rarest." Plato, *The Cratylus*, trans. Benjamin Jowett, in *The Collected Dialogues of Plato*, ed. Edith Hamilton and Huntington Cairns (New York: Pantheon, 1963), 427. In contrast to Cratylus's insistence on the natural relation between a thing and a name, and the impossibility of separating an object out from its name, Socrates opines that an entity's essence precedes its designation, and that the original legislators of names must have discerned the identity of their objects through some method other than naming (471–72). Although the legislator of the *Cratylus* bears little superficial resemblance to a more political form of lawmaker, introduction of this figure does bring names into relation with laws during the course of the dialogue. According to one exchange between Socrates and Cratylus:

> Socrates: Among legislators, there are some who do their work better and some worse?
> Cratylus: No, there I do not agree with you.
> Socrates: Then you do not think that some laws are better and others worse?
> Cratylus: No, indeed.
> Socrates: Or that one name is better than another?
> Cratylus: Certainly not.
> Socrates: Then all names are rightly imposed?
> Cratylus: Yes, if they are names at all. (463)

Cratylus's view of names as expressing the nature of their objects corresponds, in the legal realm, to the idea that laws name what is just, and that objects cannot be separated out from their names.

mistake not to recognize; as the Philosopher explains, contrasting statutes with the common law, the former "are not Philosophy as is the Common-Law, and other disputable Arts, but are Commands, or Prohibitions which ought to be obeyed."[15]

It is partly because the definitions of both the law in general and of particular legal concepts that Coke espoused in his *Institutes* and *Reports* fail, in the Philosopher's view, to conform to the dictates of reason that he finds them problematic. Instead of determining the meaning of terms in the abstract, the Philosopher maintains, Coke relied on the genealogy of words and their etymologies. As the Philosopher states, "Etymologies are no Definitions, and yet when they are true they give much light towards the finding out of a Definition; but this of Sir *Edw. Coke*'s carries with it very little of Probability." Inquiring about the boundaries of what Coke described as larceny in the *Institutes*, the Philosopher further delves into the sources for Coke's account of the crime and asks, "Is this Definition drawn out of any Statute, or is it in *Bracton*, or *Littleton*, or any other Writer upon the Science of the Laws?" Upon the Common Lawyer's admission "No; it is [Coke's] own; and you may observe by the Logick-Sentences dispersed through his Works, that he was a Logician sufficient enough to make a Definition," the Philosopher responds: "But if his Definitions must be the Rule of Law; what is there that he may not make Felony, or not Felony, at his Pleasure? But seeing it is not Statute-Law that he says, it must be very perfect Reason, or else no Law at all; and to me it seems so far from Reason as I think it ridiculous."[16] While emulating philosophical reasoning, Coke thus failed to derive philosophically acceptable results.

His errors lay in parsing concepts into too many disparate categories or in misstating the components of a particular legal notion. Thus, relying on derivations, Coke "define[d] Felony to be an Act done *Animo Felleo*; that is to say, a Bitter or Cruel Act," which the Philosopher maintains is incorrect because "there be many things made Felony by the Statute-Law, that proceed not from any bitterness of mind at all, and many that proceed from the contrary." Likewise, the Philosopher opines that "Sir *Edw. Coke* does seldom well distinguish when there are two divers Names for one and the same thing; though one contain the other, he makes them always different, as if it could not be that one and the same Man should be both an Enemy, and a Traytor."[17]

---

15. *Dialogue*, 69.
16. *Dialogue*, 6, 119.
17. *Dialogue*, 111, 106.

The Philosopher's difficulty with Coke's definitions consists in more, however, than simply a disagreement about the dictates of reason. Even if Coke's logic led him to understand "felony" in the same way the Philosopher does, this definition would not have the force that Coke had claimed for it. If Plato in the *Republic* imagined the guardians of his ideal city as philosophers, Hobbes's Philosopher opines that philosophy alone is insufficient. Only authority can secure a definition. Coke's writings on the common law, as well as the decisions and case reports of other judges, lack the power to construct or alter the meaning of legal terms.

At various points the Philosopher refers to the king or statutes as the source of definitions, observing in the context of the question whether an event has occurred at sea or on a river internal to England, and thus whether the courts of admiralty or the common law have jurisdiction, that it cannot be decided "but by the King himself," and noting in a discussion of treason that although "all Men, though of divers Opinions did Condemn it by the name of Treason," they "knew not what Treason meant, but were forced to request the King to determine it." The Philosopher likewise insists that "names imposed by Statutes are equivalent to Definitions." Judges, by contrast, lack the power to construct or alter definitions: "Have Justices of Assize any Power by their Commission to alter the Language of the Land and the received sence of words? Or in the Question in what Case Felony shall be said, is it referred to the Judges to Determine; as in the Question in what Case Treason shall be said it is referred by the Statute of *Edw.* the 3rd to the Parliament? I think not."[18]

Coke's attempt to prescribe definitions of statutory and other terms is, for this reason, hubristic; speaking of Coke's treatment of burglary, the Philosopher asserts,

> I have nothing to say against his Interpretations here, but I like not that any private Man should presume to determine, whether such, or such a Fact done be within the words of a Statute, or not, where it belongs only to a Jury of 12 Men to declare in their Verdict, whether the Fact laid open before them be Burglary, Robbery, Theft, or other Felony; for this is to give a leading Judgment to the Jury, who ought not to consider any private Lawyers Institutes, but the Statutes themselves pleaded before them for directions.[19]

---

18. *Dialogue*, 90, 102, 116, 114.
19. *Dialogue*, 121.

Despite wearing the mantle of authority in his capacity as a judge, Coke lacks the ultimate power to delineate the boundaries of a legal concept, one reserved to the sovereign, who is, for the Philosopher, identified as the King.

At the same time, however, the *Dialogue* itself seems preoccupied with providing definitions, despite constituting a philosophical work endowed with arguably less authority than Coke's own writings. A crucial moment of the *Dialogue* is, indeed, one in which the Philosopher observes, "We have hitherto spoken of Laws without considering any thing of the Nature and Essence of a Law; and not unless we define the word Law, we can go no farther without Ambiguity, and Fallacy, which will be but loss of time."[20] The subsequent discussion suggests that only philosophy—whether practiced poorly by Coke and the common lawyers or well by Hobbes's emissary the Philosopher—can furnish an account of the basis of law. The *Dialogue* thereby establishes a place for the emerging modern discipline of philosophy as the means by which to understand the source of the authority of what Hobbes calls civil law. According to this account, the flaws in Coke's definitions are the least of the lawyer's difficulties. Much more significant is the conflation, through his vision of the common law, of civil law with its own grounds, or, in other words, his understanding of the common law as self-authorizing.

Common Law, Equity, and Chancery: Sovereignty and the Grounds of Law

The *Dialogue*'s reinterpretation of the authority and source of law provides its most salient critique of the early seventeenth-century conflicts between law and equity that Coke both discussed and provoked. The form that the *Dialogue* adopts harks back not only to Plato but also, more proximately, to Christopher St. Germain's sixteenth-century dialogue *Doctor and Student*. This text staged a debate similar to that of Hobbes's work, but between a common lawyer and a doctor of divinity rather than a philosopher. The respective positions of the common lawyer and divine map, as those of the *Dialogue*'s Student and Philosopher superficially appear to as well, onto advocacy of the common law and adherence to equity. In *Doctor and Student,* though, equity maintains a different valence than in the *Dialogue*. In the former, it consists in the discretionary capacity of a judge to decide in accordance with conscience rather than law, and to create

---

20. *Dialogue*, 69.

a merciful exception that takes into account the injustice that would be perpe-trated by adhering too rigidly to statutory or common law in a particular case.[21] In the latter, by contrast, it names both that which resembles law outside of or prior to the civil law as well as the ground of legal decision making within the polity. Hobbes's *Dialogue* thus insists that philosophy has superseded religion as the privileged counterpart to civil law, but also that the relative places of com-mon law and equity should be reconceived.

From a very early moment, the relationship between the jurisprudence of equity and the Court of Chancery appeared indistinct. Although not entirely assimilated to each other, the two resembled circles shifting subtly to overlap in varying degrees according to the historical circumstances. The Court of Chancery had, according to the retrospective construction William Lambarde provided in his sixteenth-century *Archeion*, originated with the Chancellor. Often a religious figure, the Chancellor would follow the king about the country and substitute for him on important occasions. In this period, "such as then sought relief by Equity, were suitors to the King himself, who being assisted with his Chancellor and Councell, did mitigate the severity of the law in his own person, when it pleaseth him to be present; and did (in absence) either refer the same to the Chancellor alone, or to him and some other of the Council."[22] The equitable capacity of the Chancellor long remained part of his "extraordinary jurisdiction."[23] The author-ity for administering equity, and thereby rendering more comfortable the pro-crustean bed of the common law, which "otherwise, to apply one generall Law to all particular cases, were to make all *Shooes* by one *Last*, or to cut one *Glove* for all *Hands*," derived from the king's own power to exceed or correct the law.[24] Rather than simply shoring up the chancellor's position, this intimate association

21. Alan Cromartie has importantly demonstrated that the understanding of equity in *Doctor and Student* is ambivalent, in that, on the one hand, "it suggested the need for an additional jurisdic-tion that could correct the common law's procedures by reference to natural principles; but on the other it implied that equitable exceptions were actually a part of positive law." Alan Cromartie, *The Constitutionalist Revolution: An Essay on the History of England, 1450–1642* (Cambridge: Cambridge University Press, 2006), 49. As Cromartie elaborates elsewhere, application of the Chancellor's con-science represented for St. Germain not simply an exception to the rules of common law but recourse to another rule, whether laws of nature or those of custom or statute. Alan Cromartie, "*Epieikeia* and Conscience," in *The Oxford Handbook of English Law and Literature, 1500–1700*, ed. Lorna Hutson (Oxford: Oxford University Press, 2017), 320–36.

22. William Lambarde, *Archeion, or, a Discourse upon the High Courts of Justice in England* (1635), ed. Charles H. McIlwain and Paul Ward (Cambridge: Harvard University Press, 1957), 59.

23. A. H. Marsh, *History of the Court of Chancery and of the Rise and Development of the Doctrines of Equity* (Toronto: Carswell, 1890), 22–34.

24. Lambarde, *Archeion*, 69.

with the king led early seventeenth-century opponents of royal authority to critique his office and jurisdiction, culminating in an Interregnum proposal to abolish Chancery altogether.[25] Although reformers were unsuccessful in actually dispensing with the institution of Chancery, the chancellor's discretionary capacity was significantly reduced by the century's end.[26]

Although for some the jurisprudence of equity itself was tainted by its connection with Chancery and thereby the king, the rhetoric of equity and conscience remained powerful instruments in the hands of proponents of the common law.[27] The jury, in particular, one of the principal bodies charged with adjudication under the common law, was often described in a manner that suggested it implemented the jurisprudence of equity.[28] The designation "chancellor" itself became a weapon in the war over the respective places of Chancery and the common law courts; Coke at one point dubbed the jury "chancellors" (*Hixt v. Goates*), and Chancellor Ellesmere, defending his own authority in the *Earl of Oxford's Case*, insisted that Coke acted as a chancellor would in exercising the power of judicial review over statutes. Citing *Bonham's Case*, in which Coke maintained that a statute allowing an individual to sit as a judge in his own case was repugnant to the common law, Ellesmere noted: "It seemeth by the Lord Coke's Report . . . in Dr. Bonham's Case, That Statutes are not so sacred as that the Equity of them may not be examined. . . . And the Judges themselves do play the Chancellors Parts (upon Statutes, making Construction of them according to Equity, varying from the Rules and Grounds of Law, and enlarging them *pro bono publico*, against the Letter and Intent of the Makers, whereof our Books have many Hundreds of Cases)."[29] Equity was thus far from the exclusive province of the Chancellor.

---

25. *Commons Journal* 7 (October 19, 1653): 336.

26. Bernadette Meyler, "Substitute Chancellors: The Role of the Jury in the Contest between Common Law and Equity," accessed December 20, 2018, https://scholarship.law.cornell.edu/lsrp_papers/39/. As Ian Williams has elegantly demonstrated, the intimate connection between Chancery and the king's prerogative powers that conditioned the seventeenth-century conflicts over the court's role itself derived from common lawyers' readings of Bodin. Ian Williams, "Developing a Prerogative Theory for the Authority of the Chancery: The French Connection," in *Law and Authority in British Legal History, 1200–1900*, ed. Mark Godfrey (Cambridge: Cambridge University Press, 2016), 33–59. Hobbes's engagement with the debates over Chancery's power hence resonates with Bodin's treatment of the marks of sovereignty.

27. Thomas Andrew Green, *Verdict According to Conscience: Perspectives on the English Criminal Trial Jury, 1200–1800* (Chicago: University of Chicago Press, 1985), 153–99.

28. Meyler, "Substitute Chancellors."

29. *Earl of Oxford's Case* (1615), *Chancery Reports*, vol. 1: 11–12.

Doctor and Student itself suggested as much, and Edward Hake's slightly later *Epieikeia*—which not only derived its title from the Aristotelian term for equity but also was indebted to the Aristotelian notion of equity and was presented in revised form to James I in 1603—further separated the practice of Chancery from the core of the conception of equity.[30] For the Student of St. Germain's dialogue, the laws of England generously conceived include equity as a kind of penumbra. Although equity is not part of the system of English laws, it is comprehended by their general thrust. The chancellor is thus assigned the task of realizing the dictates of equity under the fiction that he is providing an exception from rather than realization of the law:

> The lorde Chaunceller must ordre his conscience after the rewles and groundes of the lawe of the realme in so moche that it had not ben moche inconuenyent to have assigned suche remedye in the Chauncery upon such equytyes for the. vii. grounde of the lawe of englande but for as moch as no recorde remayneth in the kynges courtes of no suche bylle ne of the wrytte of sub pena that is suyd thereupon therefore it is not sette as for a specyall grounde of the lawe but as a thynge that is suffred by the lawe.[31]

Although this passage represents Chancery as the institutional location for the jurisprudence of equity, it simultaneously suggests that equity is an essential correlate, if not part, of the laws of England.

The structure of *Epieikeia* further disaggregates Chancery and the jurisprudence of equity. Divided into three parts, Hake's dialogue treats first "Equity in General," then "The Equity of the Common Lawes of England," and only finally—and rather briefly—"The Equity of the Highe Courte of Chancery." In discussing the equity of the common laws, *Epieikeia* covers not only cases, the core materials of the common law, but also statutory interpretation. The arrangement of *Epieikeia* epitomizes Hake's modification of earlier notions of equity, including that which St. Germain had promulgated. *Doctor and Student* had emphasized the opposition between the equitable decision in a particular

---

30. For a fuller discussion of the Aristotelian tradition of equity and its legacy in the Renaissance, see Kathy Eden, *Poetic and Legal Fiction in the Aristotelian Tradition* (Princeton: Princeton University Press, 1986).

31. Christopher St. Germain, *Doctor and Student, or Dialogues Between a Doctor of Divinity and a Student in the Laws of England Containing the Grounds of Those Laws* (1523), ed. Christopher T. F. T. Plucknett and J. L. Barton (London: Selden Society, 1974), 105.

case and the generality of common or statutory law. St. Germain had likewise associated equity with mercy or the relaxation of standards of proof. According to the Doctor:

> Equytye is a [ryghtwysenes] that consideryth all the pertyculer cyrcum-staunces of the dede the whiche also is temperyd with the swetnes of mercye. . . . It is not possyble to make any generall rewle of the lawe but that it shall fayle in some case. And therfore makers of lawes take hede to suche thynges as may often come and not to every particuler case for they coulde not though they wolde And therfore to folowe the wordes of the lawe were in some case both agaynst Iustyce & the common welth: wherefore in some cases it is *good and even* necessary to leve the wordis of the lawe & to folowe that reason and Justyce reqyreth & to that intent equytie is ordeyned that is to say to tempre and myttygate the rygoure of the lawe.[32]

For Hake, by contrast, equity represents not a mode of judging or quality of the judge but rather an aspect of the law itself: "I conceive it somewhat cleere that if the lawe we speake of be a good lawe and well grounded, then the *Equity* that must be used to the correction of the generalitye thereof cannot be said to be the *Equitye* of the judge, but of the lawe, for otherwise the lawe muste be a lawe without *Equitye*, which weare indeede to be a lawe without justice."[33]

Furthermore, *Epieikeia*'s approach does not lead inevitably to the mitigation of punishment, as St. Germain's conception had emphasized, but in some cases extends the reach of particular statutes beyond their precise language or broadens the dictates of the common law. Hake raises the example of a man who gives his wife a poisoned apple with the intent that she consume it and perish. Because she passes it along to their child, who dies, he would not ordinarily be considered a murderer under the law. Equity, however, dictates otherwise: although "no man can be holden a felon without an intent to commit felony, yet here by the righteous exposition of this generality you see a man a felon by the only contingent sequel of an act, in which sequel he had no intent of felony."[34] Hake's separation of equity from the particularity of the judge increasingly distinguished the jurisprudence of equity from the institution of Chancery.

32. St. Germain, *Doctor and Student*, 97.
33. Edward Hake, *Epieikeia: A Dialogue on Equity in Three Parts* (1597), ed. D. E. C. Yale (New Haven: Yale University Press, 1953), 11.
34. Hake, *Epieikeia*, 68–69.

Coke, however, often conflated the two. In the prefaces to his *Reports*, Coke developed an account of the jurisprudence of the common law that established its credentials as a pillar of the English subject's liberty from time immemorial.[35] As an "ancient constitution," the common law that Coke depicted opposed the excesses of the king's prerogative and represented a bulwark against even statutory encroachments on rights. Thus Coke in 1610 opposed James I's claim that his prerogative comprehended a right to legislate by proclamation rather than through coordination with Parliament. The same year, in *Bonham's Case*, Coke explained that acts contradicting the fundamental principles of the common law would be invalid.[36] By permitting the censors of the College of Physicians to adjudicate infringements upon their charter and prescribe penalties of which they would retain a share, Parliament had, as discussed in chapter 1, violated the common law dictate that an individual cannot be a judge in his or her own case. As the court most intimately associated with the king's prerogative, Chancery too became a primary target of Coke's criticism. Although Coke directed his attention principally toward Chancery's jurisdictional contest with the courts of the common law, his vision of common law reasoning itself opposed the equitable model of adjudication.

The common law that Coke inherited lacked what twenty-first-century jurists might identify as its foremost characteristic—firm adherence in adjudication to the legal precedents set up by earlier decisions.[37] Coke was responsible for shifting jurisprudence toward an increased regard for the principles that prior cases articulated, although he did not, as T. F. T. Plucknett has demonstrated in detail in the context of *Bonham's Case*, allow precedents to entirely

---

35. J. G. A. Pocock, *The Ancient Constitution and the Feudal Law: A Study of English Historical Thought in the Seventeenth Century* (Cambridge: Cambridge University Press, 1987), 30–55.

36. Sir Edward Coke, *Reports*, in vol. 1 of *The Selected Writings and Speeches of Sir Edward Coke*, 3 vols., ed. Steve Sheppard (Indianapolis: Liberty Fund, 2003), 264–85.

37. A 1999 edition of *Black's Law Dictionary* defines precedent as "an adjudged case or decision of a court of justice, considered as furnishing an example or authority for an identical or similar case afterwards arising or a similar question of law." Henry Campbell Black and Bryan A. Garner, eds., *Black's Law Dictionary*, 7th ed. (St. Paul: West, 1999), s.v. "precedent."
The constraints provided by precedent were generally viewed as fairly pliable in common law jurisprudence up to the twentieth century. As one commentator has explained the difference, a "flexible concept of 'precedent' . . . still prevailed in the nineteenth century on one hand," whereas, on the other, a "more rigid concept of stare decisis . . . emerged in the common law in the twentieth century." Todd Zywicki, "The Rise and Fall of Efficiency in the Common Law: A Supply-Side Analysis," *Northwestern University Law Review* 97 (Summer 2003): 1617. Neil Duxbury furnishes a sketch of the earlier medieval and early modern developments regarding reliance on case citation and precedent in *The Nature and Authority of Precedent* (Cambridge: Cambridge University Press, 2008), 31–36.

dictate his own decisions.[38] In the series of prefaces to his *Reports*, Coke elaborated on the value of recording cases as he was himself doing and of making reference to earlier similar materials. Through the third, sixth, and eighth prefaces, Coke created an early canon of sources for understanding the common law, providing a litany of particular works and describing where they were to be found.[39] Coke furthermore extolled the use of recorded cases as precedent and example.

For Coke, citing precedent assisted in the task of persuading the reader of the validity of the propositions that a case put forth. As Coke wrote in the third preface, "Mine advise is, that whensoever a man is enforced to yeeld a reason of his opinion or judgement, that then hee set downe all authorities, presidents, reasons, arguments, and inferences whatsoever that may bee probably applied to the case in question; For some will be perswaded, or drawne by one, and some by another, according as the capacitie or understanding of the hearer or reader is."[40] In the sixth preface, Coke provided even more explicit instruction about citation practices. Responding to a religious individual's criticism of *Caudries Case*, Coke explained that the case simply ventriloquized established law, and that he, unlike his devout interlocutor, "quoted the Year, the Leaf, the Chapter and other certain References for the ready finding" of the "Judgments and Resolutions of the Reverend Judges and Sages of the Common Laws." According to Coke, cases also furnish informative examples of particular legal principles. In describing this function, Coke foreshadowed the case method of legal instruction still dominant at law schools today: "The reporting of particular Cases or Examples is the most perspicuous course of teaching, the right rule and reason of the law; for so did Almighty God himself, when he delivered by *Moses* his Judicial Laws, *Exemplis docuit pro Legibus*."[41]

Employment of precedent was not only conducive to these pragmatic goals of persuasion and instruction but also reflected Coke's vision of the nature of legal reasoning, a reasoning that relied on the accumulated wisdom of multiple judges rather than the perspicacity of a single individual. In accordance with this view, Coke referred to the common law as "nothing else but reason . . . an artificial perfection of reason, gotten by long study, observation, and experience,

---

38. T. F. T. Plucknett, "Bonham's Case and Judicial Review," *Harvard Law Review* 30 (1928): 30–70.

39. See Bernadette Meyler, "Towards a Common Law Originalism," *Stanford Law Review* 59 (2006): 551–600.

40. Coke, *Reports*, 60.

41. Coke, *Reports*, 155, 156.

and not of every man's natural reason."[42] Every man's natural reason might be able to arrive at the dictates of equity, and would be correlated with the equitable deployment of conscience, following Hake's comment that "*Equity* is no other thing but an exception of the lawe of God or of the lawe of Nature which is the lawe of Reason, from the generalitie of the lawe of man."[43] The reason of the common law emanated, by contrast, from the individual judge's apprenticeship in examining and understanding precedents. This mode of reasoning was distinct from that of the chancellor, who would determine cases as an individual, solely on the basis of his conscience and without reliance on the opinions of prior judges. Furthermore, the chancellor would consider each set of facts brought before him independently, without being constrained by particular precedents. In terms of both his own deployment of reason and the conspicuous absence of any reliance on example, the chancellor provided a jurisprudential contrast to Coke's conception of the common law.

Coke's efforts to establish the supremacy of the common law were, however, ultimately more institutional than jurisprudential; hence he directed his explicit criticism against Chancery and the extent of its jurisdiction rather than against equitable adjudication. In the early seventeenth century, a variety of courts were entitled to hear cases arising from the same underlying events; nor was the choice of venue insignificant, because the law applied by the disparate courts could lead one party or the other to prevail. For instance, in the case of actions for debt, the common law courts required defendants who claimed to have already fulfilled their financial obligations to show a written acquittance; without this document, the bond in the hands of the plaintiff would be sufficient to override all oral testimony and the defendant would be forced to repay the debt a second time. Chancery, however, claimed to examine the conscience of the defendant and, taking his testimony under oath, allowed it substantial weight; if the equities of the matter supported his claim for relief from the bond, the chancellor would decide in his favor.[44]

More significant than this type of "forum shopping," in which litigants engage even today, was the fact that parties could bring concurrent actions in different courts, or commence a second action in a new forum if the first was not proceeding as anticipated. In addition, an individual who was dissatisfied with

---

42. Sir Edward Coke, *Institutes*, vol. 1, in vol. 2 of *The Selected Writings and Speeches of Sir Edward Coke*, 3 vols., ed. Steve Sheppard (Indianapolis: Liberty Fund, 2003), 701.

43. Hake, *Epieikeia*, 13.

44. J. H. Baker, *An Introduction to English Legal History*, 4th ed. (London: Butterworths, 2002), 368–69, 372–73.

the outcome of a suit could ask another court to hear the case again and thereby review and potentially alter the initial judgment. The possibility that a new court might reexamine a judicial decision—in the absence of a prescribed process of appeal—left parties uncertain as to the finality of any particular determination and judges concerned about the authority of their pronouncements.

Coke was especially intent on halting Chancery's efforts to rehear cases decided at common law, for which purpose he resorted in 1616 to the writ of praemunire, originally designed to prevent individuals from appealing judgments obtained in the king's courts to the spiritual tribunals of Rome.[45] He deployed this potentially fearsome weapon—which had previously carried with it significant penalties—against those who attempted to bring actions in Chancery, trying to persuade the lawyers of the parties who had obtained judgment at common law as well as a grand jury to bring the force of the writ down upon the offending parties.[46] Coke's efforts in this regard furnished one of the reasons why King James I summarily dismissed him from office in 1616.[47]

Hobbes's *Dialogue* represents Coke's attempts to circumscribe the jurisdiction of Chancery and distinguish the capacities of the common law and other courts as misguided efforts that emanate out of a mistaken view of the nature of law. Legal authority, for the Philosopher, cannot arise from the exercise of reason alone, no matter how long the period or numerous the individuals over which that reason has accumulated. The type of reason underlying law is the natural reason identified with equity, but it becomes effectual within the polity only when

---

45. Catherine Drinker Bowen, *The Lion and the Throne: The Life and Times of Sir Edward Coke, 1552–1634* (Boston: Little Brown & Co., 1990), 362–63. According to John Cowell's *Interpreter*, a very early law dictionary:

> The church of *Rome* under pretence of her supremacie and the dignitie of Saint *Peters chaire*, grew to such an incroaching, that there could not be a benefice . . . of any worth here in England, the bestowing whereof could escape the Pope by one meanes or another. In so much, as for the most part, he graunted out Mandats of ecclesiasticall livings, before they were voide to certaine persons by his buls, pretending thereto in a great care to see the Church provided of a Successor before it needed. Whence it grew that these kinde of Buls were called *Gratiae expectativae*. . . . These provisions were so rife with us, that at the last, King *Edward* the third, that heroicall Prince, not digesting so intolerable an oppression, made a statute . . . against those that drew the Kings people out of the Realme, to answer things belonging to the kings court.

Under Richard, the punishment for violators was increased to "perpetuall banishment, forfeiture of their lands, tenements, goods, and catels." John Cowell, *A Law Dictionary: or the Interpreter of Words and Terms* (London: D. Browne, 1708).

46. John Campbell, *The Lives of the Chief Justices of England*, vol. 1 (Jersey City: Fred Linn & Co., 1881), 241–42.

47. Bowen, *The Lion and the Throne*, 362, 377.

implemented in the form of civil law by the sovereign. As civil law stands in relation to the polity so equity does to the state of nature. Equity depends on reason,
whereas civil law is a manifestation of will.

It is, in part, epistemological difficulties that render equity alone insufficient;
without the sovereign's decision, natural reason might lead individuals in disparate directions. The logic of equity itself, therefore, in the dictate to seek peace
and the mandate that each person preserve himself, leads to the conclusion that
civil law is necessary. Yet equity not only conduces toward but also retains a place
within the arena of civil law. The latter should remain consistent with equity, but
only the sovereign can pronounce the final word identifying incompatibilities.
Hence the Court of Chancery, intimately connected with the king, and the monarch himself, should be able to hear any appeal from common law courts.

The reference of the term "equity" altered during the course of Hobbes's writings. In his 1651 *Leviathan,* Hobbes had identified equity as a component of the
law of nature, whereas in the *Dialogue,* as well as in his 1668 *Behemoth,* equity generally replaces the law of nature itself. In redescribing the law of nature as equity,
the *Dialogue* elides the distinction that might be drawn between the functions of
equity on the threshold of the polity and within its confines. This conflation proves
crucial for the argument of the *Dialogue* because it allows equity both to furnish
the basis for civil law and to manifest itself as a function within the state. The law
of nature—transformed by the *Dialogue* into equity—insists upon entrance into
the social compact, while equity then polices the commonwealth's conformity with
the fundamental precepts from which Hobbes deduces the necessity of civil society
itself. Equity within the state thus becomes the basic form of law because it ensures
a coherence between the constituted state and the reasons behind its constitution.

In the *Leviathan,* Hobbes had identified equity as a component of the law of
nature, referring to it first as "also . . . a Law of Nature," then calling it "that principall Law of Nature."[48] The law of nature itself he defined as "a Precept, or generall Rule, found out by Reason, by which a man is forbidden to do, that, which
is destructive of his life, or taketh away the means of preserving the same; and to
omit, that, by which he thinketh it may be best preserved." The law of nature and
the civil law are coextensive, but until the commonwealth is erected, the laws of
nature remain qualities rather than laws; only with the aid of the sovereign power
can they transmogrify into civil law. Indeed, the designation "natural law" is
improper, according to Hobbes, because natural law lacks independent authority within the polity. Hence, "these dictates of reason, men use to call by the name

---

48. Thomas Hobbes, *Leviathan* (1651), ed. Richard Tuck (Cambridge: Cambridge University Press, 1991), 105, 195; hereafter *Leviathan.*

of Lawes, but improperly: for they are but Conclusions, or Theoremes concerning what conduceth to the conservation and defence of themselves, wheras Law, properly is the word of him, that by right hath command over others. But yet if we consider the same Theoremes, as delivered in the word of God, that by right commandeth all things, then are they properly called Lawes."[49]

The laws of nature furnish the contingent means of achieving peace in the absence of that assurance provided by the social compact: "Reason suggesteth convenient Articles of Peace, upon which men may be drawn to agreement. These Articles, are they, which otherwise are called the Lawes of Nature." At the same time, because the laws of nature impel individuals to preserve themselves, and, in doing so, to seek peace, they urge entrance into the compact and encourage members of civil society to avoid violating the compact by revolution or otherwise. Indeed, the first law of nature specifies "that every man, ought to endeavour Peace, as farre as he has hope of obtaining it," a rule that leads individuals to covenant among themselves to erect a commonwealth by institution, at the head of which the sovereign representative underwrites the search for peace and withdrawal from the state of war. Addressing the moment at which continuing adherence to the covenant is at risk, the third law of nature dictates "that men perform their Covenants made: without which, Covenants are in vain, and but Empty words. . . . [I]n this law of Nature, consisteth the Fountain and Originall of Justice." For this reason, in discussing the attempt to attain sovereignty by rebellion, Hobbes diagnoses it as a violation of the law of nature: "It is manifest, that though the event follow, yet because it cannot reasonably be expected, but rather the contrary; and because by gaining it so, others are taught to gain the same in like manner, the attempt thereof is against reason. Justice therefore, that is to say, Keeping of Covenant, is a Rule of Reason, by which we are forbidden to do any thing destructive to our life; and consequently a Law of Nature." Both because success cannot be expected to flow naturally from the revolutionary attempt and because it sets a lawless example, revolutionary action violates the law of nature that specifies men should "performe their Covenants made."[50] The laws of nature thus patrol the boundaries of the social compact, pushing individuals into a covenant with one another at the outset and thrusting them back into their agreement when they are in danger of withdrawing from it.

By the moment of the *Dialogue,* though, the term "equity" has replaced "laws of nature" as Hobbes's designation of these primordial principles that result

49. *Leviathan,* 91, 185, 111.
50. *Leviathan,* 90, 91–91, 117–18, 100, 103.

from the work of reason. The *Dialogue* equates the law of reason with equity as *Leviathan* had done with the law of nature; the Lawyer explains, "As to the Law of Reason, which is Equity, 'tis sure enough there is but one Legislator, which is God," and the Philosopher states that "Equity is the same thing with the Law of Reason." As the law of reason, equity is contrasted with civil law: "The difference between Injustice, and Iniquity is this; that Injustice is the Transgression of a Statute-Law, and Iniquity the Transgression of the Law of Reason." Discussing Bracton's claim, quoted by Coke, that "lex est sanctio justa, jubens honesta, et prohibens contraria," the Philosopher opines that it is incorrect to suppose "that a Statute made by the Soveraign Power of a Nation may be unjust. There may indeed in a Statute Law, made by Men be found Iniquity, but not Injustice."[51] Justice is therefore a correlate of civil law, whereas equity corresponds with the law of reason.

Natural reason itself, although universally shared, may not lead each person to the same result. Equity is thus an imperfect path, which may circle around civil law but is stuck in an orbit that can never reach it. Because no one is immune from errors in reasoning, and in fact the state of nature provides no vantage point from which to judge whether a path is direct or wandering, civil law appoints the sovereign as reason's voice—not because he will inevitably reason better than any other individual, but rather because someone must be designated the final arbiter; as the Philosopher inquires:

> Would you have every Man to every other Man alledge for Law his own particular Reason? There is not amongst Men an Universal Reason agreed upon in any Nation, besides the Reason of him that hath the Soveraign Power; yet though his Reason be but the Reason of one Man, yet it is set up to supply the place of that Universal Reason, which is expounded to us by our Saviour in the Gospel, and consequently our King is to us the Legislator both of Statute-Law, and of Common-Law.[52]

As the sovereign representative, the king also speaks as the designated voice for the conclusions of reason.

Nor can Coke's vision of a reason "fined and refined" by generations of judges and by years of study lead of its own accord to a just outcome. In the *Leviathan*, Hobbes compares the potential flaws in a particular person's exercise of reason with mistakes in mathematical equations:

---

51. *Dialogue*, 67, 94, 70, 69–70.
52. *Dialogue*, 67.

As in Arithmetique, unpractised men must, and Professors themselves may often erre, and cast up false; so also in any other subject of Reasoning, the ablest, most attentive, and most practiced men, may deceive themselves, and inferre false Conclusions; Not but that Reason it selfe is always Right Reason, as well as Arithmetique is a certain and infallible Art: But no one mans Reason, nor the Reason of any one number of men, makes the certaintie; no more than an account is therefore well cast up, because a great many men have unanimously approved it. And therefore, as when there is a controversy in an account, the parties must by their own accord, set up for right Reason, the Reason of some Arbitrator, or Judge, to whose sentence they will both stand, or their controversie must either come to blowes, or be undecided, for want of a right Reason constituted by Nature.[53]

In the *Dialogue*, the Philosopher presents an even dimmer view of legal reasoning; rather than drawing further analogies between the potential for flaws in mathematical and legal reasoning, he instead contrasts the two from the very outset of the discussion, opining that "the great Masters of the Mathematicks do not so often err as the great Professors of the Law."[54] Neither the agreement of the majority at a particular moment nor the consensus of judges over time can, therefore, establish the correctness of a legal principle or result.

At several points in both the *Dialogue* and *Leviathan*, Hobbes more explicitly disparages Coke's notion of the legal reasoning that underlies the common law, one that "is dispersed into so many several heads" and "hath been fined and refined, by an infinite number of Grave and Learned Men."[55] In particular, he criticizes the notion that reliance on precedent or custom—like Coke's dependence on etymologies for definitional purposes—lends the authority of law to a judicial decision. Empirically, precedents are disparate in their dictates, just as might be predicted from Hobbes's vision of the variety of outcomes consistent with the law of reason. As the Philosopher observes, "Precedents are Judgments one contrary to another; I mean divers Men, in divers Ages, upon the same case give divers Judgments." Hence, "no Record of a Judgment is a Law, save only to the party Pleading, until he can by Law reverse the former Judgment."[56] Furthermore, the mere fact that precedents do exist and coalesce does not

---

53. *Leviathan*, 33.
54. *Dialogue*, 53.
55. *Dialogue*, 61; *Leviathan*, 186–87.
56. *Dialogue*, 89, 90.

indicate that these prior cases have reached the correct result; rather, "it is possible long study may encrease, and confirm erroneous Sentences: and where men build on false grounds, the more they build, the greater is the ruin."[57]

Even if a particular principle rises to the level of constituting a custom, this custom must still accord with the prescriptions of the sovereign's reason. If the sovereign chooses to resist an established custom, even one that appears, in the language of the ancient constitution, to be immemorial, "the Length of Time shal bring no prejudice to his Right; but the question shal be judged by Equity. For many unjust Actions, and unjust Sentences, go uncontrolled a longer time, than any man can remember. And our Lawyers account no Customes law, but such as are reasonable, and that evill Customes are to be abolished: But the Judgement of what is reasonable, and of what is to be abolished, belongeth to him that maketh the Law, which is the Sovraign Assembly or Monarch."[58] The Philosopher of the *Dialogue* further opines that only those customs that accord with equity should be retained: "I deny that any Custome of its own Nature, can amount to the Authority of a Law: For if the Custom be unreasonable, you must with all other Lawyers confess that it is no Law, but ought to be abolished; and if the Custom be reasonable, it is not the Custom, but the Equity that makes it Law. For what need is there to make Reason Law by any Custom how long soever when the Law of Reason is Eternal?"[59] Thus neither precedent nor custom possesses any authority greater than the extent to which it remains in conformity with equity.

As the law of reason, equity therefore subsumes the common law. An early colloquy in the *Dialogue* suggests as much: according to the Philosopher, "It followeth then that which you call the Common-Law, Distinct from Statute-Law, is nothing else but the Law of God," to which the Lawyer responds, "In some sense it is, but it is not Gospel, but Natural Reason, and Natural Equity."[60] Coke's mistake was to insist that the common law constituted the default version of law in the commonwealth, and that equity simply supplemented its scope. Equity, Hobbes maintains, as the form in which the *Dialogue* treats natural law, itself furnishes the backdrop of civil law, and is the wellspring out of which all law, including the common law, emerges. The common law itself possesses no greater authority than equity, and is similarly subject to the sovereign's affirmation or dissent.

---

57. *Leviathan*, 187.
58. *Leviathan*, 184–85.
59. *Dialogue*, 96.
60. *Dialogue*, 67.

At the same time, equity assumes a slightly different position as one component of the civil law. While on the one hand it is the counterpart to and coextensive with the civil law for the state of nature, equity on the other hand designates a function of the civil law itself. The sovereign furnishes the point of mediation between these two aspects of equity; as the authority behind civil law, the sovereign "is not Bound to any other Law but that of Equity," and as the final point of appeal within the civil law, the sovereign must provide an equitable judgment.[61]

In its guise as a component of civil law, equity names the proper mode of judgment. Within the artificial body of the Leviathan are contained "Equity and Lawes, an artificiall Reason and Will." While the will prescribes laws, reason presents a chain of inferences that leads to the equitable resolution of a case. The ideal judge—whether of the common law courts or Chancery—must follow equity: "The things that make a good Judge, or good Interpreter of the Lawes, are, first, A right understanding of that principall Law of Nature called Equity";[62] indeed, "all Judges in all Courts ought to Judge according to Equity, which is the Law of Reason."[63] Equity is linked with the distributive justice prescribed by the law of nature, although Hobbes resists this employment of the term "justice," which should apply only in the context of civil law; as Hobbes writes in *Leviathan*: "Distributive Justice [is] the Justice of an Arbitrator; that is to say, the act of defining what is Just. Wherein, (being trusted by them that make him Arbitrator,) if he performe his Trust, he is said to distribute to every man his own: and this is indeed Just Distribution, and may be called (though improperly) Distributive Justice; but more properly Equity; which is also a Law of Nature." This version of equity relies on the operations of reason, and emphasizes equality rather than exceptionality: "The observance of this law, from the equall distribution to each man, of that which in reason belongeth to him, is called Equity, and (as I have sayd before) distributive Justice: the violation, Acceptation of persons."[64] Courts of justice may decide in accordance with statutory directives, whereas equity interprets such materials in light of the law of reason. As a result, "Justice fulfils the Law, and Equity Interprets the Law; and amends the Judgments given upon the same Law."[65]

The Philosopher is quick to specify, however, that equity amends not the laws themselves but rather erroneous judgments, whether prior precedents or earlier

61. *Dialogue*, 70.
62. *Leviathan*, 9, 47, 195.
63. *Dialogue*, 70.
64. *Leviathan*, 105, 108.
65. *Dialogue*, 100.

decisions in the same case. In his capacity as the authoritative source of the reason grounding equity, the king—or his deputy, the chancellor—is entitled to
take charge of amending judgments: "Since [lower judges] may err, and that the
King is not Bound to any other Law but that of Equity, it belongs to him alone
to give Remedy to them that by the Ignorance, or Corruption of a Judge shall
suffer damage." Indeed, Hobbes indicates that, given the resemblance among the
tasks of all courts, the only reason for the existence of the Court of Chancery
would be to provide a venue for the appeal of imperfect judgments in the courts
of common law:

> I would fain know to what end there should be any other Court of Eq-
> uity at all, either before the Chancellor or any other Person, besides the
> Judges of the Civil, or Common-Pleas? Nay I am sure you can alledge
> none but this, that there was a necessity of a Higher Court of Equity,
> than the Courts of Common-Law, to remedy the Errors in Judgement
> given by the Justices of Inferior Courts, and the errors in Chancery were
> irrevocable, except by Parliament, or by special Commission appointed
> thereunto by the King.[66]

Within the framework of the commonwealth, equity designates a type of interpretation of which the king furnishes the ultimate source.[67]

Equitable interpretation—and, in particular, that of the sovereign—proves
necessary, however, because of epistemological uncertainty. Just as reason could
lead individuals in radically disparate directions, statutes can, for Hobbes, be
understood in extremely different ways. In several areas of law—including the
definition of crimes—Hobbes focuses primarily on the intention behind an act
or statement. The Philosopher thus emphasizes, contra Coke, that the treason

---

66. *Dialogue,* 70, 94–95.
67. Philip Pettit makes a similar argument in *Made with Words: Hobbes on Language, Mind, and
Politics* (Princeton: Princeton University Press, 2008). As he explains, citing *Leviathan* and *Dialogues*:

> For Hobbes, as for contemporary legal theory, no laws, no matter how carefully formu-
> lated, are proof against rival construals. "All laws, written and unwritten, have need of
> interpretation" (L 26.21). This means that law cannot rule over human beings, strictly
> speaking, since in order to do so it would have to be self-interpreting. We have to give up
> the idea of a rule of law, then, in favor of recognizing that legislation involves legal inter-
> pretation as crucially as it does legal imposition. But if the sovereign is to impose the law,
> as all sides will agree that the sovereign should, who is to interpret it? For Hobbes, it has
> to be the individual or body in the sovereign position, or those appointed by the sovereign
> who act under the sovereign will (D 44, 68). "For else, by the craft of an interpreter the
> law may be made to bear a sense contrary to that of the sovereign, by which means the
> interpreter becomes the legislator" (L 21.20). (125–26).

statute criminalizes even the mere design or plan to kill the king; the requirement of an overt act demonstrating this intent is simply an aspect of proof, rather than an element of the offense, and should be satisfied by the defendant's words expressing intent. At the same time, the Philosopher argues that only a "voluntary unlawful act" can constitute murder.[68] The intention behind an act is thus, for Hobbes, central to whether it should be identified as a crime.

Statutes too, Hobbes opines, should be interpreted not according to their words but rather according to the legislator's intention, a method that bears significant resemblance to the traditional equitable approach.[69] As the Philosopher claims, "That is not always the Law which is signified by the Grammatical Construction of the Letter, but that which the Legislator thereby intended to be in Force." This intention is not entirely transparent, and must be discerned by examining the textual and historical context of the law; although the Philosopher admits that "the Intention . . . is a very hard matter many times to pick out of the words of the Statute," he suggests inspecting "the Preamble, the time when it was made, and the Incommodities for which it was made."[70] In the *Leviathan* as well, Hobbes had insisted that laws should be understood not simply by analyzing their explicit language but rather through examining the legislative intent, which the sovereign should attempt in various ways to make clear:

> The Perspicuity [of the laws], consisteth not so much in the words of the Law it selfe, as in a Declaration of the Causes, and Motives, for which it was made. That is it, that shewes us the meaning of the Legislator; and the meaning of the Legislator known, the Law is more easily understood by few, than many words. For all words, are subject to ambiguity; and therefore multiplication of words in the body of the Law, is multiplication of ambiguity. . . . It belongeth therefore to the Office of a Legislator . . . to make the reason Perspicuous, why the Law was made; and the Body of the Law it selfe, as short, but in as proper, and significant termes, as may be.[71]

---

68. *Dialogue*, 106–9, 148.

69. As Kathy Eden has explained, "The concept of intention . . . figures in the operation of equity—as Aristotle understands it—not only as it pertains to the agent whose actions are being judged, but also as it pertains to the legislator, according to whose intentions the laws are framed and specific legal judgments are made." Eden, *Poetic and Legal Fiction*, 42.

70. *Dialogue*, 97, 56–57.

71. *Leviathan*, 240.

Despite taking the most assiduous of precautions in their attempt to understand enacted laws, judges may not succeed in the task. Appeal to a higher court is therefore necessary. From this premise, Hobbes leaps to the conclusion that the king himself should sit in judgment on such appeals. Because of the epistemological uncertainty involved in comprehending the intent of a law, the sovereign alone can definitively resolve interpretive questions, not necessarily through diagnosing his own prior motives, but rather by treating the act of interpretation as another variety of lawgiving. Indeed both the *Leviathan* and the *Dialogue* insist on assimilating judgment with lawgiving in the final instance.

The situation seems quite different at first blush. It is, for Hobbes, the duty of judges to interpret, rather than create, laws: "In all Courts of Justice, the Soveraign (which is the Person of the Commonwealth), is he that Judgeth: The subordinate Judge, ought to have regard to the reason, which moved his Soveraign to make such law, that his Sentence may be according thereunto; which then is his Soveraigns Sentence; otherwise it is his own, and an unjust one." Unjust interpretations deviate from the law created by the sovereign; the sentence that is not in accord with the law is thus an erroneous one. At the same time, however, laws themselves differ not in kind but in degree from judgments; rather than an individual sentence, the law furnishes a general one: "All Lawes are generall Judgments, or Sentences of the Legislator; as also every particular Judgement, is a Law to him, whose case is Judged."[72]

In the extreme case, a judge's insistence on an incorrect interpretation would impermissibly alter the law itself: "No errour of a subordinate Judge, can change the Law, which is the generall Sentence of the Soveraigne." Because the authority to create the law rests ineluctably in the sovereign, only the sovereign can endow others with the ability to interpret it, lest the law be altered through this process:

> It is not the Letter, but the Intendment, or meaning; that is to say, the authentique Interpretation of the Law (which is the sense of the Legislator,) in which the nature of the Law consisteth; And therefore the Interpretation of all Lawes dependeth on the Authority Soveraign; and the Interpreters can be none but those, which the Soveraign, (to whom only the Subject oweth obedience) shall appoint. For else, by the craft of an Interpreter, the Law may be made to beare a sense, contrary to that of the Soveraign; by which means the Interpreter becomes the Legislator.[73]

---

72. *Leviathan*, 187, 197.
73. *Leviathan*, 194, 190.

The concern that inferior judges, if permitted to render unappealable decisions, would alter the laws themselves reemerges in a colloquy between the Philosopher and the Student in the *Dialogue*. When the Philosopher argues, "Since therefore the King is sole Legislator, I think it also Reason he should be sole Supream Judge," the Student replies, "There is no doubt of that; for otherwise there would be no Congruity of Judgments with the Laws."[74]

Because the *Dialogue* specifies the king as the location of sovereignty, it insists more vehemently and concretely than the *Leviathan* that the monarch himself be permitted to take charge of reviewing judgments in the final instance. Whereas the *Leviathan* speaks in terms of the "sovereign representative," which could consist in either a parliamentary or a monarchical body, the *Dialogue* has settled definitively on the king as the iconic sovereign. As a result, the Philosopher provides extensive arguments against Coke's claims that the king could not assume the place of a judge and that the chancellor, as the sovereign's representative, could not hear appeals from courts of common law.[75]

At various points during his reign, as discussed in chapter 1, King James had elaborated upon his judicial authority and had attempted to sit and deliver judgments in person. Coke, along with other judges, when consulted on this matter, concluded that "the King in his own person cannot adjudge any case, either criminall, as Treason, Felony, &c. or betwixt party and party, concerning his Inheritance, Chattels, or Goods, &c. but this ought to be determined and adjudged in some Court of Justice, according to the Law and Custom of England."[76] Coke further distinguished between the king's mode of reasoning and that of the common law, insisting that "his Majesty was not learned in the Lawes of his Realm of England. . . . [T]hey are not to be decided by naturall reason but by the artificiall reason and judgment of Law, which Law is an act which requires long study and experience, before that a man can attain to the cognizance of it."[77] This opinion did not elicit a favorable response from James, who contended that it placed him within the compass of the laws rather than above them, a position that he maintained "was Treason to affirm."[78]

On this point, as with Coke's efforts to punish those questioning verdicts obtained at common law in other courts through writs of praemunire, Hobbes vigorously defends James's claims. Although the sovereign has delegated the

---

74. *Dialogue*, 68.
75. *Dialogue*, 88–90.
76. Coke, *Reports*, 479.
77. Coke, *Reports*, 481.
78. Coke, *Reports*, 481.

judicial power to inferior judges, he reserves the right to hear appeals from the judgments of other courts in person. According to Hobbes, the king should not "in the Kings-Bench [sit] as a Spectator only," but rather if any man "appealeth to the King from any Judge whatsoever, the King may receive his Appeal; and it shall be effectual." Furthermore, Hobbes devotes an entire section of the *Dialogue* to undermining Coke's arguments for applying the writ of praemunire against those challenging judgments at common law in Chancery. Because all magistrates in England acquire their power "by Authority from the King," and the writ of praemunire is aimed against those who oppose the powers of the king's courts, every English court should be construed as similarly situated, none subject to the operations of the writ. Hobbes further argues, with respect to Chancery, that it should be construed as the ideal venue for appeals of decisions at common law. Because all law is, for Hobbes, based on the dictates of equity, a special tribunal such as Chancery would become necessary only as a place for pursuing appeals:

> I would fain know to what end there should be any other Court of Equity at all, either before the Chancellor or any other Person, besides the Judges of the Civil, or Common-Pleas? Nay I am sure you can alledge none but this, that there was a necessity of a Higher Court of Equity, than the Courts of Common-Law, to remedy the Errors in Judgement given by the Justices of Inferior Courts, and the errors in Chancery were irrevocable, except by Parliament, or by special Commission appointed thereunto by the King.[79]

Both the king and Chancery offer the possibility of an appeal based on equity from potentially erroneous judgments under the common law. At once the author of the law and an actor rather than spectator in its administration, the king, and his equitable exercise of reason, underwrites the authority of the common law while at the same time furnishing for it a final point of review.

Lawgiving and Judging: The Shift toward Statutes

By assimilating judging with lawgiving and maintaining that the sovereign— and, in the *Dialogue*, particularly the king—should control both capacities, Hobbes could have restored a notion of sovereignty based on the centrality of monarchical judgment, a conception that would accord with James I's vision

---

79. *Dialogue*, 88–89, 68, 94–95.

of his own divinely ordained authority. Instead, Hobbes's work focused attention on the generalization of judgment into legislation, placing the latter rather than the former at the core of sovereignty.[80] This shift accorded, in part, with an account of what the law of nature might require within the context of civil society. Because the goal of self-preservation lies at the center of the social compact and underpins the laws of nature, insofar as these show "the way, or means of Peace,"[81] individuals must be furnished with knowledge sufficient to achieve that end. For Hobbes, legislation rather than judgment provides the most transparent notice of what is required of the subject and what he should reasonably expect.[82] Although adherence to precedent could render judgments almost as predictable as statutory commands, Hobbes objected for other reasons to the notion that prior cases could bind judges in future disputes. It was through an emphasis on legislation alone that, Hobbes deemed, the sovereign could retain his supremacy while providing the individual with the means by which he could satisfy the obligations to which the covenant had bound him.

The centrality of self-preservation to Hobbes's political vision generates a tension between the requirement of obedience to the laws and the individual's right to save himself from death.[83] The law of nature instructs subjects to abide by the laws the sovereign promulgates, lest the commonwealth dissolve back into the state of nature and war. As the Lawyer observes, "It is also a Dictate of the Law of Reason, that Statute Laws are a necessary means of the safety and well being of Man in the present World, and are to be Obeyed by all Subjects, as the Law of Reason ought to be Obeyed, both by King and Subjects, because it is the Law of God."[84] Likewise, in *Behemoth*, A urges: "The virtue of a subject is comprehended wholly in obedience to the laws of the common wealth. To obey the laws, is justice and equity, which is the law of nature, and, consequently, is civil law in all nations of the world. . . . Likewise, to obey the laws, is the prudence of a subject; for without such obedience the commonwealth (which is every subject's

80. M. M. Goldsmith similarly observes "the primacy of legislation" for Hobbes in "Hobbes on Law," in *The Cambridge Companion to Hobbes*, ed. Tom Sorell (Cambridge: Cambridge University Press, 1996), 274–304.

81. *Leviathan*, 111.

82. In this regard, Thomas Poole helpfully insists on the necessary publicity of the laws for Hobbes. Poole, "Hobbes on Law and Prerogative," 79–84. See also Michael Lobban, "Thomas Hobbes and the Common Law," in Dyzenhaus and Poole, *Hobbes and the Law*, 54.

83. Gordon Schochet has emphasized the tension created by the coexistence of the duty of obedience to the sovereign and the right of self-preservation. Gordon Schochet, "Intending (Political) Obligation: Hobbes and the Voluntary Basis of Society," in *Thomas Hobbes and Political Theory*, ed. Mary G. Dietz (Lawrence: University Press of Kansas, 1990), 60–64.

84. *Dialogue*, 58.

safety and protection) cannot subsist."[85] Even if an individual's conscience resists the command of a particular edict, he should follow it, lest the commonwealth suffer from the distraction of being drawn in disparate directions. At the same time, however, in the extreme instance when an individual is threatened with punishment by death, he retains the right to defend himself against this end, as his demise would vitiate the very reason for entering into the covenant. Hence, in the *Leviathan*, Hobbes insists that "a Covenant not to defend my selfe from force, by force, is alwayes voyd. . . [f]or though a man may Covenant thus, Unless I do so, or so, kill me; he cannot Covenant thus, Unlesse I do so, or so, I will not resist you, when you come to kill me."[86] As a result, a person condemned to death may always resist execution of the sentence with force.

Hobbes's account of law and his focus on the legislative rather than the judicial assisted in minimizing the potential conflict between the mandate that the subject obey the laws and his ability to resist when threatened with capital punishment. The definitions of law provided in the *Leviathan* and the *Dialogue* emphasize that the law must be established in advance of any particular offense condemned under it and that it must be adequately promulgated to acquire force. As the Philosopher asserts, "A Law is the Command of him, or them that have the Soveraign Power, given to those that be his or their Subjects, declaring Publickly, and plainly what every of them may do, and what they must forbear to do."[87] Similarly, in the *Leviathan*, Hobbes maintains, "I define Civill Law in this manner. Civill Law, Is to every Subject, those Rules, which the Common-wealth hath Commanded him, by Word, Writing, or other sufficient Sign of the Will, to make use of, for the Distinction of Right, and Wrong; that is to say, of what is contrary, and what is not contrary to the Rule."[88] Civil law—as opposed to the law of nature—partakes of rules stated clearly and prior to particular applications. Hobbes's insistence on this point is aimed at ensuring that the subject be sufficiently informed about the laws to enable him to conform his behavior to them. Punishment too should be known in advance, because an individual apprised that the consequence of a particular action will be death may take sufficient steps to avoid the potential of that penalty, whereas one who lacks such information might proceed without adequate caution. Although an individual must exercise due diligence in the attempt to be informed of the dictates of the

---

85. *Behemoth*, 44.
86. *Leviathan*, 223, 98.
87. *Dialogue*, 71.
88. *Leviathan*, 183.

law, the consequences of his inability to ascertain these in advance are extreme: "The want of means to know the Law, totally Excuseth."[89]

In addition to being articulated in advance, the laws must be general in order to ensure that individuals can adequately predict their application and that no one is targeted for persecution. According to the Philosopher, "There can be no exceptions to a general Rule in law, that is not expresly made an exception by some Statute."[90] Responding in *Behemoth* to a rather extreme hypothesized situation in which the king would insist that a subject kill his own father, A maintains that such a case would never arise because the imperative could not be generalized into a law. In the unlikely circumstance that the instruction were rendered law, however, the individual would have to obey it unless he instead chose to exit the community created by the covenant. As A argues:

> By disobeying Kings, we mean the disobeying of his laws, those his laws that were made before they were applied to any particular person; for the King, though as a father of children, and a master of domestic servants command many things which bind those children and servants yet he commands the people in general never but by a precedent law, and as a politic, not a natural person. And if such a command as you speak of were contrived into a general law (which never was, nor never will be), you were bound to obey it, unless you depart the kingdom after the publication of the law, and before the condemnation of your father.[91]

We might here recall the conflict between the law of military reward and the law of gratitude in *The Laws of Candy*. For Hobbes, unlike for the author of *The Laws of Candy*, any tension that arises between the familial and political law is resolvable only through the sacrifice of the former.

Through the laws' publication, the individual subject acquires notice of them. Although the records of judicial decisions could provide similar access to the content of the laws, constraining subsequent judgments or the king's own determinations by these precedents would violate Hobbes's requirement that sovereignty remain undivided, and that the king, not his delegates, retains ultimate legal authority. Furthermore, the common law operates not by exact adherence to prior determinations but rather by extrapolation from these earlier decisions,

89. *Leviathan*, 208.
90. *Dialogue*, 152.
91. *Behemoth*, 55.

an extrapolation that Hobbes might argue would exceed what the individual should be forced to deduce about the laws.

In promoting the accessibility of law, Hobbes initially insists on an image of the law spoken by the sovereign to each individual but then elaborates upon the technologies of written dissemination that could enable the transparency he seeks. When the law assumes textual form, however, a difficulty arises: because the intention rather than the letter supplies meaning, for Hobbes, and the words of the law generate not certainty but potential confusion, the ideal of complete publicity can never be attained. In treating "civill lawes," Hobbes envisions them as the will of the sovereign entering the ears of the subject, a linguistic incursion akin to the poison purportedly poured into Hamlet's father's ear; the laws are "Artificiall Chains . . . fastned at one end, to the lips of that Man, or Assembly, to whom they have given the Soveraigne Power; and at the other end to their own Ears."[92] This vision of aural access to an oral command soon disappears, however, and Hobbes instead elaborates upon textual forms through which subjects can access the laws.

Analogizing civil law with the injunctions of the Bible, Hobbes maintains that for contemporary society, it is more important to promulgate the former than the latter. The Philosopher inquires, "What Reason can you give me why there should not be as many Copies abroad of the Statutes, as there be of the Bible?"[93] As the secular commandments of the sovereign, the laws should find a place near every hearth. Just as the Reformation allowed each individual access to the biblical text, Hobbes would like his legal reform to extend interpretive discretion to every subject. At the same time, however, he does not believe that individuals should retreat into personal and disparate opinions on the basis of such access. In *Behemoth*, B endorses public reading of the laws to the community as a means of ensuring consensus on their meaning: "The Scriptures then were nothing else but the laws of the nation, delivered unto them by Moses himself. And I believe it would do no hurt, if the laws of England also were often read and expounded in the several congregations of Englishmen, at times appointed, that they may know what to do; for they already know what to believe."[94] This public reading of the laws would render the subject more culpable for any violation: "When the Law is publiquely, and with assiduity, before all the people read, and interpreted, a fact done against it, is a greater Crime, than where men are left without such

---

92. *Leviathan*, 147.
93. *Dialogue*, 72.
94. *Behemoth*, 16.

instruction, to enquire of it with difficulty, uncertainty, and interruption of their Callings, and be informed by private men."[95]

Dissemination of the law may also occur, for Hobbes, through association with friends; the consequences of misrepresenting the law to others should in this case, however, be severe. As an alternative form of distribution, the Philosopher proposes that "the Knights of the [Shires] should be bound to furnish People with a sufficient Number of Copies (at the Peoples Charge) of the Acts of Parliament at their return into the Country; that every man may resort to them, and by themselves, or Friends take notice of what they are obliged to do; for otherwise it were Impossible they should be obeyed."[96] If the friends who provide information about the law give misleading advice, either intentionally or simply from ignorance, such action should be punished.[97]

The difficulty that remains for Hobbes, even in the utopian world where each individual would receive a copy of the laws, is that interpretation might still engender disparities. This problem becomes evident from his comparison of the law of nature and its availability for perusal in the heart with civil law and its own form of textuality. Although natural law is published to every individual *in foro interno*, and "every Subject that is in his Wits" therefore "continually carryes [it] about with him, and may read itt, if he will," it remains "the most obscure" because passion colors the extent to which anyone can access it through reason.[98] As is evident from Hobbes's discussions of reason and equity, and his conclusion that the latter cannot independently assume the tenor of law because its dictates must be established by authority, the law of nature does not lend itself readily to interpretation.

Nor do the texts of the civil law, although the likelihood of attaining an accurate understanding may increase with the constraints provided by community consensus or quasi-authoritative public interpretation. One obstacle persists ineluctably: the bare words of the statute are not determinative but must be accompanied by an extrapolation about the sovereign's intent. As Hobbes explains: "Nor is it enough the law be written, and published; but also that there be manifest signs, that it proceedeth from the will of the sovereign. There is therefore requisite, not only a Declaration of the Law, but also sufficient signes of the Author, and Authority."[99] Despite the parallel means by which Hobbes

---

95. *Leviathan*, 210.
96. *Dialogue*, 71.
97. *Leviathan*, 177.
98. *Leviathan*, 190, 191; *Dialogue*, 56.
99. *Leviathan*, 32.

urges dissemination of religious and legal texts, he would also like to ensure that the latter are not subject to as many disparate interpretations as the former. Furthermore, because Hobbes subscribes to the fiction that the intention behind the law can be accessed, in the final instance, through recourse to the sovereign's judgment, a more effective means of resolving disputes exists in the legal than in the religious arena.

Promulgation not only of the content of the laws but also of the consequences of their violation in the form of punishment is crucial for Hobbes. Like the substantive commands of the civil law, punishments must be fixed and known in advance. Dispensing with the idea that an inherent logic connects particular crimes with their punishments, the Philosopher contends that the relationship between the two is artificially constructed. As a result, common law judges cannot simply impose punishments based on reason but must rather apply an implicit or explicit command of the sovereign: "But give the authority of defining Punishments to any Man whatsoever, and let that Man define them, and right Reason has defin'd them, supposed the Definition be both made, and made known before the Offence committed. . . . [T]he Person to whom this authority of defining Punishments is given, can be no other in any place of the World, but the same Person that hath the Sovereign Power, be it one Man, or one assembly of Men."[100]

Analysis of the legal entailments of an event that bears a very strong resemblance to the Gunpowder Plot demonstrates the effect of Hobbes's theory of legal notice upon efforts to punish proto-revolutionary violence. The Philosopher inquires as to the consequences of an attempt to set fire to a residence that does not actually succeed:

> If a Man should secretly, and maliciously lay a quantity of Gun-Powder under another Mans House, sufficient to Blow it up, and set a Train of Powder in it, and set Fire to the Train, and some Accident hinder the Effect, is not this Burning? Or what is it? What Crime? It is neither Treason, nor Murder, nor Burglary, nor Robbery, nor Theft, nor (no dammage being made) any Trespass, nor contrary to any Statute. And yet (seeing the Common-Law is the Law of Reason) it is a sin, and such a sin as a Man may be Accused of, and Convicted, and consequently a Crime committed of Malice prepensed; shall he not then be Punished for the Attempt?

---

100. *Dialogue*, 140–41.

Although the law of reason demonstrates the sinfulness of the attempt, "a Judge has no Warrant from any Statute-Law, Common Law, or Commission to appoint the Punishment." At the same time, however, the king "has power to Punish him (on this side of Life or Member) as he please; and with the Assent of Parliament (if not without) to make the Crime for the future Capital."[101] Because the law of reason provides notice of the criminality of the act, the king can appoint a punishment in the absence of a previously established prohibition of the civil law. He cannot, however, push the social compact to its limits by unilaterally designating the offense capital, and must instead secure the assent of Parliament to this determination. Even with Parliament's agreement, the king may not render the crime capital in this particular case; actual rather than theoretical notice is required before imposition of the ultimate punishment within the commonwealth.

Equity, Pardoning, and Self-Preservation: Legalizing Forgiveness

If designating crimes and their punishment in advance, combined with providing notice of the content of the laws and the consequences of resisting them, furnishes one means of reconciling the goal of the individual's self-preservation with the civil order of the commonwealth, pardoning provides another. The alternative, for Hobbes, to performing in accordance with the covenant is to be forgiven this obligation.[102] Pardoning cannot, however, be counted upon in advance, and it therefore exceeds the contractual structure of civil society. It thus constitutes the sovereign representative's fulfillment of one of the laws of nature: that of insisting upon forgiveness with regard to the achievement of a future peace. It also provides the most effective response to the dangers posed by the man who has escaped from the constraints of the social contract, especially when many such individuals have banded together to undertake a set of revolutionary deeds. The Act of Oblivion exemplifies this approach to pardoning.

At first blush, Hobbes's account of pardoning partakes of the conventional aspects of equity that fail to find a place in his understanding of the concept. The individual granting a pardon provides forgiveness as a form of discretionary mercy in the civil sphere. Both equity as traditionally conceived and pardoning rely on the individualized determination of the king or judge, and are associated

---

101. *Dialogue*, 121–22.
102. Hobbes's account here foreshadows that of Arendt discussed in the Postlude.

with remission rather than punishment. At the same time, however, pardoning generally takes place after judgment rather than in the process of judicially achieving an equitable result. In addition, pardoning violates the principle that an individual should not serve as a judge in his own case; indeed, because solely the one injured should furnish a pardon, it is only the unjust pardon that would conform to the normal rule. The other moment when such judgment in one's own case is permissible, for Hobbes, involves the situation of self-preservation. Pardoning and self-preservation again demonstrate themselves mirror images at this moment. A deeper difficulty with the analogy between equity and pardoning, however, arises from Hobbes's understanding of the Act of Oblivion, through which pardoning itself becomes generalized and legislative in nature in the same way as equity.

Throughout his work, Hobbes continually insists that one of the laws of nature obliges the individual and the sovereign to forgive or pardon a wrongdoer who repents. The same rationale underlies this law of nature as underwrites the social compact more generally; if civil society is designed for the promotion of peace, pardoning materially aids in attaining the aimed-for goal. Forgiveness under this account lacks the purity of an act done for itself and instead acquires an instrumental quality. As Hobbes maintains in *De Cive*: "The fift precept of the Law of nature is: *That we must forgive him who repents, and asketh pardon for what is past; having first taken caution for the time to come.* The *pardon* of what is past, or the remission of an offence, is nothing else but the granting of *peace* to him that asketh it, after he hath *warr'd* against us, & now is become peninent."[103] Renumbering the laws of nature, the *Leviathan* announces: "A sixth Law of Nature, is this, *That upon caution of the Future time, a man ought to pardon the offences past of them that repenting, desire it.* For Pardon, is nothing but granting of Peace; which though granted to them that persevere in their hostility, be not peace, but Feare; yet not granted to them that give caution of the Future time, is signe of an aversion to Peace; and therefore contrary to the Law of Nature."[104] Pardoning thereby provides an assurance of peace for the future, and constitutes a strategic move in the attainment of civil society.

Pardoning proves especially useful in combating a continuing threat of revolution. Although individuals are not justified in joining the violence of civil war, once the struggle has reached a certain point, they may be allowed—and even

---

103. Thomas Hobbes, *De Cive: The English Version* (1647), ed. Howard Warrender (Oxford: Clarendon Press, 1983), 67; hereafter *De Cive*.

104. *Leviathan*, 106.

obliged by necessity—to take up arms to preserve themselves. These subjects' right to employ violence for the goal of self-preservation is, however, extinguished once they receive an offer of pardon, because the prospect of remission of their punishment for crimes removes the fear of death:

> In case a great many men together, have already resisted the Soveraign Power unjustly, or committed some Capitall crime, for which every one of them expecteth death, whether have they not the Liberty then to joyn together, and assist, and defend one another? Certainly they have: For they but defend their lives, which the Guilty man may as well do, as the Innocent. There was indeed injustice in the first breach of their duty; Their bearing of Arms subsequent to it, though it be to maintain what they have done, is no new unjust act. And if it be onely to defend their persons, it is not unjust at all. But the offer of pardon taketh from them, to whom it is offered, the plea of self-defence, and maketh their perseverance in assisting, or defending the rest, unlawfull.[105]

Both pardoning and self-preservation operate outside the contractual order in another respect as well: each instance represents a particular kind of excess over the social compact. Whereas forgiveness excuses performance of the individual's covenant, the act of preserving oneself without regard to it is premised on the assumption that the covenant is ineffectual. For Hobbes, forgiveness partakes of the gift, in opposition to the contract. Only through forgiveness is an individual exempted from his obligations, including, presumably, those acquired under the social compact: "We are freed from *Covenants* two wayes, either by performing, or by being forgiven: By performing, for beyond that we oblig'd not our selves. By being for-given, because he whom we oblig'd our selves to by forgiving, is conceiv'd to return us that *Right* which we past over to him; for, forgiving, implies *giving* . . . a conveyance of Right to him to whom the gift is made."[106] One can never count on a gift or forgiveness in the future, from either a human or a divine entity; unlike contractual expressions, words promising gifts in the future lack consideration and therefore cannot be binding.[107] When forgiveness does arrive, however, it restores to an individual his natural right that had been contracted away. Seeking self-preservation is, similarly, a form of self-enforcement of a natural right that remains even in the context of

---

105. *Leviathan*, 152.
106. *De Cive*, 57; see also *Leviathan*, 97.
107. *De Cive*, 54–55, 61.

civil society, an act premised on the assumption that the covenant has already broken down.

In each case, a third party who can judge the merits of the dispute is absent from the theoretical landscape. Only inside the world created by the covenant can the nominally objective position of the third, as represented by the judge, arise. One of the laws of nature that Hobbes emphasizes—and on which Coke had also insisted in *Bonham's Case*—specifies that, under the social compact, no individual should judge in his own case: "And seeing every man is presumed to do all things in order to his own benefit, no man is a fit Arbitrator in his own cause: and if he were never so fit; yet equity allowing to each party equall benefit, if one be admitted to be Judge, the other is to be admitted also; & so the controversie, that is, the cause of War, remains, against the Law of nature."[108] Pardoning and self-preservation constitute the two exceptions to this rule. When the prospect of preserving oneself at the expense of the commonwealth arises, only the individual who engages in such activity can judge the merits of his position: "Now whether the means which he is about to use, and the action he is performing, be necessary to the preservation of his Life, and Members, or not *he himself*, by the right of nature, must *be judg*; for say another man, judg that it is contrary to right reason that I should judg of mine own peril: why now, because he judgeth of what concerns me, by the same reason, because we are equall by nature, will I judge also of things which doe belong to him."[109] Similarly, only the one injured can, by right, pardon the perpetrator; the sovereign's act of pardoning subjects who have harmed others constitutes a wrong. When the Philosopher asks, "If a Man do you an injury, to whom (think you) belongeth the Right of pardoning it?," the Lawyer answers, "Doubtless to me alone, if to me alone be done that injury."[110]

The question of who received an injury is not always transparent, however, and may implicate the structure of the social compact itself. The compact is constituted, for Hobbes, not generally by a covenant between sovereign and subjects, but rather by an agreement among the future members of the commonwealth themselves to institute a society for whom a sovereign representative will exist.[111]

---

108. *Leviathan*, 109. We have already seen, in chapters 1 and 3, how *Measure for Measure* and *The Laws of Candy* set up Angelo and Antinous, respectively, as judges in their own case to the extent that they engage in a form of self-condemnation that views the law as self-executing rather than requiring an intermediary to apply it.

109. *De Cive*, 47.

110. *Dialogue*, 152.

111. *Leviathan*, 121–22. The exception that proves the rule may be, as Gordon Schochet argues, sovereigns by acquisition, who "enter into reciprocal agreements with their subjects." Schochet, "Intending (Political) Obligation," 61.

When the covenant is violated through revolutionary violence, or, as in the case of Charles I, the king is deposed or beheaded, not just the sovereign representative but the people themselves suffer injury. Hence, the Student elaborates that both the subject and the king possess the right of pardoning an injury "done to both." At the same time, Hobbes at several points maintains that the king always possesses a residual right to pardon with a view to establishing future peace and analyzes the form of various pardons as structurally gifts of the king. According to the Philosopher, in the relevant statute there is "a clause for the saving of the Kings Regality, From Which may be inferr'd, that the King did not grant away that power [to pardon], when he thought good to use it for the Commonwealth." The king should nevertheless provide compensation in such a case to those who have suffered injury.[112] In the *Leviathan*, Hobbes analyzes charters of pardon as gifts from the king to his subjects, ones that adopt the first-person singular form of address: "The phrase of a Charter is *Dedi, Concessi, I have given, I have granted*."[113] Although the Philosopher in the *Dialogue* acknowledges that charters may be laws as well as grants, he assiduously maintains that Coke erred in asserting that charters of pardon could be provided only by Parliament, and in advocating that Parliament should, in general, take charge of all pardoning.[114]

Hobbes's stance on the king's capacity to pardon—even when another subject, or the covenant itself, rather than his own person has been injured—renders more puzzling his concession that it was appropriate for the Act of Oblivion to be passed by Parliament. The Philosopher initially resists the Student's formulation

---

112. *Dialogue*, 152, 153.

113. *Leviathan*, 200.

114. *Dialogue*, 72, 152. Coke had elaborated his views on the king's power of pardoning in 1607, as well as in his *Institutes*, but the text of the former discussion was published only posthumously, in the twelfth volume of his *Reports*, in 1656. Coke, *Reports*, 441. One of his main objections in that context to the king's exercise of the pardon power when subjects of public welfare were involved consisted in the concern that such a pardon would violate the rights of the king's subjects. Hence Coke argued that "although . . . the King shall have the suit solely in his name for the redress of it, yet by his pardon he cannot discharge the Offender, for this, that it is not only in prejudice of the King, but in damage of the Subjects" (*Reports*, 439). Giving the example of a decaying bridge that a subject has an obligation to repair, Coke explained that, because of the duty owed to other subjects, as well as to the king, the king may pardon a fine owed on the bridge but not the obligation to repair it eventually (*Reports*, 440). In addition, the king may not pardon a breach of the peace before it occurs because, "inasmuch as [the agreement to keep the peace] be made to the King solely; yet inasmuch as this is made for the benefit and safety of the subjects of the King, in such Case it cannot be discharged" (*Reports*, 441). To extrapolate to the revolutionary case, the king could not release the subject from his or her covenant in advance of resistance because such a release would detrimentally affect other subjects. At the same time, Coke acknowledged that pardon might be granted, in the similar instance he described, after a breach of the peace had already occurred.

of the Act of Oblivion as a pardon accomplished by "the King *and* Parliament" and insists that "the King *in* Parliament" passed the act.[115] His grounds for this assertion are that "the pardoning of Injury, belongs to the Person that is Injur'd. Treason and other Offences against the Peace, and against the Right of the Soveraign are Injuries done to the King." When the Student explains that the nature of the commonwealth's prior dissolution meant that everyone was injured, not just the sovereign representative, and hence it was necessary for Parliament to collaborate in the pardon, the Philosopher summarily assents: "The Act of *Oblivion*, without a Parliament could not have passed, because, not only the King, but also most of the Lords, and abundance of Common People had received Injuries; which not being pardonable, but by their own Assent, it was absolutely necessary that it should be done in Parliament, and by the assent of the Lords and Commons."[116] Taken to its logical conclusion, the Student's reasoning would lead to the notion that every subject should have participated in the pardon, not just the king and Parliament.[117] If the sovereign representative in the form of the king alone could be insufficient, how would the addition of Parliament solve the difficulty? The answer lies in the implicit assumption that the House of Commons better represents the position of the people than the king himself. Indeed, the Philosopher's concession represents a concession about the appropriate form of the sovereign representative, according to which the numerosity of the elected Commons proves capable of embodying the interest of the people more concretely than the majesty of the king. The conditions for passing the Act of Oblivion thus indicate something about the structure of the state itself; despite Hobbes's insistence on the king's exclusive authority, his conclusion that the king and Parliament should together pass the Act of Oblivion endows Parliament with a substantive role in the polity.

As its title suggests, the Act of Oblivion was in fact a law, and is represented by Hobbes as law-like and, therefore, distinct from the conventional, individualized pardon. First announcing its resemblance to a parliamentary general pardon, the *Dialogue* proceeds to explain how the Act of Oblivion creates an even more universally applicable rule. Whereas quibbles might arise as to what kinds of crimes would be included in a parliamentary general pardon, only those persons specifically excepted from the scope of the Act of Oblivion could be prosecuted;

---

115. *Dialogue*, 76; emphasis added.

116. *Dialogue*, 76.

117. Here we might think back to *The Laws of Candy*, which, although operating on the register of forgiveness rather than pardon, does in fact take the Student's point to its logical conclusion, insisting that each individual forgive the one who has injured him or her before the state can be restored.

everyone else would be able to call upon the Act of Oblivion as a general matter as an absolute defense against any accusation related to the English Revolution:

> By the late Act of *Oblivion*, which pardoned all manner of offences committed in the late Civil War, no question could arise concerning Crimes excepted. First, because no Man can by Law accuse another Man of a Fact, which by Law is to be forgotten. Secondly, because all Crimes may be alledged, as proceeding from the Licentiousness of the time, and from the silence of the Law occasion'd by the Civil War, and consequently (unless the offenders Person also were excepted, or unless the Crime were committed before the War began) are within the Pardon.[118]

Although not mandating, for Hobbes, that subjects *actually* forget historical events, the act, in prescribing oblivion, mandates a legal forgetting of crimes that occurred.[119] The act indeed provides an odd example of a legal fiction, as it is impossible to imagine that a law titled an "Act of Oblivion" could actually cause subjects to forget the events to which it refers rather than furnishing an additional incentive for them to remember.

The generality of the act itself conduces, like the generality of civil laws, to peace. If equity speaks against the acceptation of persons, pardons violate that prescription, and may themselves do what is perceived as violence against the offender. The "cheerful acceptation" of a gift, or of forgiveness, bespeaks "such an honour done to the obliger, as is taken generally for retribution." Indeed, Hobbes describes the need to accept forgiveness as "hatefull" in the same way as that of receiving retribution. It is out of fear of receiving pardon that some men grow into rebellion, because "when they have engaged themselves beyond hope of justification, [they] fall also upon the Supreme Authority, for feare of punishment, or shame of receiving pardon."[120] Precisely the individual quality of pardoning generates this shame; at the same time that the pardon is given, an acknowledgment

---

118. *Dialogue*, 158. The existence of an Act of Oblivion could in fact be employed as a defense in the context of a prosecution. Hence the Marquess of Argyll, a former ally of Charles I who had then taken the side of the Commonwealth during the Interregnum, adduced several earlier Acts of Oblivion when attempting (unsuccessfully) to defend himself against a 1661 prosecution for treason. *The Marques of Argyll His Defenses against the Grand Indytement of High Treason Exhibited against Him to the Parliament in Scotland* (London, 1661), 33, 53, 95.

119. *Dialogue*, 157–58. There may be some resemblance here to Hobbes's interest in political silence, which Jonathan Scott has discussed in "The Peace of Silence: Thucydides and the English Civil War," in *Hobbes and History*, ed. G. A. J. Rogers and Thomas Sorrell (London: Routledge, 2000), 112–36.

120. *Leviathan*, 71, 74.

that it is required must be received. The generality of the Act of Oblivion obviates the necessity for this acknowledgment and operates, as it were, from behind the veil of ignorance, with the universality of a law. Rather than occurring after judgment, or even in the context of judgment, it erases the possibility of judicial action in advance for an entire category of persons and acts.

Charles I, Charles II, and the Act of Oblivion: Pardoning for the Future

Despite the Philosopher's expressions of surprise at the unprecedented nature of the Act of Oblivion Parliament passed upon the restoration of King Charles II to the British throne, such statutes had existed earlier, as discussed in chapter 5, and, during the course of the Civil War, Charles I's successive proposals for a similar Act of Oblivion had occasioned some controversy with Parliament. Charles II had indeed, in a sense, inherited the Act of Oblivion from his father, who, in his final missive to his son, had instructed him to take the course of mercy rather than revenge against the insurgents when he would finally return to the throne. Although earlier Acts of Oblivion and abortive attempts at achieving them had existed, the 1660 act did constitute an innovation in at least one way: it was the first such gesture to occur upon the reestablishment of a government after revolution. Its placement at the commencement of the reign of King Charles II was crucial not only because of the content of the Act of Oblivion itself but also because the structure of its enactment and implementation assisted in constituting the government to come.

Pardoning and oblivion fall within the same species but diverge from each other in various particulars. An Act of Oblivion constitutes, in a sense, a general pardon, and is often accompanied with phrases so suggesting, like that of "free and general pardon."[121] The Act of Oblivion is thus in its character more law-like than a conventional pardon, observing the norm of generality that Hobbes ascribed to law itself. Nevertheless, acts of oblivion, including the one Charles II promulgated, may depart from the standpoint of generality and exempt particular individuals from their purview. A pardon likewise recognizes the existence and culpability of a crime before remitting punishment, whereas an act of oblivion instead insists upon forgetting. In these respects the Act of Oblivion controverts

---

121. Charles's 1660 act itself contained this language, calling itself "The Kings Majesties most Gracious, Free and General Pardon, Indempnity, and Oblivion."

several of the fundamental underpinnings of the pardon itself, emphasizing a general rather than an individualized decision, a legislative rather than a judicial determination, and an erasure rather than forgiveness of the crime.

A fulfillment of one of the Hobbesian laws of nature—that one should pardon those desirous of pardon in order to achieve peace—the Act of Oblivion functioned as a strategy for the future and as a means of reaffirming a social compact that had been breached. At the same time, however, and despite Hobbes's emphasis on the unified sovereignty of the king, the Act of Oblivion itself shifted focus from judgment to lawgiving, and in this shift awakened the possibility of a concomitant transfer of authority from king to Parliament. Although it would take until the eighteenth century's explosion of legislation to reach William Blackstone's emphasis on parliamentary supremacy in his *Commentaries on the Laws of England*, the Act of Oblivion and Hobbes's account of the king's power as first legislative, then judicial, already sketched out the trajectory of this alteration.[122] In the Act of Oblivion, the goals of the revolution have, in a sense, been achieved rather than forgotten; from the act itself it was but a short step to extending the generality of the laws to the generality of the lawmaker in the form of Parliament.

Although Charles's Declaration of Breda had assured his restored subjects of his inclination toward pardoning, some delay intervened between this speech and Parliament's action on the subject. Indeed, conflict broke out almost immediately during the parliamentary deliberations; one member had injudiciously claimed that those who first began the Civil War were as guilty as those who had ultimately executed Charles I, a statement that drew great resistance and would have led to punishment had the Parliament not been simultaneously considering mercy, pardon, and indemnity. The time intervening between the Declaration of Breda and Parliament's passage of the Act of Oblivion was construed by some as indicating the king's retraction of his promises; as a result, and in response to these criticisms, Charles renewed his pleas to Parliament in favor of the act.[123]

---

122. Legislation proliferated during the eighteenth century. Randall McGowen, for example, notes the explosion in statutes criminalizing forgery, among other capital offenses. Randall McGowen, "The Bloody Code?," in *Law, Crime and English Society, 1660–1830*, ed. Norma Landau (New York: Cambridge University Press, 2003), 117–18. It is also generally acknowledged that Blackstone's *Commentaries* emphasized legislative sovereignty more than its jurisprudential predecessors had. David Lieberman, *The Province of Legislation Determined: Legal Theory in Eighteenth-Century Britain* (Cambridge: Cambridge University Press, 1989), 48–55.

123. "The Convention Parliament, 1st sess., April 25, 1660," in *The History and Proceedings of the House of Commons*, vol. 1, *1660–1680* (London, 1742), 4–5, 13–14, 15–16.

The language of the act itself, as well as Charles's speech accompanying it, suggested two central purposes: to avoid the possibility of continued struggle based on the revolutionaries' assumption that they remained in danger, and, counterintuitively, to enable harsher punishment of future treasonous activity. In service of the former goal, the act announced the king's desire "to bury all seeds of future Discords and remembrance of the former, as well in his own Breast as in the Breasts of his subjects one towards the other."[124] Even the memory of the discords, not simply their consequences in punishment, would be eliminated; oblivion was not a velleity but was actually enforced by the act. Anyone who, within three years of its passage, "presume[d] maliciously to call or alleadge of or object against any other person or persons, any Name or Names, or other Words of Reproach, any way tending to revive the Memory of the late Differences, or the Occasions thereof," would be forced to pay the aggrieved individual a fairly significant fine.[125] As the controversy leading up to passing the act had demonstrated, even discussing the revolutionary sequence of events could stir turmoil and lead to reputational harms that could spur continued violence.

At the same time, however, Charles insisted that his character for mercy would not lead him into a permissive reign. The oblivion specified in the act covered a precise time period—from January 1, 1637, to June 4, 1660—and Charles accorded considerable significance to this delineation. As he announced, subdividing time into that included within the purview of the statute, that between the time designated and that in which he spoke, and all future time,

> all I do very willingly pardon . . . that are pardon'd by this Act of Indemnity, to that Time which is mention'd in the Bill: Nay, I will tell you, That, from that Time to this Day, I will not use great Severity, except in such Cases where the Malice is notorious, and the Public Peace exceedingly concern'd. But for the Time to come, the same Discretion and Conscience, which dispos'd me to the Clemency I have express'ed (which is most agreeable to my Nature) will oblige me to all Rigour and Severity, how contrary soever it be to my Nature, towards those who shall not now acquiesce, but continue to manifest their Sedition and Dislike of the Government, either in Actions or Words.[126]

---

124. An Act of Free and General Pardon, Indemnity and Oblivion, 12 Cha. 2 cap. XI (1660). Hereafter Act of Oblivion.

125. Act of Oblivion. This feature of the act connects back to Hobbes. As Stephen Holmes has elaborated, Hobbes was obsessed with "the politics of name calling." Stephen Holmes, "Political Psychology in Hobbes' *Behemoth*," in Dietz, *Thomas Hobbes and Political Theory*, 128.

126. "Convention Parliament," 17.

The same equitable characteristics of discretion and conscience that led Charles to seek out an act of oblivion thus become the justification for enhancing the severity of punishment for the future.

The language of the act itself, finally, demonstrated some anxiety about the generality of its scope. In its attempt to cover all contingencies, the Act of Oblivion included various catalogues of the circumstances it intended to comprehend. The act thus enumerated all of the categories of activities it would cover, and insisted that it should be read *as if* it resembled a traditional pardon for very specific offenses:

> [The] said Free Pardon, Indempnity and Oblivion, shall be as good and effectual in the Law to every of his said subjects, Bodies corporate, and others before rehearsed, in, for, and against all things which be not hereafter in this present Act excepted and foreprized, as the same pardon, Indempnity, and Oblivion should have been, if all Offices, Contempt, Forfeitures, Causes, Matters, Suits, Quarrels, Judgments Executions, penalties, and all other things, not hereafter in this present Act excepted and foreprized, had been particularly, singularly, especially and plainly named, rehearsed and specified, and also pardoned by proper and expresse Words and Names.

The act likewise provided for its own use as a defense by the "singular" subject in a particular court case despite its "general Words, Clauses, and Sentences."[127]

In the *Dialogue*, Hobbes revisits the act's concern about its own application in the particular case, focusing on the fear that a specific individual or instance might not be comprehended within the general language of the law. The Philosopher attempts to elaborate two justifications for considering the parliamentary pardon complete, and not subject to exception within courts of law. As he opines:

> By the late Act of *Oblivion*, which pardoned all manner of offences committed in the late Civil War, no question could arise concerning Crimes excepted. First, because no Man can by Law accuse another Man of a Fact, which by Law is to be forgotten. Secondly, because all Crimes may be alledged, as proceeding from the Licentiousness of the time, and from the silence of the Law occasion'd by the Civil War, and consequently (unless the offenders Person also were excepted, or unless the Crime were committed before the War began) are within the Pardon.[128]

---

127. Act of Oblivion.
128. *Dialogue*, 158.

Hobbes's first rationale refers to the act's own choice of oblivion over pardoning, while the second provides a ground for that rationale in Hobbes's own philosophy. The Act of Oblivion was, according to this conjunction of reasons, justified in choosing forgetting over pardoning because the Interregnum constituted a rupture within the legal order, a "silence of the Law" that returned individuals to the state of nature. The memory of the law runs back, paradoxically, only to those points at which the law spoke rather than remaining silent; it is, indeed, a rather self-regarding memory. The default of the law is, therefore, oblivion rather than punishment for the exceptional time of the Revolution, and the law must, unlike in ordinary times, specifically single out any individuals it wishes to punish for their actions within that moment. Hence the Act of Oblivion contained a long litany of those who would be excepted from its scope and could be prosecuted rather than pardoned.

Although the Act of Oblivion eschews the monarchical theater of pardoning of plays like *Measure for Measure*, it entails another kind of performance for the subject, one toward which Hobbes's thought would have particularly inclined him. As Paul Kottman has argued, Hobbes's Leviathan generates a politics without a scene: "The 'visible power' of the Leviathan belongs to no *scene*, no localizable context; instead, its power derives from the fact that it transcends any particular locality and casts its shadow over the entire visible realm."[129] While Monica Vieira has read Kottman as opposing a theatrical understanding of Hobbes, this vision of a politics without a scene can actually be reconciled with the theatricality of concealment in Hobbes.[130] As David Runciman has elaborated, in seeking peace, deception or concealment of belief is acceptable for Hobbes; hence "sovereigns might lie, deceive, and dissemble . . . in the pursuit of peace. Equally, loyal subjects should be willing to conceal the truth about themselves in their public professions of faith if to do otherwise would be to undermine the foundations of civil order."[131] Conversely, Kinch Hoekstra has read the fool in *Leviathan* who endorses breaking covenants as an explicit advocate of such action rather than a silent dissenter and has explained the particularly grievous quality of such speech for Hobbes.[132] Consistent with these accounts of the justifications for a display of silence, the refusal of speech that the Act of Oblivion commands of subjects distributes the performance of fidelity

---

129. Paul A. Kottman, *A Politics of the Scene* (Stanford: Stanford University Press, 2008), 88.

130. Monica Vieira, *The Elements of Representation in Hobbes* (Leiden: Brill, 2009), 78.

131. David Runciman, *Political Hypocrisy: Masks of Power, from Hobbes to Orwell and Beyond* (Princeton: Princeton University Press, 2008), 40.

132. Kinch Hoekstra, "Hobbes and the Fool," *Political Theory* 25, no. 5 (October 1997): 620–54.

to the state throughout the populace. The Act of Oblivion thereby replaces the spectacular display of the sovereign's power with a less visible and more pervasive mode of performance.

Despite his insistence upon the sovereignty of the king, Hobbes's conceptions of equity and pardoning conduced not to a vision of the sovereign as the Schmittian figure "who decides on the state of exception,"[133] but instead to an account of sovereign lawgiving that rested on a natural law version of equity standing outside the state as well as an equitable mode of interpretation and judgment applying the law within political institutions. It is perhaps inevitable, however, that once pardoning enters into the service of the future, or the renewing of the state, it will lose its singularity and acquire the quality of a normal law. As Jacques Derrida wrote of hospitality, "*The* law [of hospitality] is above the laws. It is thus illegal, transgressive, outside the law, like a lawless law, *nomos anomos*, law above the laws and law outside the law. . . . But even while keeping itself above the laws of hospitality, *the* unconditional law of hospitality needs the laws, it *requires* them."[134] Similarly, *the* law of forgiveness requires laws of pardoning yet must not become subsumed by them, as in Hobbes's or Charles II's visions of the Act of Oblivion.

Once forgiveness—and, even more so, oblivion—is commanded, it ceases to retain the qualities essential to the concept, those of singularity and non-exchange. Although what is in question here is indeed the capacity to forgive the unforgivable, or the revolutionary act, the mode that Hobbes and Charles II select for doing so simply reinstitutes sovereignty as a law-like rule. Derrida described this dynamic of the fall of the possibility of a pure forgiveness into the realm of the political-legal institution:

> In the case at once exceptional and exemplary of the right of grace, where what exceeds the juridico-political inscribes itself in the constitutional law in order to found itself; well, *there is and there is not* this personal head-to-head or face-to-face, which one could think is required by the very essence of forgiveness. Even there, where is should engage only in absolute singularities, it cannot *manifest* itself in some fashion without calling on a third, the institution, sociality, the transgenera-

---

133. Schmitt, *Political Theology*, 5.
134. Jacques Derrida, *Of Hospitality: Anne Dufourmantelle Invites Jacques Derrida to Respond* (Stanford: Stanford University Press, 2000), 79.

tional heritage, or the survivor in general; and first on that universalizing instance which is language.[135]

Like James I before them, Hobbes and Charles II invoked pardoning in service of the reestablishment of sovereignty, yet their efforts at doing so shifted the place of sovereignty gradually in the direction of Parliament rather than the king. Just as James had institutionally displaced judgment onto Parliament, Hobbes recentered focus from the judgment or exceptional pardon that could constitute the monarch's sovereignty onto a notion of lawgiving that was more appropriate to Parliament than to the king.

---

135. Jacques Derrida, *On Forgiveness*, in *On Cosmopolitanism and Forgiveness*, trans. Mark Dooley and Michael Hughes (London: Routledge, 2001), 47–48.

POSTLUDE / Pardoning and Liberal Constitutionalism

Within the history of political theory, pardoning was characterized by Jean Bodin as one of the marks of sovereignty and by Immanuel Kant as the act that most enhances the majesty of the king. According to this tradition, pardoning itself constitutes a display of sovereignty, and the location of the pardon power indicates the place of sovereignty within the state. The pardon, however, sits ill with liberal political theory. Rather than treating all citizens as equal under law, the pardon exempts an individual or group from punishment; an advantage for some could thus seem an injustice to others, especially those harmed by what has been pardoned. At the same time, pardoning revolutionary violence may, as a form of what Thomas Hobbes would consider seeking peace, serve the interests of the entire future citizenry, for whom the continuation or renewal of the state is enabled. As Alexander Hamilton claimed in *Federalist* 74, "in seasons of insurrection or rebellion, there are often critical moments, when a well-timed offer of pardon to the insurgents or rebels may restore the tranquility of the commonwealth; and which, if suffered to pass unimproved, it may never be possible afterwards to recall."[1] When it takes on the guise of amnesty, as in Hamilton's example, pardoning may itself constitute the political community for the sake of which it is given.

If the identity of those for whom and before whom the pardon is given has remained vexed, the connection between the one who pardons and the sovereign appeared much clearer from Bodin forward. Even within the American constitutional context, the pardon power that Article II accords the president has often seemed an undemocratic residue of the king's monarchical authority.[2] Indeed, it may never have appeared more so than in the Trump era. The structure of sovereignty analyzed by Carl Schmitt illuminates the nature of the

---

1. Alexander Hamilton, *Federalist* no. 74, in *The Federalist Papers* (New York: Tribeca Books, 2009), 215–16.

2. Kathleen Moore, *Pardons: Justice, Mercy, and the Public Interest* (Oxford: Oxford University Press, 1989), 25–26.

relationship between pardoning and sovereignty. Although Schmitt himself devoted little attention to the pardon power, referring to it only in passing in *Constitutional Theory*, his account of the exception shares critical features with the dynamics of pardoning.

Nor is the isomorphism between pardoning and the exception simply an anti-liberal Schmittian innovation. At the heart of the liberal tradition against which Schmitt launched his attacks, Immanuel Kant's writings themselves suggest both the necessity of pardoning in proto-revolutionary situations and the incompatibility of the pardon power with the liberal state grounded in the rule of law, or what we might call constitutionalism. Analysis of Kant's work on and around pardoning demonstrates the extent to which he remained captured both by the connection between sovereignty and pardoning that we have seen enacted in the seventeenth-century English tradition and by the notion that pardoning might be required to preserve the polity from proto-revolutionary violence. Furthermore, like Hobbes, he continued at least nominally to link the power of pardoning with the king. It was in part precisely this association, however, that led Kant to resist the entailments of the pardon power, a power that served to aggrandize the king in the sight of his subjects and contravened the lawful character of the state—a principle on which Kant simultaneously insisted. The pardon hence proves an exception within the Kantian corpus as much as in the Schmittian critique.

The fundamental mistake shared by Kant and Schmitt—and spawned by the tradition we have seen playing out within early modern English drama and politics—may be the insistence upon linking pardoning with sovereignty. To the extent that something like pardoning could be detached from sovereignty, it could be retained without compromising liberal constitutionalism. Although she refrained from fully elaborating the implications of the concept, what Hannah Arendt termed forgiveness—an ethical act between individuals that yet possesses political consequences—might furnish such a substitution for the sovereign pardon. The plays treated in chapters 3 and 4—*The Laws of Candy* and *The Bondman*—likewise suggest ways of circumventing pardoning, either by emphasizing forgiveness among subjects or citizens, as Arendt does, or by insisting on a conception of clemency that resembles an equitable approach to law. These possible ways forward have never been taken up within the sphere of contemporary politics, which, recognizing the anomalous character of pardoning, has let it atrophy without adequate replacements.

The significance of this atrophy for criminal law has been widely discussed.[3] The consequences are, however, not confined to that realm. The absence of an appealing model for pardoning in contemporary politics possesses consequences for the nature of the political bond. In his writings on pardoning, Jacques Derrida emphasized the significance of a "pure" pardon, which "would be a pardon without power: unconditional but without sovereignty."[4] For Derrida, the purity of the pardon is fundamentally compromised not only by a link with sovereignty but also by its instrumental deployment. Hence he contends:

> Each time that the pardon is in the service of an end, even if it were noble and spiritual (financial or spiritual redemption, reconciliation, salvation), each time that it tends to re-establish a normality (social, national, political, psychological) by a work of mourning, by some therapy or ecology of the memory, then the "pardon" is not pure, nor is its concept. The pardon is not, it should not be, normal, normative, normalizing. It should remain exceptional and extraordinary, by proof of the impossible: as if it could interrupt the ordinary course of historic temporality.[5]

This linkage of pardoning "in the service of an end" with the "re-establish[ment of] normality" would render justifications for pardoning like Hamilton's impure. It would further seem to contravene any political use of pardoning. In connecting the pardon in service of an end and the goal of "re-establish[ing] normality," Derrida here paints with too broad a brush. A non-sovereign version of the pardon could serve the goal of founding or refounding a state without rendering the result "normal." Instead, it could help to generate new bases for the relations among political subjects or citizens and assist in the creation of a different form of political organization. The tragedy of Trump's pardons, according to this view,

---

3. Margaret Colgate Love, among others, has written extensively about this phenomenon. Margaret Colgate Love, "The Twilight of the Pardon Power," *Journal of Criminal Law and Criminology* 100 (Summer 2010): 1169.

4. Jacques Derrida, "The Century and the Pardon," *Le monde des débats* 9 (December 1999), trans. Greg Macon (2001), http://fixion.sytes.net/pardonEng.htm. In French, the primary meaning of the word "pardon" is forgiveness, not the juridical usage as in English, which would generally be translated as "faire grâce à" or "droit de grâce." Nevertheless, the term is sometimes deployed in legal contexts, generating an ambiguity that Derrida and others have used to productive effect. Although I cite Derrida's shorter essays on pardoning that have appeared in French and English, the basis for my discussion of his contribution is the as yet unpublished seminar "Le parjure et le pardon" (1997–1999).

5. Derrida, "The Century and the Pardon."

would be not his introduction of politics into the process but rather his implicit reassertion of the bond between pardoning and sovereignty. Under an alternative model, the pardon used for the ends of the state would itself generate a new basis for politics within that very state. It is this possibility to which the remainder of the Postlude attempts to lend shape.

The Pardon as Exception

According to the now familiar mantra at the opening of *Political Theology*, "sovereign is he who decides on the exception [*Souverän ist, wer über den Ausnahmezustand entscheidet*]."[6] The exception, or emergency, as Schmitt defines it, "can at best be characterized as a case of extreme peril, a danger to the existence of the state, or the like."[7] The necessity of a decision on the exception controverts the possibility of a completely self-sufficient *Rechtsstaat*, or state characterized by the rule of law, and demonstrates the inevitably political—rather than exclusively legal—character of any constitution. As he explains in *Constitutional Theory*, the modern constitution must contain both *Rechtsstaat* and political elements: "For the Rechtsstaat understanding, the law is essentially a norm," whereas "'political' means a concept of law that, in contrast to the Rechtsstaat, results from the political form of existence of the state and out of the concrete manner of the formation of the organization of rule."[8] The mistake of liberal constitutional theory, in Schmitt's view, is to confuse the "constitution" with "constitutional law." As he explains: "The distinction between constitution and constitutional law . . . [is] possible because the essence of the constitution is not contained in a statute or in a norm. Prior to the establishment of any norm, there is a fundamental *political decision by the bearer of the constitution-making power*. In a democracy, more specifically, this is a decision by the people; in a genuine monarchy, it is a decision by the monarch."[9] The political decision both precedes the establishment of the norm and intervenes at the moment of the emergency to reground the *Rechtsstaat*. The sovereignty of the constitution-making power reveals itself again when a decision is rendered on the exception.

---

6. Carl Schmitt, *Political Theology: Four Chapters on the Concept of Sovereignty*, trans. George Schwab (Chicago: University of Chicago Press, 2006), 5.

7. Schmitt, *Political Theology*, 6.

8. Carl Schmitt, *Constitutional Theory*, trans. Jeffrey Seitzer (Durham: Duke University Press, 2008), 187.

9. Schmitt, *Constitutional Theory*, 75, 77.

Rather than recognizing the inevitably political component of the constitution, the bourgeois *Rechtsstaat* instead attempts to regulate the emergency from within constitutional law by "spell[ing] out in detail the case in which law suspends itself."[10] Many of the post-Weimar constitutions of Latin America and the post-Soviet ones of eastern Europe attempted to avoid the abuse of emergency powers in precisely such a manner, depriving the executive of the capacity to decide, limiting the duration of the emergency, or protecting certain fundamental rights against abrogation during the period of exception.[11]

The effort to constrain the exception through constitutional law coincides with the *Rechtsstaat's* failure to disclose the source of sovereign power. As Schmitt contends, the *Rechtsstaat* "aspires, in fact, to not answer the question of sovereignty and to leave open the question of which political will makes the appropriate norm into a positively valid command. As noted, this must lead to concealments and fictions, with every instance of conflict posing anew the problem of sovereignty." Despite these supposed fictions and subterfuges, "inside every political unity, there can only be one bearer of the constitution-making power," and the constitution must rest "either on the monarchical or the democratic principle, on the constitution-making power of the prince or that of the people." The fictions in question may result either from a compromise within the constitution—one that defers to the future the ultimate question of who will exercise sovereignty—or a refusal of the decision entirely. Whereas the Weimar Constitution (1919) arrived at the most fundamental political decision—that the "German Reich is a constitutional democracy"—the 1875 constitutional laws of the French National Assembly attempted to leave open whether the state would be a monarchy or a republic. Notwithstanding this effort, however, the popular rejection in 1877 of the steps that the Third Republic's president, Patrice de Mac-Mahon, had taken to ensure a conservative government created a precedent ensuring the republican rather than monarchical character of France.[12] In the absence of a decision embodied in constitutional laws, political precedent thus supplied the requisite determination of the identity of the sovereign. As this

---

10. Schmitt, *Political Theology*, 14.

11. Many of these measures are catalogued in Venelin I. Ganev, "Emergency Powers and the New East European Constitutions," *American Journal of Comparative Law* 45 (Summer 1997): 585–612; and Gabriel Negretto and Jose Rivera, "Liberalism and Emergency Powers in Latin America: Reflections on Carl Schmitt and the Theory of Constitutional Dictatorship," *Cardozo Law Review* 21, no. 5–6 (May 2000): 1797–1823.

12. Schmitt, *Constitutional Theory*, 187, 105, 86–88, 82–83.

example suggests, constitutional law may hold open a gap that practice steps in to fill.

While Schmitt devotes little attention to pardoning in *Constitutional Theory*—or in his other works—the position and specifications of the pardon power in the Weimar Constitution suggests a compromise akin to those he does discuss. The clauses pertaining to pardoning immediately followed the notorious Article 48, the grant of emergency powers to the president of the Reich that later furnished Hitler with a legal excuse for suppressing individual rights.[13] As they specified, "The president exercises the right of pardon [*das Begnadigungsrecht*] for the Reich. Reich amnesties [*Reichsamnestien*] require a Reich statute."[14] Harking back to the logic of monarchy, Article 49 first endowed the president with the power of pardoning. This strategy is consistent with what Schmitt identifies as the grant of pseudo-monarchical capacities to

---

13. Article 48 of the Weimar Constitution reads:

1. If a *Land* does not fulfill its duties according to the Reich Constitution or Reich statutes, the president can compel it to do so with the aid of armed force.
2. If in the German Reich the public security and order are being significantly disturbed or endangered, the president can utilize the necessary measures to restore public security and order, if necessary with the aid of armed force. For this purpose, he may provisionally suspend, in whole or in part, the basic rights established in Articles 114, 115, 117, 118, 123, 124, 153.
3. The president must inform the Reichstag without delay of all the measures instituted according to section 1 or section 2 of this article. The measures must be set aside at the request of the Reichstag.
4. In the case of immediate danger, the *Land* government can institute for its territory the type of measures designated in the second section on an interim basis. The measures can be set aside at the demand of the president or the Reichstag.
5. A Reich statute determines the details.

Schmitt treats this article at length in a number of works, including not only *Constitutional Theory* but also *Legality and Legitimacy, Political Theology, Der Hüter der Verfassung*, and *Die Diktatur*. According to his claim, Article 48 allowed the president to effect a fundamental alteration in the form of government. Despite the enumeration of only certain individual rights that could be suspended, the grant of the power to suspend implied a broader capacity to abrogate liberties; furthermore, the president's capacity to interfere with the jurisdiction of the *Länder* fundamentally altered the constitutional structure of federalism; finally, allowing presidential measures the force of law rendered the president superior to the Reichstag because "he unites in himself lawmaking and legal execution and can enforce directly the norms he establishes, which the ordinary legislature of the parliamentary legislative state cannot do, so long as it respects the separation of powers with its distinction between law and legal application so essential for the legislative state." Carl Schmitt, *Legality and Legitimacy*, trans. Jeffrey Seitzer (Durham: Duke University Press, 2004), 70–83.

14. Weimar Constitution, Article 49.

the president within the bourgeois *Rechtsstaat* in order to generate a separation or balance of powers.[15] At the same time, however, the Weimar Constitution attempts to cabin even this allowance of authority rather than simply weighing other parliamentary powers against it. Distinguishing between "amnesty" and "pardon," the document limits the president's pardon by allocating amnesty to parliament. This strategy stands in contrast to Hamilton's comments in *Federalist* 74 about the scope of the pardon power as well as the Supreme Court's subsequent interpretation of the U.S. Constitution in *United States v. Klein* (1871), a decision insisting that "pardon includes amnesty. It blots out the offense pardoned and removes all its penal consequences. . . . [I]t is clear that the legislature cannot change the effect of such a pardon any more than the executive can change a law."[16]

Pardoning (or *Begnadigung*) and amnesty (or *amnestie*) do differ substantially; whereas pardoning in its legal acceptation, according to the *Oxford English Dictionary,* denotes a "remission, either free or conditional, of the legal consequences of crime," amnesty consists in "forgetfulness, oblivion; an intentional overlooking" or "an act of oblivion, a general overlooking or pardoning of past offenses, by the ruling authority." While pardoning usually occurs after conviction and simply removes punishment, amnesty or oblivion encourages forgetting the entire set of underlying events and suspending the question of culpability or innocence. The pardon generally touches an individual, while an amnesty covers a collectivity. And since at least the seventeenth century, efforts have been made in constitutional theory to restrict the pardon power of the king or chief executive by giving legislatures control over amnesty.[17]

Nevertheless, the boundaries between pardoning and amnesty remain murky. General pardons were granted by the king and Parliament well before any efforts to divide amnesty from pardon or Parliament from monarch.[18] More

---

15. Schmitt, *Constitutional Theory*, 315–17.

16. *United States v. Klein,* 80 U.S. 128 (1872), 147–48.

17. The legislative nature of the 1660 Act of Oblivion following the restoration of King Charles II to the English throne furnishes one example of an allocation of amnesty power to Parliament. A more recent episode involving a struggle between Congress and the president over amnesty in the U.S. context occurred in the aftermath of the Civil War and is detailed in Jonathan Dorris, *Pardon and Amnesty under Lincoln and Johnson* (Chapel Hill: University of North Carolina Press, 1953).

18. Krista Kesselring treats the dynamics of such general pardons in the sixteenth century at length in *Mercy and Authority in the Tudor State* (Cambridge: Cambridge University Press, 2003), 56–90.

recently, within the French setting, Vladimir Jankélévitch called attention to the possible proximity of forgiveness and forgetting in attacking statutes of limitations in *L'imprescriptible*. At the beginning of that polemic, Jankélévitch asks, "Est-il temps de pardoner, où tout au moins d'oublier?," seeming to assimilate forgiveness with forgetting.[19] Statutes of limitations on crimes might themselves constitute a very broad form of amnesty.

Delineating the precise limits of the concepts of pardoning and amnesty itself requires a decision and may occasion conflict among the branches, as it did when Congress sparred with Presidents Lincoln and Johnson about their authority to grant amnesty to members of the former Confederacy after the end of the Civil War.[20] Article 49's attempt to require a Reich statute for amnesty, while allowing the president to exercise the pardon power, hence leaves open the further determination of the boundary between pardoning and amnesty; in this way it resembles the political compromises within constitutional law that Schmitt identifies and seems to await the gloss upon its meaning provided by future practice.

As with the state of exception, the Weimar Constitution tried to circumscribe pardoning by placing it within a separation of powers framework. In Schmitt's view, and in accord with his challenge elsewhere to the very possibility

---

19. Vladimir Jankélévitch, *L'imprescriptible* (Paris: Éditions du Seuil, 1986), 17. Derrida treats this aspect of Jankélévitch's theory in "To Forgive: The Unforgivable and the Imprescriptible," in Jacques Derrida, *Love and Forgiveness for a More Just World*, ed. Hent de Vries and Nils F. Schott (Columbia: Columbia University Press, 2015), 144–81. Whereas Jankélévitch in at least this context assimilates forgiveness with forgetting, Derrida insists that "forgiving is not forgetting (another enormous problem)." Derrida, "To Forgive," 23, 25–26. Many have noted the seeming incompatibility between Jankélévitch's account of forgiveness in *L'imprescriptible* and his more purely philosophical account in the subsequent book *Le pardon*. There he maintains that one can forgive even an unforgettable and inexcusable crime. Vladimir Jankélévitch, *Le pardon* (Paris: Montaigne, 1967), 204. Kevin Hart furnishes a plausible explanation of the difference, focusing on the distinction between the unpardonable and unforgivable on the one hand and the imprescriptible on the other: "One might take the whole of 'Should We Pardon Them?' (1965) to be a long, anguished counter-example to the case developed in *Forgiveness* (1967), one given both before and after the fact and not explicitly considered in the book. That would be a mistake, for the essay on Germany's role in the Shoah is concerned with another matter entirely, the imprescriptible rather than the unpardonable." Kevin Hart, "Guilty Forgiveness," in *Vladimir Jankélévitch and the Question of Forgiveness*, ed. Alan Udoff (New York: Lexington, 2013), 52. Ethan Kleinberg has persuasively argued that both of Jankélévitch's works must be seen as responses to the juridical debates about the punishment of crimes against humanity in the aftermath of the Holocaust. Ethan Kleinberg, "To Atone and to Forgive," in Udoff, *Vladimir Jankélévitch and the Question of Forgiveness*, 147.

20. Jonathan Dorris describes this conflict in detail in *Pardon and Amnesty under Lincoln and Johnson*.

of separating powers,[21] the efforts of Article 48 to limit the president's decision on the exception remained of only nominal efficacy:

> According to article 48 of the German constitution of 1919, the exception is declared by the president of the Reich but is under the control of parliament, the Reichstag, which can at any time demand its suspension. This provision corresponds to the development and practice of the liberal constitutional state, which attempts to repress the question of sovereignty by a division and mutual control of competences. But only the arrangement of the precondition that governs the invocation of exceptional powers corresponds to the liberal constitutional tendency, not the content of article 48. Article 48 grants unlimited power.[22]

The same might be said of Article 49. To the extent that the president is, in the first instance, entitled to exercise the pardon on behalf of the state, the restriction

---

21. Criticizing the pluralist theory of the state espoused in the Anglo-American context by G. D. H. Cole and Harold Laski, Schmitt contends in *The Concept of the Political* that it cannot answer the essential question of "which social entity . . . decides the extreme case and determines the decisive friend-and-enemy grouping." Schmitt, *The Concept of the Political*, trans. George Schwab (Chicago: University of Chicago Press, 1996), 43. Likewise, as William Scheuerman demonstrates, Schmitt rejected the view that legislative and executive power could be definitively separated. William Scheuerman, *Carl Schmitt: The End of Law* (New York: Rowman & Littlefield, 1999), 26–30; William Scheuerman, *Between the Norm and the Exception: The Frankfurt School and the Rule of Law* (Cambridge: MIT Press, 1997), 75–76.

Giorgio Agamben's analysis in *State of Exception* illuminates the connection between the effacement of a strict separation of powers and the condition of emergency itself; according to Agamben, "In our discussion of the state of exception, we have encountered numerous examples of this confusion between acts of the executive power and acts of the legislative power; indeed, as we have seen, such a confusion defines one of the essential characteristics of the state of exception." Giorgio Agamben, *State of Exception*, trans. Kevin Attell (Chicago: University of Chicago Press, 2005), 38. Peter Lindseth explains in "The Paradox of Parliamentary Supremacy":

> For Schmitt, the traditional precepts of the separation of powers inherited from nineteenth-century European public law (at the core of which was the deliberative, elected parliament) simply could not be reconciled with the exigencies of modern governance and the interventionist demands of the "total state." . . . His basic argument was that, in the aftermath of World War I, developments not just in Germany and France but also in Britain and the United States (the four "Great Powers" on which he chose to focus) reflected a similar breakdown in the constitutional boundary between legislative and executive power, to the obvious benefit of the latter. . . . [H]owever, only Germany had, in his view, taken this process to its logical conclusion by completely eliminating any semblance of "separation of powers," opting instead for a system of "governmental legislation."

Peter Lindseth, "The Paradox of Parliamentary Supremacy: Delegation, Democracy, and Dictatorship in Germany and France, 1920s–1950s," *Yale Law Journal* 113 (May 2004): 1358–59.

22. Schmitt, *Political Theory*, 11. *Legality and Legitimacy*, composed in 1932, contains a more elaborated discussion of how exactly Article 48 shifts power to the executive over the legislative branch. Schmitt, *Legality and Legitimacy*, 70–71.

of his power in the case of amnesty appears only belatedly and is itself subject to circumscription. The discretionary decision on the pardon, like that on the emergency, determines what constitutes a pardon as well as when it should be employed.

The connections between the pardon and the exception extend further than the proximity of Articles 48 and 49 of the Weimar Constitution. The decision on the exception and the determination to pardon resist circumscription by rule. Similarly, the specification of procedures for the declaration of emergency and the maintenance of restrictions on its scope have been notoriously insufficient in delineating the boundaries of states of exception.[23] This is the case in part because what is perceived to be at stake is the very existence of the state itself; as Schmitt elaborates, "The state suspends the law in the exception on the basis of its right of self-preservation."[24] Such a Hobbesian account of the exception finds an analogy in the pardon power as well. Seeking peace was, for Hobbes, as we have seen, the primary dictate of natural law, and pardoning furnished the principal way of achieving peace within an already constituted—although perhaps revolutionarily overturned—polity. Finally, both the exception and the pardon—like the other attributes of sovereignty—partake of theological roots. According to Schmitt, "The exception in jurisprudence is analogous to the miracle in theology."[25] The pardon itself, as an act of free gift, or grace, is likewise associated with the sovereignty of a Christian god, whose mercy displays a power even greater than that of judgment.

Even Schmitt appears to acknowledge this connection in a passage furnishing his most suggestive remarks about pardoning. Resisting the notion that the liberal state had managed to efface its own agency through law, Schmitt claimed:

> Whoever takes the trouble of examining the public law literature of positive jurisprudence for its basic concepts and arguments will see that the state intervenes everywhere. At times it does so as a *deus ex machina*, to decide according to positive statute a controversy that the independent act of juristic perception failed to bring to a generally plausible solution; at other times it does so as the graceful and merciful lord who proves by pardons and amnesties his supremacy over his own laws. There always exists the same inexplicable identity; lawgiver, executive power, police,

---

23. This phenomenon becomes apparent in Agamben's "brief history of the state of exception." Agamben, *State of Exception*, 11–22.

24. Schmitt, *Political Theory*, 12.

25. Schmitt, *Political Theory*, 36.

pardoner, welfare institution. Thus to an observer who takes the trouble to look at the total picture of contemporary jurisprudence, there appears a huge cloak-and-dagger drama, in which the state acts in many disguises but always as the same invisible person. The "omnipotence" of the modern lawgiver, of which one reads in every textbook on public law, is not only linguistically derived from theology.[26]

Here the state operates in dramatic terms, either serving as a *deus ex machina* or playing in a "cloak-and-dagger drama," its many personae substituting for a single surreptitious power. The *deus ex machina* form of the decision assumes a place analogous to that of the pardon. Despite the seemingly automated quality of the positivist state, it reaches out in various characters to affect what would otherwise seem a uniform rule of law.[27]

Late in his career, after the dire consequences of his theories had become all too evident under the Third Reich, Schmitt would turn to an actual play— Shakespeare's *Hamlet*—to illuminate the relationship between aesthetics and history as well as between drama and sovereignty. A final intervention in the exchange between Schmitt and Walter Benjamin, and a response to the latter's use of Schmitt's thesis on sovereignty in his 1927 *Origin of German Tragic Drama*, Schmitt's *Hamlet or Hecuba: The Intrusion of Time into the Play* sees in the character Hamlet the formation of a myth, one that Jennifer Rust and Julia Lupton have aptly glossed as, in part, "the myth of sovereignty *as* presence."[28] The identification of Hamlet with a Schmittian sovereign might, at first blush, appear strange; as Schmitt himself describes Hamlet, he is a "procrastinator and dreamer . . . who cannot take the decision to act," an incapacity that would seem to accord poorly with the decisionism of *Political Theology*.[29] It is not exactly Hamlet's stance with respect to the decision, however, that renders him mythic

---

26. Schmitt, *Political Theory*, 38.

27. The only other extended discussion I have found of the connection between pardoning—or mercy—and the exception in Schmitt occurs in Christoph Menke, *Reflections of Equality*, trans. Howard Rouse and Andrei Denejkine (Stanford: Stanford University Press, 2006), 177–97. Menke sees in mercy, however, and Schmitt's treatment of it, an alternative to the kind of exception represented by the dictator. Mercy instead, under his view, allows for the adequation of the law to the subject. He thus focuses not on the relationship between pardoning and sovereignty but instead on the nature of mercy's effect on the application of the law.

28. Jennifer Rust and Julia Lupton, "Schmitt and Shakespeare," in Carl Schmitt, *Hamlet or Hecuba*, ed. and trans. David Pan, Jennifer Rust, and Julia Reinhard Lupton (New York: Telos Press, 2009), xxviii, xxxvii.

29. Schmitt, *Hamlet or Hecuba*, 9.

but rather what that postponement of the decision signals about his connection with the historical figure of King James I.

The failure of decision in *Hamlet*, or "the transformation of the figure of the avenger into a reflective, self-conscious melancholic," itself indicates the "intrusion" (*Einbruch*) of history. As Schmitt writes: "The philosophizing and theologizing King James embodied namely the entire conflict of his age, a century of divided belief and religious civil war. The distortion that differentiates the Hamlet of this drama from all other avenger figures and that is otherwise inexplicable . . .—in short, the Hamletization of the avenger—finds a suitable explanation only here, in James. It is here that the connection between present history and tragedy emerges."[30] Just as James here manifests himself in Hamlet, the "conflict of his age" imposes itself on James. Hamlet may represent both James and this conflict, but the form of representation is "personalized" rather than "impersonated."[31] The immediacy of the connection between Hamlet and James, and between James and the "conflict of his age," transcends "play" and renders *Hamlet* tragedy rather than *Trauerspiel*. Referring to the "unplayability [*Unverspielbarkeit*] of the tragic," Schmitt therefore explains that "in distinguishing *Trauerspiel* and tragedy, we can recognize that incontrovertible core of a singular historical reality that transcends every subjective invention and can then understand its elevation to myth."[32] It is not just sovereign indecision but rather the historical problem to which that sovereign indecision points that renders Hamlet a mythic figure for the future.

The nature of this historical problem, however, remains less than perspicuous. On one level, Schmitt insists upon a rather blunt comparison between Queen Mary Stuart's supposed culpability for the death of her husband—the future King James's father—and Gertrude's potential guilt in the demise of Hamlet's father, both of which subjects are "taboo." Likewise, he associates the treatment of the ghost in *Hamlet* with Catholic and Protestant debates about the demonic quality of such apparitions and, in particular, the adolescent James's intervention in these debates with his 1597 *Daemonologie*. More broadly, however, the problem concerns not only the division between Catholics and Protestants—and among various types of Protestants—that plagued seventeenth-century England, but also the hypothesis of the "divine right of kings," which in Schmitt's view furnished King James's "true life's task, his existential problem."[33]

---

30. Schmitt, *Hamlet or Hecuba*, 26.
31. Rust and Lupton, "Schmitt and Shakespeare," xl.
32. Schmitt, *Hamlet or Hecuba*, 40, 52.
33. Schmitt, *Hamlet or Hecuba*, 15–18, 28, 29.

When James was writing and ruling, the prelude to the English Revolution had, in Schmitt's view, already commenced. Because James's concerns would lead neither to the "state" characteristic of the continental European countries of the eighteenth century, nor to the maritime economic empire of England, which Schmitt analyzed in *The Nomos of the Earth*, he was destined "to disappear from the stage of world history" and to remain in the modern consciousness only to the extent that the myth of Hamlet contains his relic.[34] If the myth of Hamlet furnishes this remainder and reminder of James, another seventeenth-century myth—that of the Leviathan—carried forward greater consequences for European political development, somewhat to Schmitt's chagrin.

In analyzing Hobbes's image for the commonwealth in an earlier book from 1938, Schmitt claimed that the figure of the Leviathan gestured in two directions, one a personalist vision unifying all of the components of the state into a single figure, and the other a mechanistic and machinic one.[35] Whereas the first interpretation connected back to James himself and the Stuarts more generally, the second pointed forward to the continental European theories of the state.[36] As Victoria Kahn has persuasively argued, Schmitt's disillusion with the Hobbesian image of the Leviathan, the doubleness of which prevented Hobbes's philosophy from being received as decisionist and instead paved the path for the future liberal state, itself sent Schmitt back to search the seventeenth century for another hero of decisionism, which he ultimately located in Hamlet.[37] The passage from *Political Theology* quoted earlier, however, explaining the *deus ex machina* mode of the state's intervention, indicates the potential return of the person—or at least the god—in even the machine of the liberal state. The drama therefore continues as the god is put back into the machine. The pardon and the *deus ex machina* subsist only as the residue of the personalist sovereign in Schmitt's account though; rather than being identified with the divine right monarch, they are personae adopted by the otherwise mechanistic state. At the same time, however, their existence may hinder the closure of the liberal state.

Schmitt's fascination with Hamlet and the Leviathan, images emanating from seventeenth-century England, might suggest a further engagement with the political developments of that century and the relationship of dramatic

---

34. Schmitt, *Hamlet or Hecuba*, 62, 65.

35. Carl Schmitt, *The Leviathan in the State Theory of Thomas Hobbes: Meaning and Failure of a Political Symbol*, trans. George Schwab (Chicago: University of Chicago Press, 1996), 34–35.

36. Schmitt, *The Leviathan*, 79–80, 86.

37. Victoria Kahn, "Hamlet or Hecuba: Carl Schmitt's Decision," *Representations* 83, no. 1 (Summer 2003): 80.

spectacle to what transpired. Oddly, though, by positing the historical anoma-lousness of James's theories and their lack of inheritors, as well as claiming that Hobbes influenced continental Europe more than England itself, Schmitt man-aged to gloss over the space between *Hamlet* and Hobbes and to ignore the con-test over sovereignty contained there, the very contest with which this book has been concerned.

In addition, by concentrating on the respective roles of monarch and legisla-ture or, in their English incarnations, king and Parliament, Schmitt neglected the crucial role of the judiciary in the struggle among powers in seventeenth-century England. As we have seen, the king's capacity to pardon was, in the early seven-teenth century, challenged by and itself challenged the regularity of common law decision making. The pardon thereby became a site for staging conflicts among not simply two but three forms of authority in the state. Indeed, the common law component of the contest among powers may, more than the parliamentary aspect, have set the stage for the constitutional elements of the tradition of liberal constitutionalism, elements that come to the fore in the writings of Immanuel Kant.

Liberalism and the Sovereign Pardon

Although Kant's work is associated with the inauguration of Enlightenment reason and politics, and it promulgates a vision of sovereignty that is largely legislative rather than judicial, a certain singularity of sovereignty remains in *The Metaphysics of Morals*, one associated with the king's act of pardoning. Hobbes, in reaffirming monarchical sovereignty and the sovereign's identity as the source of both laws and their interpretation, had shifted away from James I's notion of the king as judge toward a model of sovereignty based on lawgiv-ing, and, hence, one that could be applied just as easily to Parliament as to the king. Kant, by contrast, while seeming to prioritize lawgiving—in the context of both individual ethics and the polity in general—allows space for the par-don, a pardon that presents the tragicomic resolution of the revolutionary situ-ation. Thus at the origins of modern liberalism lies an exception to the general rule of law.

The pardon intervenes, in Kant's writings, at the intersection between two dramas—that of, on the one hand, the revolution itself, which, although poten-tially partaking of the sublime, must simply be interpreted by the world audi-ence as a tragedy on the order of the beautiful; and that of, on the other hand, the sovereign, who, in staging the pardon, dramatizes his own majesty. In *The*

Metaphysics of Morals, Kant describes the pardon both theatrically and with great ambivalence:

> Of all the rights of a sovereign, the *right to grant clemency* to a criminal *(ius aggratiandi)*, either by lessening or entirely remitting punishment, is the slipperiest one for him to exercise for it must be exercised in such a way as to show the splendor [*Glanz*] of his majesty, although he is thereby doing injustice [*unrecht zu tun*] in the highest degree.—With regard to crimes of *subjects* against one another it is absolutely not for him to exercise it; for here failure to punish *(impunitas criminis)* is the greatest wrong against his subjects. He can make use of it, therefore, only in case of a wrong done *to himself (crimen laesae maiestatis)*. But he cannot make use of it even then if his failure to punish could endanger the people's security [*dem Volke selbst in Ansehung seiner Sicherheit Gefahr erwachsen könnte*].—This right is the only one that deserves to be called the right of majesty.[38]

Through pardoning, the sovereign commits an "injustice in the highest degree" that proves invisible to the people and instead enhances "the splendor of his majesty." Kant theatricalizes this "injustice in the highest degree," which derives from a display staged for the benefit of public opinion—the *Ansehung* of the people. The sovereign thus "shines" (*glänzen*) in the eyes of his subjects through the graciousness of his pardon. Pardon emerges here, however, as a responsibility that the sovereign should assume only in relation to himself, an act of forgiving someone who would injure him as a singular entity—but always *qua* sovereign.[39] Kant assigns for pardoning the narrow space between circumstances

---

38. Immanuel Kant, *The Metaphysics of Morals*, trans. Mary Gregor (Cambridge: Cambridge University Press, 1996), 109–10. The German text is quoted from Immanuel Kant, *Werkausgabe*, ed. Wilhelm Weischedel (Frankfurt am Main: Suhrkamp, 1977).

39. Kant's discussion of pardoning here generates several parallels with his brief treatment of "equity" in the "Introduction to the Doctrine of Right." In excluding "equity" from the purview of his investigation in the *Doctrine of Right,* Kant maintains that although equity as a category involves right, it comprehends cases "for which no judge can be appointed to render a decision," because the conditions of right are ill-defined or undefined. Since no one can provide evidence sufficient for a judge removed from the situation to render a verdict, Kant concludes that "only where the judge's own rights are concerned, and he can dispose of the case for his own person, may and should he listen to equity, as, for example, when the crown itself bears the damages that others have incurred in its service and for which they petition it to indemnify them." Kant, *Metaphysics of Morals*, 27. The sovereign provides the exemplary figure in this instance, as in that of pardoning, while in both circumstances, the one executing the decision must be one of the affected parties, thus reducing the juridical situation from three components to two. The difference between determining an equitable solution and

in which political subjects would be injured by the absence of punishment—pardon defined here as an omission rather than a positive act—and those that, since involving only the sovereign, permit him the right to pardon.[40]

This sliver constricts further when considered in the context of Kant's statements elsewhere defining sovereignty and discussing the nature of revolution. These remarks reveal the near impossibility of injuring the sovereign without simultaneously challenging the people, and also demonstrate that the ultimate offense against the sovereign would constitute the most unpardonable deed. Indeed, the right to pardon is accurately described as "the slipperiest," not because it can ever be exercised rightly, but because it always engenders injustice and constitutes the element of sovereignty lying outside the law.[41]

In a footnote to a passage in "Part Two: Public Right," Kant discusses the ultimate violence against a sovereign, that of "formal execution" (*der förmlichen Hinrichtung*), which he vehemently distinguishes from "murder" (*der Mord*), and employs as one example the trial and decapitation of Charles I during the English Revolution. The difference between "formal execution" and "murder" that Kant stresses, however, is undermined when he concludes that Charles and Louis XVI could not actually have been subjected to the first crime but instead were victims of the second and less egregious one. This confusion is made possible by the fact that the king functions as both a physical individual and a symbolic placeholder, so that any attack against his literal body could signal either formal execution or murder. In order to ensure that he was targeted as sovereign rather than simply as individual, one would need to discover a revolutionary procedure that—like slander—operated on a symbolic rather than a material level. Asserting in the main text the principle that "a people cannot offer any resistance to the legislative head of a state which would be consistent with right, since a rightful condition is possible only by submission to its general [*allgemein*] legislative will," Kant further articulates the paradox of rebellion against the sovereign by explaining that the people's will would then be supreme, thereby negating the analytic

---

pardoning, however, is that the former still deals with a right on the part of the one petitioning, while the latter constitutes a right of the sovereign himself.

40. There are echoes here of Sir Edward Coke's account of the constraints on the king's ability to pardon, discussed in chapters 1 and 6.

41. Despite the fact that Kant defines the sovereign as the lawgiving power, his examples most frequently employ the figure of the absolute monarch, or "autocrat," a circumstance that facilitates comparison with James I's comments on the sovereign, whom he too conceives as an absolute monarch, despite the legislative powers of Parliament. Kant, *Metaphysics of Morals*, 111. In all forms of government, however, one can imagine a sovereign body that would decide on an exception to its own laws.

supremacy of the sovereign. He finally concludes with the summation: "This is self-contradictory, and the contradiction is evident as soon as one asks who is to be the judge in this dispute between people and sovereign (for, considered in terms of rights, these are always two distinct moral persons). For it is then apparent that the people wants to be the judge in its own suit."[42] Crucially here, Kant determines that since no "objective" standpoint can be attained, resolving the issue proves impossible. The opposition between people and sovereign cannot be reconciled.

Since Kant claims that judgment has reached an insoluble quandary when the people are pitted against their sovereign, it should not be surprising that he refers in his footnote to the case of the British monarch Charles I. Having created the High Court of Justice in 1649, the House of Commons proceeded to execute Charles for committing treason during the Civil War.[43] When introducing the spectacle of Charles's death, Kant adds imaginary onlookers, alleging:

> It is the formal *execution* of a monarch that strikes horror [*Schaudern*] in a soul filled with the idea of human beings' rights, a horror that one feels repeatedly as soon as and as often as one thinks of such scenes [*Auftritt*] as the fate of Charles I or Louis XVI. But how are we to explain this feeling [*Gefühl*], which is not aesthetic feeling (sympathy, an effect of the imagination by which we put ourselves in the place of the sufferer) but moral feeling resulting from the complete overturning of all concepts of rights? It is regarded as a crime that remains forever and can never be expiated (*crimen immortale, inexpiabile*), and it seems to be like what theologians call the sin that cannot be forgiven [*vergeben*] either in this world or the next.[44]

As Kant explains, this feeling occurs because the criminal, here identified with the people, rather than simply making himself an exception to his own—in principle universalizable—maxim, instead sets his maxim against the dictates of reason; thus, the fact that it takes place "beyond human reason," or, in other words, violates the humanity of man, occasions the horrific quality of this crime, and perhaps also the reference to a theological analogy in the attempt to explain it. Although the passage denies aesthetic sympathy, the audience's reaction to a

---

42. Kant, *Metaphysics of Morals*, 96, 97.

43. See David Lagomarsino and Charles T. Wood, *The Trial of Charles I: A Documentary History* (Hanover: Dartmouth College Press, 1989).

44. Kant, *Metaphysics of Morals*, 97.

tragedy, it retains the dramatic structure, so that the spectators simply experience a different generic drama, one connected with the sublime.

We can now return to the initial issue of the space left over for pardoning between the sovereign's right and the endangerment of the people, examining the paradoxical nature of Kant's double demand through a final passage. In this section of *The Doctrine of Right*, Kant asserts that the sovereign should remit capital punishment if the greater part of his citizenry would be eliminated by the *lex talionis* system of justice that Kant usually advocates. Although in speaking of pardoning, Kant claims that it constitutes the sovereign's only "right of majesty," he yet refers to this mitigating function also as "an act of the right of majesty which, as clemency [*Begnadigung*], can always be exercised only in individual cases," setting the two deeds almost indiscernibly close together. Again in this passage, Kant employs dramatic terminology to describe the situation, maintaining:

> If . . . the number of accomplices (*correi*) to such a deed is so great that the state, in order to have no such criminals in it, could soon find itself without subjects; and if the state still does not want to dissolve, that is, to pass over into the state of nature, which is far worse because there is no external justice at all in it (and if especially it does not want to dull the people's feeling [*das Gefühl*] by the spectacle [*das Spektakel*] of a slaughterhouse), then the sovereign must also have it in his power, in this case of necessity (*casus necessitatis*), to assume the role of judge (to represent him [*vorzustellen*]) and pronounce a judgment that decrees for the criminals a sentence other than capital punishment . . . which still preserves the population.[45]

If the civil order were to devolve again into the state of nature, the remaining individuals would be adversely affected, so here the amelioration of punishment, like pardon, allows for the well-being of lawful subjects. While the aggregate of the people cannot kill the king, the king as the representative of sovereign generality likewise cannot annihilate all his subjects. The hypothetical example that Kant invokes, however, since it involves such a large number of people, could be seen as an allusion to revolutionary violence as well. This conception would put the event on the verge of the unpardonable, lacking only the assassination of

---

45. Kant, *Metaphysics of Morals*, 108, 107. Yet again, the sovereign here assumes a judicial as well as legislative role. In *Measure for Measure* (2.1.235–40), the bawd Pompey similarly asserts that the new laws are too harsh since they will result in eliminating the entire populace.

the sovereign himself. In order to retain the concept of legality here, the crime against legality must be pardoned and the law of the unpardonable compromised. This passage describes what should occur on the other side of revolution, but only if the revolution has failed in its ultimate goal, that of deposing the monarch; we receive no advice here on how to respond when the sovereign no longer exists and thus lacks the capacity to pardon.

Within Kant's narrative, the king stages his pardon both to accentuate his majesty in the eyes of his subjects and to transform what might, for the world audience, have been the sublime spectacle of the revolutionary overturning of law into a tragicomedy restoring the constitutional state. In both respects, the pardon shifts the signification of the performance for those watching, yet it fails to allow the "groundlings" of the polity or international community a means of participating more actively in the performance. In scattered comments, Hannah Arendt indicates the potential for rescuing the spectator from his passivity by replacing the sovereign's pardon of proto-revolutionary violence with the individual's forgiveness of the revolutionary act. Rather than furnishing a sovereign manifestation of political will, this forgiveness would arrive as an ethical gesture that yet carried implications for the reconstitution of the state.

Forgiveness and Refounding

Arendt concludes the section of *The Human Condition* on "action" by considering two complementary concepts, those of forgiving and promising—both of which establish the other-regarding quality of action and, hence, its political dimension. As she additionally explains, both forgiving and promising also affect the temporality of the world of action; while forgiving supposedly "serves to undo the deeds of the past," promising "serves to set up in the ocean of uncertainty, which the future is by definition, islands of security without which not even continuity, let alone durability of any kind, would be possible in the relationships between men."[46] Although forgiving and promising each provides a plurality for the political that Arendt deems lacking in a Platonic politics, she identifies them as inherently moral rather than immediately political. Forgiving, in particular, is not described within the context of a recognizable political sphere but instead assumes an interpersonal quality; verging on a religious type

---

46. Hannah Arendt, *The Human Condition* (1958; Chicago: University of Chicago Press, 1998), 237.

of redemption, it was supposedly "discovered" by Jesus of Nazareth. Promising appears to make up this deficit, as Arendt insists that it provides the only viable basis for the concept of sovereignty, and, in doing so, transforms that political principle.[47] Given the intimate connection Arendt diagnoses between forgiving and promising, it is somewhat surprising that when she rejects sovereignty as traditionally conceived in *On Revolution*, and insists upon the significance of the American Revolution's experience of promising, forgiveness appears nowhere on the horizon. Regardless of the causes of this absence, it may be useful for dissociating pardoning from sovereignty to imagine how forgiveness might have operated in *On Revolution*.

Dealing with beginnings, *On Revolution* focuses primarily on a comparison between the French and American revolutions and their respective capacities to continue the process of recommencement. Forgiveness, as Arendt describes it in *The Human Condition*, should assist in this task, the attempt to reformulate the present in a manner that exceeds the potential of the past. Calling forgiveness "the exact opposite of vengeance," she explains that, whereas the latter simply reinforces the initial deed by perpetuating a "chain reaction," the former realizes human agency, since "it is the only reaction that acts in an unexpected way and thus retains, though being a reaction, something of the original character of action."[48] When Arendt then elucidates the triangulation of forgiveness, vengeance, and punishment, the final element differentiated from but not opposed to the others, her account recalls Hegel's description of the relationship between revenge and retribution in *The Philosophy of Right*.

Whereas revenge (*die Rache*), for Hegel, remains personal, a "particular caprice of the subjective will [*subjectiven Willens*],"[49] retribution (*die Wiedervergeltung*)[50] represents the cancellation (*Aufheben*) of the crime. Although acknowledging that retribution may adopt the same form of arbitrary external equivalence as the *lex talionis*'s "eye for an eye," Hegel insists that it instead establishes an inner equality of value between crime and punishment. Rather than being imposed

---

47. Arendt, *Human Condition*, 245–56, 238, 245.

48. Arendt, *Human Condition*, 240–41.

49. G. W. F. Hegel, *Elements of the Philosophy of Right*, ed. Allen W. Wood, trans. H. B. Nisbet (Cambridge: Cambridge University Press, 1991), §101, Addition (H). The German is quoted from G. W. F. Hegel, *Grundlinien der Philosophie des Rechts*, vol. 7 of *Werke* (Frankfurt am Main: Suhrkamp, 1971). The "Additions" to the *Philosophy of Right* contain the notes on Hegel's lectures compiled by Eduard Gans.

50. Although it is accurate to translate Hegel's term as "retribution," the German might be more aptly rendered "retaliation," since etymologically *Wiedervergeltung* implies a paying back. The word thus conjures a connection with the *lex talionis*.

from without, retribution is entailed by the concept of the crime itself: "What is at first sight objectionable about retribution is that it looks like something immoral, like revenge, and may thus be interpreted as a personal matter. Yet it is not the personal element, but the concept [*Begriff*] itself which carries out retribution."[51]

If we align Arendt's punishment with Hegel's retribution and pair vengeance with revenge, the nature of the relationship between forgiveness and punishment becomes apparent. Since Arendt conceives of forgiveness as "an eminently personal (though not necessarily individual or private) affair," an act that occurs for the sake of the other and does not pass through the objective determination of the state, it subsists on the same level as revenge.[52] Punishment, like forgiveness, however, also represents an end to the cycle of crime, in contrast to vengeance; as Hegel, whom Arendt follows here, asserts, "Revenge, as the positive action of a *particular* will, becomes *a new infringement*; because of this contradiction, it becomes part of an infinite progression and is inherited indefinitely from generation to generation." We have seen, however, that for Hegel, retribution is implicit within the crime itself; in the terms of Aeschylus's *Oresteia*, an example Hegel often invokes in the context of revenge and retribution, "the Eumenides sleep, but crime awakens them; thus the deed brings its own retribution with it."[53] Rather than allowing for the appearance of the new, which forgiveness could permit, punishment continues within the constraints of the concept evoked by the crime.

Applying this triangulated structure to the revolutionary scene reveals that forgiveness might serve to break the deleterious pattern according to which the revolution brings about its own failure. According to Arendt, only a revolutionary redefinition of revolution led to our current understanding of the term as referring to innovation rather than cyclical return. As she asserts, "The modern concept of revolution, inextricably bound up with the notion that the course of history suddenly begins anew, that an entirely new story, a story never known or told before, is about to unfold, was unknown prior to the two great revolutions at the end of the eighteenth century."[54] In discussing the English Revolution, Arendt adds content to this claim by reminding her readers that the designation "revolution" emerged only at the moment when the monarchy was to be restored.

---

51. Hegel, *Philosophy of Right*, §101, and §101 Addition (H).
52. Arendt, *Human Condition*, 241.
53. Hegel, *Philosophy of Right*, §102, §101 Addition (H)
54. Hannah Arendt, *On Revolution* (1963; London: Penguin, 1990), 28.

Although this cyclical vision of revolution was superseded, another inheritance of the term's astronomical derivation remains: the notion of its irresistibility, or, as Arendt puts it, "the fact that the revolving motion of the stars follows a pre-ordained path and is removed from all influence of human power." The modern concept of revolution's unstoppable force she identifies with "the idea of histori-cal necessity" and with Hegel, whom she views as the thinker of such necessity.[55]

To this Hegelian vision of history, and its inheritance in Marx, both of which she presents in fairly reductive terms, Arendt opposes the revolutionary attempt to attain freedom. Such freedom—envisioned not merely as liberation but more substantively as "participation in public affairs, or admission to the public realm"—Arendt insists upon as the only justifiable goal of violence.[56] Consisting in the ability to act within the political sphere, the freedom Arendt espouses stands in contrast with the modern concept of freedom of the will and the politi-cal principle corresponding to it—that of sovereignty. Arendt elaborates upon her concept of freedom most explicitly in the essay "What Is Freedom?," the les-sons of which *On Revolution* internalizes. She describes her vision of freedom in terms of the classical *polis*, arguing that "freedom was an exclusively political concept" in Greek and Roman antiquity and, furthermore, that "freedom as a political phenomenon was coeval with the rise of the Greek city-states."[57] These contexts provide an example, for Arendt, of her claim that "the *raison d'être* of politics is freedom, and its field of experience is action."[58]

Western philosophical and religious traditions, and, in accordance with them, modern political thought, have instead emphasized free will.[59] Jean-Jacques

---

55. Arendt, *On Revolution*, 43, 47, 48.

56. Arendt, *On Revolution*, 32. Explaining why the use of violence is not sufficient to define an event as a revolution, Arendt elaborates that "violence is no more adequate to describe the phenom-enon of revolution than change; only where change occurs in the sense of new beginning, where violence is used to constitute an altogether different form of government, to bring about the forma-tion of a new body politic, where the liberation from oppression aims at least at the constitution of freedom can we speak of revolution." Arendt, *On Revolution*, 35. Approaching Arendt's distinction between violence and freedom from the vantage point of the former rather than the latter, Beatrice Hanssen has confirmed that "the only politically acceptable limit case[s] of violence [for Arendt] were democratic revolutions—her grand exemplar being the American Revolution—which consisted of nation-founding acts of violence, animated by a revolutionary spirit that unfailingly espoused the ideals of 'public freedom, public happiness, public spirit.'" Beatrice Hanssen, *Critique of Violence: Between Poststructuralism and Critical Theory* (London: Routledge, 2000), 30.

57. Hannah Arendt, "What Is Freedom?" (1961), in *Between Past and Future* (London: Penguin Books, 1993), 157; Arendt, *On Revolution*, 30.

58. Arendt, "What Is Freedom?," 146.

59. Arendt, "What Is Freedom?," 156–65. Although Arendt regards both the philosophical and Christian concepts of freedom as centered on the will, she distinguishes Augustine's *City of God* and

Rousseau, as the preeminent thinker of sovereignty in terms of the general will, thus furnishes the exemplary object of Arendt's critique.[60] In *What Is Freedom?* Arendt juxtaposes Rousseau's conception of the sovereign will and her own insistence on a community constructed through promising, highlighting a distinction that emerges more obliquely in *On Revolution*:

> In reality Rousseau's theory stands refuted for the simple reason that "it is absurd for the will to bind itself for the future"; a community actually founded on this sovereign will would be built not on sand but on quicksand. All political business is, and always has been, transacted within an elaborate framework of ties and bonds for the future—such as laws and constitutions, treaties and alliances—all of which derive in the last instance from the faculty to promise and to keep promises in the face of the essential uncertainties of the future.[61]

Not the sovereign will but the promise, which, like forgiveness, is a manifestation of that sphere of action in which freedom is experienced, constitutes the condition of possibility for politics.[62] At the same time, freedom in the form of action constitutes the interruption of a cycle and the arrival of the unexpected, observed from the vantage point of the outsider as a miracle; as Arendt writes, "Every act, seen from the perspective not of the agent but of the process in whose framework it occurs and whose automatism it interrupts, is a 'miracle'—that is, something which could not be expected."[63]

The principal problem, she claims, with a Hegelian or post-Hegelian approach is that it views revolution not from the perspective of the actors, which she sees as the properly political point of view, but instead from that of

---

"the sayings of Jesus of Nazareth" on the one hand from the Pauline tradition on the other; whereas the latter emphasizes freedom as an outgrowth of will, the former, according to Arendt, envisions freedom as a function of faith, the work of which is the miracle. Arendt, *Human Condition*, 167, 168. Arendt's tentative approval of Jesus's stance on freedom accords with her claim in *The Human Condition* that Jesus discovered forgiveness.

60. Arendt, "What Is Freedom?," 163–65. Arendt identifies Carl Schmitt as the modern inheritor of Rousseau's understanding of sovereignty as a phenomenon of the will. Arendt, "What Is Freedom?," 296.

61. Arendt, "What Is Freedom?," 163–64.

62. This emphasis on promising suggests, of course, the relevance of the social contract, the Hobbesian version of which is discussed in chapter 6. Forgiveness and promising are, in a sense, combined in *The Laws of Candy*, treated in chapter 3, because forgivenesses are exchanged in a manner that suggests the refounding of the state.

63. Arendt, "What Is Freedom?," 169.

the spectator—which instead produces a philosophy of history.[64] Described as a drama, revolution is then either played for the spectator, and thereby manifests itself according to a logic of necessity, or is lived by the actors, who discover freedom. In other words, what Arendt views as happening in Hegel is the reinstatement of the fundamentally foreign nature of revolutions—like that of the starry heavens. The cyclical quality of revolution is thus realized in a modified form within the French Revolution's inability to achieve the goal of freedom.

The opposition between the inevitability of natural phenomena and the freedom of human affairs that Arendt describes in the context of revolution can also, however, be found in the section of *The Human Condition* on "acting." In that context, forgiving and promising together permit escape from the constraints of necessity. The duality of perspectives on revolution is there anticipated by the doubleness of viewpoints on man: "Just as, from the standpoint of nature, the rectilinear movement of man's life-span between birth and death looks like a peculiar deviation from the common natural rule of cyclical movement, thus action, seen from the viewpoint of the automatic processes which seem to determine the course of the world, looks like a miracle." Action itself—and, in particular, forgiving, which can occur only, or at least without the risk of great danger, between men—controverts the natural process of cyclical movement from which the concept of revolution was first derived.[65]

Arendt's conception of forgiveness, like that staged during the seventeenth century in *The Laws of Candy*, bypasses the connection between pardoning and sovereignty that Bodin proposed and that Hobbes, Kant, and their followers reaffirmed. Allowing for the possibility of a drama in which the participants are also the protagonists, and in which citizens do not simply serve as spectators to the scene of sovereign forgiveness, the line of Arendt's thought suggests that the moment between the beginning of revolution—or perhaps even the prospect of revolution—and its shutting down might furnish an opportunity for freedom, an opportunity that could be seized through forgiveness as well as promising. Although she herself did not pursue the political implications of forgiveness in *On Revolution*, *The Laws of Candy* indicates how such forgiveness might operate. Even more centrally, Arendt's treatment of forgiveness demonstrates that sovereignty need not be inextricably linked with pardoning and that simply conceiving of the pardon in sovereign form divests it of an important ethical component. With this insight arrives the potential to move beyond the impasse

---

64. Arendt, *On Revolution*, 52–53.
65. Arendt, *Human Condition*, 246, 238.

that pardoning faces within liberal constitutionalism along lines that early seventeenth-century dramatists may have envisioned more clearly than we can today. The imagined world of Jacobean tragicomedy may not have exhausted its political potential with audiences of the seventeenth century and can still reveal new alternatives to our own stalemate.

Kant associated pardoning with a particular kind of staging of the splendor of the king's majesty, one trumped only by the horror of the spectacle of revolutionary and counterrevolutionary violence. This theatrical version of the pardon scene as affirming the height of the sovereign above the people manifests itself in the spectacular finales of early seventeenth-century plays like Shakespeare's *Measure for Measure*, in which Duke Vincentio returns and remits both the punishments that have accrued in his absence and those he himself has just imposed. Such a staging is countered by another kind of drama, that of *The Laws of Candy*, in which forgiveness comes from a stranger or a friend and is passed among citizens to reconstitute the state.

Those setting up the foundations for liberal constitutionalism, like Kant, failed to generate a new account of pardoning that would render it an important component of either the rule of law or democracy, rather than a relic of monarchical sovereignty. Hence the pardon seems to fit more naturally into the antiliberal Schmittian account of politics than into the contemporary U.S. constitutional order. Such a result was not, however, inevitable; an alternative, non-sovereign conception of pardoning that appeared in early modern drama presented an alternative basis for the act, one that was never implemented in politics.

APPENDIX A

The plays included on this list stem from a review of all tragicomedies listed within the period from 1600 to 1660 in Alfred Harbage's *Annals of English Drama, 975–1700*, 3rd ed. (London: Routledge, 2013), supplemented by a review of some comedies and the entire published oeuvre in the Beaumont and Fletcher canon as well as the works attributed to Philip Massinger.

1. John Dymock (?), *Il Pastor Fido, or the Faithful Shepherd* (translating Giovanni Battista Guarini's *Il Pastor Fido*, first performed 1601, closet?)—published 1602
2. William Shakespeare, *Measure for Measure* (first performed 1604)—published 1623
3. John Fletcher, *The Faithful Shepherdess* (first performed 1608)—published ca. 1609
4. Thomas Heywood, *The Royal King and the Loyal Subject* (1602–1618)—published 1637
5. Francis Beaumont and John Fletcher, *Philaster* (first performed ca. 1608–1610)—published 1620
6. William Shakespeare, *Cymbeline* (first performed ca. 1611)—published 1623
7. Thomas Middleton (?), *The Nice Valour, or, the Passionate Mad-Man* (first performed ca. 1615–16)—published 1647
8. John Fletcher, *The Loyal Subject* (ca. 1616–1619)—published 1647
9. John Fletcher, *The Pilgrim* (1621)—published 1647
10. John Ford, *Laws of Candy* (ca. 1619–1623)—published 1647
11. John Fletcher and Philip Massinger, *The Prophetess* (1622)—published 1647
12. Beaumont and Fletcher canon (disputed), *The Faithful Friends* (ca. 1604–1626)—published 1812
13. Philip Massinger, *The Bondman* (1623)—published 1624
14. John Fletcher, *A Wife for a Month* (1624)—published 1647 (very conditional pardon)

15. Thomas Heywood, *The Captives, or, The Lost Recovered* (1624)—published from manuscript in 1885

16. Philip Massinger, *The Parliament of Love* (1624)—published from manuscript in 1929

17. *The Partiall Law* (c. 1615–1630)—published from manuscript in 1908

18. *Dick of Devonshire* (1626)—published from manuscript in 1905

19. Philip Massinger, *The Great Duke of Florence* (1627)—published 1636

20. John Ford, *The Queen, or the Excellency of her Sex* (ca. 1621–1633)—published 1653

21. Lodowick Carlell, *The Deserving Favourite*—published 1629

22. Richard Brome, *The Queen's Exchange* (ca. 1629–1631)

23. Philip Massinger and John Fletcher, *A Very Woman* (licensed 1634)—published 1655

24. Richard Brome, *The Queen and Concubine* (ca. 1635–1640)—published 1659

25. William Strode, *The Floating Island* (1636)—published 1655

26. William Rider, *The Twins* (1635)—published 1655 ("Lets cosen the Politian once more; if all agree with me lets pardon him, and conquer hate with love since all proves well.")

27. Henry Killigrew, *The Conspiracy* (1635)—published 1638

28. William Cartwright, *The Royal Slave* (1636)—published 1639

29. James Shirley, *The Duke's Mistress* (1636)—published 1638

30. William Cartwright, *The Lady Errant* (1628–1638)—published 1651

31. William Davenant, *The Fair Favourite* (1638)—published 1673

32. Robert Mead, *The Combat of Love and Friendship* (1638)—published 1654

33. Lewis Sharpe, *The Noble Stranger* (ca. 1638–1640)—published 1640

34. Richard Brome, *The Lovesick Court* (ca. 1632–1640)—published 1659

35. James Shirley, *The Gentleman of Venice* (1639)—published 1655

36. John Gough, *The Strange Discovery* (ca. 1624–1640)—1640

37. Richard Fanshawe, *The Faithfull Shepherd* (translation of Guarini's *Il Pastor Fido*)—published 1647

38. James Shirley, *The Court Secret* (1642, unacted)—published 1653

39. Francis Quarles, *The Virgin Widow* (ca. 1640–1642, privately acted)—1649 (very similar marriage structure at end as at end of *M for M*, but gender reversed)

40. Cosmo Manuche, *The Just General* (closet)—published 1652

41. George Gerbier D'Ouvilly, *The False Favourit Disgrac'd* (closet)—published 1657

42. William Chamberlaine, *Love's Victory* (1658, operatic show)—published 1658
43. H.B., *The Female Rebellion* (ca. 1657–1659, closet)—published 1872
44. William Davenant, *The Siege of Rhodes II* (ca. 1657–1659)—published 1663
45. Robert Howard, *The Blind Lady* (1660, closet)—published 1660
46. Cosmo Manuche, *The Banish'd Shepherdess* (1659–60)—MS
47. John Fountain, *The Rewards of Virtue* (1661, unacted)—published 1661

James Compton, "Political Treatise" [name given by Luke Beattie]

The former constitution of this realme being so well known to all, and the late changes so visible, I shall not loose so muche time as to make a vaine rehearsall of passed ages or spend so muche of my paines to no effect as to manifest my owne opinion by any descantation on what is past, I holding it for granted that those who inwardly repine must now outwardly submit, so that what on that subject can bee written will neither more confirme them in their opinions should my treatise tend that way or change them were it to another subject, neither can I thinke a fluent pen sufficient to blunt a sharpe sword so that those who approve the present condition of affairs need no confirmation, nor will not easily bee persuaded to the contrary all things then being as they are I shall only declare my judgement how most for the future all may tend to the honor and wellfare of this nation.

First I heare a rumor of a new representative, a thing the report whereof may do muche good as to the keeping still some turbulent spirits, who desire for a while to rule, and thinke it their due to govern, but I should thinke it strange if those who with so muche judgement, industry and courage have obtaind their seats at helme should after all their labor leave the possession (now it is growing to the pleasures of peace and plenty) to [others] to enjoy the chiefe fruits of their toiles and cares, and content themselves with the bare gleanings of so glorious an harvest, neither do I thinke the stormes as yet so well allaied, as it can conduce to this nations quiet to trust the rudder with less skillful pilots.

Another report is of an act of indemnitie, or of oblivion stille it what you please, the reallitie of this would worke more good then the flying fame that fills so many minds with expectation. It cannot bee exprest how many spirits it would lay past power of being conjured up again since the discreete penning might forgive past crimes which have not alltogether scaped unpunisht neither, and yet so threaten future faylors that it will make all content to sleepe in quiet and rest in peace under their own vine, their feares overcome by affection.

Some may thinke this maxim rather propounded for the Cavaliers benefit then the States safety but if with unpartiall eys it bee looked into, it will bee found muche more tending to future tranquillitie of this commonwealth then to their advantage, though both will reape muche by it, the cavalier satisfaction and the commonwealth securitie. Nothing is more fatall to a nations ruine then to bee in continuall dread of plots and conspiracies, when their owne vigilance and care in discovery, often incites their enemies to things not before dreamed on, and through them they perceive the lineaments of treachery, as one sees a well limbd picture set behind a transparent Christall, the way to free a state from these fears and jealousies, is to remove not onely all occasions but all possibilities of thriving by being their open or secret enemies, their are two things that principally stir up commotions and broils in state, the first is where no solid law is provided for the punishment of suche offenders, for their the hops of advantage may bee vast, the danger small, and if it chance that suche treasons thrive not yet if punishment bee inflicted, though not greater then the offence deserves, yet not what the law in former times held forth, it shall bee imputed for injustice, and breed ill blood. A second cause of the raising war or taking other waies to change a present forme of government, is when the rulers bind not themselves by some apparent act, from oppressing any they have promised to forgive, but that the delinquent is never sure after all composition, but still liable to all inconveniencies ["Whereas" crossed out] nay [lately] on all occasions, acts have bin made to their prejudice and [it is] in my opinion advantageous to the safety of the state, this then will prompt men to thoughts of change, libertie of person and quiet possession of ones owne being the desire of mans heart, whiche if not assured offend or offend not, will make them hold no hazard to greate to purchase the one and obtaine the other, so that a cleere and free pardon for the past, opening the gates of mercie to all by past offenders, and bolting them forever against all future delinquencies, will bee the sole means of removing all possibilitie of danger from inbred commotions[.]

BIBLIOGRAPHY

The Act of Oblivioun (Jun. 4, 1563). In *Acts of the Parliaments of Scotland*. Vol. 2, edited by Thomas Thomson and Cosmo Innes.

Acts and Ordinances of the Interregnum, 1642–1660. Ed. C. H. Firth and R. S. Rait for the Statute Law Committee. Vol. 2. Holmes Beach, FL: Wm. Gaunt, 1969.

Adams, J. Q. *The Dramatic Records of Sir Henry Herbert, Master of the Revels, 1623–1673*. New Haven: Yale University Press, 1917.

Adams, Norma. "Review." *Speculum: A Journal of Medieval Studies* 28, no. 1 (January 1953): 164–66.

Aeschylus. *The Oresteia*. Trans. David Grene and Wendy Doniger O'Flaherty. Chicago: University of Chicago Press, 1989.

Agamben, Giorgio. *Homo Sacer: Sovereign Power and Bare Life*. Trans. Daniel Heller-Roazen. Stanford: Stanford University Press, 1998.

———. *Stasis: Civil War as a Political Paradigm*. Trans. Nicholas Heron. Stanford: Stanford University Press, 2015.

———. *State of Exception*. Trans. Kevin Attell. Chicago: University of Chicago Press, 2005.

———. *Le temps qui reste: Un commentaire de l'Épître aux Romains*. Trans. Judith Revel. Paris: Bibliothèque Rivages, 2000.

Albrecht, Louis. *Neue Untersuchungen zu Shakespeares* Mass für Mass. Berlin: Weidmannsche Buchhandlung, 1914.

Ardolino, Frank. *Apocalypse and Armada in Kyd's* Spanish Tragedy. Kirksville, MO: Sixteenth Century Essays & Studies, 1995.

Arendt, Hannah. *Eichmann in Jerusalem: A Report on the Banality of Evil*. London: Penguin, 1994.

———. *The Human Condition*. 1958. Chicago: University of Chicago Press, 1998.

———. *Lectures on Kant's Political Philosophy*. Ed. Ronald Beiner. Chicago: University of Chicago Press. 1982.

———. *On Revolution*. 1963. London: Penguin, 1990.

———. *On Violence*. New York: Harcourt Brace & Co. 1969.

———. "What Is Freedom?" 1961. In *Between Past and Future*. London: Penguin Books, 1993. 143–71.

Aristophanes. "Frogs." In *Aristophanes II*. Loeb Classical Library. Cambridge: Harvard University Press, 1989. 293–437.

Aristotle. *Poetics*. Trans. S. H. Butcher. New York: Hill and Wang, 1961.

———. *The Poetics*. Trans. Stephen Halliwell. Loeb Classical Library. Cambridge: Harvard University Press, 1991.

Arnold, Oliver. *The Third Citizen: Shakespeare's Theater and the Early Modern House of Commons*. Baltimore: Johns Hopkins University Press, 2007.

Astington, John. *English Court Theatre, 1558–1642*. Cambridge: Cambridge University Press, 1999.

Augustine. *Confessions II*. Loeb Classical Library. Cambridge: Harvard University Press, 1988.

Austin, J. L. *How to Do Things with Words*. Cambridge: Harvard University Press, 1975.

Bailey, Rebecca. "Staging 'a Queene opprest': William Habington's Exploration of the Politics of Queenship on the Caroline Stage." *Theatre Journal* 65, no. 2 (May 2013): 197–214.

Baines, Barbara. "Assaying the Power of Chastity in *Measure for Measure*," *Studies in English Literature, 1500–1900*, no. 2 (1990): 283–301.

Baker, J. H. "Common Lawyers' Libraries, 1450–1650." In *Collected Papers on English Legal History*. Vol. 2. Cambridge: Cambridge University Press, 2013. 697–708.

——. *An Introduction to English Legal History*. 4th ed. London: Butterworths, 2002.

——. "The Third University of England." In *The Common Law Tradition: Lawyers, Books, and the Law*. London: Hambledon Press, 2000. 3–28.

——. "Westminster Hall, 1097–1997." In *The Common Law Tradition: Lawyers, Books, and the Law*. London: Hambledon Press, 2000. 247–62.

Barbour, Reid. *English Epicures and Stoics: Ancient Legacies in Early Stuart Culture*. Boston: University of Massachusetts Press, 1998.

Barish, Jonas. *The Antitheatrical Prejudice*. Berkeley: University of California Press, 1985.

Barton, Anne. *The Names of Comedy*. Toronto: University of Toronto Press, 1990.

Barton, Sir Dunbar Plunket. *Links between Shakespeare and the Law*. London: Faber & Gwyer, 1929.

Baumgold, Deborah. "When Hobbes Needed History." In *Hobbes and History*. London: Routledge, 2000. 25–43.

Beattie, Luke. "How Were the Anonymous Castle Ashby Play Manuscripts Created, and Why?" Ph.D. dissertation, University of Exeter, 2011.

——. "Theatrical Potential in the Cavalier Plays of James Compton, Third Earl of Northampton," *Studies in Theater and Performance* 33, no. 1 (January 2014): 96–106.

Beck, Lewis White. *A Commentary on Kant's* Critique of Practical Reason. Chicago: University of Chicago Press. 1960.

Beckett, Samuel. *Fin de partie*. Paris: Minuit, 1957.

Bellamy, Elizabeth Jane. "Plato." In *The Oxford History of Classical Reception in English Literature*. Vol. 2, 1558–1660. Ed. Patrick Cheney and Philip Hardie. Oxford: Oxford University Press, 2015. 503–15.

Benjamin, Walter. *The Origin of German Tragic Drama*. Trans. John Osborne. London: Verso, 1998.Bernard, Richard. *A Key of Knowledge for the Opening of the Secret Mysteries of St. Johns Mysticall Revelation*. London: Felix Kynaston, 1617.

Bernthal, Craig. "Staging Justice: James I and the Trial Scenes of *Measure for Measure*." *Studies in English Literature, 1500–1900*, no. 32 (1992): 247–69.

Bertman, Martin. "Hobbes' Science of Politics and Plato's *Laws*." *Independent Journal of Philosophy* 2 (1978): 47–53.

Black, Henry Campbell, and Bryan A. Garner, eds. *Black's Law Dictionary*. 7th ed. St. Paul: West, 1999.

Blackstone, William. *Commentaries on the Laws of England: A Facsimile of the First Edition of 1765–1769*. 4 vols. Chicago: University of Chicago Press, 1979.

Bland, Mark. "The Appearance of the Text in Early Modern England." *Text* 11 (1998): 91–154.

Bodin, Jean. *On Sovereignty: Four Chapters from* The Six Books of the Commonwealth. Ed. and trans. Julian H. Franklin. Cambridge: Cambridge University Press, 1992.

The Six Bookes of a Commonweale. Trans. Richard Knolles. London: G. Bishop, 1606. Reprinted in *The Six Bookes of a Commonweale.* Ed. Kenneth Douglas McRae. Harvard Political Classics. Cambridge: Harvard University Press, 1962.

——. *Les six livres de la République.* Paris: Fayard, Corpus des Oeuvres de Philosophie en Langue Française, 1986.

Botero, Giovanni. *The Reason of State.* Trans. P. J. Waley and D. P. Waley. London: Routledge, 1956.

Bowen, Catherine Drinker. *The Lion and the Throne: The Life and Times of Sir Edward Coke, 1552–1634.* Boston: Little Brown & Co., 1990.

Boyer, Allen D. *Sir Edward Coke and the Elizabethan Age.* Stanford: Stanford University Press, 2003.

Boyes, J. F. *Illustrations of the Tragedies of Aeschylus from the Greek, Latin, and English Poets.* Oxford: J. Vincent, 1842.

Braden, Gordon. *Renaissance Tragedy and the Senecan Tradition: Anger's Privilege.* New Haven: Yale University Press, 1985.

Brightman, Thomas. *A Revelation of the Apocalyps.* Amsterdam: Iudocus Hondius & Hendrick Laurenss, 1611.

Brooks, Christopher. *Law, Politics, and Society in Early Modern England.* Cambridge: Cambridge University Press, 2008.

Burgess, Glenn. *The Politics of the Ancient Constitution: An Introduction to English Political Thought, 1603–1642.* University Park: Penn State University Press, 1992.

Burnett, Anne Pippin. *Revenge in Attic and Later Tragedy.* Berkeley: University of California Press, 1998.

Bushnell, Rebecca. *Tragedies of Tyrants: Political Thought and Theater in the English Renaissance.* Ithaca: Cornell University Press, 1990.

Calendar of State Papers, Domestic Series, of the Reign of James I: 1619–1623. Ed. Mary Anne Everett Green. London: Longman, Brown, 1858.

Calvin, John. *Calvin's Commentary on Seneca's* De Clementia. Ed. Ford Lewis Battles and André Malan Hugo. Leiden: E. J. Brill, 1969.

Campbell, John. *The Lives of the Chief Justices of England.* Vol. 1. Jersey City: Fred Linn & Co., 1881.

Capp, Bernard. "The Political Dimension of Apocalyptic Thought." In *The Apocalypse in English Renaissance Thought and Literature: Patterns, Antecedents and Repercussions.* Ed. C. A. Patrides and Joseph Wittreich. Manchester: Manchester University Press, 1984. 93–124.

Cartwright, William. *The Lady-Errant: A Tragi-Comedy.* In *The Plays and Poems of William Cartwright.* Ed. G. Blakemore Evans. Madison: University of Wisconsin Press, 1951. 81–162.

Cascardi, Anthony. *Consequences of Enlightenment.* Literature, Culture, Theory Series. Cambridge: Cambridge University Press, 1999.

A Catalogue of the Library of Sir Edward Coke. Ed. W. O. Hassall. Yale Law Library Publications. New Haven: Yale University Press, 1950.

The Cavaliers Jubilee: or, Long Look'd for Come at Last: viz. the Generall Pardon. London: William Ley, 1652.

Cavell, Stanley. *The Claim of Reason: Wittgenstein, Skepticism, Morality, and Tragedy.* New York: Oxford University Press, 1982.

——. *Disowning Knowledge in Six Plays of Shakespeare.* Cambridge: Cambridge University Press, 1987.

Cawdrey, Robert. *The First English Dictionary, 1604: Robert Cawdrey's* A Table Alphabeti-call. Ed. John Simpson. Oxford: Bodleian Library, 2007.

Charles II. *Declaration to All His Loving Subjects of the Kingdome of England and Domin-ion of Wales.* London: John Field, 1651.

——. *His Majesties Gracious Speech to the House of Peers, the 27th of July, 1660 concern-ing the Speedy Passing of the Bill of Indempnity & Oblivion.* London: Christopher Barker and John Bill, 1660.

Cheneval, Francis. *The Government of the Peoples on the Idea and Principles of Multilat-eral Democracy.* New York: Palgrave Macmillan, 2011.

Christianson, Paul K. *Reformers and Babylon: English Apocalyptic Visions from the Refor-mation to the Eve of the Civil War.* Toronto: University of Toronto Press, 1978.

Die Chronik des Otto von St. Blasien. Ed. Horst Kohl. Leipzig: Franz Dunder, 1881.

Cicero, Marcus Tullius. "De Inventione." In *Cicero: On Invention, Best Kind of Orator, Topics.* Trans. H. M. Hubbell. Loeb Classical Library. Cambridge: Harvard Univer-sity Press, 1949. 1–348.

Cinthio, Giraldi. *On the Composition of Comedies and Tragedies.* In *Sources of Dramatic Theory I: Plato to Congreve.* Cambridge: Cambridge University Press, 1991. 123–28.

Cogswell, Thomas. *The Blessed Revolution: English Politics and the Coming of War, 1621–4.* Cambridge: Cambridge University Press, 1989.

Cojjeius, Henricus. *Disputatio Juris Gentium, de Postliminio in Pace, et Amnestia.* Frank-furt: Christopher Zeitler, 1691.

Coke, Sir Edward. *Institutes.* In vol. 2 of *The Selected Writings and Speeches of Sir Edward Coke.* 3 vols. Ed. Steve Sheppard. Indianapolis: Liberty Fund, 2003. 571–1184.

——. *Reports.* In vol. 1 of *The Selected Writings and Speeches of Sir Edward Coke.* 3 vols. Ed. Steve Sheppard. Indianapolis: Liberty Fund, 2003.

Commons Debates, 1621. Ed. Wallace Notestein, Frances Helen Relf, and Hartley Simp-son. 7 vols. New Haven: Yale University Press, 1935.

Compton, James, Earl of Northampton. "Political Treatise." MS. British Library, MS ADD 60282.

"The Convention Parliament, 1st sess., April 25, 1660." In *The History and Proceedings of the House of Commons.* Vol. 1. *1660–1680.* London, 1742. 2–25.

Coquillette, Daniel R. *The Civilian Writers of Doctors' Commons, London: Three Centuries of Juristic Innovation in Comparative, Commercial, and International Law.* Berlin: Duncker and Humblot, 1988.

Cormack, Bradin. *A Power to Do Justice: Jurisdiction, English Literature, and the Rise of the Common Law.* Chicago: University of Chicago Press, 2007.

Cover, Robert. "The Supreme Court, 1982 Term: Foreword: *Nomos* and Narrative." *Har-vard Law Review* 97, no. 1 (1982): 4–68.

Cowell, John. *A Law Dictionary: or the Interpreter of Words and Terms.* London: D. Browne, 1708.

——. *The Institutes of the Lawes of England.* London: Thomas Roycroft, 1651.

Cromartie, Alan. *The Constitutionalist Revolution: An Essay on the History of England, 1450–1642.* Cambridge: Cambridge University Press, 2006.

——. "*Epieikeia* and Conscience." In *The Oxford Handbook of English Law and Literature, 1500–1700.* Ed. Lorna Hutson. Oxford: Oxford University Press, 2017. 320–36.

Cromwell, Oliver. "An Act of General Pardon and Oblivion." London: John Field, 1651.

Cunningham, Karen. "Opening Doubts upon the Law: *Measure for Measure.*" *A Com-panion to Shakespeare's Works.* Vol. 4. Ed. Richard Dutton and Jean E. Howard. Oxford: Blackwell, 2003. 316–32.

Dauncey, John (?). *The History of His Sacred Majesty Charles II*. London: James Davies, 1660.

DeChalus, Camila. "In Virginia, Ex-Felons Find Empowerment in the Voting Booth." www.cnn.com/2016/11/05/politics/virginia-felons-voting-rights. November 5, 2016.

De Libellis Famosis. 77 Eng. Rep. 250 (K.B. 1605).

de Man, Paul. *Aesthetic Ideology*. Ed. Andrzej Warminski. Theory and History of Literature Series. Minneapolis: University of Minnesota Press, 1996.

Derrida, Jacques. "Before the Law." In *Acts of Literature*. Ed. Derek Attridge. London: Routledge, 1992. 181–220.

——. "The Century and the Pardon." *Le monde des débats* 9 (December 1999). Trans. Greg Macon (2001). http://fixion.sytes.net/pardonEng.htm.

——. *Of Hospitality: Anne Dufourmantelle Invites Jacques Derrida to Respond*. Stanford: Stanford University Press, 2000.

——. *On Forgiveness*. In *On Cosmopolitanism and Forgiveness*. Trans. Mark Dooley and Michael Hughes. London: Routledge, 2001. 27–61.

——. *The Politics of Friendship*. Trans. George Collins. Verso, 1997.

——. "To Forgive: The Unforgivable and the Imprescriptible." In *Love and Forgiveness for a More Just World*. Ed. Hent de Vries and Nils F. Schott. New York: Columbia University Press, 2015. 144–81.

Dewar-Watson, Sarah. "Aristotle and Tragicomedy." In *Early Modern Tragicomedy*. Ed. Subha Mukherji and Raphael Lyne. Cambridge: Cambridge University Press, 2007. 15–27.

Dick of Devonshire. Oxford: Malone Society, 1955.

Diehl, Huston. "'Infinite Space': Representation and Reformation in *Measure for Measure*." *Shakespeare Quarterly* 49, no. 4 (1998): 393–410.

Dollimore, Jonathan. "Surveillance and Transgression in *Measure for Measure*." In *Political Shakespeare: New Essays in Cultural Materialism*. Ed. Jonathan Dollimore and Alan Sinfield. Ithaca: Cornell University Press, 1985. 72–87.

Dorris, Jonathan. *Pardon and Amnesty under Lincoln and Johnson*. Chapel Hill: University of North Carolina Press, 1953.

Dryden, John. "Essay of Dramatic Poesy." In *Sources of Dramatic Theory I: Plato to Congreve*. Ed. Michael J. Sidnell. Cambridge: Cambridge University Press, 2008. 269–90.

Duxbury, Neil. *The Nature and Authority of Precedent*. Cambridge: Cambridge University Press, 2008.

Dworkin, Ronald. *Law's Empire*. Cambridge: Harvard University Press, 1988.

Dymock, John (?). *Il Pastor Fido, or the Faithfull Shepherd*. Translation of Giovanni Battista Guarini's *Il Pastor Fido*. London: Thomas Creede, 1602.

Dyzenhaus, David. "*Leviathan* as a Theory of Transitional Justice." In *NOMOS LI: Transitional Justice*. Ed. Melissa S. Williams, Rosemary Nagy, and Jon Elster. New York: NYU Press, 2012. 180–217.

Eden, Kathy. *Poetic and Legal Fiction in the Aristotelian Tradition*. Princeton: Princeton University Press, 1986.

Edwards, Philip. "The Sources of Massinger's *The Bondman*." *Review of English Studies* 15, no. 57 (1964): 21–26.

Elster, Jon. *Closing the Books: Transitional Justice in Historical Perspective*. Cambridge: Cambridge University Press, 2004.

——. "Coming to Terms with the Past: A Framework for the Study of Justice in the Transition to Democracy." *European Journal of Sociology* 29, no. 1 (May 1998): 7–48.

Euripides. *Fragments*. Vol. 2. Trans. and ed. Christopher Collard and Martin Cropp. Cambridge: Harvard University Press, 2011.

Evrigenis, Ioannis. *Images of Anarchy: The Rhetoric and Science in Hobbes's State of Nature*. Cambridge: Cambridge University Press, 2016.

Ewbank, Inga-Stina. "'Striking too short at Greeks': The Transmission of *Agamemnon* to the English Renaissance Stage." In *Agamemnon in Performance, 458 BC to AD 2004*. Ed. Fiona Macintosh, Pantelis Michelakis, Edith Hall, and Oliver Taplin. Oxford: Oxford University Press, 2005. 37–52.

Fanshawe, Richard. *The Faithfull Shepherd*. Translation of Giovanni Battista Guarini's *Il Pastor Fido*. London: R. Raworth, 1647.

Felman, Shoshana. "Theaters of Justice: Arendt in Jerusalem, the Eichmann Trial, and the Redefinition of Legal Meaning in the Wake of the Holocaust." *Critical Inquiry* 27, no. 2 (Winter 2001): 201–38.

The Female Rebellion: A Tragicomedy. Glasgow: W. Anderson Eadie, 1872.

Fenves, Peter. *A Peculiar Fate: Metaphysics and World-History in Kant*. Ithaca: Cornell University Press, 1991.

Figgis, John Neville. *The Divine Right of Kings*. New York: Harper & Row, 1965.

Filmer, Robert. "Observations upon Aristotle's Politiques." In *Patriarcha and Other Writings*. Ed. Johann P. Sommerville. Cambridge Texts in the History of Political Thought. Cambridge: Cambridge University Press, 1991. 235–86.

——. *Patriarcha*. In *Patriarcha and Other Writings*. Ed. Johann P. Sommerville. Cambridge Texts in the History of Political Thought. Cambridge: Cambridge University Press, 1991. 1–68.

Finch, Henry. *Nomotexnia; cestascavoir, un description del Common Leys dangleterre solonque les rules del Art*. London, 1613.

Finkelpearl, Philip J. *John Marston of the Middle Temple: An Elizabethan Dramatist in His Social Setting*. Cambridge: Harvard University Press, 1969.

Fisch, Jörg. *Krieg und Frieden im Friedensvertrag*. Stuttgart: Klett-Cotta, 1979.

Fletcher, John. *The Pilgrim*. In *Dramatic Works in the Beaumont and Fletcher Canon*. Vol. 6. Ed. Fredson Bowers. Cambridge: Cambridge University Press, 2008. 111–224.

Fletcher, John, et al. *The Fair Maid of the Inn*. In *Dramatic Works in the Beaumont and Fletcher Canon*. Vol. 10. Ed. Fredson Bowers. Cambridge: Cambridge University Press, 2008. 553–658.

Fletcher, John, with Nathan Field and Philip Massinger (?). *The Knight of Malta*. In *Dramatic Works in the Beaumont and Fletcher Canon*. Vol. 8. Cambridge: Cambridge University Press, 2008. 345–482.

Ford, John. *The Collected Works of John Ford*. Vol. 1. Ed. Gilles Monsarrat, Brian Vickers, and R. J. C. Watt. Oxford: Oxford University Press, 2012.

——. *The Collected Works of John Ford*. Vol. 2. Ed. Brian Vickers. Oxford: Oxford University Press, 2017.

Ford, John (with Philip Massinger?). *The Laws of Candy*. In *The Collected Works of John Ford*. Vol. 3. Ed. Brian Vickers. Oxford: Oxford University Press, 2017. 1–132.

Forman, Valerie. *Tragicomic Redemptions: Global Economics and the Early Modern English Stage*. Philadelphia: University of Pennsylvania Press, 2008.

Fortier, Mark. "Equity and Ideas: Coke, Ellesmere, and James I." *Renaissance Quarterly* 51, no. 4 (1998): 1255–81.

Foucault, Michel. *Discipline and Punish*. Trans. Alan Sheridan. 2nd ed. New York: Vintage, 1995.

———. *Society Must Be Defended*. Trans. David Macey. New York: Picador, 2003.

Fraser, Antonia. *Faith and Treason: The Story of the Gunpowder Plot*. New York: Doubleday Anchor Books, 1997.

Friedrich, Carl J. *Constitutional Reason of State: The Survival of the Constitutional Order*. Providence: Brown University Press, 1957.

Frisch, Andrea. *Forgetting Differences: Tragedy, Historiography, and the French Wars of Religion*. Edinburgh Critical Studies in Renaissance Culture. Edinburgh: Edinburgh University Press, 2015.

Fulbeck, William. *A Parallele or Conference of the Civil Law, the Canon Law, and the Common Law of this Realme of England*. London: Adam Islip, 1601.

———. *The Second Part of the Parallele, or Conference of the Civill Law, the Canon Law, and the Common Law of this Realme of England*. London: Adam Islip, 1602.

Fulton, Thomas C. "'The True and Naturall Constitution of that Mixed Government': Massinger's *The Bondman* and the Influence of Dutch Republicanism." *Studies in Philology* 99 (2002): 152–77.

Gadamer, Hans-Georg. "Poetry and Mimesis." In *The Relevance of the Beautiful and Other Essays*. Ed. Robert Bernasconi. Trans. Nicholas Walker. Cambridge: Cambridge University Press, 1987. 115–22.

———. "The Relevance of the Beautiful." In *The Relevance of the Beautiful and Other Essays*. Ed. Robert Bernasconi. Trans. Nicholas Walker. Cambridge: Cambridge University Press, 1987. 1–53.

Ganev, Venelin I. "Emergency Powers and the New East European Constitutions." *American Journal of Comparative Law* 45 (Summer 1997): 585–612.

Gardiner, Samuel R. "The Political Element in Massinger." *Contemporary Review* 28 (1876): 495–507.

———, ed. *Lords' Debates in 1621*. London: Camden Society, 1870.

Garrett, Martin, ed. *Massinger: The Critical Heritage*. London: Routledge, 1991.

Gaunt, Peter, ed. *The English Civil War: The Essential Readings*. Oxford: Blackwell, 2000.

Gauthier, David. "Hobbes: The Laws of Nature." *Pacific Philosophical Quarterly* 82 (February 2003): 258–84.

Gewirtz, Paul. "Aeschylus' Law." *Harvard Law Review* 101, no. 5 (March 1988): 1043–55.

Gibbons, Brian. *Jacobean City Comedy*. London: Routledge, 2017.

Goldhill, Simon. *Aeschylus: The Oresteia*. 2nd ed. Cambridge: Cambridge University Press. 2004.

———. *Reading Greek Tragedy*. Cambridge: Cambridge University Press, 1986.

Goldsmith, M. M. "Hobbes on Law." In *The Cambridge Companion to Hobbes*. Ed. Tom Sorell. Cambridge: Cambridge University Press, 1996. 274–304.

Goodwin, Thomas. *The Great Interest of States and Kingdoms*. London: R. Dawlman, 1646.

Green, Adwin Wigfall. *The Inns of Court and Early English Drama*. 1931. New Haven: Yale University Press, 1965.

Green, Thomas Andrew. *Verdict According to Conscience: Perspectives on the English Criminal Trial Jury, 1200–1800*. Chicago: University of Chicago Press, 1985.

Gross, Allen. "Contemporary Politics in Massinger." *Studies in English Literature* 6, no. 2 (1966): 279–90.

Guarini, Giambattista. "Compendio della poesia tragicomica." In *Sources of Dramatic Theory I: Plato to Congreve*. Ed. Michael J. Sidnell. Cambridge: Cambridge University Press, 1991. 149–59.

Gulley, Ervene. "'Dressed in a little Brief Authority': Law as Theater in *Measure for Measure*." In *Law and Literature Perspectives*. Ed. Bruce L. Rockwood. New York: Peter Lang, 1996. 53–80.

Gurr, Andrew. *The Shakespearean Stage, 1574–1642*. 3rd ed. Cambridge: Cambridge University Press, 1992.

Habington, William. *The Queene of Arragon, A Tragi-Comedie*. In *A Select Collection of Old English Plays*. 4th ed. Ed. W. Carew Hazlitt. Vol. 13. London: Reeves & Turner, 1875. 322–409.

Hake, Edward. *Epieikeia: A Dialogue on Equity in Three Parts*. 1597. Ed. D. E. C. Yale. New Haven: Yale University Press, 1953.

Hale, John. "Watchmen on the Ramparts: *Hamlet*'s Opening Image." *Hamlet Studies* 17 (1995): 98–101.

Hall, Jerome. *The General Principles of Criminal Law*. 2nd ed. Indianapolis: Bobbs-Merrill Company, 2005.

——. "Nulla Poena sine Lege." *Yale Law Journal* 47, no. 2 (December 1937): 165–93.

Halley, Janet E. "Equivocation and the Legal Conflict over Religious Identity in Early Modern England." *Yale Journal of Law and the Humanities* 3 (1991): 33–52.

Halper, Louise. "*Measure for Measure*: Law, Prerogative, Subversion." *Cardozo Studies in Law and Literature* 13, no. 2 (Fall 2001): 221–64.

Hamilton, Alexander. *Federalist* no. 74. 1788. In *The Federalist Papers*. New York: Tribeca Books, 2009, 215–16.

Hanssen, Beatrice. *Critique of Violence: Between Poststructuralism and Critical Theory*. London: Routledge, 2000.

Harbage, Alfred. *Annals of English Drama, 975–1700*. 3rd ed. London: Routledge, 1989.

Hart, James S. *Justice upon Petition: The House of Lords and the Reformation of Justice, 1621–1675*. London: Routledge, 1992.

Hart, Kevin. "Guilty Forgiveness." In *Vladimir Jankélévitch and the Question of Forgiveness*. Ed. Alan Udoff. New York: Lexington, 2013. 49–66.

Hassall, W. O., ed. *A Catalogue of the Library of Sir Edward Coke*. New Haven: Yale University Press, 1950.

Hayne, Victoria. "Performing Social Practice: The Example of *Measure for Measure*." *Shakespeare Quarterly* 44 (1993): 1–29.

Hegel, G. W. F. *Elements of the Philosophy of Right*. Ed. Allen W. Wood. Trans. H. B. Nisbet. Cambridge Texts in the History of Political Thought. Cambridge: Cambridge University Press, 1991.

——. *Frühe Schriften (Werke 1)*. Frankfurt am Main: Suhrkamp, 1971.

——. *Grundlinien der Philosophie des Rechts*. Vol. 7 of *Werke*. Frankfurt am Main: Suhrkamp, 1971.

——. *Phänomenologie des Geistes*. Stuttgart: Philipp Reclam 1987.

——. *The Phenomenology of Spirit*. Trans. A. V. Miller. Oxford: Oxford University Press, 1977.

——. "The Spirit of Christianity." In *Early Theological Writings*. Trans. T. M. Knox. Chicago: University of Chicago Press, 1975.

Herrup, Cynthia. *The Common Peace: Participation and the Criminal Law in Seventeenth-Century England*. Cambridge Studies in Early Modern British History. Cambridge: Cambridge University Press, 1989.

——. "The King's Two Genders." *Journal of British Studies* 45, no. 3 (July 2006): 493–510.

——. "Negotiating Grace." In *Politics, Religion and Popularity in Early Stuart Britain: Essays in Honor of Conrad Russell.* Ed. Thomas Cogswell, Richard Cust, and Peter Lake. Cambridge: Cambridge University Press, 2002. 124–42.

——. "The Punishing Pardon: Some Thoughts on Penal Transportation." In *Penal Practice and Culture: Punishing the English, 1500–1700.* Ed. Paul Griffiths and Simon Devereux. New York: Palgrave Macmillan, 2004. 121–38.

Heywood, Thomas. *The Captives.* London: Malone Society, 1953.

Hobbes, Thomas. *Behemoth; or, the Long Parliament.* 1682. Ed. Ferdinand Tönnies. Chicago: University of Chicago Press, 1990.

——. *De Cive: The English Version.* 1647. Ed. Howard Warrender. Oxford: Clarendon Press, 1983.

——. *A Dialogue between a Philosopher and a Student of the Common Lawes of England.* 1681. Ed. Joseph Cropsey. Chicago: University of Chicago Press, 1971.

——. *Leviathan.* 1651. Ed. Richard Tuck. Cambridge: Cambridge University Press, 1991.

——. *Thomas Hobbes, Man and Citizen (De Homine & De Cive).* 1647. Ed. Bernard Gert. Indianapolis: Hackett, 1991.

Hoekstra, Kinch. "The *De Facto* Turn in Hobbes's Political Philosophy." In *Leviathan after 350 Years.* Ed. Tom Sorell and Luc Foisneau. Oxford: Oxford University Press, 2004. 33–73.

——. "Hobbes and the Fool." *Political Theory* 25, no. 5 (October 1997): 620–54.

——. "A Lion in the House: Hobbes and Democracy." In *Rethinking the Foundations of Modern Political Thought.* Ed. Annabel Brett and James Tully. Cambridge: Cambridge University Press, 2006. 191–218.

Holmes, Oliver Wendell. *The Common Law.* New York: Dover Publications, 1991.

Holmes, Stephen. "Political Psychology in Hobbes' *Behemoth*." In *Thomas Hobbes and Political Theory.* Ed. Mary G. Dietz. Lawrence: University Press of Kansas, 1990. 120–52.

Honig, Bonnie. *Democracy and the Foreigner.* Princeton: Princeton University Press, 2001.

Horkheimer, Max, and Theodor Adorno. *Dialectic of Enlightenment.* Trans. John Cumming. New York: Continuum, 1998.

Howell, T. B. *State Trials.* London: T. C. Hansard, 1816.

Hurnard, Naomi. *The King's Pardon for Homicide before A.D. 1307.* Oxford: Clarendon Press, 1969.

Hutson, Lorna. *The Invention of Suspicion: Law and Mimesis in Shakespeare and Renaissance Drama.* Oxford: Oxford University Press, 2008.

——. "Proof and Probability: Law, Imagination, and the Form of Things Unknown." In *New Directions in Law and Literature.* Ed. Elizabeth Anker and Bernadette Meyler. Oxford: Oxford University Press, 2017. 144–59.

——, ed. *Oxford Handbook of English Law and Literature, 1500–1700.* Oxford: Oxford University Press, 2017.

Hutson, Lorna, and Victoria Kahn, eds. *Rhetoric and Law in Early Modern Europe.* New Haven: Yale University Press, 2001.

Jain, Pranav. "John Sadler (1615–1674): Religion, Common Law, and Reason in Early Modern England." *Columbia University Journal of Politics and Society* 26, no. 2 (Spring 2016). www.helvidius.org.

James VI and I. *Basilicon Doron.* In *Political Writings.* Ed. Johann P. Sommerville. Cambridge Texts in the History of Political Thought. Cambridge: Cambridge University Press, 1994. 1–61.

——. *Fruitfull Meditation*. In *Workes*. London: Robert Barker, 1616. 81–88.

——. *Paraphrase on Revelation*. In *Workes*. London: Robert Barker, 1616. 1–80.

——. *Premonition*. In *Workes*. London: Robert Barker, 1616. 287–338.

——. Speech to Parliament of 9 November 1605. In *Political Writings*. Ed. Johann P. Sommerville. Cambridge Texts in the History of Political Thought. Cambridge: Cambridge University Press, 1994. 147–58.

——. Speech to Parliament of 21 March 1609. In *Political Writings*. Ed. Johann P. Sommerville. Cambridge Texts in the History of Political Thought. Cambridge: Cambridge University Press, 1994. 179–203.

——. *The Trew Law of Free Monarchies*. In *Political Writings*. Ed. Johann P. Sommerville. Cambridge Texts in the History of Political Thought. Cambridge: Cambridge University Press, 1994. 62–84.

——. *Triplici Nodo*. In *Political Writings*. Ed. Johann P. Sommerville. Cambridge Texts in the History of Political Thought. Cambridge: Cambridge University Press, 1994. 85–131.

——. *Workes*. London: Robert Barker, 1616.

James, Bishop of Winton. "Preface to the Reader." In *Workes*. London: Robert Barker, 1616.

Jankélévitch, Vladimir. *L'imprescriptible*. Paris: Éditions du Seuil, 1986.

——. *Le pardon*. Paris: Montaigne, 1967.

Jardine, David, ed. *Criminal Trials*. Vol. 2. *The Gunpowder Plot*. London: Charles Knight, 1835.

Jayne, Sears. *Plato in Renaissance England*. Dordrecht: Kluwer Academic Publishers, 1995.

Jonson, Ben. *The Alchemist*. In *The Selected Plays of Ben Jonson*. Vol. 2. Ed. Martin Butler. Cambridge: Cambridge University Press, 1989. 3–146.

——. *Bartholomew Fair*. In *The Selected Plays of Ben Jonson*. Vol. 2. Ed. Martin Butler. Cambridge: Cambridge University Press, 1989. 147–298.

——. *Ben Jonson*. Ed. C. H. Herford and Percy Simpson. 11 vols. Oxford: Clarendon Press, 1954–1963.

——. *Discoveries: A Critical Edition*. Ed. Maurice Castelain. Paris: Librairie Hachette, 1906.

Journal of the House of Commons. Vol. 7. 1651–1660. 1802. 336. [October 19, 1653.]

Journal of the House of Lords. Vol. 3. 1620–1628. 1767–1830. 210–13. [Proceedings of February 21, 1624.]

Kahn, Victoria. "Hamlet or Hecuba: Carl Schmitt's Decision." *Representations* 83, no. 1 (Summer 2003): 67–96.

——. "The Passions and the Interests in Early Modern Europe: The Case of Guarini's *Il Pastor Fido*." In *Reading the Early Modern Passions: Essays in the Cultural History of Emotion*. Ed. Gail Kern Paster, Katherine Rowe, and Mary Floyd-Wilson. Philadelphia: University of Pennsylvania Press, 2004. 217–39.

——. *Wayward Contracts: The Crisis of Political Obligation in England, 1640–1674*. Princeton: Princeton University Press, 2004.

Kant, Immanuel. *The Conflict of the Faculties*. Trans. Mary J. Gregor and Robert E. Anchor. New York: Abaris, 1979.

——. *Critique of Judgment*. Trans. J. H. Bernard. New York: Hafner, 1951.

——. *Critique of Practical Reason*. Trans. Lewis White Beck. New York: Macmillan, 1993.

——. *Lectures on Ethics*. Trans. Louis Infield. Indianapolis: Hackett, 1979.

———. *The Metaphysics of Morals*. Trans. Mary Gregor. Cambridge Texts in the History of Political Thought. Cambridge: Cambridge University Press, 1996.

———. *Observations on the Feeling of the Beautiful and Sublime*. Trans. John T. Goldthwait. Berkeley: University of California Press, 1960.

———. *Werkausgabe*. Ed. Wilhelm Weischedel. Frankfurt. am Main: Suhrkamp, 1977.

Kantorowicz, Ernst. *The King's Two Bodies: A Study in Medieval Political Theology*. Princeton: Princeton University Press, 1997.

Kaplan, M. Lindsay. *The Culture of Slander in Early Modern England*. Cambridge: Cambridge University Press, 1997.

Kendall, Gillian Murray, ed. *Shakespearean Power and Punishment*. London: Associated University Presses, 1998.

Kernan, Alvin. *Shakespeare, the King's Playwright: Theater in the Stuart Court, 1603–1613*. New Haven: Yale University Press, 1995.

Kerrigan, John. *Revenge Tragedy: Aeschylus to Armageddon*. Oxford: Clarendon Press, 1996.

Kesselring, Krista. *Mercy and Authority in the Tudor State*. Cambridge Studies in Early Modern British History. Cambridge: Cambridge University Press, 2003.

Killigrew, Thomas. *Claracilla: A Tragae-Comedy*. London: Thomas Cotes, 1641.

The King James Study Bible. Ed. C. J. Scofield. Uhrichsville, Ohio: Barbour Publishing. 1999.

Kleinberg, Ethan. "To Atone and to Forgive." In *Vladimir Jankélévitch and the Question of Forgiveness*. Ed. Alan Udoff. New York: Lexington, 2013. 143–58.

Klimchuk, Dennis. "Hobbes on Equity." In *Hobbes and the Law*. Ed. David Dyzenhaus and Thomas Poole. Cambridge: Cambridge University Press, 2012. 165–85.

Kottman, Paul A. *A Politics of the Scene*. Stanford: Stanford University Press, 2008.

Lagomarsino, David, and Charles T. Wood. *The Trial of Charles I: A Documentary History*. Hanover: Dartmouth College Press, 1989.

Lamb, Mary Ellen. "Shakespeare's 'Theatrics': Ambivalence toward Theater in *Measure for Measure*." *Shakespeare Studies* 20 (1987): 129–46.

Lambarde, William. *Archeion, or, a Discourse upon the High Courts of Justice in England*. 1635. Ed. Charles H. McIlwain and Paul Ward. Cambridge: Harvard University Press, 1957.

Langbein, John. *The Origins of Adversary Criminal Trial*. Oxford Studies in Modern Legal History. Oxford: Oxford University Press, 2001.

Langbein, John, Renee Lettow Lerner, and Bruce P. Smith. *The History of the Common Law: The Development of Anglo-American Legal Institutions*. New York: Aspen Press, 2009.

Lee, Daniel. *Popular Sovereignty in Early Modern Constitutional Thought*. Oxford: Oxford University Press, 2016.

Lesaffer, Randall. "From Lodi to Westphalia." In *Peace Treaties and International Law in European History from the Late Middle Ages to World War One*. Cambridge: Cambridge University Press, 2004.

Levine, Caroline. *Forms: Whole, Rhythm, Hierarchy, Network*. Princeton: Princeton University Press, 2015.

Levinson, Marjorie. "What Is New Formalism?" *PMLA* 122, no. 2 (March 2007): 558–69.

Lieberman, David. *The Province of Legislation Determined: Legal Theory in Eighteenth-Century Britain*. Cambridge: Cambridge University Press, 1989.

Lewalski, Barbara K. "Biblical Allusion and Allegory in *The Merchant of Venice*." *Shakespeare Quarterly* 13, no. 3 (1962): 327–43.

Limon, Jerzy. *Dangerous Matter: English Drama and Politics, 1623/24.* Cambridge: Cambridge University Press, 1986.

Lindseth, Peter. "The Paradox of Parliamentary Supremacy: Delegation, Democracy, and Dictatorship in Germany and France, 1920s–1950s." *Yale Law Journal* 113 (May 2004): 1341–1415.

Little, Arthur L., Jr. "Absolute Bodies, Absolute Laws: Staging Punishment in *Measure for Measure.*" *Shakespearean Power and Punishment.* Ed. Gillian Murray Kendall. London: Associated University Presses, 1998. 113–29.

Lloyd, Lodowick. *A Briefe Conference of Divers Lawes: Divided into certaine Regiments.* London: T. Creede, 1602.

Lobban, Michael. "Thomas Hobbes and the Common Law." In *Hobbes and the Law.* Ed. David Dyzenhaus and Thomas Poole. Cambridge: Cambridge University Press, 2012. 39–67.

Lord, Louis. *Aristophanes: His Plays and His Influence.* London: George G. Harrap & Co., 1925.

Lorenz, Philip. *The Tears of Sovereignty: Perspectives of Power in Renaissance Drama.* New York: Fordham University Press, 2013.

Love, Margaret Colgate. "The Twilight of the Pardon Power." *Journal of Criminal Law and Criminology* 100 (Summer 2010). 1169–212.

Lovell, Colin Rhys. "The 'Reception' of Defamation by the Common Law." *Vanderbilt Law Review* 15 (1962): 1051–72.

Lupton, Julia Reinhard. *Citizen-Saints: Shakespeare and Political Theology.* Chicago: University of Chicago Press, 2005.

Lyotard, Jean-François. *The Differend: Phrases in Dispute.* Trans. Georges Van Den Abbeele. Theory and History of Literature Series 46. Minneapolis: University of Minnesota Press, 1988.

———. *Lessons on the Analytic of the Sublime (Kant's "Critique of Judgment," §§23–29).* Trans. Elizabeth Rottenberg. Stanford: Stanford University Press, 1994.

MacKay, Maxine. "*The Merchant of Venice*: A Reflection of the Early Conflict between Courts of Law and Courts of Equity." *Shakespeare Quarterly* 15, no. 4 (1964): 371–75.

Maguire, Nancy Klein. *Regicide and Restoration: English Tragicomedy, 1660–1671.* Cambridge: Cambridge University Press, 1991.

Majeske, Andrew. "Equity's Absence: The Extremity of Claudio's Prosecution and Barnardine's Pardon in Shakespeare's *Measure for Measure.*" *Law and Literature* 21, no. 2 (2009): 169–84.

Manuche, Cosmo. *The Banish'd Shepherdess.* In Patrick Kennedy Canavan. "A Study of English Drama." Ph.D. dissertation, University of Southern California, 1950. Also available in MS at British Library, Add. MS 60273; Huntington Library, MS EL 8395.

———. *The Just General: A Tragi-Comedy.* London: G. Bedell, 1652.

Mansfield, Harvey. *Taming the Prince: The Ambivalence of Modern Executive Power.* Baltimore: Johns Hopkins University Press, 1993.

The Marques of Argyll His Defenses against the Grand Indytement of High Treason Exhibited against Him to the Parliament in Scotland. London, 1661.

Marsh, A. H. *History of the Court of Chancery and of the Rise and Development of the Doctrines of Equity.* Toronto: Carswell, 1890.

Massinger, Philip. *The Bondman: An Antient Storie.* Ed. Benjamin Townley Spencer. Princeton: Princeton University Press, 1932.

Mathie, William. "Justice and Equity: An Inquiry into the Meaning and Role of Equity in the Hobbesian Account of Justice and Politics." In *Hobbes's "Science of Natural Justice."* Ed. C. Walton and P. J. Johnson. Dordrecht: Martinus Nijhoff, 1987. 257–76.

May, Larry. "Hobbes on Equity and Justice." In *Hobbes's "Science of Natural Justice."* Ed. C. Walton and P. J. Johnson. Dordrecht: Martinus Nijhoff, 1987. 241–52.

McGowen, Randall. "The Bloody Code?" In *Law, Crime and English Society, 1660–1830.* Ed. Norma Landau. New York: Cambridge University Press, 2003. 117–38.

McManaway, James G. "Philip Massinger and the Restoration Drama." *ELH* 1, no. 3 (December 1934): 276–304.

McQueen, Alison, *Political Realism in Apocalyptic Times.* Cambridge: Cambridge University Press, 2018.

Menke, Christoph. *Reflections of Equality.* Trans. Howard Rouse and Andrei Denejkine. Stanford: Stanford University Press, 2006.

Merritt, J. F. *The Social World of Early Modern Westminster: Abbey, Court and Community, 1525–1640.* Manchester: Manchester University Press, 2005.

Meyler, Bernadette. "Law, Literature, and History: The Love Triangle." *UC Irvine Law Review* 5, no. 2 (June 2015): 365–92.

——. "Substitute Chancellors: The Role of the Jury in the Contest between Common Law and Equity." ssrn.com.

——. "Towards a Common Law Originalism." *Stanford Law Review* 59 (2006): 551–600.

Mirabellius, Dominicus. *Polyanthea.* Lyon: Vignon, 1600.

——. *Polyanthea Nova.* Ed. Josephus Langius. Lyon: Zetzner, 1604.

Monsarrat, Gilles. "John Ford: The Early Years (1586–1620)." In *The Collected Works of John Ford.* Vol. 1. Ed. Gilles Monsarrat, Brian Vickers, and R. J. C. Watt. Oxford: Oxford University Press, 2012. 12–38.

Montagu, Elizabeth. *An Essay on the Writings and Genius of Shakespear Compared with the Greek and French Dramatic Poets.* 1769. Eighteenth Century Shakespeare 12. London: Frank Cass and Co., 1970.

Moore, Kathleen. *Pardons: Justice, Mercy, and the Public Interest.* Oxford: Oxford University Press, 1989.

Morgan, Edmund S. *Inventing the People: The Rise of Popular Sovereignty in England and America.* New York: Norton, 1988.

Mukherji, Subha. *Law and Representation in Early Modern Drama.* Cambridge: Cambridge University Press, 2006.

Mukherji, Subha, and Raphael Lyne, eds. *Early Modern Tragicomedy.* Cambridge: D. S. Brewer, 2007.

Murrin, Michael. "Revelation and Two Seventeenth-Century Commentators." In *The Apocalypse in English Renaissance Thought and Literature: Patterns, Antecedents and Repercussions.* Ed. C. A. Patrides and Joseph Wittreich. Manchester: Manchester University Press, 1984. 125–47.

Negretto, Gabriel, and Jose Rivera. "Liberalism and Emergency Powers in Latin America: Reflections on Carl Schmitt and the Theory of Constitutional Dictatorship." *Cardozo Law Review* 21, no. 5–6 (May 2000): 1797–1823.

Nelson, Eric. *The Greek Tradition in Republican Thought.* Cambridge: Cambridge University Press, 2004.

Nicol, David. "Review of *Measure for Measure.*" *Early Modern Literary Studies* 10, no. 2 (September 2004): 13.1–8.

Norbrook, David. *Writing the English Republic: Poetry, Rhetoric and Politics, 1627–1660.* Cambridge: Cambridge University Press, 2000.

Nussbaum, Martha. "Equity and Mercy." *Philosophy and Public Affairs* 22, no. 2 (Spring 1993): 83–125.

——. *Poetic Justice: The Literary Imagination and Public Life.* Boston: Beacon Press, 1995.

——. *Political Emotions: Why Love Matters for Justice.* Cambridge: Harvard University Press, 2015.

——. *The Therapy of Desire.* Princeton: Princeton University Press, 1994.

——. *Upheavals of Thought: The Intelligence of Emotions.* Cambridge: Cambridge University Press, 2001.

Ohler, Norbert. "Krieg und Frieden am Ausgang des Mittelalters." In *Krieg und Frieden im Übergang vom Mittelalter zur Neuzeit.* Mainz: Philipp Von Zabern, 2000. 1–12.

Oliphant, E. H. C. *The Plays of Beaumont and Fletcher: An Attempt to Determine Their Respective Shares and the Shares of Others.* New Haven: Yale University Press, 1927.

O'Neill, Onora. "Vindicating Reason." In *The Cambridge Companion to Kant.* Ed. Paul Guyer. Cambridge: Cambridge University Press, 1992. 280–308.

Papy, Jan. "Erasmus's and Lipsius's Editions of Seneca: A 'Complementary Project'?" *Erasmus of Rotterdam Society Yearbook* 22 (2002): 10–36.

Pareus, David. *Commentary upon the Divine Revelation of the Apostle and Evangelist John.* Trans. Elias Arnold. Amsterdam: C.P., 1644.

The Partiall Law: A Tragi-Comedy by an Unknown Author. Ed. Bertram Dobell. London: Published by the editor, 1908.

Patrides, C. A., and Joseph Wittreich, eds. *The Apocalypse in English Renaissance Thought and Literature: Patterns, Antecedents and Repercussions.* Manchester: Manchester University Press, 1984.

Patterson, Annabel. *Censorship and Interpretation: The Conditions of Writing and Reading in Early Modern England.* Madison: University of Wisconsin Press, 1984.

Pearce, Robert R. *A History of the Inns of Court and Chancery.* London: Richard Bentley, 1848.

Peltonen, Markku. *Classical Humanism and Republicanism in English Political Thought, 1570–1640.* Cambridge: Cambridge University Press, 1995.

Pettit, Philip. *Made with Words: Hobbes on Language, Mind, and Politics.* Princeton: Princeton University Press, 2008.

Plato. *The Collected Dialogues of Plato.* Ed. Edith Hamilton and Huntington Cairns. New York: Pantheon, 1963.

——. *The Cratylus.* Trans. Benjamin Jowett. In *The Collected Dialogues of Plato.* Ed. Edith Hamilton and Huntington Cairns. New York: Pantheon, 1963. 421–74.

——. *The Laws.* Books 1–6. Trans. R. G. Bury. Loeb Classical Library. Cambridge: Harvard University Press, 1926.

——. *The Laws.* Books 7–12. Trans. R. G. Bury. Loeb Classical Library. Cambridge: Harvard University Press, 1926.

——. *The Laws.* Trans. A. E. Taylor. In *The Collected Dialogues of Plato.* Ed. Edith Hamilton and Huntington Cairns. New York: Pantheon, 1963. 1225–1516.

——. *The Republic.* Trans. Paul Shorey. In *The Collected Dialogues of Plato.* Ed. Edith Hamilton and Huntington Cairns. New York: Pantheon, 1963. 575–844.

Plaute. *Amphitryon.* Ed. Charles Guittard. Paris: Flammarion, 1998.

Plautus. *Amphitryon.* Trans. Constance Carrier. In *Plautus: The Comedies.* Vol. 1. Ed. David R. Slavitt and Palmer Bovie. Baltimore: Johns Hopkins University Press, 1995. 1–64.

Plucknett, T. F. T. "Bonham's Case and Judicial Review." *Harvard Law Review* 30 (1928): 30–70.

———. *Concise History of the Common Law*. Rochester, NY: Lawyers Coop Publishing, 1956.

Pocock, J. G. A. *The Ancient Constitution and the Feudal Law: A Study of English Historical Thought in the Seventeenth Century*. Cambridge: Cambridge University Press, 1987.

Pollard, Tanya. "Tragicomedy." In *The Oxford History of Classical Reception in English Literature*. Ed. Patrick Cheney and Philip Hardie. Vol. 2. 1558–1660. Oxford: Oxford University Press, 2012. 419–32.

Pontanus, Jacobus. *Poeticarum institutionum*. Ingolstadt: David Santori, 1594.

Poole, Adrian. *Tragedy: Shakespeare and the Greek Example*. Oxford: Basil Blackwell, 1987.

Poole, Thomas. "Hobbes on Law and Prerogative." In *Hobbes and the Law*. Ed. David Dyzenhaus and Thomas Poole. Cambridge: Cambridge University Press, 2012. 68–96.

Posner, Richard A. "Law and Commerce in *The Merchant of Venice*." In *Shakespeare and the Law: A Conversation among Disciplines and Professions*. Ed. Bradin Cormack, Martha C. Nussbaum, and Richard Strier. Chicago: University of Chicago Press, 2013. 147–55.

Prest, Wilfred. "The Dialectical Origins of Finch's *Law*." *Cambridge Law Journal* 36, no. 2 (1977): 326–52.

Prynne, William. *Health's Sickness: Or, a Compendious and Briefe Discourse; Prouing, the Drinking and Pledging of Healthes, to be Sinfull*. London: Augustine Mathewes, 1628.

Quarmby, Kevin A. *The Disguised Ruler in Shakespeare and His Contemporaries*. Oxford: Routledge, 2016.

Randall, Dale B. J. *Winter Fruit: English Drama, 1642–1660*. Lexington: University Press of Kentucky, 1995.

Rechner, Leonhard. *Aristophanes in England: Eine literarhistorische Untersuchung*. Frankfurt am Main: M. G. Martens, 1914.

Rhodes, Neil. "The Controversial Plot: Declamation and the Concept of the 'Problem Play.'" *Modern Language Review* 95, no. 3 (July 2000): 609–22.

Ross, Richard. "The Commoning of the Common Law: The Renaissance Debate over Printing English Law." *University of Pennsylvania Law Review* 146, no. 2 (January 1998): 323–461.

Runciman, David. *Political Hypocrisy: Masks of Power, from Hobbes to Orwell and Beyond*. Princeton: Princeton University Press, 2008.

Russell, Conrad, ed. *The Origins of the English Civil War*. New York: Barnes and Noble Books, 1973.

———. *Parliaments and English Politics, 1621–1629*. Oxford: Oxford University Press, 1979.

———. "Topsy and the King: The English Common Law, King James VI and I, and the Union of the Crowns." In *Law and Authority in Early Modern England: Essays Presented to Thomas Garden Barnes*. Ed. Buchanan Sharp and Mark Charles Fissel. Wilmington: University of Delaware Press, 2007. 64–80.

Rust, Jennifer, and Julia Lupton. "Schmitt and Shakespeare" In Carl Schmitt, *Hamlet or Hecuba: The Intrusion of Time into the Play*. Ed. David Pan, Jennifer Rust, and Julia Reinhard Lupton. New York: Telos Press, 2009. xv–li.

Sadler, John. *Rights of the Kingdom: or, Customs of our Ancestors. Touching the Duty, Power, Election, or Succession of our Kings and Parliaments*. London: Richard Bishop, 1649.

St. Germain, Christopher. *Doctor and Student, or Dialogues Between a Doctor of Divinity and a Student in the Laws of England Containing the Grounds of Those Laws*. 1523. Ed. Christopher T. F. T. Plucknett and J. L. Barton. Publications of the Selden Society, vol. 91. London: Selden Society, 1974.

Salmon, J. H. M. "Stoicism and Roman Example: Seneca and Tacitus in Jacobean England." *Journal of the History of Ideas* 50, no. 2 (April–June 1989): 199–225.

Sanderson, William. *A Compleat History of the Life and Raigne of King Charles from His Cradle to His Grave*. London: Humphrey Moseley, 1658.

Santner, Eric L. *The Royal Remains: The People's Two Bodies and the Endgames of Sovereignty*. Chicago: University of Chicago Press, 2011.

Sayles, G. O. *The Medieval Foundations of England*. 2nd ed. London: Methuen & Co., 1950.

Scaliger, Julius Caesar. *Poetices libri septem*. Trans. C. J. McDonough. In *Sources of Dramatic Theory I: Plato to Congreve*. Ed. Michael J. Sidnell. Cambridge: Cambridge University Press, 1991. 98–110.

Scheuerman, William. *Between the Norm and the Exception: The Frankfurt School and the Rule of Law*. Cambridge: MIT Press, 1997.

——. *Carl Schmitt: The End of Law*. New York: Rowman & Littlefield, 1999.

Schiesaro, Alessandro. *The Passions in Play: Thyestes and the Dynamics of Senecan Drama*. Cambridge: Cambridge University Press, 2003.

Schleiner, Louise. "Latinized Greek Drama in Shakespeare's Writing of *Hamlet*." *Shakespeare Quarterly* 41 (1990): 29–48.

Schmitt, Carl. *The Concept of the Political*. Trans. George Schwab. Chicago: University of Chicago Press, 1996.

——. *Constitutional Theory*. Trans. Jeffrey Seitzer. Durham: Duke University Press, 2008.

——. *The Crisis of Parliamentary Democracy*. Trans. Ellen Kennedy. Cambridge: MIT Press, 1996.

——. *Hamlet or Hecuba: The Intrusion of Time into the Play*. Ed. David Pan, Jennifer Rust, and Julia Reinhard Lupton. New York: Telos Press, 2009.

——. *Hamlet oder Hekuba: Der Einbruch der Zeit in das Spiel*. Düsseldorf: E. Diederichs, 1956.

——. *Legality and Legitimacy*. Trans. Jeffrey Seitzer. Durham: Duke University Press, 2004.

——. *The Leviathan in the State Theory of Thomas Hobbes: Meaning and Failure of a Political Symbol*. Trans. George Schwab. Chicago: University of Chicago Press, 1996.

——. *The Nomos of the Earth in the International Law of* Jus Publicum Europaeum. Trans. G. L. Ulmen. New York: Telos Press, 2006.

——. *Political Theology: Four Chapters on the Concept of Sovereignty*. Trans. George Schwab. Chicago: University of Chicago Press, 2006.

——. *Verfassungslehre*. Munich: Duncker und Humblot, 1928.

Schochet, Gordon J. "Intending (Political) Obligation: Hobbes and the Voluntary Basis of Society." In *Thomas Hobbes and Political Theory*. Ed. Mary G. Dietz. Lawrence: University Press of Kansas, 1990.

Schuhmann, Karl, Piet Steenbakkers, and Cees Leijenhorst. "Hobbes and the Political Thought of Plato and Aristotle." In *Selected Papers on Renaissance Philosophy and on Thomas Hobbes*. Dordrecht: Springer, 2004. 191–218.

Scott, Jonathan. "The Peace of Silence: Thucydides and the English Civil War." In *Hobbes and History*. Ed. G. A. J. Rogers and Thomas Sorrell. London: Routledge, 2000. 112–36.

Segal, Charles. *Language and Desire in Seneca's* Phaedra. Princeton: Princeton University Press, 1986.

Sellars, John. *Stoicism*. Berkeley: University of California Press, 2006.

Seneca the Elder. *Controversiae*. In *Declamations*. Vol. 2. Trans. M. Winterbottom. Loeb Classical Library. Cambridge: Harvard University Press, 1974. 2–483.

Seneca, Lucius Annaeus. *Annaei Senecae Philosophi Opera, Quae Existant Omnia*. Ed. Justus Lipsius. Antwerp: Plantin-Moretus, 1605.

——. "De Beneficiis." In *Moral Essays*. Vol. 3. Trans. John W. Basore. Loeb Classical Library. Cambridge: Harvard University Press, 1935.

——. "De Clementia." In *Moral Essays*. Vol. 1. Trans. John W. Basore. Loeb Classical Library. Cambridge: Harvard University Press, 1928. 356–449.

——. *Epistles 1–65*. Loeb Classical Library. Cambridge: Harvard University Press, 1917.

——. *Epistles 66–92*. Trans. Richard M. Gummere. Loeb Classical Library. Cambridge: Harvard University Press, 1920.

——. *The Workes of Lucius Annaeus Seneca newly inlarged and corrected by Thomas Lodge D.M.P.* London: William Stansby, 1614.

Shakespeare, William. *All's Well That Ends Well*. Ed. G. K. Hunter. 3rd ser. London: Arden Shakespeare, 2006.

——. *King Lear*. Ed. R. A. Foakes. 3rd ser. London: Arden Shakespeare, 1997.

——. *Measure for Measure*. Ed. J. W. Lever. 2nd ser. London: Arden Shakespeare, 1994.

——. *The Merchant of Venice*. Ed. John Russell Brown. 2nd ser. London: Arden Shakespeare, 1985.

——. *The Norton Facsimile: The First Folio of Shakespeare*. Ed. Charles Hinman. 2nd ed. New York: W. W. Norton & Co., 1996.

Shapiro, Barbara. "Law Reform in Seventeenth-Century England." *American Journal of Legal History* 19 (1975): 280–312.

——. *Political Communication and Political Culture in England*. Stanford: Stanford University Press, 2012.

Shell, Susan Meld. *The Embodiment of Reason: Kant on Spirit, Generation, and Community*. Chicago: University of Chicago Press, 1996.

Sheppard, J. T. *Aeschylus and Sophocles: Their Work and Influence*. London: George G. Harrap & Co., 1927.

Shuger, Debora K. *Political Theologies in Shakespeare's England: The Sacred and the State in* Measure for Measure. New York: Palgrave, 2001.

Sir Edward Coke's Ownership List. Holkham Hall Library, Norfolk, n.d.

Skinner, Quentin. *Reason and Rhetoric in the Philosophy of Thomas Hobbes*. Cambridge: Cambridge University Press, 1996.

——. "Why Shylock Loses His Case: Judicial Rhetoric in *The Merchant of Venice*." In *The Oxford Handbook of English Law and Literature, 1500–1700*. Ed. Lorna Huston. Oxford: Oxford University Press, 2017. 97–120.

Sokol, B. J., and Mary Sokol. *Shakespeare's Legal Language: A Dictionary*. London: Continuum, 2000.

Sommerville, J. P. "The Ancient Constitution Reassessed: The Common Law, the Court and the Language of Politics in Early Modern England." In *The Stuart Court and Europe: Essays in Politics and Personal Culture*. Cambridge: Cambridge University Press, 1996. 39–64.

——. Introduction to *Political Writings* by James VI and I. Cambridge Texts in the History of Political Thought. Cambridge: Cambridge University Press, 1994. xv–xxix.

——. "Lofty Science and Local Politics." In *Cambridge Companion to Hobbes*. Ed. Tom Sorell. Cambridge: Cambridge University Press, 1996. 246–73.

——. *Royalists and Patriots: Politics and Ideology in England, 1603–1640*. 2nd ed. London: Routledge, 2014.

Spencer, Janet. "Staging Pardon Scenes: Variations of Tragicomedy." *Renaissance Drama* 21 (1990): 55–89.

Stacey, Peter. *Roman Monarchy and the Renaissance Prince*. Cambridge: Cambridge University Press, 2007.

Staley, Gregory A. *Seneca and the Idea of Tragedy*. Oxford: Oxford University Press, 2010.

Stanton, Timothy. "Hobbes and Schmitt." *History of European Ideas* 37 (2011): 160–67.

Steggle, Matthew. "Aristophanes in Early Modern England." In *Aristophanes in Performance, 421 BC–AD 2007: Peace, Birds, and Frogs*. Ed. Edith Hall and Amanda Wrigley. London: Modern Humanities Research Association and W. S. Maney & Son, 2007. 52–65.

Steiger, Heinhard. "Peace Treaties from Paris to Versailles." In *Peace Treaties and International Law in European History from the Late Middle Ages to World War One*. Ed. Randall Lesaffer. Cambridge: Cambridge University Press, 2004. 59–102.

Stobaei, Ioannis. *Anthologii*. Ed. Otto Hense. Vol. 3. Berlin: Weidmannos, 1894.

Stoddart, Jessie. "Constitutional Crisis and the House of Lords, 1621–1629." Ph.D. dissertation, UC Berkeley, 1966.

Sykes, H. Dugdale. Review. *Review of English Studies* 4, no. 16 (1928): 456–63.

Syme, Holger Schott. "(Mis)Representing Justice on the Early Modern Stage." *Studies in Philology* 109, no. 1 (Winter 2012): 79–80.

——. *Theatre and Testimony in Shakespeare's England: A Culture of Mediation*. Cambridge: Cambridge University Press, 2011.

Teitel, Ruti. *Transitional Justice*. New York: Oxford University Press, 2000.

Tennenhouse, Leonard. *Power on Display*. New York: Methuen, 1986.

Thayer, C. G. *Ben Jonson: Studies in the Plays*. Norman: University of Oklahoma Press, 1963.

Tomlinson, Sophie. *Women on Stage in Stuart Drama*. Cambridge: Cambridge University Press, 2005.

Tuck, Richard. *The Rights of War and Peace: Political Thought and the International Order from Grotius to Kant*. Oxford: Oxford University Press, 2001.

——. *The Sleeping Sovereign: The Invention of Modern Democracy*. Cambridge: Cambridge University Press, 2016.

Turner, Robert. "Giving and Taking in Massinger's Tragicomedies." *Studies in English Literature, 1500–1900* 35, no. 2 (Spring 1995): 361–81.

Vickers, Brian. 'Counterfeiting' Shakespeare: Evidence, Authorship, and John Ford's *Funerall Elegye*. Cambridge: Cambridge University Press, 2002.

Vieira, Monica. *The Elements of Representation in Hobbes*. Leiden: Brill, 2009.

Viroli, Maurizio. *From Politics to Reason of State: The Acquisition and Transformation of the Language of Politics, 1250–1600*. Cambridge: Cambridge University Press, 1992.

Visconsi, Elliott. *Lines of Equity: Literature and the Origins of Law in Later Stuart England*. Ithaca: Cornell University Press, 2008.

Waith, Eugene M. "Controversia in the English Drama: Medwall and Massinger." *PMLA* 68, no. 1 (March 1953): 286–303.

——. "John Fletcher and the Art of Declamation." *PMLA* 66, no. 2 (March 1951): 226–34.

——. *The Pattern of Tragicomedy in Beaumont and Fletcher*. New Haven: Yale University Press, 1952.

Ward, Ian. *Shakespeare and the Legal Imagination*. Law in Context. London: Butterworths, 1999.

Watt, Gary, and Paul Raffield, eds. *Shakespeare and the Law*. Oxford: Hart Publishing, 2008.

West, Robin. "The Anti-Empathic Turn." *NOMOS LIII*. Ed. James Fleming (2011): 243–88.

White, Hayden. "The Politics of Historical Interpretation." In *The Content of the Form: Narrative Discourse and Historical Representation*. Baltimore: Johns Hopkins University Press, 1987. 58–82.

Whitman, James Q. *The Origins of Reasonable Doubt: Theological Roots of the Criminal Trial*. Yale Law Library Series in Legal History and Reference. New Haven: Yale University Press, 2016.

Williams, Ian. "Developing a Prerogative Theory for the Authority of the Chancery: The French Connection." In *Law and Authority in British Legal History, 1200–1900*. Ed. Mark Godfrey. Cambridge: Cambridge University Press, 2016. 33–59.

Williams, Melissa, and Rosemary Nagy. Introduction. In *NOMOS LI: Transitional Justice*. Ed. Melissa S. Williams, Rosemary Nagy, and Jon Elster. New York: NYU Press, 2012. 1–30.

Wills, Gary. *Witches and Jesuits: Shakespeare's* Macbeth. New York Public Library Series. New York: Oxford University Press, 1995.

Willson, David. *James VI and I*. London: J. Cape, 1963.

Wilson, Luke. *Theaters of Intention: Drama and the Law in Early Modern England*. Stanford: Stanford University Press, 2000.

Winston, Jessica. *Lawyers at Play: Literature, Law, and Politics at the Early Modern Inns of Court, 1558–1581*. Oxford: Oxford University Press, 2016.

Wiseman, Susan. *Drama and Politics in the English Civil War*. Cambridge: Cambridge University Press, 1998.

Wolfe, Jessica. *Homer and the Question of Strife from Erasmus to Hobbes*. Toronto: University of Toronto Press, 2015.

Woolrych, Humphry W. *The Life of the Right Honourable Sir Edward Coke, Knt.* London: J. & W. T. Clarke, 1826. Reprint, South Hackensack, NJ: Rothman Reprints, 1972.

Wormald, Jenny. "'*Basilikon Doron*' and '*The Trew Law of Free Monarchies.*'" In *The Mental World of the Jacobean Court*. Ed. Linda Levy Peck. Cambridge: Cambridge University Press, 1991. 36–54.

Yoshino, Kenji. *A Thousand Times More Fair: What Shakespeare's Plays Teach Us about Justice*. New York: HarperCollins, 2001.

Young, Michael. "Buckingham, War, and Parliament: Revisionism Gone Too Far." *Parliamentary History* 4 (1985). 45–69.

Zaller, Robert. *The Parliament of 1621: A Study in Constitutional Conflict*. Berkeley: University of California Press, 1971.

Zemon Davis, Natalie. *Fiction in the Archives: Pardon Tales and Their Tellers in Sixteenth-Century France*. Stanford: Stanford University Press, 1987.

Zywicki, Todd. "The Rise and Fall of Efficiency in the Common Law: A Supply-Side Analysis." *Northwestern University Law Review* 97 (Summer 2003). 1551–633.

INDEX

CPSIA information can be obtained
at www.ICGtesting.com
Printed in the USA
FSHW020551310719
60555FS